MERCER UNIVERSITY

MERCER UNIVERSITY PRESS

Endowed by

TOM WATSON BROWN

and

THE WATSON-BROWN FOUNDATION, INC.

An Officer of the Old Guard

LEWIS STEVENSON CRAIG

1807–1852

William Harris Bragg

MERCER UNIVERSITY PRESS
Macon, Georgia
MMXX

MUP/ H995

Published by Mercer University Press
1501 Mercer University Drive
Macon, Georgia 31207

25 24 23 22 21 20   5 4 3 2 1

Books published by Mercer University Press are printed on acid-free paper that meets the requirements of the American National Standard for Information Sciences—Permanence of Paper for Printed Library Materials.

Printed and bound in the United States.

This book is set in Adobe Caslon Pro and Georgia (display)

Cover/jacket design by Burt&Burt.

Cataloging-in-Publication Data from the Library of Congress
Names: Bragg, William Harris, author.
Title: An Officer of the Old Guard : Lewis Stevenson Craig 1807-1852 / Willilam Harris Bragg.
Other titles: Lewis Stevenson Craig 1807-1852
Description: Macon, Georgia : Mercer University Press, 2020. |
Includes bibliographical references and index. |
Identifiers: LCCN 2020027727 | ISBN 9780881467642 (hardback)
Subjects: LCSH: United States. Army. Infantry Regiment, 3rd--Biography. | Craig, Lewis Stevenson, 1807-1852. | Craig, Lewis Stevenson, 1807-1852--Diaries. | United States. Army—Officers—Biography. | United States—History, Military—19th century.
Classification: LCC UA29 3d .B73 2020 | DDC 355.0092 [B]—dc23
LC record available at https://lccn.loc.gov/2020027727

For the Descendants and Namesakes of

Lewis Stevenson Craig,
Brevet Lieutenant Colonel,
Third U. S. Army Infantry
(1807-1852)

In Memoriam

Craig Barrow, M.D.
(1876-1945)

Craig Barrow, Jr.
(1906-1978)

and to

Craig Barrow III

INHERITORS • PRESERVERS • EXEMPLARS

I will bear true allegiance to the United States of America
and…will serve them honestly and faithfully
against all their enemies and opposers whatsoever….

—From Lewis Stevenson Craig's printed officer's commission,
signed at Fredericksburg, Virginia,
October 24, 1837

Contents

Preface

> It is very seldom that the preface of a work is read; indeed, of late years, most books have been sent into the world without any. I deem it, however, advisable to write a preface, and to this I humbly call the attention of the courteous reader, as its perusal will not a little tend to the proper understanding and appreciation of this volume.
>
> —George Borrow, *The Bible in Spain*, 1843

In the *Democratic Review* for summer 1845, founding editor John O'Sullivan demanded that the United States annex the young Republic of Texas as was then being debated in the U.S. Congress. More importantly, O'Sullivan argued not only for immediate statehood for Texas, but also for America to accept its "manifest destiny to overspread the continent allotted by Providence" and expand to the Pacific Ocean. That same summer found Lewis Stevenson Craig serving as a 1st lieutenant in the Third U.S. Infantry. Within only three years, Craig's regiment would pass into legend as "The Old Guard" and would help push America's borders to the western sea, just as expansionists such as O'Sullivan had insisted.

In mid-1845, Craig's Third Infantry formed part of a 3800-man "U.S. Army of Occupation" concentrated on the disputed Mexican-American border at Corpus Christi. This tiny Gulf coast settlement lay either in northeastern Mexico's Tamaulipas province, or in San Patricio County, on the southwestern border of the Republic of Texas. Precisely which republic had the better claim to Corpus Christi constituted a question that had thus far defied diplomacy.

Texas annexation and statehood would come by the end of December 1845. Whether this was a permanent arrangement of Texas's western border would be decided through the "arbitrament of the sword": a brief Mexican-American war (April 1846–February 1848), in which the Third Infantry would achieve fame and Lewis Craig would earn successive promotions. The war not only decisively brought Texas into the United States—it also added to the nation a vast area of more than 500,000 square miles. The war also would give the victorious American republic a lengthy Pacific coastline of over 1200 miles, after California's 840-mile coast (formerly belonging to Mexico) was added to the shorelines of Oregon and Washington, territories ceded to the U.S. in 1846 by Great Britain.

In retrospect—and in keeping with the term coined by John O'Sullivan—Craig and those other officers and men who had campaigned in Mexico would later be called "Agents of Manifest Destiny." In that category, few men personified American expansion as well as Craig, who lived his entire forty-five years within that momentous half-century, 1803–1853, when the American domain south of Canada expanded to its greatest extent.

Fittingly, Craig's places of birth and burial marked in time and distance the republic's progress from sea to sea. Born in 1807 in Richmond—Atlantic river port and capital of Virginia, first of Britain's American colonies—Craig was bound for a soldier's grave on a Pacific promontory that lay over twenty-five hundred miles from the Old Dominion. By the time of Craig's death in 1852, extraordinary events had transformed the fifteen-star American flag that flew over Richmond at his birth to a banner emblazoned with thirty-one stars, with more to be added from territory won or purchased from Mexico.

Nonetheless, at Craig's birth Imperial Spain still held titular claim to the Floridas, while exercising little control over them. These turbulent Spanish provinces formed the southernmost natural border of the United States east of the Mississippi, stretching from Baton Rouge to St. Augustine. Pen and sword would bring these southern lands into American possession by 1819, while Craig was still a boy. Nonetheless, pacification and settlement of the area between the Gulf and the Atlantic would demand decades of fighting the Seminole Indians.

Ultimately, Craig would be introduced to combat in the greatest of these conflicts, the "Florida War" of the late 1830s and early 1840s, later called the Second Seminole War. Consequently, it would be as a battle-tested veteran officer that he would earn rapid advancement during the subsequent war with Mexico. Afterward, Craig would play an important role in the exploration and survey of the U.S.-Mexican border between El Paso, Texas, and San Diego, California.

In 1853, a year after Craig's death, the Gadsden Treaty added almost 30,000 square miles to the area won from Mexico through war. This purchase constituted the final addition of territory to a national domain now bounded by the Atlantic and the Pacific and containing more than three million square miles. Thus, only eight years after John O'Sullivan had advocated manifest destiny, the United States had indeed "overspread the continent," with Lewis Craig in the vanguard.

Lewis Craig's participation in completing America's ocean-to-ocean expansion seems fitting. He was a proud Virginian at a time when the Old Dominion continued to stand in the forefront of American affairs—military, judicial, and political—thus granting a unique esteem and patrimony to its citizens. Consequently, Craig, as a Virginian "Agent of Manifest Destiny," offers a focus for understanding the expanding America of the antebellum period—in terms of military history, certainly. But because of Craig's remarkable antecedents and extraordinary family, Craig's life contributes to understanding other aspects of American culture, society, and even literature in the decades before the War Between the States.

During Craig's youth, the U.S. Military Academy at West Point had produced most of the nation's military officers. But Craig himself would receive an officer's commission through appointment from civilian life. Arguably, that circumstance rested in great degree on the fact that Craig—in terms of family, upbringing, and education—was a gentleman. The term then referred to much more than conduct or deportment; it denoted a particular place in the social hierarchy of America: a class concept imported from England and rooted in Virginia as nowhere else among the Crown colonies.

Ironically, the Craig family, a late addition to the oldest English colony, had only recently become gentlefolk. Indeed, just a century before Lewis Craig reached Corpus Christi, his Anglo-Scottish grandfather, the London goldsmith James Craig, had arrived at Yorktown. Never a gentleman in the social hierarchy of his time, James Craig had crossed an ocean to seek his fortune. His exertions and foresight propelled his elder son, Lewis's father, Adam, upward in Virginia society, so that Lewis, unlike Adam himself, would be born a gentleman.

This book will present Lewis Craig's life, particularly its military dimension, strangely foreshadowed at his birth and fortuitously reinforced during his school years. The prologue and chapter 1 relate the circumstances of Craig's early life, ending with his commissioning as an officer of the U.S. Army. Chapter 2 covers Craig's service in the Florida War, his marriage, and the birth of his only child, along with his garrison duties at Fort Jesup, Louisiana, and Jefferson Barracks, Missouri. Chapters 3 and 4 deal with Craig's experiences during the Mexican War, while chapter 5 describes his service with the U.S.-Mexican Boundary Commission and concludes with his death. Craig's legacies to his comrades and survivors, and the lives after his death of his widow and daughter, form the subjects of the epilogue.

Craig left journals and letters that support much of chapters 3, 4, and

5 with his own words. Those portions of his writings set out in the text have had to be only lightly edited, with occasional misspellings silently corrected and paragraphing and some missing punctuation (except in the case of A.M. and P.M.) likewise supplied. The abundant capitalizations of the time have not been modernized, though spellings have been updated, as in "endeavor," instead of "endeavour." Rare omissions (for length) are represented by ellipses (…). Whenever possible, forenames have been supplied for individuals represented only by surnames. For readers' convenience, the sections from Craig's journals have, in most cases, been uniformly formatted by date.

As for the approach of this book to its subject, "the purpose here has not been to interpret history apart from the time when these events occurred, but rather to record them in the spirit of those times." These words were written in 1972 by the most eminent Georgia historian of the twentieth century, E. Merton Coulter (1890–1981), now not only unfashionable among academic historians, but much maligned. His words appear here in hope that this book will at least come near the factually correct history that Dr. Coulter always championed against ideological, politically correct history, which was burgeoning in his later years.

This book is meant for a general readership, a fact which has called for somewhat idiosyncratic citations. The historian Byron Farwell somewhat unfairly called footnotes a "crutch of poor writers" in his un-footnoted 1963 biography of Sir Richard Francis Burton, whose own use of lengthy footnotes Farwell deplored and attacked. Anthony Grafton, on the other hand, author of an entire book titled *The Footnote: A Curious History* (1997), quotes an anecdote in which the presence of footnotes on a page is compared to someone attempting romance upstairs, but having to go constantly downstairs to answer the door.

Where footnotes were concerned, Dr. Coulter followed general academic practice in most of his articles and books, with the exception of his oft-reprinted history of Georgia, originally published in 1933 and re-issued "revised and enlarged" in 1947 as *Georgia: A Short History.* In the original version, Dr. Coulter commented that he had "felt it unnecessary to encumber the pages with footnotes," and in his revision he held to his "position against peppering [his] pages" with them.

For this book, an adaptation of Dr. Coulter's practice in *Georgia: A Short History* has been employed; that is, short citations have been grouped "at the end of the book and arranged according to chapters." Additionally, within the transcripts of Craig's journals (along with some bridging paragraphs), bracketed explanations (often, but not always) appear for terms and subjects that can be explained briefly but would normally appear as footnotes.

As for Lewis Stevenson Craig, his memory was destined to be kept green not only by his family but also, among many others, by the military fraternity he cherished. As noted by John Russell Bartlett, a companion of Craig's last adventure, Craig "was an officer of whom the army and the nation had just cause to feel proud....His genuine kindness of heart, honesty of purpose, and rigid adherence to duty...won for him a large circle of devoted friends among civilians, as well as among his brother officers."

No officer—and no gentleman—could desire a better epitaph.

E PLURIBUS
UNUM

Brevet Lieutenant Colonel Lewis Stevenson Craig, Third Regiment, U. S. Army Infantry, from an oil portrait, artist unknown, shoulder straps later retouched to reflect promotion.

Courtesy Mr. and Mrs. Craig Barrow III

Richmond, Virginia, from Church Hill, with Thomas Jefferson's state capitol building in the distance, overlooking the James River.

Courtesy Maryland Historical Society

In his residence on Grace Street in the shadow of Church Hill, Richmond's foremost court clerk, Adam Craig, and his wife raised seven children, the last of whom was Lewis Craig.
Courtesy The Valentine, *Richmond, Virginia, photograph by Maurice J. Duke*

The Richmond Theatre Fire horrified the young American republic. Over seventy people died in the conflagration, most of them women, including an elder sister of Lewis Craig.
Courtesy New York Public Library

Fredericksburg, Virginia, Rappahannock river port, was Lewis Craig's adopted home. This view shows the town from Ferry Farm, where George Washington spent his boyhood.

From Henry Howe's Historical Collections of Virginia *(1852)*

Roger Jones, Adjutant General of the U.S. Army from 1825 until his death in 1852. His tenure bracketed Lewis Craig's entire military career.

From L. H. Jones, Captain Roger Jones of London and Virginia *(1891)*

Beginning his career as a captain during the War of 1812, David Twiggs by 1861 was one of the four senior generals in the U. S. Army. As colonel of Dragoons, he was Lewis Craig's first commanding officer, and also led the division in which Craig served until the end of the Mexican War.

Courtesy David M. Rubenstein Rare Book & Manuscript Library, Duke University Libraries

Ten years Twiggs' junior, William S. Harney was his equal in profanity and his superior in general violence. He served as Twiggs' second-in-command in the Florida War and briefly commanded Twiggs' division in Mexico.

Courtesy Missouri Historical Society

Thomas Jesup, famed as the nonpareil of U. S. Army Quartermaster Generals, also enjoyed considerable success as a combat general in the war against the Seminoles.

Courtesy Army Quartermaster Museum, Fort Lee, Virginia

Fort Mellon, on Lake Monroe, one of Florida's multiplicity of temporary palisade forts. From this fort General Jesup hoped to lead a war-ending campaign against the Seminole Indians.

Courtesy State Archives of Florida, Florida Memory

Only briefly a leader of the Seminoles during the Florida War (1835–42), Osceola took part in the massacres that sparked the war in December 1835 and, captured in late October 1837, died early the next year. Ironically, Osceola would become the Florida War's only participant to be lionized as a heroic figure.

Courtesy National Portrait Gallery

Of the two great Whig generals who won national fame in the Mexican War, it would be Zachary Taylor, hero of Monterrey and Buena Vista, who would be elevated to the U. S. Presidency, succeeding Democrat James Knox Polk.

Courtesy Digital Public Library of America

William J. Worth took credit for ending the Florida War and, after a shaky start, won additional fame in the war with Mexico.

Courtesy Digital Public Library of America.

Founded in 1822, Fort Jesup, Louisiana, often served as a duty station for the Third Regiment, U. S. Infantry. The building shown is a reconstruction of the officers' quarters.

Courtesy Louisiana Digital Library.

One of the U. S. Army's principal soldier-savants, Ethan Allen Hitchcock perfected the Third Regiment in both drill and devotion to duty.

Courtesy Library of Congress

Elizabeth Church, one among a constellation of beautiful daughters of the President of the University of Georgia, met First Lieutenant Lewis Craig in Tallahassee, Florida, during the Florida War and married him in Athens, Georgia, soon thereafter.
Courtesy Malcolm Bell III

In this lithograph view of the University of Georgia, issued during the 1850s, the institution's first building, "Old College," appears at the center, partly screened by trees. Likewise constructed in 1806, the original President's House (unshown in this view) stood near and to the left of Old College, and was the childhood home of the Church children. In 1849, the Churches moved to a new official residence, a roomy masonry structure located where the university's Main Library now stands.

Courtesy Hargrett Rare Book and Manuscript Library, University of Georgia

Named Sarah Church Craig after her maternal grandmother, the Craigs' only child was always called Sallie, and her likeness accompanied her father into Mexico and to the Pacific.

Courtesy Malcolm Bell III

The encampment of the U. S. Army of Occupation in 1846 at Corpus Christi, with drilling underway at center.

Courtesy Beinecke Digital Collections, Yale University

House-to-house street fighting marked one of the deadliest phases of the Battle of Monterrey.

Courtesy Library of Congress

Monterrey taken, Craig and several officers ascended Saddleback Mountain to survey the territory American arms had gained.

Courtesy Library of Congress

At Vera Cruz, the elements of the U.S. Army were brought ashore by purpose-built U.S. Navy surf boats. Rapidly invested and bombarded, the city soon surrendered.

Courtesy Library of Congress

Winfield Scott, who led the U.S. Army from Vera Cruz to victory at Mexico City, took a personal interest in the career of fellow Virginian Lewis Craig.

Courtesy Library of Congress

The Third Regiment's deft use of the bayonet at the battle of Cerro Gordo led to the honor of becoming the lone U. S. regiment allowed to parade with bayonets fixed.

Alonzo Chappel, "Battle of Cerro Gordo" from Henry Dawson's Battles of the United States, by Sea and Land *(1858)*

The victors at Vera Cruz and Cerro Gordo, the men of Twiggs' Division were subject of a panoramic image showing them drawn up at Puebla, before the advance on Mexico City.

Courtesy Massachusetts Historical Society

John Magruder in his artillery officer's uniform. A close friend of Lewis Craig, Magruder and Craig were linked as the Padierna battle opened.

From Year Book of the American Clan Gregor Society *(1914)*

Covering a massive U.S. troop movement, John B. Magruder's outgunned battery (top left) was supported on the slopes below by Craig's small command.

Courtesy U. S. Army Center of Military History

Lewis Craig suffered a near-mortal wound at Churubusco, but the battle ended with the Third Regiment's flag first to be displayed on the walls of the fortified Mexican convent.

Courtesy U. S. Army Center of Military History

Lewis Craig's Third Regiment passed into legend as "The Old Guard" as General Scott entered Mexico City with his battered veterans.

Courtesy New York Public Library

William C. Dawson, U.S. Senator from Georgia, long acted as a Whig kingmaker and became the valued political patron of Lewis Craig.

From Men of Mark in Georgia, *Vol. 2 (1910)*

John Russell Bartlett, sketched by a colleague during the U.S.-Mexican Boundary Survey. Commissioner Bartlett left a detailed account and numerous evocative images of the survey's explorations, though in retrospect his activities served mainly as an interruption between two more successful surveys.

Courtesy John Carter Brown Library

Veteran frontiersman John Cremony served as Commissioner Bartlett's interpreter. Among Lewis Craig's many admirers among commission personnel, Cremony left his own account of his exploits, *Life among the Apaches*.

Courtesy California Faces: Selections from The Bancroft Library Portrait Collection

A West Point graduate and dedicated officer, Amiel Weeks Whipple served in all three major U. S.-Mexico boundary surveys and became a confirmed "hero-worshipper" of Lewis Craig.

Courtesy Brady Image Collection, National Archives

Commissioner Bartlett's rendering of El Paso, Texas. Over one thousand miles of rugged, mostly parched territory lay between El Paso and San Diego.

Courtesy John Carter Brown Library

Santa Rita del Cobre, New Mexico, long served as a center of Mexican copper-mining. Its old presidio was refurbished by Lewis Craig as Cantonment Dawson, eastern headquarters of the U.S.-Mexican Boundary Commission.

Courtesy John Carter Brown Library

A major complication for the boundary survey was working within the nexus of the Mexico raiding trails of the "Copper Mines Apaches," led by the redoubtable Mangus Colorado.

From Bartlett's Personal Narrative , *Vol. 1 (1854)*

Commissioner Bartlett spent a scant two weeks at Santa Rita del Cobre before setting out south to return former Apache captive Inez Gonzalez to her family in Mexico. Lewis Craig would not see him again until the winter of 1851–52. Bartlett's sketch depicts the customary attire of the men attached to the commission party, usually bearded, in a country where water was too scarce for shaving.

Courtesy John Carter Brown Library

The Gila River villages of the peaceful Pima Indians represented an important way station on the road to the Pacific.

Courtesy John Carter Brown Library

The Colorado River, looking up the Gila. This confluence formed the only major water barrier on the trail to San Diego and was crossable only by ferriage.

Courtesy John Carter Brown Library

The mission of San Diego de Alcala in "Old San Diego," was the first founded of the California missions in 1769. The mission, secularized by 1834, had become headquarters of John Magruder when Lewis Craig knew it.

Courtesy John Carter Brown Library

Disastrously unreliable, the wells at Alamo Mocho formed a desolate landmark where a portion of the San Diego trail crossed briefly into Mexico.

From Bartlett's Personal Narrative, *Vol. 2 (1854)*

Clad in their shrouds, the murderous deserters William Hays and John Condon prepare to ascend the gallows, witnessed by an assemblage of soldiers and Indians at the old San Diego mission.

Courtesy San Diego History Center

Elizabeth Church Craig, shown in later years, after her marriage to James Robb. Her face shows the effects of years caring for Confederate prisoners of war in Chicago, as well as the inroads of terminal illness.
Courtesy Malcolm Bell III

Sallie Craig always revered the memory of her officer father. After the Civil War, she married former Confederate officer Middleton Pope Barrow, who had named a new cannon of the Troup Artillery in her honor.

Courtesy Malcolm Bell III

Middleton Pope Barrow, shown in his Confederate uniform. A graduate of both the University of Georgia and its law school, Barrow devoted his public career to politics and the law and briefly served as U. S. Senator from Georgia.

Courtesy Hargrett Rare Book and Manuscript Library, University of Georgia

Lewis Stevenson Craig's headstone, Point Loma, California, is surrounded by the markers of the dead of San Pasqual.

Private Collection

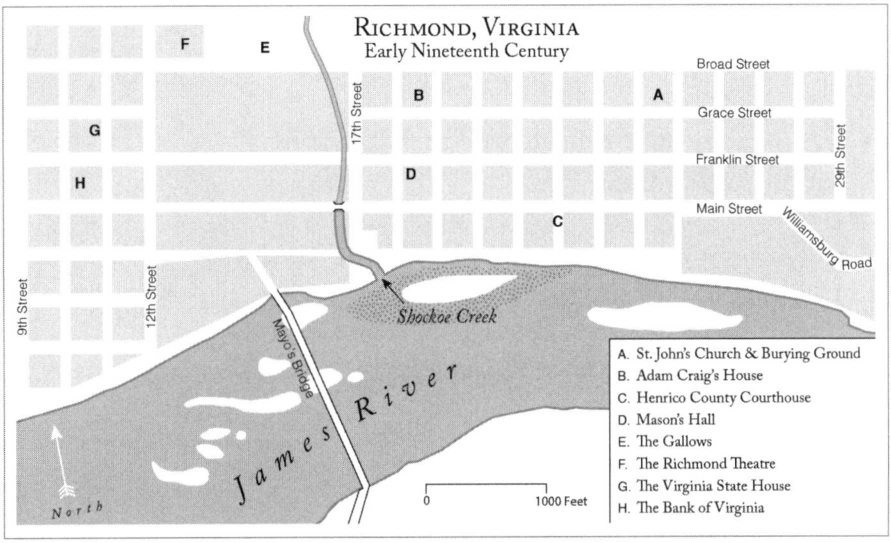

Richmond.

After Richard Young, A Plan of the City of Richmond, Virginia *(1809)*

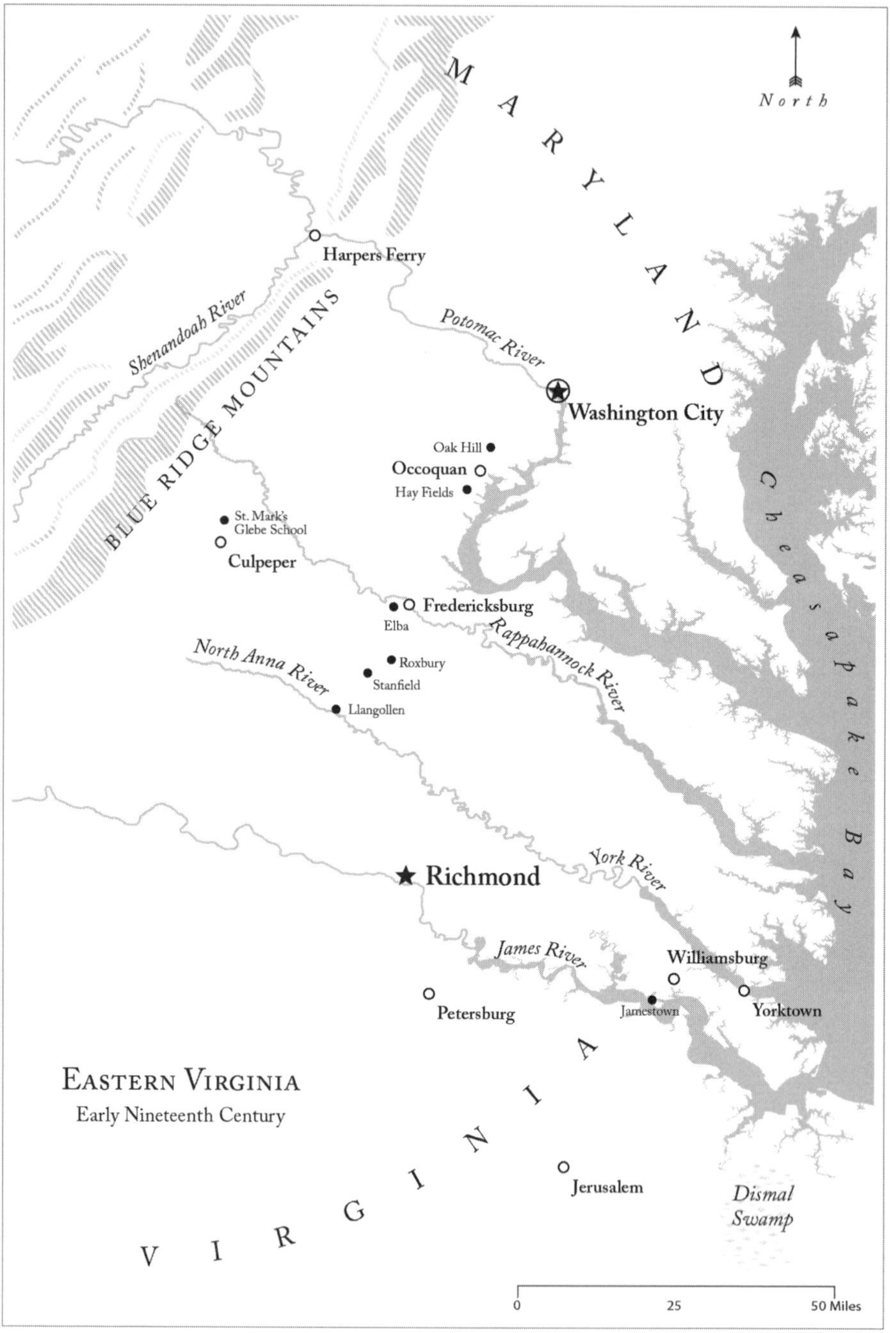

Eastern Virginia.

After "Virginia, Maryland, and Pennsylvania," in James Truslow Adams, ed., Atlas of American History *(New York: Charles Scribner's Sons, 1943), plate 128.*

The Floridas.

After "Seminole Wars, 1816–1842," Atlas of American History *(New York: Charles Scribner's Sons, 1943), plate 103.*

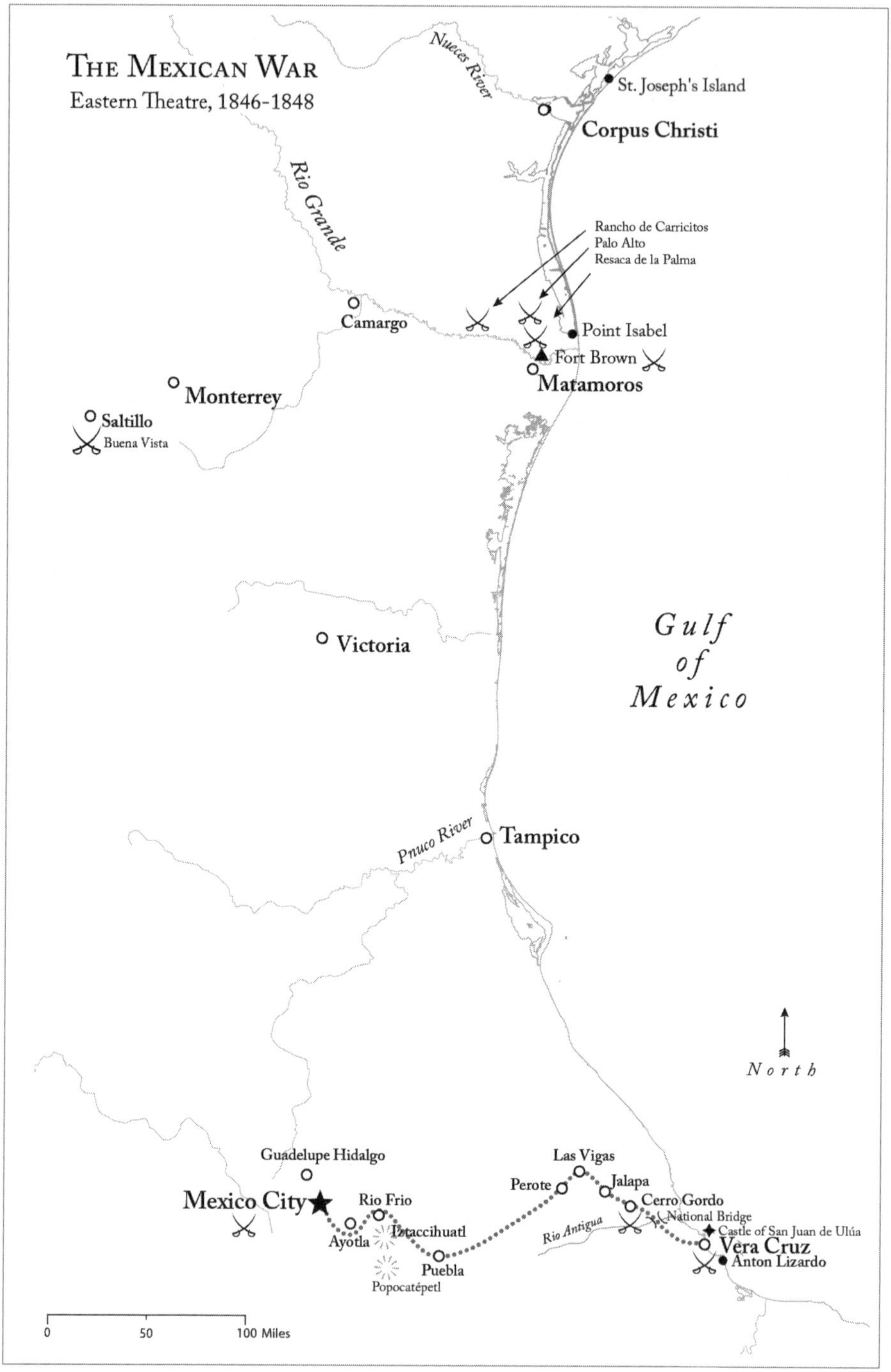

Eastern Theater of the Mexican War.

After "Battlegrounds," in Edward D. Mansfield's The Mexican War *(New York, A. S. Barnes, 1850), facing ch. 1.*

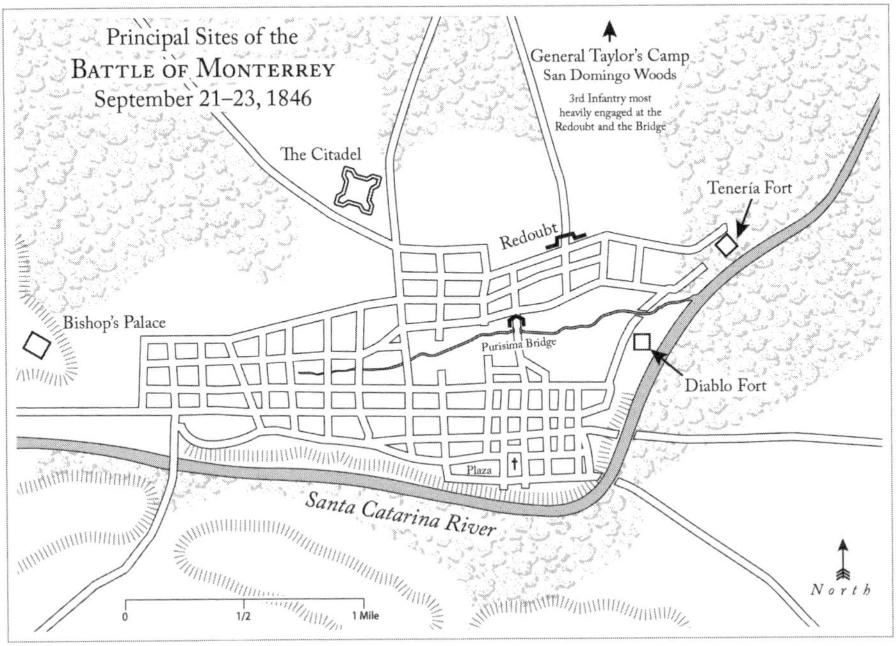

The Battle of Monterrey, Mexico.

After "The Battle of Monterrey," in Rives, The United States and Mexico, *opposite 2:262.*

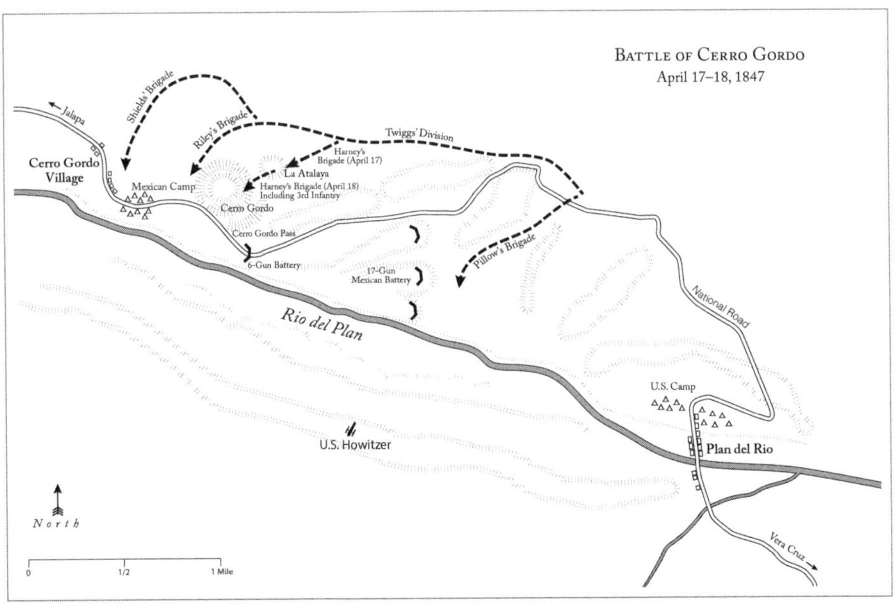

The Battle of Cerro Gordo, Mexico.

After "Cerro Gordo," in Rives, The United States and Mexico, *opposite 2:396.*

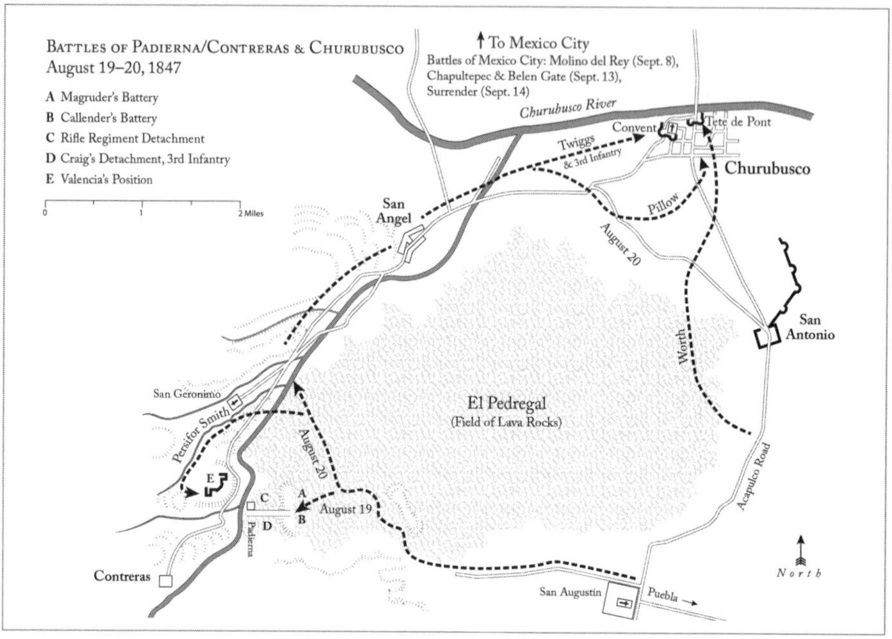

The Battles of Padierna/Contreras & Churubusco.

After "Contreras and Churubusco," in Rives, The United States and Mexico, *between 2:460–61.*

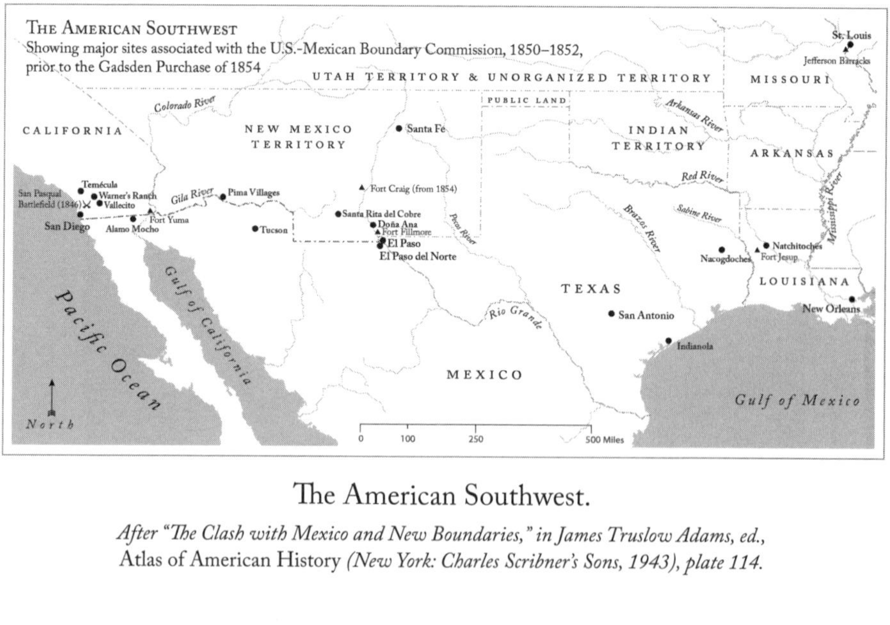

The American Southwest.

After "The Clash with Mexico and New Boundaries," in James Truslow Adams, ed., Atlas of American History *(New York: Charles Scribner's Sons, 1943), plate 114.*

Prologue

Portents

Coming events cast their shadow before.
—Thomas Campbell, "Lochiel's Warning"

On April 25, 1807, at Richmond, as the snowmelt-swollen James River roared over its granite shoals, Lewis Stevenson Craig was born in his family's house on Grace Street. Soon the Virginia capital itself became even more clamorous. The town's population of some five thousand doubled, as throngs crowded to the city to witness "the nation's first great legal spectacle"—the indictment and trial, on a hanging charge of treason—of former vice president Aaron Burr, who had been brought prisoner to Richmond the previous month. Oblivious to the hurly-burly, the newborn Lewis spent the months until Burr's surprising September acquittal securely cradled in the Craig house near the foot of Church Hill. Meanwhile, in the columned capitol a half-mile west on Shockoe Hill, the Burr drama played out in the crowded House chamber.

Although birth portents are retrospective (as well as outmoded since the days of the Roman historian Livy), someone glancing at the events of Craig's life—including his happiest years as a U.S. Army officer—might find it befitting that the Burr trial, with its plentiful martial associations, formed the backdrop for the boy's birth and early infancy. Many of the trial's participants (the defendant, the judge, many witnesses, and even some of the spectators) embodied decades of American military history—past, present, and future. They formed a virtual parade of American war chiefs from the Revolution onward.

Not only born of war, Craig's America had grown to early maturity embattled. Consequently, its military leaders customarily enjoyed respect and renown, as well as opportunities for political leadership. And, even after exchanging military for political power, many officers continued to be identified by their field grade military ranks, in preference to their civil titles. This was true for most of the former officers who entered the Richmond courtroom.

Defendant Aaron Burr, for instance, although he had been honored with the vice-presidency, the nation's second highest political office, would be referred to as "Colonel Burr" during his trial, both in court and in print—although he had resigned his Continental Army commission almost thirty years earlier. In many minds, moreover, Burr was constantly accompanied by the shade of a higher-ranking officer: General Alexander Hamilton, whom Burr had killed in a July 1804 duel.

Even so, towering over the military reputations of both Burr and Hamilton stood that of the Great Exemplar, revolutionary General and Commander-in-Chief George Washington, on whose wartime staff both Burr and Hamilton had served. For all those attending the Burr trial, General Washington loomed inescapably, and not only in ever-present memory. As the trial's attendees daily made their way to and from the courtroom, they passed Washington's life-size marble statue, as it loomed from its pedestal beneath the soaring State House rotunda, as accurate a replica of the general as a life-mask, exact physical measurements, and the genius of sculptor Jean-Antoine Houdon could make it. True, Washington had also been the Great Exemplar as the first president of the United States, but, in priority, he had been eulogized by Major General Henry Lee as "first in war" soon after his unexpected death eight years earlier.

Military motifs had served as General Washington's inspiration when, in the last years of his life, he became deeply involved in the planning and construction of the new U.S. capital that bore his name. He had helped see to it that the Federal City's architecture would suggest military strength and grandeur to citizens and visitors, as well as to the army officers who would look to Washington City for their orders and hoped-for advancement.

Several choices made by General Washington and his advisers had contributed to the national capital's marked martial aspect: those neoclassical elements like pediments, columns, arches, colonnades, and domes were meant to evoke the strength and splendor of ancient Rome, the greatest military power of ancient times. Monumental scale likewise figured significantly in the general's plans, in particular where the dwelling house of the commander-in-chief was concerned: during Lewis Craig's lifetime there would be no residence in the United States larger than the President's House in Washington City.

Near the turn of the eighteenth century, the association of American military power with that of ancient Rome might have appeared to be a combination of hope and pretension. After all, Rome at its height had boasted an army of more than 645,000 men while General Washington had never led more than seventeen thousand soldiers into battle. Indeed, during the War for Independence, the U.S. Congress had never been able to raise more than 89,600 troops in a single year.

Nonetheless, America's emulation of Roman war power would proceed rapidly. During Craig's boyhood, in the impending War of 1812, a massive U.S. army of over half a million men would be raised, comparable in numbers to the immense army that would make Napoleon master of Europe during the same period. Not a standing army like Napoleon's, the American republic's war force comprised over 450,000 militiamen serving short enlistments though the regular force, including the U.S. Navy and the U.S. Marines, would be recruited to over 55,000 men. And, as General Washington had firmly established, this and all other succeeding U.S. armies would campaign under civilian, not military, control, and would not be standing armies. Prior to war with Mexico in the 1840s, the U.S. peacetime army would never exceed 6,500 men.

To the regular army's officers, who decried the regular reductions in the force, the U.S. Congress—mindful of the people's aversion to standing armies—would seldom be considered an ally. In times of uneasy peace that often threatened to explode into war, the army was never allowed to reach, much less surpass, 7,000 men in peacetime until the 1840s.

Rather than depending on the halls of Congress, the republic's men of war would more often direct their attention to another location in Washington's columned city: a massive brick building centered with a two-story Corinthian colonnade. This was the War Department, positioned by General Washington just east of and adjacent to the Executive Mansion itself.

From the War Department, the Secretary of War, the adjutant general, and the departmental staff officers would control the destinies of the officers of the U.S. Army. And they would usually constitute the court of last resort for those embroiled in the eternal controversies of the service. Although British troops would prove in 1814 that the War Department building could be burned (torched like the neighboring Executive Mansion), its function could not be destroyed, and the structure itself would be rebuilt by 1820.

Omnipresent in the American mind, General Washington's deeds and works would continue to be revered decades after his death, not only by a grateful public but by the U.S. Army officer corps as well. Indeed, as late as 1847, with Craig and his comrades campaigning in faraway Mexico, Washington's birthday would be celebrated, most conspicuously before the notable American victory on the field of Buena Vista.

During Craig's youth, Washington would remain a living memory to many prominent Americans. At the Burr trial, for example, one of General Washington's former officers (and most enthusiastic admirers) would be presiding judge: U.S. Supreme Court Chief Justice John Marshall. Since Burr's alleged treasonous plotting had taken place on Blennerhassett Island—in the Ohio River on the distant western border of the Old Dominion—the case had been sent to the Federal court in Richmond, then located in Marshall's circuit. There in early April the chief justice decided that the Burr case would go before a grand jury in May. As the trial wound down in autumn, Marshall was pleased to welcome publication of the fifth and last volume of his mammoth biography of the general, which emphasized Washington's military greatness. Like other writers of the time, Marshall also preferred officers who were gentlemen: he pictured the "military paragons" of the Revolution as patricians, with Washington as "the epitome of patrician leadership."

John Marshall had been with Washington at Valley Forge during the bitter winter of 1777–1778, as had Hamilton and Burr. There the American army had been introduced by Baron Friedrich von Steuben to the vital intricacies of drill, a necessity in transforming an armed mob into an effective fighting force, a learned exercise without which an army might as well not take the field—and a discipline that Craig would later conspicuously master as an officer.

Although the Valley Forge army had seen much of death and would soon see more, Washington emphasized duty and patriotism and self-sacrifice by drawing on Roman history, as interpreted by one of his favorite British writers, Joseph Addison. The general particularly valued Addison's 1713 play, *Cato: A Tragedy*, and had an amateur performance staged for his soldiers at Valley Forge. In one of the most memorable scenes, Cato—a senator of the Roman republic who opposed the dictatorship of Julius Caesar and was soon to kill himself rather than lose his freedom—greets his dead son, killed in battle and borne to him on his comrades' shields:

> Welcome, my son! here lay him down, my friends,
> Full in my sight, that I may view at leisure
> The bloody corse, and count those glorious wounds.
> —How beautiful is death, when earn'd by virtue!
> Who would not be that youth? What pity is it
> That we can die but once to serve our country!

Another Roman hero gave his name to a society of officers—including Marshall, Burr, and Hamilton—who survived the Revolutionary War: an exclusive organization created in 1783, the hereditary Society of the Cincinnati. It took its name from the warrior Cincinnatus, who had left his fields to defeat Rome's enemies, and then, with Rome secure, had returned to his plow. Washington himself had served as the Society's first president, and General Hamilton as the second, both serving until their deaths. Among the members was Lewis Craig's uncle, David Miller of Williamsburg, who had been an officer of the Third Virginia Infantry Regiment of the Continental Line.

As one of the Cincinnati, Miller was entitled to the Society's handsome eagle badge, designed, like part of Washington City, by Pierre L'Enfant. It, like the organization's tribute in name to the Roman military hero, forged another link between the new American republic and Eternal Rome. Later, the United States government would also adopt the eagle as a symbol, though not the usual generic one, but an American bald eagle.

General Washington's own identification with Cincinnatus was fittingly emphasized by his statue in the Richmond State House. As a reminder that both the Roman general and Washington had returned to their farms after the enemy's defeat, a marble plow rested at the base of the Washington sculpture—though the general's sword was ready nearby, hanging from a column of bound rods of office, the symbol for millennia of governmental power and judicial authority.

As a member General Washington's party, the Federalists, Chief Justice Marshall stood in political opposition to then-commander-in-chief, Thomas Jefferson, founder of the anti-administration party, known hereafter as the Democrats (one of several party labels, confusingly including "Republicans"). Jefferson hated Burr, did not love his cousin Marshall, and pulled what strings he could to guarantee that a hempen rope would terminate Burr's life as surely as a leaden ball had killed Hamilton.

Marshall, however, owed some gratitude to Burr for his final major act as vice president: his impartial handling of the U.S. Senate impeachment proceedings against one of Marshall's Federalist associate justices. This political prosecution by the Democrats failed; thus, it served to strengthen the highest court and assured Marshall's lifetime position on the bench, where he would remain until his death in 1835.

President Jefferson himself did not appear in Richmond for the 1807 trial despite a subpoena. He preferred to divide his time between his Monticello gardens and the Federal City, to him so unpleasant that he longed to leave it behind permanently. Nonetheless, Jefferson was constantly kept posted on the progress of the trial and occasionally sent advice to Burr's prosecutors.

Although little interested in military matters, Jefferson had founded the U.S. Military Academy at West Point in 1802, and soon thereafter had projected American military power across the Atlantic. Jefferson also knew that the Federalists, having created the U.S. military establishment, had made it top-heavy with officers from their party. West Point, in addition to other more direct actions, was meant to effect a change in the officer corps that favored the Democrats at the Federalists' expense.

Nonetheless, for various reasons, the Federalist party itself would die by around 1816. Partisan influence on the War Department (and within it), however, would never wane, and Lewis Craig would witness political power intervening for good and ill throughout his military career. Additionally, he, as many other officers, would eventually protect himself to some extent by acquiring a political patron of his own in the U.S. Congress, U.S. Senator William C. Dawson of Georgia.

In Richmond, somewhat ironically, the matter at trial—Burr's alleged treason—sprang from one of Jefferson's greatest successes as president: the Louisiana Purchase. Until this mammoth land acquisition in 1803, the American republic had been confined to that region east of the Mississippi River won from Britain during the Revolutionary War of 1775–1783. Although the Americans had plainly finished with kings, the United States remained bounded on three sides by monarchs' domains, whose kings were not through with the Americans. On maps of the time, the British Canadas to the north and Spanish lands to the west and south seemed to enclose the United States like a pair of monstrous jaws.

Spain, in particular, as overlord of the Mississippi River, would for decades vex the western citizens of the newly independent nation, as Spanish officials at the port of New Orleans controlled and often hampered American commerce on the great river. In Kentucky, restless frontiersmen, weary of waiting for their national government to secure free navigation of the river for them, had begun to plot their own unilateral accommodation with Spain, or, if not, to solve their problem militarily.

Then, in 1803, Spain suddenly transferred all of Louisiana to France—at first a frightening prospect for Americans since, instead of belonging to the feeble Spanish Empire, the huge area to the west was now the property of the restless, aggressive Napoleon. Almost miraculously, Napoleon soon sold the immense area to the United States. Thus, several strokes of a pen (along with payment of fifteen million dollars to France's dictator) made American cities (and future duty stations of Lewis Craig) of both New Orleans, capital of Lower Louisiana, and—almost eight hundred miles upriver—St. Louis, Upper Louisiana's capital city.

Jefferson's acquisition of the Louisianas had immediately added over 820,000 square miles of land to the United States and made the Rocky Mountains the nation's westernmost border. Furthermore, Jefferson now considered America's southwest border to be the Rio Grande, as French claims suggested, though he was content for diplomacy to convince the Spanish of the fact. Time would show that force would be necessary. In any case, the Democrat Jefferson had actually lagged behind the plans of the Federalist Alexander Hamilton, who in the 1790s had become convinced of the importance to the American republic of nothing less than "wresting Latin America from Spanish control."

In part, Hamilton was reacting to the perilous international situation. Europe had been engulfed in war since 1792 and with war had come disruptions of trade in the Americas, along with tremors of democratic revolt throughout the Latin American colonies. Peace would not come to Europe until 1815, by which time America itself had been drawn into the conflict although, happily, the nation had emerged more unified than ever. By 1826 the New World colonies of Spain and Portugal would achieve their independence, and the burgeoning United States, through the Monroe Doctrine of 1823, would have warned the powers of Europe that the days of colonization in the western hemisphere were over.

In the early 1800s, before all these events, Aaron Burr—without employment or reputation, but retaining important military, political, and diplomatic connections—would see in a weaker, younger United States various circumstances that seemed perfectly matched for such a man as he, who could plan deeply and act quickly as events dictated.

In the Richmond courtroom, however, to the despair of his prosecutors, it developed that Burr had been so acutely subtle, had made his plans so murky, and had relied so heavily on contingency that, even to posterity, confusion would long exist regarding his actual project. Despite wild rumors, however, Burr's actual goal appears to have been more modest than Hamilton's: Burr would have been satisfied with Mexico and its fabulous gold and silver mines.

But had Burr actually harbored a desire to cut away the Lower Mississippi Valley from the United States, his clandestine collaborator would have proved indispensable. General James Wilkinson—fellow plotter since March 1805—was senior officer of the U.S. Army and soon-to-be governor of Upper Louisiana (1805–1807). A Marylander and Revolutionary War veteran, Wilkinson had been a Kentuckian since 1784, eight years before Kentucky had achieved statehood. A leader of the state's secessionist element, he and his frontier followers had long felt that Kentucky would flourish more richly out of the union.

In attempting unilaterally to secure for Kentucky trade concessions from the Spanish at New Orleans, Wilkinson had earlier sworn allegiance to Spain. For over two decades the general would remain a paid informant, known to his Spanish masters as Secret Agent No. 13. Despite numerous rumors of Wilkinson's questionable activities, President Jefferson in late 1803 had chosen him—together with the new governor of Lower Louisiana, young William C. C. Claiborne of Virginia—to serve as one of the commissioners overseeing France's transfer of the new purchase to the United States.

As for Burr, beyond question he intended to descend from the Ohio with the nucleus of an army, hoping it would be recruited into thousands from the restless frontiersman in Kentucky, as well as from adventurers from Tennessee and Mississippi—and perhaps even from some soldiers of Wilkinson's command. Very early in the plotting, one of the Kentuckians disclosed that conquest, not western secession, was the object of Burr's conspiracy. As the Kentuckian wrote to Wilkinson, "Mexico glitters in our eyes—the word is all we wait for."

So Burr's army was in fact bound for New Orleans, which Burr thought he could easily take from Governor Claiborne, them notably unpopular with the majority French Creole population. With its point of embarkation secured, the Burr expedition would be transported across the Gulf, perhaps by elements of the U.S. Navy (in the event that war with Spain had broken out) or perhaps by ships of the Royal Navy, as Burr had tried to arrange. The Americans would land at Vera Cruz. There, like "stout Cortez," Burr would march his men west to take Mexico City, capital of New Spain, where rich veins of gold and silver were mined just to the north.

As he laid his plans, Burr had exhibited an uncanny ability to attract the full cooperation of several major American military figures—daring officers who had won public acclaim in America's wars from the late 1700s to the early 1800s. But he had provoked the bitter enmity of a few others as well.

Among the more newly minted heroes among Burr's associates was Admiral Thomas Truxtun, who appeared briefly for the defense at the trial, attired plainly in civilian clothing. Hero of the naval Quasi-War (1798–1800) against Revolutionary France, Truxtun had instantly won fame when his U.S.S. *Constellation* had captured near the island of Nevis the French warship *L'Insurgente*, winning the first victory for the recently formed U.S. Navy. Truxtun was suspected of arranging for ships to ferry Burr's troops to Vera Cruz, a charge he strenuously denied. The admiral noted, however, that he thought Burr's Mexican invasion had been predicated on war breaking out between the United States and Spain, as had recently almost happened; this probably represented the major contingency on which Burr had counted.

Against Burr, foursquare for the prosecution, appeared "General" William Eaton. He had resigned from the U.S. Army as a captain in 1797 but had been complimented with a general's rank by the brother of the Bashaw of Tripoli, the storied Muslim stronghold in the southwest Mediterranean. As a prosecution witness, the voluble Eaton contrasted flamboyantly with the dignified, black-clad Burr.

Never reluctant to attract attention, Eaton wore in Richmond the exotic trappings of a traveler from the Levant. Sporting a forbidding black hat and vivid clothing—including a brilliant Turkish sash—Eaton frequently regaled his fellow tipplers in the capital's taverns, for he remained widely celebrated in the American republic as "the hero of Derne," the Tripolitan port that he had captured in 1805. At that time, as a newly appointed U.S. Navy lieutenant, Eaton had marched a tiny army of Arabs and Tripolitans—along with a group of U.S. Marine and Navy volunteers—on a 500-mile march across the desert to Derne. Significantly, the U.S. Marines had there first planted the American flag on foreign soil, and peace had soon followed.

More than a decade earlier, Eaton's military service had meshed more closely with Lewis Craig's future career as an Indian fighter. Eaton had first been commissioned a captain during the Northwest Indian War (1790–1795), which had been successfully concluded by General Anthony Wayne. As an officer in Wayne's Legion of the United States, especially created for Indian warfare, Eaton was among the men sent to build Fort Recovery. It was constructed on the site of the "Battle of a Thousand Slain" of November 1791, where General Arthur St. Clair's army had suffered the greatest defeat ever to be inflicted by Indians on a U.S. force. This debacle Wayne would avenge at the Battle of Fallen Timbers in August 1794. Arguably, Wayne's creation of the Legion and his leading it to the new Republic's first decisive victory entitled him to be called "the Father of the Regular Army."

The lineal predecessor of Lewis Craig's own Third U.S. Infantry had fought victoriously at the Fallen Timbers victory as the First Sub-Legion. From that time its officers and men (and their successors in the Third Regiment) would wear white as the distinctive color of their "cap ornaments and uniform facings," originally part of General Wayne's plan to foster *esprit de corps*. The First Sub-Legion was itself successor to the 700-man First American Regiment of 1784, which Congress had established rather than providing the small peacetime U.S. Army requested by General Washington. By various consolidations and permutations, the First Sub-Legion would in 1815 finally become the Third U.S. Infantry Regiment, Craig's "Old Guard."

General Wayne would not himself live to witness this transformation. He died in 1796, aged only fifty-one. But one of Wayne's major enemies and betrayers—Burr's co-conspirator, General James Wilkinson—would survive for decades to come. An arch-traitor surpassing even Benedict Arnold, Wilkinson in his time had betrayed not only Wayne but George Washington and George Rogers Clark as well. And, whether or not Burr was trying to create a secession movement in the states along the Mississippi, Wilkinson himself had in 1787 already sworn to Spain that he would do so.

Now the most valuable prosecution witness at the Burr trial, General Wilkinson arrived late in Richmond. Portly and pretentious and clad in a gaudy uniform of his own design, Wilkinson served as President Jefferson's most valuable ally during the legal proceedings.

A proud recipient of the patronage of both the Democrat Jefferson and the Federalist Hamilton, Wilkinson was to exercise command over the U.S. army longer than any other general of his time. In 1807 he was also serving as governor of the Louisiana territory, and his tardy arrival at the Burr trial ostensibly was due to continued concerns about a Spanish incursion in late 1806 across the Sabine River, the border between Spanish Texas and the U.S. Territory of Louisiana. As Secret Agent No. 13, Wilkinson had himself suggested that Spain act aggressively along the Sabine, but he had apparently been surprised by the incursion's timing. Nonetheless, he and his Spanish counterpart had "defused" the situation before war broke out by establishing a demilitarized zone on the Louisiana-Texas border. For this service, Wilkinson sent a demand for over 150,000 pesos to the Spanish viceroy in Mexico City.

Along with suggesting a heavy Spanish force be stationed along New Spain's border with the United States, Wilkinson had also advised the Spaniards in 1804 to send "a sufficient body of chasseurs to intercept" the Missouri River expedition of Captain Meriwether Lewis and Lt. William Clark and either to "force them to retire or take them prisoners." Captain Zebulon Pike, whom Wilkinson had ostensibly sent west on another exploration of Lower Louisiana, was also ordered to bring back Wilkinson intelligence on the roads between Louisiana and Santa Fe, Wilkinson's choice as a staging point for a north-to-south invasion of Mexico, though unbeknownst to Pike. Meanwhile, as additional advice to the Spaniards, Wilkinson had counseled them to support diplomatically the Southeastern Indians' removal across the Mississippi. There, Wilkinson argued, the Indians' consequent hatred of the Americans would make them an excellent human buffer between New Spain and the United States.

Wilkinson's treasonous activities had long been suspected, and many were surprised that he continued to hold posts of responsibility. Among those who deplored Wilkinson (and attacked him in print) was young

Washington Irving. Irving's forename represented an obvious tribute to George Washington—like those of so many in his and later generations; his own five-volume biography of the general would appear between 1855 and 1859.

The young New Yorker attended the Richmond trial some dozen years before reaching fame as one of the founders of American literature. Something of a Burr sympathizer, he delightedly described the first brief courtroom confrontation between Wilkinson and Burr, leaving no doubt whom he admired:

> Burr was seated with his back to the entrance, facing the judge, and conversing with one of his counsel. Wilkinson strutted into Court…[and] stood for a moment swelling like a turkey cock, and bracing himself for the encounter of Burr's eye. The latter did not take any notice of him until the judge directed the clerk to swear Gen. Wilkinson; at the mention of the name Burr turned his head, looked him full in the face with one of his piercing regards, swept his eye over his whole person from head to foot…and then coolly resumed his former position, and went on conversing with his counsel as tranquilly as ever. The whole look was over in an instant…a slight expression of contempt played over his countenance, such as you show on regarding any person to whom you were indifferent, but whom you considered mean and contemptible.

In the end, General Wilkinson's testimony proved insufficient to engineer Burr's conviction. And only posterity would see Wilkinson's own treachery in all its garish colors. Incredibly, he would survive a quite thorough court-martial in 1811, and it was only when Wilkinson failed militarily on the Canadian front in the War of 1812 that his "tainted reputation" finally caught up with him. Discharged from the army in 1815, he finally reached Mexico in 1822. There he would end his days in 1825, speculating in land and hoping forlornly that retired president Thomas Jefferson would respond to his many letters. When in 1847 the soldiers of the U.S. Army followed the path blazed by Cortez to triumph at Mexico City, the bones of James Wilkinson would await them, lying there in an unmarked grave.

By 1807 all but Wilkinson among the officers described above had either perished or left their days of prominence behind them all of the officers described above but Wilkinson had left their days of prominence behind them. But two observers present at Burr's trial had many campaigns ahead of them, both military and political. One, much more conspicuous by his behavior, was a tall man of around forty—apparently a frontiersman and no gentleman—with his long red hair tied with an eel skin at the back of his neck. Unseen, a chunk of lead lodged painfully (and permanently) near his heart, the souvenir of a May 1806 duel that his opponent had failed to survive. This was General Andrew Jackson of the Tennessee state militia, who as U.S. general and president would cut through many of the Gordian knots that had so far bedeviled American expansion.

Jackson would break the Creeks in 1814, defeat the British the next year at New Orleans, and rampage through the Floridas in 1818, speeding their sale to the United States by Spain three years later. During the presidential administration of Virginian James Monroe, Jackson would offer to take Cuba as well, if properly reinforced, but an alarmed John Calhoun, Secretary of War, feared Jackson intended also to invade Mexico.

In 1807 Richmond, Jackson's fervent attempts to testify in Burr's defense were blocked by the defendant's attorneys, who had found the Tennessean's grand jury testimony too inflammatory. Denied his role in court, Jackson instead delivered pro-Burr harangues to crowds outside the Capitol, rants so intemperate that some onlookers thought him mad.

Only slightly less conspicuous than General Jackson, Winfield Scott, the remaining man, was both younger and taller than Jackson—a gangly giant, in fact, at six feet four inches, with an ego in proportion—an apprentice lawyer who had just reached his twenty-first birthday in summer 1807. Most significantly for Lewis Craig, in later years Scott would come to be his commander, friend, and patron, and would grow to understand Craig's character as well as anyone.

Of these two, Burr himself personally knew only Jackson (who had several times hosted Burr at the Hermitage and only narrowly escaped being charged as one of Burr's confederates). Nonetheless, Burr was quite taken with Scott. The tall young man would have stood above any crowd (and above Jefferson, Jackson, and even Washington, for that matter). But to improve his view in the packed courtroom, he had clambered onto the rear door's "massive bronze lock" to watch the proceedings. Noticing Scott, Burr instantly classed him as the "most magnificent youth in Virginia." Though impressed by Burr's dignity and self-possession during the proceedings, Scott judged Burr guilty as charged of treason and considered that his execution would have been both exemplary and beneficial to the health of the republic.

Burr was acquitted of treason in September 1807, and the next month his murder indictment from the Hamilton duel was quashed. Entering self-imposed exile, he wandered through Europe, unsuccessfully attempting to secure support for his Mexican scheme. Burr would finally return to a quiet legal practice (and genteel poverty) in New York City. There he would ultimately die in his bed in 1836—not, as he would have preferred, wealthy and full of honors, but certainly, at age eighty, full of years.

Ironically, being a victim of a political prosecution had helped save Burr from the gallows. The Federalist chief justice had defined "treason" more narrowly than the Democrat president had wished, and Burr's acquittal also arguably saved Jefferson's posthumous reputation, for it prevented him from being remembered as the president who had used the law to murder a political foe.

As for Andrew Jackson, politically, Scott and Craig would later unite in opposition against him while respecting him as fighting man. The two would support the Whig party that arose in the 1830s in opposition to "King Andrew." With this name, the Whigs christened Jackson as a tyrant and identified themselves with the Whigs of the Revolution who had opposed King George III. Much later, Scott would go on to become the Whigs' last standard bearer in the presidential election of 1852. Although Scott would then outlive the party, which died soon thereafter, the Whigs would only barely survive Craig.

As would Craig less prominently, Scott would attain his greatest distinction in war, not politics. Scott's national reputation would continuously grow from first fame as a heroic brigadier in the War of 1812 to his becoming the longest-serving commanding general of the United States Army, 1841–1861.

In fact, an incident during the Burr trial led Scott to his military career. In late June 1807, the British warship H.M.S. *Leopard* attacked, defeated, and boarded the U.S.S. *Chesapeake* off the Virginia coast near Norfolk; its boarding party then proceeded to seize several sailors as deserters from the Royal Navy. The news shook Richmond like a thunderclap, and Scott joined those who rushed seaward as militiamen. By the next year, as British-American relations continued to deteriorate, the army was expanded, with Scott soon appointed to a captaincy.

After victories against the British in Canada, Scott would end the war as a U.S. army general, as would Andrew Jackson, after his own triumph over the British at New Orleans. Their successes had been such that there was even a suggestion that both Scott and Jackson be raised to lieutenant general, a rank previously held by George Washington alone.

From the 1812 war's conclusion to Craig's death in 1852, the military threat of Great Britain would remain. It would raise itself again in both Texas and California and would continue to preoccupy the minds of the U.S. officer corps, along with other possible threats from Europe. But the British threat would steadily recede. It would be into the remnants of the dying Spanish Empire and its successor state the Republic of Mexico that Lewis Craig would follow the Stars and Stripes, as he successfully practiced the profession of arms.

Chapter 1

From the Old Dominion

By what sweet charm I know not, the native land draws all men,
and never allows them to forget her.
—Ovid, Book 1, *Epistulae ex Ponto*

I.

As a proud Virginian, Lewis Stevenson Craig's participation in completing America's ocean-to-ocean expansion seems entirely appropriate. His pride in his native Virginia alone was reason enough. By the time Craig reached his majority, Virginia was well along in earning its identification as "Mother of Presidents." While Washington, of course, had come first, Craig was born within the period of the "Virginia Dynasty" of U.S. presidents, which began with Thomas Jefferson in 1801 and continued with James Madison and James Monroe until 1825. Afterward augmented by William Henry Harrison and John Tyler between 1841 and 1845, there would also be a brief coda (1849–1850) provided by Craig's future commander in Northern Mexico, Zachary Taylor.

General Taylor, with predecessors like Washington and Harrison, would also help support the later idea of the Old Dominion as the "Mother of Generals." Many additional war chieftains would be born in Virginia over the next century, far exceeding the number of those Virginians who served chief executive.

Ironically enough—where national expansion was concerned—Virginia, first founded in 1607 of the permanent Atlantic seaboard English colonies, had originally included much of the territory that Craig would assist in annexing to the United States. Indeed, where the broad expanse of North America was concerned, Craig's Virginia, according to its 1609 charter, had not only stretched to the Pacific, but had encompassed the bulk of the land occupied by the future United States, along with a sizeable portion of Canada. Small wonder that England's oldest American colony was sometimes called "the continent of Virginia." Or that in 1705 Virginia historian Robert Beverley "confidently foresaw the day when Virginia's settlements would reach 'the *Californian* Sea.'"

Even after the British crown had in 1783 relinquished its trans-Mississippi claims and lost Virginia itself as the result of the American Revolution, the Old Dominion had retained in her "Northwest Territory," south of the Great Lakes and east of the Mississippi, an area larger than France. And, though the Virginians ceded this territory to the Confederation government in 1784, Virginia would remain the largest of the American states for almost four decades more, even after much of the state below the Ohio River had become the state of Kentucky. And, as for the union created under the U.S. Constitution of 1787, Virginia stood preeminent among the states that constructed it.

Second-generation Virginians both, Winfield Scott and Lewis Craig embodied the fact that Virginia was not the sole preserve of the descendants of the seventeenth-century colonists. Where family military traditions were concerned, however, Scott's warrior ancestry was unquestionable. His grandfather, James Scott, had been among the losers in the Jacobite Rebellion of 1745, prompting his emigration to the Old Dominion. There Scott's father, William, had fought on the victorious side in the American Revolution.

For Lewis Craig there was no recent ancestral prompting toward military service. His own paternal grandfather, James Craig, had been a goldsmith of Scottish extraction, his topographic surname suggesting Scotland's rugged terrain, the most mountainous in Great Britain. James's parents, goldsmiths both, had been purveyors to the gentry and the aristocracy in London's Haymarket district. In the mid-1740s their son had made the four-thousand-mile voyage to Virginia, seeking to improve his fortunes. In the Old Dominion he would encounter the source of the masses of tobacco whose numerous East London warehouses encroached even on Tower Hill. At the time of James's voyage out, many "both in the colonies and the mother country, had come to regard Virginia and tobacco as synonymous." As the young man first made his way from Yorktown port to his new home in Williamsburg, he saw fields where tobacco leaves unfurled like pound notes—appropriately enough, since tobacco itself often served as Virginia currency.

For many years James Craig would conduct business at the sign of the Golden Ball on Williamsburg's Duke of Gloucester Street near the

Raleigh Tavern. He and his family lived behind the shop and in a dormer-lighted half-story above. Having arrived in Virginia's capital with the cachet of having come from London in his favor, James for many years would continue to import his goods from across the Atlantic. His regular supplier was John Norton of London and Yorktown.

James Craig specialized in jewelry at the Golden Ball. Among his customers, for one, George Washington purchased from him various finger rings and ornamental buttons, as well as golden earrings for his stepdaughter. Later James added to his inventory such luxury items as timepieces. Additionally, his dexterity and competence at such meticulous work as clock-making led to other commissions. Thomas Jefferson, for example, came to the Golden Ball for the repair of such delicate instruments as his perspective glass and his microscope.

Postponing marriage until the late 1750s, James Craig had found a good match in Anne Stevenson, a daughter of Virginia's prosperous "middling classes," with family connections in Williamsburg, Petersburg, and elsewhere. Thus, through his marriage, James Craig entered the "tangled cousinry" of the Old Dominion, as would the four children—two sons and two daughters—who were born to the couple over the next decade. The first of the four, Lewis Craig's father, was born in 1759. At the stone font laboriously transported from Jamestown to Bruton Parish Church, the infant was appropriately christened "Adam," as the first male Craig to be born in the New World Eden.

Determined to see his elder son become a prosperous gentleman, not a tradesman like himself, James in the early 1770s had apprenticed Adam to Virginia Secretary of State James Waller for training as a county court clerk. For seven years Adam learned and labored in Waller's office, a one-story fireproof brick structure down the street from the Golden Ball, close at hand to the capitol.

Intended to serve as an indispensable officer of one of the colony's county courts, Adam looked forward to being centrally seated below the gentleman justices, between bench and bar. There he would oversee judicial proceedings' proper form and documentation and be consulted on points of law by the justices, few of whom were lawyers. Such a clerkship often represented steadier returns than a lawyer's practice, with a sizeable monthly salary and the promise of many fees as well—all without the constant traveling from court to court that many lawyers necessarily undertook to make a living.

Though trained to serve the king, Adam Craig made an easy transition to acting as an official of the independent state of Virginia. In May 1776, during the "Interregnum" after the outbreak of war, Adam—already described in the legislation as "Adam Craig, Gentleman"—was selected to number "thirteen thousand three and thirty three" pounds of new currency. Several years earlier, his England-born father had realized that he was no longer a loyal royal subject: as a free Virginian, the elder Craig had in 1769 joined the Non-Importation Association organized by George Washington.

Soon Adam was made an assistant clerk to the General Court, the state's highest judicial body, a position he would hold for decades. In announcing Craig's election, the Assembly added to his name the courtesy title "Esquire," often considered even more flattering than "Gentleman." Adam Craig was not yet twenty. Mid-1777 found the House of Delegates electing Craig to be Virginia's Muster Master General, with the responsibility "to ascertain and report every month the effective state of the Army, for the payment of the men and officers."

Adam Craig would not be slow to proclaim his gentleman status symbolically. For use on legal documents, he owned an armorial seal, its stamp-end set with a fine topaz, deeply incised with a Craig coat-of-arms and the Latin motto "Liber et Fidelis" (Free and Faithful). Ownership of such a valuable instrument suggested more than wealth and position: it also served as an additional declaration that Adam Craig was a gentleman in the social hierarchy, with his family recognized as gentry, ranking in English usage second only to the aristocracy.

A heraldic, martial display like a coat-of-arms fit well with Lewis Craig's subsequent decision to follow the profession of arms. For, although the words "gentleman" and "gentry" were often allied with other soft-sounding terms (gentility, gentle birth, gentle blood), they had arisen from the violence of the medieval era: the original gentlemen were warriors, and their armorial bearings proclaimed them as such. They were armigers—arms-bearers. Fittingly, then, Lewis Craig, as a military officer, would follow the centuries-old calling of the gentleman-warrior.

In 1794 when James Craig died, aged around seventy, his daughter Ann Craig Miller was "lent for her life" his lots, house, and furnishings on Duke of Gloucester Street. The residue of his estate amounted to less than

£100, more than half of which represented the monetary value of Nan, the bondswoman who had presumably cooked and cared for James during his last years. Any funds remaining after payment of his debts, Craig's will ordered divided equally between his two sons. In addition, James left Adam, "the best of sons," his "Table Clock." He also testified to Adam's superior business acumen by noting that he had "relieved" his father "in many distressing situations." After Ann Miller's death all the Williamsburg property was to go to "Adam Craig and his heirs forever." Mrs. Miller, then thirty, would survive for a half-century more, outliving not only her brother Adam, but two of Adam's heirs as well. (It would ultimately fall to Adam Craig's son-in-law, Robert Stanard, to sell the Craig property in 1845.)

To her nephew Lewis Stevenson Craig (who himself would outlive her by only eight years), Mary Craig Miller represented the only direct family link to his London-born grandfather and to his Williamsburg-born father. Consequently, Lewis Craig's frequent visits to Williamsburg probably included visits to his aunt, with, perhaps, sharing of family lore. Judging only by the spirited personality Ann Miller conveys in her will, she appears to have been the type of aunt who could spin fascinating tales out of the Craig family's past—as well as from her husband's exploits during the Revolution, which had included service in South Carolina (including time as a prisoner of war in Charleston) and participation in the Siege of Yorktown in 1781.

Ann's brother Adam, now a trained court clerk, had moved to Richmond in April 1780—the first month that government business left Williamsburg permanently. Adam was tasked with transporting the state documents to their new location and arranging them appropriately.

Ironically, British general Benedict Arnold's recent burning of much of Richmond heralded more good fortune for Adam Craig. The capital also served as seat of Henrico County, and a great number of the county's records had been burned by Arnold's men, through the county clerk's "neglect of duty." When the negligent clerk was forced to resign, the county chose Adam Craig as its new clerk, a post he would hold for the rest of his life.

This office was added to yet another clerkship to which Craig had been appointed the previous July when the City of Richmond had been incorporated. The town fathers had chosen Adam Craig to be the Clerk of the Hustings Court (the Richmond city court), and he had given his £1,000 bond, the same as for his county clerk position. Craig would serve ably in this office for over twenty years.

Though public officials were allowed to hold more than one post, the number of burdensome offices that Craig held (and competently administered) occasioned some amazement. Craig's several jobs took him to the capitol on Shockoe Hill for state business and to the courthouse on Church Hill for his city and county duties. At the capitol he served not only as assistant clerk of the General Court, but also—as an officer of the General Assembly—as clerk of such committees as religion, courts of justice, and trade.

With his work divided between Richmond's two principal hills, Craig in 1784 decided to build a house between them, but closer to the courthouse. The year was an auspicious one. Late the previous year the news arrived that the peace treaty ending the late war had finally been signed between the United States and Great Britain. Richmond had celebrated joyously with "illuminations, fire-works, banqueting, and, finally, a ball."

Craig's Richmond house, where his son Lewis would be born in 1807, was situated on a full block fronting Grace Street, between 18th and 19th streets. Grace Street ran west toward Capitol Square, and the courthouse lay southeast a few blocks away. The house, still extant, gives the appearance of two two-story houses combined to create a backwards "L," with the base not fronting Grace Street, but the corner at Grace and 19th. An antebellum memoirist described it as a "pleasant, rural-looking residence....The green slope in rear of the house was washed at its base by a clear rivulet," a tributary of Shockoe Creek. Inside was "a graceful stairway, with slim balusters and mahogany rail," floors of "random-width pine," and "dark marble" mantels.

Craig's small office at the courthouse was insufficient for all the business he conducted. Along with advising the gentleman justices on points of law, Craig and his assistants kept meticulous minutes of county court proceedings and made multiple copies of the rafts of legal documents the court system produced: "county records, court cases, indentures, deeds, wills." Although the court only met every two months, the clerk had to be available daily to the citizens. On the other hand, the Hustings Court—"practically the legislative, judicial, and executive body of Richmond"—met monthly, with jurisdiction over all "cases occurring within the city of

Richmond."

Craig alone could not himself hope to do all the work for the three courts, so, as county court clerk, he hired and trained assistants and also received some aid from the budding lawyers who "read the law" in his well-stocked library. There they found not only the standard authorities but also all "the laws passed by the Assembly as soon as they were printed." Though not allowed to practice law, a county clerk "possessed an influence far beyond the legal powers of his office," became "an expert in the law through experience," and, as had been the case in colonial times, "guided the justices in many cases."

Craig's attendance at the capitol occurred principally during the General Assembly's sessions. Where his city and county duties were concerned, he arranged to be at the courthouse only when the courts were in session. Otherwise, he (or one of his deputies) could be found, as marked on the Richmond map, at the "Henrico & Hustings Court Office," a "very small Dutch-roofed house," built to his order on the southwestern corner of his Grace Street lot. As time went on, those assisting Craig or reading law with him were allowed bed and board on his premises, first in the residence itself, then in a sort of legal student barracks in his side yard, with its own detached kitchen.

Having worked steadily in Richmond since 1780, making himself vital to the workings of the law in Virginia's capital, Adam Craig decided in 1787 to marry and start a family. For his wedding he traveled quite far afield from Richmond, to the eastern shore of the Virginia peninsula, below Yorktown. There in the small, marlstone Charles Parish Church, on the sixth of July, "in the 12th Year of the Commonwealth," the Reverend Joseph Davenport married Adam Craig and Mary Mallory, whose planter father, William, owned three plantations in the vicinity of the Poquoson River.

Craig's father-in-law owned several slaves, but he apparently concentrated less on plantation agriculture than on raising cattle, sheep, and hogs. Although a townsman, Adam Craig would come to own plantations on the Chickahominy River and considerable acreage in Kentucky, together with much real estate in and around Richmond and in several other Virginia counties. Craig would also own over twenty slaves, some of them Richmond domestic servants, others laboring as field hands on his Chickahominy lands.

The extent to which slave-owning proclaimed Adam Craig's ascent into the gentry cannot be known, but it seems probable that it accomplished two other declarations related to his having become a gentleman—his church and fraternal organization memberships.

Where slave-owning was concerned, slave masters occupied the apex of antebellum Virginia society, and many whites and a few free blacks worked to establish themselves in that status. British visitors to Virginia before the Revolutionary War often criticized the "parvenu character of the colony's ruling class." One observer in particular targeted the link between gentry status and slave-owning, asserting that, in Virginia, a man "may be a gentleman without having any Virtue at all" provided he has "Money, Negroes, and land enough." Regarding "the still culturally new but economically established gentry" who had made their status hereditary, this critic exclaimed bitterly against a system that allowed a son to be "a Gentleman by the Negroes and land given him by his father."

Soon after Adam Craig arrived in Richmond (where 66 percent of the 124 households owned one slave or more), he became concerned over one aspect of urban slavery, and he signed a June 1782 petition to the Virginia House of Delegates that asserted

> that many persons have suffer'd their Slaves to go about and to hire themselves and pay their masters for their hire, and others under pretense of putting them free set them out to live for themselves and allow for their masters such hire as they can agree, by which mean the said Slaves live in a very idle and disorderly manner, and in order to pay their masters their due hire are frequently stealing in the neighborhoods in which they reside.

The petitioners wished "such pernicious practices ended," and put part of the blame for the situation on a 1782 "liberal act of manumission," but the century would turn before the legislature acted. In 1806, a new law required "all manumitted blacks to leave the state within a year after receiving their freedom on pain of being reclaimed and sold as slaves."

Between 1782 and 1800, Adam Craig witnessed an evolution of both white public opinion and state law from the vantage point of his various clerkships. As clerk of the Hustings Court, which had jurisdiction over the offenses of slaves and freedmen in Richmond, Craig was familiar with the statistics, which showed that most criminal charges involved theft.

In 1800, during James Monroe's governorship, Craig—as clerk of the Court of Oyer and Terminer—recorded the case against the freedman Gabriel and his followers for planning a rebellion, apparently inspired by the volcanic Caribbean slave revolt in Haiti (then called Saint-Domingue), which had raged since 1791. Consequently, city and state authorities had grown more punitive. Gabriel and some two dozen others were convicted and ordered hanged at the Richmond gallows west of Shockoe Creek.

Along with slave-ownership, Adam Craig's faithful membership in the Anglican Church of his youth, known as the Episcopal Church since 1789, also proclaimed gentry status. In the 1780s, Thomas Jefferson and James Madison had not only disestablished the Virginia church—which had been supported by the people's taxes as the established church since 1610—they had all but destroyed it. Indeed, the condition of the church was almost as dire as described (with both exaggeration and sly pleasure) by New England historian Henry Adams: "The Virginia gentry stood by and saw their churches closed, the roofs rot, the aisles and pews become a refuge for sheep and foxes, the tombstones of their ancestry built into strange walls or turned into flagging to be worn by the feet of slaves."

Nonetheless, Adams admitted, "Good society in Virginia recognized no other religion....'Sure I am of one thing,' was the remark in the Virginia legislature of an old-fashioned Federalist, with powdered hair, three-cornered hat, long queue, and white top-boots,—'Sure I am of one thing, that no *gentleman* would choose any road to heaven but the Episcopal.'"

One could quite easily join a church, but entrance into exclusive fraternal organizations could be more difficult, particularly into those considered the preserves of Virginia gentlemen. This was certainly the case with Freemasonry. In 1773 a Williamsburg lodge was founded while Adam Craig remained James Waller's student, but in 1782, then in his early twenties, Adam was admitted to the lodge, which included, among others, faculty members from the College of William and Mary and future president James Monroe. Adam Craig (and his friend John Marshall) would later be among the Richmond gentlemen who in 1785 organized Richmond Lodge, No. 10, Ancient Free & Accepted Masons. Claimed as the "first Masonic edifice in America," their hall on Church Hill, had been "launched" on the same day of "the laying of the corner-stone of the Virginia State Capitol." This hall, attended throughout his life by Adam Craig, stood on Franklin Street near his home. Craig, Marshall, and their fellow Masons (and fellow gentlemen) in 1792 also organized the Richmond Royal Arch Chapter, No. 3, A.F. & A.M. As one of the Masonic songs of the time noted,

> We make it plainly to appear
> By our behavior everywhere,
> That when you meet with Masons there,
> You meet with gentlemen.

II.

Between 1788 and 1805, five children came to the marriage of Adam Craig, gentleman, and his wife, Mary Mallory Craig: William Mallory (born 1788), Jane Stith (1793), James (1795), Ann (1797), Mary Mallory (1800), and Arnett (1805). Even before his family began to grow, Adam Craig had begun to plan for his children's future provision by purchasing lands in Kentucky that would constitute much of his legacy to them.

Adam's professional family expanded even more rapidly and numerously. Of Adam Craig's many students in law, the one destined for greatest fame was his distant cousin Andrew Stevenson, son of the Reverend James Stevenson, rector of St. Mark's parish in Culpeper County. Stevenson served as one of Craig's assistants from 1800 until 1805, when he was admitted to the Virginia bar. He eventually became Speaker of the U.S. House of Representatives, serving from 1827 to 1834. From 1836 to 1841, Stevenson was posted to the Court of St. James's as U.S. ambassador, and thus was present for the 1837 coronation of Queen Victoria, whose name would characterize the remainder of the nineteenth century. Through the Craigs' esteem for this promising young man and his family, their youngest daughter was named for Andrew Stevenson's mother, born Frances Arnett Littlepage, who would later privately educate the older Craig daughters.

Moreover, the boy born in 1807 as the last of the Craig children provided an opportunity to honor not only the Stevensons but also one of the most remarkable men of the early republic, General Lewis Littlepage, the illustrious half-brother of Frances Littlepage Stevenson. Born in 1762, Littlepage had commanded no American armies but had led several European ones. In 1801 he had visited the clerk's establishment on Grace Street to visit his nephew Andrew and to present the young scholar with some of his law books. Though Adam Craig and Littlepage had never before met, they shared the bond of being brother Masons.

Littlepage had only recently returned from decades of adventures across the Atlantic. In 1780 his first sojourn to Europe had taken him to Spain as an assistant to John Jay, the U.S. Continental Congress's minister to the royal court. Ultimately falling out with Jay (to the extent of challenging him to a duel), Littlepage had soon found more suitable employment as a soldier of fortune.

Returning briefly to Virginia, Littlepage had secured the patronage of Patrick Henry, then governor of Virginia and fellow native of Hanover County. With Henry's letter of introduction to General George Washington, Littlepage stayed as an overnight guest at Mount Vernon in November 1785.

The future U.S. president described Littlepage as "an extraordinary character," mentioning particularly his service on the staff of the Duke de Crillon during the spectacular but futile siege of British Gibraltar (1779–1783). Washington's interest in the Gibraltar siege was more than intellectual: this lengthy military operation, conducted by the French and their Spanish allies, had actually represented the European front of the American Revolution.

Returning to Europe in 1786, Littlepage had served for many years the doomed last king of Poland, Stanislaus II, and thus became known as "The King's Chevalier." In the late 1780s, he was involved with Captain John Paul Jones in successful naval operations against the Turks in the Black Sea.

Unfortunately, as the Polish king's envoy to Imperial Russia, Littlepage had easily won—and dangerously lost—the affections of Catherine the Great. After Poland vanished in the final partition of 1795, the empress forbade Littlepage to accompany the king into exile, where the luckless monarch died in 1798. Following further adventures and controversies, Littlepage returned in 1801 to his native Virginia.

The last of Adam and Mary Craig's children was therefore christened Lewis Stevenson Craig, a compliment to the Chevalier Littlepage, his nephew Andrew Stevenson, and, by extension, the Stevenson family itself. In retrospect, this connection of Lewis Craig to Lewis Littlepage seems particularly fitting. As a prominent Virginian historian later commented, Littlepage occupied a place at the forefront of "two generations of adventurers" from the Old Dominion, "famous Virginians who carried the frontiers of the Union to the Rio Grande and the Pacific." Among those later adventurers, Lewis Stevenson Craig was destined to take his own place.

The newborn Lewis Craig had been oblivious to the dramatic events at the state capitol in 1807 and would continue unconscious of the tragic circumstances that would prevent him from ever knowing his family's full circle. Adam Craig's health had been declining since the time of the Burr trial as he was being slowly killed by consumption. His newspaper obituary in May 1808 obliquely noted the lingering nature of his illness with a line of verse from the British poet William Mason: "Beside the couch, Death took his patient stand / And menaced oft, and oft withheld the blow."

Adam Craig, then a relatively young forty-seven, appears to have brought on the final crisis himself by overusing a folk remedy for pulmonary complaints. Inhaling the fumes of burning pine straw, he had fatally seared his air passages. He left an estate worth over $100,000 (mainly land, slaves, and bank stock)—the twenty-first-century equivalent of over two million dollars. Except for the eldest, William, who had demanded his portion early, each of the children was left with a legacy of over $15,000—today's equivalent of over $300,000—for their "maintenance and education."

As the youngest child, however, Lewis Craig was two decades from his majority, and thus the most vulnerable of his father's survivors. Other family deaths, along with sibling estrangements and questionable business decisions by his older brothers, would ultimately work to trap Lewis Craig in a tangled legal thicket that he found impossible to escape until 1836. Lewis's two brothers—William, named for Mary Craig's father; and James, named for his father's father—appear to have generally viewed Lewis as a complication to their own legacies. In the Craig family, where each newborn was often first known as "the little stranger," Lewis's fragmented childhood and youth would work to keep him always a stranger from much of his remaining family.

Lewis's four sisters, however, appear to have welcomed him. Jane, the eldest, was fourteen when her youngest brother arrived, and she seems to have given him more maternal affection than his mother ever did. The other three sisters also helped care for their young brother, particularly since, at the beginning, Mrs. Craig was recovering from what had been a difficult pregnancy. Of the sisters, Ann was near Jane's age, with Mary next. Arnett the youngest, was little older than Lewis.

Not only was Lewis left fatherless (and with no memory of his father), but his entire family now also experienced an abrupt end to what had been ever-increasing prosperity. Instead, Adam Craig's heirs would be engaged for over two decades in an increasingly rancorous division of his large estate. Lewis's elder brothers, of whom James would become his first guardian, engaged in a certain amount of wheeling and dealing with the estate, as they began to cast their eyes about for suitable wives.

It would be the older sisters—all acclaimed beauties (as often seems the case, but in this instance verified by all the sources)—who progressed more quickly toward marriage, endowed by their father's will with handsome dowries. Jane, the first to marry, chose a diligent young lawyer, Robert Stanard of Stanfield, a large plantation to the north in Spotsylvania County, south of Fredericksburg.

The Craig-Stanard marriage would occur during a period of mourning born of a family tragedy. On December 26, 1811, Jane's younger sister Ann left the Craig house for the last time, as a short carriage ride took her uphill to the Richmond Theatre. Toward the performance's end, a fire broke out and quickly consumed the frame building. Ann and one hundred other Richmonders perished, including the mayor of Richmond and the president of the Bank of Virginia. Future president John Tyler, kept home only by chance, expressed his horror and relief in a letter that also mourned the loss of Ann Craig, "a most lovely woman."

The Richmond Theatre fire created despondency not only in Richmond but across a nation already dreading another war with Britain, which would indeed break out in five months. For those who considered theatergoing to be of doubtful morality, the catastrophe also became an occasion for soul-searching. The blaze had broken out after the main play, during a scene (adapted from Matthew Lewis's notorious novel *The Monk*) that included a candlelit chandelier. Richmond's grieving citizens determined that the theater would not be rebuilt. Instead, with so many of the dead unidentifiable, all the ashes were buried together in a masonry crypt on the site, over which a large church was then constructed.

Called the Monumental Church, it proved to be a massy, primitive-looking building whose façade looked back past Greece and Rome to ancient Egypt for its design. At the church's entrance, a pyramidal memorial stone recorded the names of Ann Craig and the fire's other victims.

Though not quite five at the time of Ann's death, Lewis could scarcely have been unaware of the abject grief that descended on the house when his sister was lost. But the boy would remain in Richmond for only five more years before traveling to the Stanards' new home in Fredericksburg. Lewis soon fell in love with the area, its hills and dales, and the town's connection to the sea, the Rappahannock River.

The young George Washington had lived at Ferry Farm across the river. Perhaps Lewis copied Washington by trying to throw a rock across the Rappahannock (apparently the origin of the myth of Washington's throwing a silver dollar over the Potomac). In any case, Lewis had claimed a new home. From there he would travel to boarding schools, first in Culpeper County and then in southern Spotsylvania County, before returning to Fredericksburg as his residence of choice.

During his Richmond childhood, Lewis and his friends probably spent time exploring the woods east of Church Hill and scaling the steep bluff above the Craig house that led to the upper level of Grace Street. In warm weather there was swimming, rock-throwing, and the launching of wooden branches in the nearby James River, "studded here and there with bright islands" and "brawling" through its rocky shoals. And, always there was the less active pastime of standing in wait at the head of Mayo's bridge, observing those who entered and left the town, and hoping for something dashing and colorful—like a contingent of U.S. cavalry.

Lewis would begin to split his time between Richmond and Fredericksburg after Jane's move there, and he would soon become more familiar with the Rappahannock River than the James. Moreover, south of Fredericksburg at Robert Stanard's Stanfield, he could hunt when he grew older, with hounds or on horseback, as he had been unable to do in Richmond. Nearby, other members of the Stanard family resided at a larger plantation, Roxbury. Through Jane's marriage, the Stanards had now become Lewis's family, and over the years he would happily resort to both the Stanard plantations.

Jane Craig Stanard had been in Fredericksburg only a few months when war broke out with Britain in June 1812. Nonetheless, the war did not encroach measurably on daily life until its last months, when the Chesapeake area became a major theater of war. With Fredericksburg vulnerable to the smaller warships of the British navy, some families moved further into the Virginia interior or temporarily evacuated, as Jane did. Her time of greatest anxiety came in August 1814 when, with Washington City's public buildings in ruins, she worried (needlessly as it happened) that Robert Stanard would have his name drawn in the Spotsylvania militia draft and be sent to the battle front.

For good or ill, such state militias (in Virginia and the other states) would form the bulk of American forces in the War of 1812. But most of the Old Dominion's military-age males, such as Lewis's elder brothers, would spend the war going about their business. Though boasting a population of almost 900,000, Virginia contributed only some 70,000 militiamen to the war effort, for varying terms of brief service. Consequently, a major pastime of James Craig during the war was courtship and marriage, which further served to draw the Craig siblings toward Fredericksburg.

The most flamboyant personality of the Craig family, James greatly enjoyed the social life offered by Jane's new surroundings. As the largest town of its region, Fredericksburg drew the planter families (and their daughters) to balls and other festive gatherings. At one of them James encountered Nancy Fox, whose father, Captain John Fox of Oak Hill Plantation, had extensive land holdings to the north in Potomac-bordered Prince William County. In early 1814 James Craig married Nancy, his "little sun beam," as he described her. And, since Captain Fox presided over a large family—including seven more daughters—one of Nancy's sisters also was available for William Craig. He accordingly married Mary Bronough Fox in summer 1817 when Lewis was ten.

Jane's move to Fredericksburg in 1812 had left her mother, Mary Mallory Craig, at home with her twelve-year-old daughter Mary, and "the children" as they were described in letters: Arnett, seven, and Lewis, five. Mrs. Craig was oppressed by her widowhood. Added to her grief at the untimely deaths of her husband and daughter was the increased responsibility for her younger children, duties previously shared with both Ann and Jane. Even with the help of servants, Mrs. Craig felt confined by her maternal obligations. Although some of Adam Craig's astute friends served as his executors, Mrs. Craig, made executrix, proved unequal to the task. She was particularly burdened by the litigation that seemed inevitably to cluster around the administration of the large estate.

Jane Stanard's return to Richmond for the 1812 Christmas season had marked the last time Lewis Craig's family gathered together in the house on Grace Street. Thoughts of Ann at the previous Christmas must have loomed inescapably since, across Shockoe Valley, the grim facade of the Monumental Church loomed, a forceful reminder of the family's recent tragedy.

At the Craig house, however, much had been done to produce forward-looking thoughts. In preparation for the Christmas gathering, the house had been painted inside and out, to the frank amazement of Mrs. Craig. Jane, fast becoming the de facto head of the family as far as Lewis was concerned, prolonged her stay until February 1813. She would remain the sibling most attentive to young Lewis, sending him marbles, toys, and books from Fredericksburg during his Richmond childhood, and sacks of gingerbread cookies and other treats later when he was away at school. During his holidays Lewis would usually visit with the Stanards in Fredericksburg.

Unfortunately, by the time Jane and Robert Stanard returned to Richmond permanently in 1819, the Craig family would be irrevocably split. The physical separation of Mrs. Craig and her eldest daughter had created numerous problems. Mrs. Craig, literate but never comfortable with writing, used her "amanuensis" young Mary for her few missives, while at the same time reproaching Jane, much the better correspondent, for a lack of letters.

To Jane's great disappointment, her mother also resisted visiting her in Fredericksburg. Particularly upsetting to Jane, Mrs. Craig did not stay with her during her first confinement in November 1812, which concluded with a miscarriage. Mrs. Craig was present at the birth of her first grandchild, Robert Craig Stanard, in April 1814 and visited again in fall 1815. But, by May 1817, Jane, now the mother of three children, was reduced to begging her mother to come visit them in Frederickburg.

Later in 1817, Jane was stunned to discover the reason for her mother's puzzling lack of family feeling. Apparently, since shortly after Adam Craig's death, Mrs. Craig had been courted by one of her husband's executors, Samuel Paine, and had formed an "ill-placed attachment" with him. They wed in November 1817.

Although Jane had appreciated Paine's assistance to her mother with business matters, she never suspected the possibility of a union and considered Paine—a tradesman and speculator in public securities—an insultingly inappropriate successor to Adam Craig. At great emotional cost, Jane terminated all contact with her mother, both from Fredericksburg and upon her return to Richmond.

By the time of his mother's remarriage, Lewis Craig had embarked on what would become a decade of boarding school education, 1816–1826. From early childhood he had shown an aptitude for reading and a fascination with books. Nonetheless, higher education, such as his brother-in-law Robert Stanard had received at the College of William and Mary, played no part in his plans. Lewis's was to be a preparatory education ample for what he then hoped to be: a country gentleman living on his own lands, the life for which the legacy from his father had prepared him.

The education young Lewis received would, however, prove more than adequate for his ultimate profession as an army officer. In particular he learned a very legible hand and a prose style direct and unornamented. Additionally, as his love of reading expanded, his choices in books became broader and deeper, preparing him for respectable discourse among the more enlightened members of the officer class, as he would later discover.

As Winfield Scott certainly did, Lewis probably enjoyed the novels of Sir Walter Scott, which appeared regularly between 1814 and 1832. In fact, just as General Scott could enjoy Sir Walter's tales of his ancestral Jacobites, Lewis Craig could find—in *The Fortunes of Nigel* (1822), as one of the novel's major historical figures—George Heriot, the Scottish "goldsmith of goldsmiths," so rich that he loaned money to King James I.

Fittingly, both of Lewis's teachers—the Reverend John Woodville at St. Mark's Glebe and John Lewis at Llangollen School (each a relation of Craig to one degree or another)—valued military service. And the Reverend Woodville particularly admired the character and exploits of Craig's namesake, General Lewis Littlepage. Indeed Woodville hero-worshiped Littlepage to the degree that he requested burial beside "the King's Chevalier" in the Masonic Cemetery at Fredericksburg, a wish that would be granted.

The Rev. Woodville's St. Mark's Glebe School was located in rural Culpeper County, over one hundred miles from Richmond, but only forty miles northwest of Fredericksburg. An area of often steep hills and scattered deep woods, the county produced mainly wheat and corn, with some tobacco as well. The glebe itself, essentially a parcel of land set aside for the benefit, support, and residence of the minister of nearby St. Mark's

Episcopal Church, served as the location of the boarding school.

The glebe where Craig's education began followed a once-common pattern in Anglican Virginia. It lay some miles from St. Mark's Church, the simple but stylish rectangular masonry structure covered by a shingle-clad hip roof where the Reverend Woodville officiated. Illuminated by arched windows, the building contained within a version of the liturgical floor plan of Bruton Parish Church in Williamsburg.

Students at the glebe school paid for bed and board, pens and paper and ink, and in return received a basic education that did not skimp on religion. Craig's older brothers as well as several of his cousins had received their schooling there. The church lay in a fork formed by the Hazel River and the Rappahannock, so was frequently called the Little Fork Church. Although neither watercourse was visible from church or glebe, the Blue Ridge Mountains rose prominently to the west, and would remain one of Craig's fond memories of his early school days.

During Craig's time at Woodville's school (1816–1822), there was one unusual occurrence. Perhaps unsurprisingly, it took place in December 1820, almost exactly a year after Lewis's mother had "very suddenly" died. His elder brother William, then his guardian, received a letter from the boy suggesting, in William's words, that he was "destitute of whole clothing" and wished William to send for him. But when Lewis arrived at Hay Fields, William's farm near Occoquan, he came "neatly and warmly clad" in clothing already supplied by Mr. Woodville and Robert Stanard.

Although the boy had needed more clothing (and was no doubt also grieving and homesick), William received him with little patience or sympathy. He implored Jane by letter, "for God's sake prevail on some good steady man to become his guardian."

Pleading poverty, William also asked Jane and Robert Stanard to provide Lewis with two books the Reverend Woodville said he needed—Sallust, on the wars of the late Roman Republic, in the original Latin, and a copy of Morrell's Latin dictionary, for the schoolmaster thought the boy would "make a very good classical scholar."

By this time William Craig was indeed poor, and had been involved in litigation with his father-in-law, John Fox, almost from the beginning of his 1817 marriage to Mary Fox. Suits and countersuits would continue into the 1830s. According to Captain Fox, despite a marriage contract executed to protect Mary Fox from her already deeply indebted husband,

William, had succeeded in liquidating much of the property attached to Mary's 300-acre estate: "Negroes to the value of more than $500 and Timber, etc., to the value of $2000." These funds, deposed John Fox, "had been spent and wasted" to the profit of "sharpers, gamblers, and tavern keepers" by a man "habitually addicted to the intemperate use of intoxicating liquors."

With brother James as his next guardian, Lewis continued his education (1822–1826) thirty miles southwest of Fredericksburg at Llangollen, poetically named by founder and schoolmaster John Lewis in honor of his Welsh heritage. A remarkable institution, Llangollen offered excellent college preparation for those inclined, and the finest of gentlemen's education for those who were not.

Schooling for a few young women was offered also, along with bed and board. The female dormitory occupied the massive residence's half-story, and, prudently, was accessible only by a stairway in the bedroom of Mr. and Mrs. Lewis. Unusually, the house was warmed by several fireplaces, whose two broad chimneys rose along the ridge line, away from the gables.

For young men interested in the profession of arms, Llangollen also presented a perfect opportunity to begin separating the romance of war from reality, for the boys' section was a military school. The young men wore uniforms and slept downhill from Lewis's residence in log-cabin barracks near a small stream. Their meals, however, were taken in the large kitchen in the house's cellar.

Cold baths, the only type available for male students, were taken in an unusual building partially constructed over a spring-fed stream west of the residence. Adjacent but unconnected to Mr. Lewis's small office and study, the bath house contained a plank enclosure that trapped water for bathing, with the overflow continuing to run downhill to join the creek near the barracks.

Llangollen offered a young man a spectrum of activities devoted to work and play, devised to create the sound mind in the sound body prescribed by the Romans. The classroom's book studies and oral exercises were balanced by the commands and evolutions of the drill field. But opportunities for play were not neglected, whether students were frolicking nearby in the rocky North Anna River, less than a mile away, or ice skating on a nearby pond, as weather allowed.

Though John Woodville had been a superior teacher, John Lewis was an extraordinary one. A "man of parts," as the phrase went, the schoolmaster excelled in several fields, and in his time would become a published novelist, poet, and mathematician. A cavalry officer during the recent war, he could authoritatively explain to his charges the roles of horse and rider in combat. An ardent admirer of the patriot fathers, he was also a confirmed Southern nationalist.

For a young patriot such as Lewis Craig, there could hardly have been a better place to be situated in 1826 than Llangollen. The fiftieth year of the independence of the republic would be enthusiastically celebrated in the months leading up to and following July 4, not least in Virginia. John Lewis was sure to see that his students share in the newspaper accounts as well as local celebrations of the jubilee: "colorful military bands; ceremonial cannon blasts" and "much patriotic oratory." Especially gratifying to Virginians was the special attention given by the visiting Marquis de Lafayette, who not only paid his respects at Washington's Mount Vernon, but went as well to Yorktown, Williamsburg, and Charlottesville.

The patriot fathers often displayed their enthusiasm for the classics—those of Rome in particular—a passion that John Lewis shared and was reflected in Llangollen's curriculum. Among their assignments, the young men were given Virgil to read, study, and translate, another exemplar of "arms and the man," as the young students read of Aeneas leading his warriors ever westward from Troy, following the sun.

Despite John Lewis's martial interests and his emphasis on discipline, Llangollen's head was not a brutal taskmaster, as was common in the day. When one of his charges did wrong, he considered that a beating would represent a double failure on his part. Consequently, where discipline was concerned, he strove to lead by example, and to show that self-discipline was discipline in its finest form. During Lewis Craig's career as an army officer, he would in great part mirror John Lewis's training.

By 1826, when Lewis, nineteen, left Llangollen, his family had undergone many changes. Jane and Robert Stanard had returned permanently to Richmond in 1818, leaving young Lewis, now a confirmed citizen of Fredericksburg, behind with other relations. In 1820 Mary Mallory Craig had died, followed the next year by her second husband, Samuel Paine. In 1822 Arnett, the sister closest to Lewis in age, married Philip W. Claiborne, a kinsman of Governor Claiborne of New Orleans. As had been the case with Lewis's brothers and the Fox ladies, there was also a Claiborne brother for sister Mary, although she wouldn't marry George Claiborne until 1827.

With all of his siblings wed by 1827 and Lewis Craig approaching his majority, it might have seemed likely that he would soon marry. That he would not take a wife until 1843 resulted in part from a series of calamities that had struck in 1824.

Foremost among them was the April 1824 death of Jane Craig Stanard. Jane—always the most affectionate and solicitous of Lewis's siblings and, in her way, much more of a mother to Lewis than Mary Craig—had suffered from the time of Lewis's birth from a series of emotional blows. At that time Adam Craig's lingering death had begun. And, soon after her father died, so did Frances Stevenson, Jane's revered teacher, soon followed by her husband, the Reverend James Stevenson, father of the estimable Andrew.

During Jane's courtship by Robert Stanard, the Stevensons' bereaved spinster daughter, Elizabeth, proved a gloomy and demanding correspondent, capable of beginning a letter, without salutation, "'Tis the dark and solemn hour of midnight & all is silent as the chill cold grave around me. I alone am awake in the house." Tragically, as Jane's marriage approached, Elizabeth made a long-anticipated visit to Richmond only to die with Ann Craig in the theater fire. This horrifying incident formed an unbelievably doleful prelude to the Stanards' wedding and subsequent removal to Fredericksburg, soon to be threatened by the war with Britain.

Jane's Fredericksburg days had also been marked by loneliness, despite her growing family and occasional visits from young Lewis. Mary Craig neglected Jane, while her husband followed his political career to Richmond and his growing law practice to teeming Norfolk and elsewhere. Although a frequent, thoughtful, and understanding correspondent, Robert was too often absent. He learned mainly from Jane's letters the various demands of running the household without him (including dealing with a drunken and destructive domestic servant) and of answering calls for assistance from relatives and friends. Robert was away, for example, when Jane took upon herself the grim duty of suckling a friend's dying baby, necessarily taken from its mortally ill mother, only to see both of them perish.

The Stanards' move to Richmond, into a spacious mansion opposite the capitol grounds, made for a welcome change, but did not end Jane's self-imposed estrangement from her mother. And Mary Craig's sudden death left Jane desolate. Some writers have thought Jane descended into madness. Instead, she was actually slowly dying of consumption, the same malady that had killed her father.

Americans of the early 1800s were more closely acquainted with death than later generations. But Jane's multiple bereavements had been more wrenching than those many of her time experienced, as the above inventory demonstrates. Her unusual experiences, now followed by what she called a "death-like sickness," with the listlessness and pallor (but with blooming lips and cheeks), all brought on by wasting disease—all these suggest the adjective "Poesque," and rightly so.

Edgar Allan Poe had known and platonically loved Jane in the last months before her death in April 1824. At that time he was just fourteen-year-old "Eddie" Poe, a close friend of Jane's eldest child, "Rob" (Robert Craig Stanard), who was only two years younger than Rob's uncle Lewis Craig.

Nine-year-old Rob idealized young Eddie. It was Poe's athleticism, however—not any aesthetic sense—that won him the allegiance of many of his fellow schoolboys. Most famously he had completed a heroic swim across the James River (no doubt while thinking of Lord Byron's 1810 conquest of the Hellespont) and had returned to shore exhausted and sunburned to a lobster red. Unlike posterity, Poe's youthful friends would be unsurprised at his enlistment in the U.S. Army in 1827, or his admittance to the U.S. Military Academy in 1829.

Two centuries of mythmaking have made the true lineaments of the relationship between Lewis Craig's dying sister and the author-to-be difficult to discern. But even one short conversation would have apprised them both of much in common. Jane must have seen Poe's actress mother perform at the Richmond theater—the 24-year-old Mrs. Poe herself had died of consumption shortly before the theater fire. The Monumental Church, which marked the spot where Mrs. Poe had acted and Ann Craig had died, was attended by Poe's guardians, the Allans, and consequently was the one Poe attended as well. Additionally, Poe's mother was buried in the graveyard of St. John's, on the bluff not far distant from Jane's place of birth on Grace Street.

In any case, Poe was struck by Jane's ethereal beauty, as well as by her kindness. He in later years remembered "how Mrs. Stanard had taken his hand, when they first met, welcoming him so kindly and gently as to leave him speechless." Her death jolted him, and whether or not he long kept vigil at her grave in Shockoe Cemetery, as legend has it, it would be in character.

In any case, the evidence confirms that Jane was indeed the inspiration of Poe's poem titled "To Helen," one of his loveliest lyrics. And she was certainly among the inspirations of one of Poe's most haunting subjects, the early death of a beautiful woman.

By the time "To Helen" was first published in 1831, Poe had no doubt learned of another tragedy in Jane's and Rob's family—the fate of Lewis Craig's niece, Jane's six-year-old daughter and namesake, who burned to death when her dress ignited as she stood before a fireplace in the Stanard residence.

Poe's sense of loss at Jane Stanard's death must give at least an indication of what Lewis Craig must have felt. And Jane's interest in Lewis and her attention to his welfare, had they continued, might have worked against the forces that were now brought into play.

After the death of his mother, Mary Craig Paine, and William Craig's withdrawal, Lewis was required to go into court to ask for another guardian to be appointed. The family encouraged him to pick his brother James as best suited, and James consequently made the required bonds to protect Lewis's inheritance. But in 1824, financial reverses caused James also to withdraw as guardian.

James's suggestion for successor was his brother-in-law, Elijah T. Fox, whose very name strongly (though anachronistically) suggests that of a Dickensian villain. Perhaps because of blandishments such as promising to purchase for the young man a 500-acre plantation (called Elba) on the Rappahannock River west of Fredericksburg, Lewis went into court and requested that Fox be James Craig's successor. Consequently, Fox became Lewis's guardian in May 1824, only a few days after Jane's death and burial, and James transferred Lewis's bank stock to Fox in July of the same year.

Fox's conduct as guardian was suspicious from the start. He persuaded two fellow Prince William County residents to join him as guarantors and shortly thereafter persuaded a second set unknowingly to do the same. It was the second group of guarantors, alarmed that they were about to be liable for fraudulent behavior on Fox's part, who went to court to prevent this action.

This should have been the end of the matter. But the case was plagued from the first by conflicting jurisdictions. Some of the motions were filed in Prince William County, some in Spotsylvania County, and the issuer of the bonds was the Bank of Virginia in Richmond's Henrico County.

In the ongoing litigation, Craig himself was served with a subpoena in October 1827, only a year after he had left Llangollen and some months before he reached his majority. At about the same time, the case *Lewis v. Craig* was heard, resulting in Elijah Fox being directed to pay John Lewis for Lewis Craig's last year of education. Soon thereafter, Fox left the scene permanently. Court papers noted tersely that Fox was "no longer an inhabitant of Virginia," and it was said that he had left the Old Dominion under circumstances suggesting he would not return.

The litigation now progressed between the guarantors, Lewis Craig, and the Bank of Virginia, which Craig charged should not have allowed his stock to be sold. Incredibly, the litigation ground on until 1836. A lower court, having decided against the Bank of Virginia, ordered the bank to pay Lewis over $9000, but the bank appealed to the Virginia Supreme Court. The justices decided for the Bank of Virginia, but, after further argument by Robert Stanard, who had entered the case late in the process, the Virginia Supreme Court also decided to make the second guarantors liable. The extent to which Craig succeeded in being repaid by the guarantors is unknown.

This process of legal wrangling continued throughout Craig's twenties. It is difficult to determine, given time and legal fees, what portion of his various legacies in land, slaves, and bank stock remained when the cases concluded. Lewis Craig's legal situation suggested in part the actual case on which Charles Dickens based Jarndyce and Jarndyce in *Bleak House,* as examples of "the futility and length of certain civil court cases." What is certain is that Lewis's biggest personal loss came from another transaction with Fox. It regarded Elba, which Lewis Craig would always call "my plantation."

James Craig, who appears to have been culpable in much of this ordeal, was deeply involved in the Elba episode. Despite conflicting testimony, the most plausible scenario is that Fox and James Craig purchased Elba as an investment and future residence for Lewis Craig. Fox himself lived at Elba from 1825 to 1827, and his ward, Lewis, probably stayed there when not at John Lewis's school.

During negotiations Fox "offered" Elba to Lewis Craig, but court documents don't show Lewis's becoming grantee of the plantation until May 1829, two years after Fox absconded. Less than two years later, aged twenty-four, Craig sold Elba, presumably due to financial problems born of the continuing litigation.

It is also difficult to determine how much the financial policies of President Andrew Jackson, in office 1829–1837, diminished whatever legacy remained to Craig after his court ordeals. Jackson's bank policies certainly turned some former allies into enemies, and the Panic of 1837 created widespread distress. In Virginia, Jackson's opponents the Whigs would carry the state in the off-year election of 1838.

In any case, the Jacksonian financial crisis is unnecessary in explaining Lewis Craig's partiality to the Whigs and his admiration for Henry Clay of Kentucky, who had named and helped organize the party in 1834. The Whig party, after all, was, among other things, the party of the gentry.

Having been confined to Fredericksburg and environs for a decade, Lewis Craig was ready to move on. Whether or not he had entertained dreams of one day serving his country as a U.S. army officer, he proceeded now to embark on his years of military service, which would end only with his death. But, at Lewis's age, West Point could hardly be a possibility. Two years younger than Lewis, Edgar Poe had arrived for his brief sojourn at the military academy at age twenty-one; Lewis was then twenty-eight.

Meanwhile, war had broken out with the Seminole Indians in the Floridas, and in 1836 Congress responded favorably to Floridians' pleas to create a second regiment of Dragoons to serve there. The First Regiment, created in 1833 as a result of the Black Hawk War, had been "mounted for speed, yet trained and equipped to fight both mounted and dismounted." These Dragoons had served well as Indian fighters on the northern plains, and it was hoped that similar Dragoons would become a valuable addition to the forces fighting the Florida War. Their fearsome name alone conjured up the famous Napoleonic Dragoons, whose fire-belching carbines had been associated with the dragons of myth.

The officers of the Second Regiment of Dragoons could not be furnished entirely by the U.S. Military Academy, because of increasing demands for officers for the war, along with floods of resignations, many from officers who refused to travel to the Floridas to fight the Seminoles. Consequently, direct appointments were allowed for those gentlemen who wished to become officers and could secure political support. Usually these men were from the same "social base" as the West Pointers, and therefore could secure the necessary recommendations from members of the U.S. Congress.

Not only was Lewis Craig undeniably a gentleman, he had connections equal to any. By 1837, Andrew Stevenson had become one of the nation's principal statesmen and was in the first of five years' service as U.S. Ambassador to Great Britain. Moreover, Craig's brother-in-law Robert Stanard had by 1837 also served as member and speaker of the Virginia House of Delegates, as a member of the Virginia Constitutional Convention of 1829–1830, and as a U.S. district attorney.

These were only two of the prominent Virginians who would have helped Craig. But a specific member of the U.S. Congress led members of the Virginia delegation in recommending to Secretary of War Joel R. Poinsett that Lewis Stevenson Craig be commissioned an officer of the U.S. Dragoons. He was Senator William H. Roane, grandson of Patrick Henry and the son of Judge Spencer Roane—a member with Andrew Stevenson of the powerful Richmond Junto, a group of Democrat grandees who, from the 1820s through the 1830s, controlled Virginia state patronage.

Lewis Craig received his commission as an officer of the Second Regiment of Dragoons in October 1837. It would be some time before he would again be seen by his friends, relations, and neighbors. Soon, however, it became widely known that Lewis Craig had left Fredericksburg, bound for the Floridas to fight the Indians.

Chapter 2

To the Floridas

> The Florida War's "peculiar nature" offered "constant occasion for the display of zeal, energy, and talent, and patient endurance of hardship and privation, but few opportunities for the more brilliant exhibitions of those qualities which attract and fix attention in the presence of an enemy "worthy of a soldier's blade."
>
> —Brigadier General William J. Worth

I.

As a career officer in the United States Army, Lewis Stevenson Craig was "born" in East Florida on January 25, 1838. On that day, as a three-month 2nd lieutenant in the Second Regiment of Dragoons, Craig first led troops into battle. At that time, he also received a form of martial baptism as he charged at the head of his men through Seminole musket fire into the dark waters of the Loxahatchee River. By day's end, with the enemy put to flight, Craig and a fellow lieutenant had received that highly valued distinction for combat officers: commendation by name in the commanding officer's report of the engagement. This officer noted that fifteen of the Second Dragoons (with specific mention of lieutenants Lewis Craig and Charles May) had located "more than sixty warriors" on the far bank of the river and had "attacked them, and, in about ten or fifteen minutes, dispersed them…." *The Army & Navy Chronicle* and other journals soon printed the full report, widely disseminating the news of Craig's achievement.

Craig had rapidly been transformed from a long-suffering victim of "the law's delay" into an exemplary leader of men. As recently as October 1837, Craig had been a civilian, accustomed to a comfortable, unregimented life in town and country. Then, on October 24, 1837, in Fredericksburg, he had received and formally signed and accepted his 2nd lieutenant's commission, along with a certificate requiring his oath "to bear true allegiance to the United States of America," to "serve them honestly and faithfully against all their enemies and opposers whatsoever" and to "observe and obey the orders of the President of the United States and the orders of the officers appointed" over him, "according to the Rules and Articles for the government of the Armies of the United States."

Perhaps unsurprisingly, given Fredericksburg's plentiful military associations, the justice of the peace who witnessed and countersigned Craig's oath certificate was Hugh Mercer Patton, grandson and namesake of Gen. Hugh Mercer, a Revolutionary War hero who had fallen at Princeton in 1777. Moreover, two of General Mercer's descendants in the Patton line would themselves later make considerable military contributions to the armies of both the Southern Confederacy and the United States.

With his acceptance and certificate posted to Secretary of War Joel Poinsett in Washington City, Craig hastened south, probably via the recently opened rail line to Richmond, where a Rocketts Landing river steamer took him to the great Virginia port of Norfolk. There a sea-going steamship carried him to Savannah, Georgia, for passage on yet another river steamer—a shallow-draft, side-wheel vessel that churned south down the inland waterway, between the mainland and Georgia's and East Florida's barrier islands. Arriving at the mile-wide mouth of the St. Johns River, his craft pushed into the river mouth's shallow waters, bumped over its shifting masses of sand, and then glided into open water. Craig had arrived in the Floridas.

To some, the Florida territory was classed as singular—simply a vast, rough-edged peninsula, resembling a wide flint blade that pushed south, toward the island of Cuba and separated the Atlantic Ocean from the Gulf of Mexico. But, according to the federal census of 1830, there were actually four Floridas. Craig would serve in two of them, first in East Florida, where the old capital of St. Augustine had stood since its founding by the Spaniards in 1565.

East Florida occupied most of the peninsula south of the Georgia border and east of the Suwannee River and was bordered by both the Gulf and the Atlantic. In East Florida, Craig would serve mainly along and near the three-hundred-mile St. Johns River. Florida's greatest river, it seeped from a southern marshland near the ocean and flowed north, roughly parallel to eastern coast; then the river turned sharply east to empty into the ocean past Jacksonville. Although stretches of the St. Johns routinely failed to maintain navigable depth, the twisting river remained vital to the U.S. Army's steamer-based military operations in East Florida.

On East Florida's Gulf Coast, Craig would later briefly be stationed at Fort Brooke, near Tampa Bay. This post represented the planned culmination of the Florida War itself, for near here most of the Seminoles were gathered for transportation—first to New Orleans, then up the Mississippi and west by way of the Arkansas River to Indian Territory. North of Fort Brooke, Craig would also see service for short periods at a string of other forts in East Florida's interior.

Craig would be sent to neither South Florida nor West Florida. South Florida comprised vast Monroe County, which sprawled below East Florida. The county's uppermost border was an invisible line stretching diagonally some 160 miles from Charlotte Harbor on the Gulf to Hillsboro Inlet on the Atlantic. Quite thinly populated and difficult to access when not impenetrable, South Florida included the forbidding Everglades, along with the long westering line of unbridged Florida Keys.

West Florida, according to Spanish claims, had originally stretched from the Apalachicola River to the Mississippi and had included the town of Baton Rouge. But—between 1810 and 1819—rebellion, war, and diplomacy had established West Florida's western border at the Perdido River, and all previously disputed territory beyond had been allotted to Louisiana, Mississippi, and Alabama. Ultimately, in 1821, Spain had surrendered all the Floridas east of the Perdido to the United States. West Florida then was confined to the area of the panhandle between the Perdido and the Apalachicola, with the area beyond, between the Apalachicola and Suwannee rivers, called Middle Florida.

West Florida and Middle Florida had served as the major battlegrounds of the First Seminole War (1818–1819). This brief conflict formed something of a sequel to the War of 1812, during which the British had used Spanish Florida as a base—in particular West Florida's capital, Pensacola. The British had encouraged the Creeks, along with the Seminoles, to attack the farms and settlements on the American southern border, onslaughts that continued after war's end.

An abandoned British fort on the Apalachicola River became a stronghold from which the hostiles raided farms and settlements and attacked U.S. shipping on the river. This large earthwork came to be called the "Negro Fort" and was occupied by several hundred black allies of the

Seminoles. When in summer 1816 fire from a U.S. Navy gunboat had exploded the fort's magazine, killing most of the garrison, the Seminoles increased their raiding into Georgia. Attacks and U.S. counterattacks continued into the next year, most prominently at Fowltown, taken and destroyed in November 1817 by Gen. Edmund Pendleton Gaines of Virginia.

Major General Andrew Jackson, now "the Hero of New Orleans," was dispatched into the Floridas by President James Monroe. Soon he had taken West Florida's Pensacola, as well as the Middle Florida port of St. Marks, summarily hanged two Seminole leaders and two British instigators, handily defeated the Seminoles, and burned Indian villages across lower Middle Florida all the way to the Suwannee.

Spain, now convinced that it should rid itself of its "profitless possession," sold Florida to the United States in 1819. When it became a U.S. territory in 1821, Andrew Jackson served briefly as territorial governor and was favored by having the St. Johns River hamlet of Cow Ford named Jacksonville in his honor.

Middle Florida (bounded by the Apalachicola and Suwannee rivers) would contribute most importantly to Lewis Craig's future, both in military and personal terms. The most agriculturally rich and most populous of the Floridas and the domain of an elite planter class, Middle Florida would form the backdrop for the final operations of the Florida War, as the Second Seminole War was then known. There Craig would proudly serve under an exemplary officer whom he would come to revere and emulate. And there also Craig would persuade an attractive young lady from Georgia to become his wife.

The four Floridas encompassed over 55,000 square miles and were credited by the U.S. Census Department with an 1830 population of around 34,000—18,000 whites and 16,000 blacks (mostly slaves), so that the entire territory's population was quite small, roughly equal to the number of people who in 1830 lived in Charleston, South Carolina.

In addition to the census population, an estimated five thousand Seminole Indians were dispersed throughout the largely unmapped territory; they were the targets of the military campaign that Craig had joined. There had been earlier, unsuccessful attempts to persuade the Indians to dwell on reservations. But, from 1830, official U.S. government policy had demanded the removal of all of the Southeastern Indians to lands west of the Mississippi and north of the Red River.

Of the five major tribes of the American Southeast, the Seminoles would resist deportation most fiercely. To Florida's scattered white population, the Seminoles represented a threat to life, limb, and property (and black Floridians, slave or free, could also be subject to killing or capture). As a political matter, the Seminoles blocked the Florida territory's hope of reaching the required population needed to transform it into one of the United States. As a military matter, although deploying possibly as few as 1500 warriors, the Seminoles proved willing to attack settlements not only in Florida, but in Georgia as well. They were also considered probable allies of any European invaders of the United States, a serious concern of the republic's military establishment. In any case, it would prove almost impossible to dislodge the Seminoles from the near-wilderness where they farmed and hunted and herded and wished to be left alone, a hostile region that would prove their most valuable ally.

Virginians of Lewis Craig's generation had little reason for understanding the Florida Indians. As anomalous as the Floridas themselves, the Seminoles had not existed as a separate people in 1607, when the first hundred English settlers had arrived on the Virginia coast and been received by the arrows of a small war party from the 20,000 Indians who then populated Virginia.

Colonist George Percy's description of the first contact between colonists and natives closely resembled many attacks of the Florida War: "At night…there came Savages creeping upon all foures…like Beares…[who] charged us very desperately in the faces…. After they had spent their Arrowes, and felt the sharpnesse of our shot, they retired into the Woods with a great noise, and so left us." Such tactics were part of what had long been called "the skulking way of war," and the Seminoles were masters of it.

Although the English had nearly been annihilated by the Virginia Indians in the early years, there were 15,000 English settlers by 1650, and the iron law of numbers ultimately prevailed. By the time Craig left his home on the Rappahannock, only a few hundred Indians remained in Virginia, restricted to various reservations.

When compared to the Lower South's other four "Civilized Tribes" (Mississippi's Chickasaws and Choctaws, Georgia's and Alabama's Creeks, and the Cherokees of Georgia and North Carolina), the

Seminoles were not only the least numerous and historically youngest group, but those who least supported chattel slavery. The other four tribes would take several thousand slaves with them as property to Indian territory, but true plantation slavery did not exist among the Seminoles. They held few slaves, most of whom enjoyed a kind of "benevolent bondage," which allowed them virtual independence for the price of an annual tribute of produce or stock.

Moreover, since the Floridas had long offered a refuge for runaway Southern slaves, many of them, often called the "Black Seminoles," had separate, independent villages near those of the Indians, with whom they allied themselves only in war. The Seminoles—unlettered like all the other Lower South tribes except the Cherokees, and mostly not conversant in English—depended on some of the bilingual Black Seminoles for service as translators and bargainers, while the U.S. Army often used some of these blacks not only as translators but often as guides, sometimes with disastrous results. In general, unlike those Florida Indians who regretfully chose peace and removal to war and ruin (and were then often murdered by the war leaders), the Black Seminoles adamantly opposed deportation, fearing that they would be re-enslaved rather than sent to Indian Territory.

The Black Seminoles thus presented a major complication, not present in the removal of the other tribes. Where many white Southerners were concerned (and probably to third-generation slaveholding Virginians like Lewis Craig, in particular), they represented the specter of slaves in arms, a common Southern nightmare since the widespread massacres of the Haitian Revolution of 1791–1804.

Additionally, it had been only six years since Nat Turner's 1831 insurrection in southeastern Virginia's Southampton County, and that bloody uprising endured as a fresh and horrifying memory, feared as presaging future murderous slave rebellions. Although trials at the county seat of Jerusalem had culminated in the executions of Turner and over fifty others for killing over fifty innocent whites, there had also been a wave of indiscriminate white reprisals that had left over 120 innocent blacks dead.

The Southampton Revolt had jarred Craig's Virginia to the extent that the House of Delegates seriously debated the abolition of slavery in the 1831–1832 session. Chillingly, in November 1831, the governor of Virginia had included in his annual message an anonymous, threatening letter that referred to the historic Haitian bloodbath with a promise of "approaching carnage."

In some minds, Nat Turner's revolt was also connected to both black abolitionist pamphleteer David Walker's 1829 call for "violence and revolt," and white abolitionist William Lloyd Garrison's radical newspaper *The Liberator*, published since January 1831. From this point, slaves throughout the Southern states were restricted in their movements, watched more closely than ever, and denied everything from literacy to fowling pieces to independent worship. In stark contrast, the Black Seminoles meanwhile cooperated with their Indian allies and freely roamed the Floridas with muskets, attacking settlers and fighting U.S. troops.

II.

In late October 1837 Craig's easy journey up Florida's St. Johns River brought him his first look at a region that must have seemed to him as outlandish as Borneo. Like many travelers before him on the wide watercourse, here he first encountered the peculiarity of sailing south to go upriver. And here also he first saw alligators—rows of them, basking along riverbanks thickly lined with trees, whose overhanging branches bore long clumps of trailing moss, drooping ominously like trophy scalps.

Craig's immediate destination lay over fifty miles from the St. Johns' mouth, to a point where dark and deep Black Creek cut through the western bank and flowed into the river. Twelve miles farther upstream at the creek's fork stood Fort Heilman—a major U.S. army supply depot, as well as the headquarters post of the Second Dragoon Regiment in late 1837. Fort Heilman had been named for a U.S. Army officer who, in common with most of the Florida War's army deaths past and to come, had died of disease.

Adjacent to the fort was the small settlement of Garey's Ferry, where travelers to and from Jacksonville could cross by flatboat. To the U.S. Army this depot was indifferently known as Black Creek, Fort Heilman, or Garey's Ferry. Nonetheless, anyone expecting the village and the fort to resemble the peninsula's many crude villages and miserable outposts had to be surprised by this settlement—"There were frame houses with glass in window sashes; steam-boats were moored to the banks of the stream; and a stirring business-like air prevailed everywhere."

The fort's environs were crowded with soldiers of all kinds—regulars, volunteers, and militia—all of them taking a dim view of the others. The regulars considered the volunteers to be meddling amateurs and the militia to be worse, with their brief enlistments and arrogance. The regulars were often viewed by the others as pretentious, condescending, and overeducated. There were grains of truth in all these prejudices.

At the fort there were also numerous supporting personnel and various army contractors working among the various storage houses. Usually there were also numerous war refugees from the interior, many of them "crackers" whom the regulars thought worse than the Indians. And there, bound for the plantations of Middle Florida, were coffles of slaves, considered by some Northern officers in particular as constituting the major reason for the war—and far from a sufficient one in their view.

From Fort Heilman's military stores 2nd Lieutenant Craig presumably secured his first uniform, weapons, and gear. From that time until his death, Craig's trunk would contain these accoutrements and all his other worldly possessions as an army officer, similar in most respects to those effects to be posthumously inventoried fifteen years later: a pillow, two blankets, a bag of assorted clothing, a small writing desk (with paper, journal, pen, ink, and pencil), and a box containing coffee, sugar, and assorted patent medicines.

Like all officers, Craig also took with him a small collection of books: perhaps *The Book of Common Prayer*; certainly the officers' "Bible"—the 1835 revised edition of General Winfield Scott's *General Regulations for the Army*, containing all the information regarding officers' rights and perquisites, as well as chapter and verse on professional officers' most oft-studied topics: pay, promotion, and transfers.

Most vital to line officers of all grades, General Scott's *Infantry-Tactics*, based on Napoleonic practice and adopted by the U.S. Army in 1835, had to be closely studied. Craig had to understand his copy and teach others below him to do so. The book contained almost all an officer needed to learn and to drum into his troops, whether in platoon, company, or regiment, including "the principles and the mechanism of the step, the position of the body, and the manual and bearing of arms."

Scott's *Tactics* also included the wording and meaning of a bewildering number of commands, and the prompts of field musicians that accompanied them, all of which had to be thoroughly mastered. There was no room for uncertainty on a battlefield, "where the penalty for confusion or misunderstanding could be fatal." As mounted infantry, the Dragoons had already learned even more commands peculiar to their status in the camps of instruction, which Craig had to learn from them, having missed their months of training. But infantry tactics remained paramount, for the Dragoons were mounted infantry, with their horses mainly their means of reaching the battle line, where they were to be deployed as foot soldiers.

Once the military essentials were mastered, there were opportunities in camp and field for other reading. For history reading, Craig seems most often to have turned to accounts of Napoleon and his marshals. For pleasure, he enjoyed Laurence Sterne's satiric *Tristram Shandy*, episodic enough to be picked up and put down at random, full of humor about eighteenth-century military life and lore, with occasional veins of sentiment.

In charge of Craig's trunk and accoutrements from this point until his last day was Willis, formerly a slave of William Craig's wife, and now Craig's body servant, courtesy of William's wrecked fortunes. Willis would accompany Lewis Craig in this and all future campaigns. He would be one among the small army of officers' "waiters"—most of them black bondsmen—whose food, clothing, and maintenance were provided by the government at the rate due a private, through a supplementary allowance to officers' pay.

As a 2nd lieutenant, Craig earned $40 monthly, an amount not likely to restore his fortunes or make him rich. For that matter, neither would have a full colonel's pay of less than $100 a month have done so. A 2nd lieutenant's annual salary of $480, however, has been calculated as having purchasing power of over $13,000 in twenty-first-century dollars. Craig, however, was serving his country as he wished to do, and, in addition to his pay, he would always be provided with food, clothing, shelter, and medical care.

At Fort Heilman, during the first two weeks of November 1837, Craig joined the Second Dragoons for what was an unprecedented gathering—there, for the first time since the regiment's creation, most of the officers and men of the ten companies were together in one place. Those companies raised east of the Mississippi had been trained at Fort Hamilton, New York, and had arrived by steamer. Those recruited west of the Mississippi had received their training (and, in some cases, their first horses), at Jefferson Barracks, south of St. Louis. From Jefferson Barracks, those companies had then ridden with their commander in a grand cavalcade across the southeast to the "seat of war" in the Floridas. Along the way, these new dragoons had been welcomed with appreciation, even adulation, in such places as Georgia's capital of Milledgeville.

Native Georgian Colonel David Twiggs, born in 1790, had led this cross-country march. Twiggs was a second-generation Indian fighter. His father, Georgia Militia general John Twiggs, had fought the British-allied Cherokees and Creeks during the American Revolution, and in 1793 he had led an expedition that sought to punish the harrying Creeks in their Chattahoochee villages. David Twiggs himself had fought the British-allied Red Sticks in the Creek War of 1813–1814 and the Spanish-allied Seminoles in the First Seminole War of 1818–1819. He was also destined to participate in a third and final Seminole war, 1855–1858. Over six feet tall and bull-necked, but otherwise bearish in shape and temperament, Colonel Twiggs was well-matched with his second-in-command, Lieutenant-Colonel William S. Harney.

A Tennessean ally of Andrew Jackson, Harney, then in his late thirties, was, like Twiggs, a confirmed Democrat, and was always eager to claim political persecution from Whig superior officers. A veteran of northwestern frontier service in the First Dragoons, Harney, as later recalled by fellow Dragoons officer (and later U.S. Secretary of War and Confederate president) Jefferson Davis, was "physically, the finest specimen of a man I ever saw.... Tall, straight, muscular, broad-chested and gaunt-waisted...one of...'nature's noblemen.'"

Nonetheless, Harney also possessed a temper even more volatile than that of Twiggs. In 1834 Harney had so brutally whipped a slave woman named Hannah that she had died, although a Missouri trial jury had accepted Harney's plea of not guilty at his 1835 trial. Unsurprisingly, the Seminoles would find to their cost that Harney could be a cruel and relentless enemy, ready to match atrocity for atrocity.

Incorrigible cursers, Twiggs and Harney had matching reputations for casual, ceaseless profanity, remarkable even in a profession where swearing was commonplace. In his memorandum book, perhaps as an oblique comment on the bad language of Twiggs and Harney, Lewis Craig copied from *Tristram Shandy* a famous quotation, in which Tristram's uncle, Capt. Toby Shandy, a veteran of the War of the Grand Alliance, is provoked into swearing (after having sadly noted, "Our armies swore terribly in Flanders"). Arguing with his body servant, Cpl. Trim (over whether Toby's brother officer, Lt. Le Fever, will die), Uncle Toby wearies of Trim's repeated assurances that Le Fever will surely perish (which indeed he does), and finally reaches the end of his patience:

> "He shall not die, by G__," cried my uncle Toby.
> —The *ACCUSING SPIRIT* which flew up to Heaven's chancery with the oath, blush'd as he gave it in; and the *RECORDING ANGEL*, as he wrote it down, dropp'd a tear upon the word, and blotted it out forever.

Twiggs and Harney, aside from overworking the Accusing Spirit, both epitomized "Old Army" officers, and had no more graduated from the U.S. Military Academy than Craig had. Craig would continue to serve under them as they increased in rank during the Mexican War. Twiggs and Harney would have long careers, and in January 1861 would represent exactly half of the serving generals in the U.S. Army, along with Winfield Scott and John Wool, all four of them recipients of an education on the battlefield rather than at West Point.

Lewis Craig probably didn't see the Second Dragoons' colonel and lieutenant colonel together until the regiment concentrated later in the month for the winter campaign. From Fort Heilman, Craig joined a Dragoon detachment bound upriver to Volusia, another army depot, on the east bank of the St. Johns. There Craig presumably was provided with his first horse, since the Dragoons then began a cross-country march to Fort Mellon, on the south bank of Lake Monroe. They were led by the Florida army's commanding general, fifty-year-old Virginian Thomas Jesup, conspicuous then for his brilliant, longtime service as the U.S. Army's quartermaster general. If nothing else, Jesup's force would be not only well-supplied but also well-led.

Arriving at Fort Mellon on November 26, Craig saw the first frontier fortification in his experience that had been named for an officer killed in battle, in this case Capt. Charles Mellon of the 2nd U.S. Artillery. Mellon had fallen the previous February during a Seminole attack on the ground where the fort stood; there he had been buried, and there he still lies. Fort Mellon was neither the first nor the last of the Florida War's many forts to be named for an officer who died in the performance of his duty; most forts were memorials to such war dead. Craig himself would later command one of these crude Florida frontier strongholds, and, on the opposite end of the continent, he would ultimately receive the honor of having an adobe fortification named in his memory.

For the Dragoons, two other Florida forts would figure more prominently—and troublingly—in the history of the regiment. One was Fort Lane, soon to be constructed twenty miles to the southeast of Fort Mellon, and named for Colonel John F. Lane, originally a captain in the Second Dragoons. In late 1836 he had been raised to the colonelcy of a regiment of 750 Creek warriors gathered to fight the Seminoles. After an arduous march, Lane had retired to his tent, sat on his cot, placed the point of his sword before his right eye, and, whether from exhaustion or fever, leaned over and pushed it into his brain.

To the northwest, the second, Fort Wheelock would be built, named for a lieutenant in the First Dragoons, West Pointer Thompson Wheelock of Massachusetts. After the hard-fought but victorious Battle of Micanopy the previous summer, he had placed his pistol barrel in his mouth and pulled the trigger.

Were both these deaths the consequence of the mental strain of a war fought in miserable conditions against an often invisible enemy? Some classed Lane's death as suicide while others ascribed it to accident or fever; Wheelock's could less persuasively have been so interpreted. In any case, the circumstances of the Florida War presented a severe test of much more than a man's physical strength and stamina.

No matter how these forts had come by their names, all those that Craig encountered—and the one he later commanded in Middle Florida—followed similar patterns. British soldier of fortune, journalist, and novelist Mayne Reid—who served in Mexico with Florida War officers—provided a lively set of instructions for constructing such a fort:

> To fortify against an Indian enemy, proceed as follows:
>
> Obtain a few hundred trees [pine or palmetto]; cut them into lengths of eighteen feet; split them up the middle; set them in a quadrangle, side by side, flat faces inward; batten them together; point them at the tops; loophole eight feet from the ground; place a staging under the loopholes...hang a strong gate.... Build strong [cabins] within the enclosure...loophole them also—against the contingency of the stockade being carried; and, this done, your fort is finished.

With more elaborate forts, two or more corners would support machicolated blockhouses, with wall loopholes, as well as "murder holes" in the floor for firing downward at enemies who came beneath the overhanging structure. But most of these ad hoc frontier strongholds were simple stockades, bare of blockhouses, and all of them, when no longer needed, would soon enough collapse into the forest floor, there to decay and disappear.

One of many such "throwaway" army forts Craig would encounter, Fort Mellon was of "rude" construction and "temporary intent"—built "at little expense, to be abandoned with as little loss." It was nothing like those immense masonry piles Craig would encounter at St. Augustine and in Mexico, "with angles and embrasures, bastions and battlements, curtains, casemates, and glacis."

With his routine established at Fort Heilman, Craig found his new life as an officer structured by beating drum or sometimes sounding bugles: he arose at "Reveille," heard "Retreat" at sunset, and retired at "Tattoo." At "Assembly" Craig assisted in forming his company's men (usually from fifty to sixty-four Dragoons, with Craig's particular responsibility a platoon—half the total), whose own favorite signals were probably "Peas-upon-a-trencher" for breakfast and "Roast beef" for dinner or drawing provisions. The drummers also provided many other signals for camp and on the march. For the Dragoons, just after "Reveille" and twice more during the day came "Stable-call," for "watering, feeding, and attending to the horses."

More important to morale than the drum and bugle signals was the "music" of the regimental bands. A month after the Dragoons and other regiments converged on Fort Mellon, an infantry officer recorded in his journal that on December 10, "the band of music of the 2nd Regt. Dragoons arrived from Garey's Ferry & for the last two nights we have been favored with their fine music."

Such bands' repertoires ranged from popular ditties like "Cigars and Cognac," to patriotic tunes—including the rollicking "Yankee Doodle" and the stately "Hail, Columbia," then the republic's unofficial national anthem. But all-too-frequently heard in the war zone was "The Dead March," from Handel's *Saul*, with its plaintive fifes and muffled drums; it had been linked to American military funerals ever since the 1797 obsequies for George Washington.

Notably, soon after the Florida War had broken out, this solemn march had been played in early 1836 at the mass burial of Maj. Francis L. Dade and over one hundred of his men, massacred in late 1835. Col. Twiggs had served as one of Gen. Edmund Gaines's brigadiers in the force that had gone to the site and identified the dead. Afterwards, the soldiers had then interred the remains in three grave-pits and marked the site with a spiked cannon, partly sunk vertically into the ground.

Three generals had tried unsuccessfully to bring the Seminoles to bay in 1836, including Winfield Scott, who discovered that Napoleonic strategy worked better on the fields of Europe than in the sloughs of Florida. Much of the 1836 fighting centered on the Cove of the Withlacoochee, a river stronghold of the Indians near the Gulf coast, which long defied conquest. As others recognized, there was an echo of the Napoleonic War in Florida, but it harked back to the guerilla war that had baffled Napoleon in Spain, not the French army's sweeping movements across the rolling plains to the northeast.

Craig's time at Fort Mellon no doubt introduced him to the history and lore of the war to date, as well as to one the most pleasant pastimes of armies in the field. Often at night the officers would gather around the campfire, at first to learn about each other and their native states, then to swap stories, tell jokes, and talk of family and home. Some would have guitars as part of their *impedimenta* and, to drive away the mind's "azure demons," would lead songs or sing solo.

As a proud Virginia native, Lewis Craig would always use the Old Dominion as his touchstone when encountering new states, territories, and countries—and would almost always find them inferior by comparison. Of these, his Florida duty posts would present the greatest contrasts. As had many before him, he found a region of confounding extremes in weather, as well as of remarkable hostility, not only from the warring natives but also from much of the flora and fauna.

Although the sea breezes of East Florida's St. Augustine settlement had drawn health-seeking invalids from the upper states since the 1820s, the soldiers sent to fight the Florida War in the interior more often found the territory a place of "death, contagion, and unnatural sleep." Despite occasional cold snaps, stifling heat and drenching humidity constituted the norm for troops on the march, with, for variety, black thunderstorms, and, in some areas, occasional sandstorms in those flat areas where deep sand made marching wearisome.

More often, too much water was the problem. Millennia before, the Florida peninsula had been the last region of the lower South to emerge from the ancient sea, and much of it appeared to long to submerge once again. Its myriad marshes and swamps "gave peculiar and strenuous character" to military operations, regularly slowing troop movements by foot and horse, and often defying the passage of wagons and artillery. Additionally, the region's opaque streams were always of indeterminate depth—although perhaps appearing shallow, a horseman could suddenly find himself up to his saddle skirts, if not abruptly swimming, and foot soldiers not uncommonly found themselves wading up to their chests.

There were, of course, hills along the territory's north-central spine, together with numerous forests, as well as wide prairies dotted with island-like hammocks—small or of many acres—supporting oaks, cypress, and other trees, and thickly underlain by rank growth.

In general, a daunting number of the Floridas' plants were spiked, barbed, or keenly edged. And, among the characteristic palms that dominated more open lands, the trunks of the cabbage palmetto and the leaf palm were often latticed with rough leaf stems resembling interwoven sword blades, while the *Yucca aloifolia* actually appeared to sprout its own sharp green daggers.

The handsome royal palm did not suggest weaponry as such, but its dignified crown of drooping fronds suggested those down-bending feathers of ostriches and other birds that decorated the turbans of the Seminole war leaders, perhaps emulating the palm foliage. Such colorful and elaborate headpieces, however, were most common as Seminole finery, worn at parleys and treaty signings. As warriors, the Seminoles wore clothing of textiles and leathers that blended with their surroundings—long shirts, leggings, and moccasins; sometimes they wore portions of U.S. Army uniforms. Their regalia they usually carried in their packs.

Some Floridian fauna seemed benign and were also edible—turkey and deer added variety to a soldier's diet, as did the massive green turtles of the coastal areas. But the reptiles were often fearsome—there were six kinds of poisonous snakes—including that adept swimmer, the cottonmouth moccasin—as well as rattlesnakes of several varieties.

Most disturbingly exotic to Northern soldiers, and many from the South as well, was the alligator, usually not aggressive (and often happily used as targets for distant rifle practice), but with dangerous, tooth-studded jaws and a smashing tail rapidly deployed when surprised or threatened. More likely to injure the unwary, however, was the alligator snapping turtle, which could grow up to two hundred pounds and bite through a broom handle.

Miniscule annoyances there were aplenty, from flightless insects like fleas and chiggers, to flyers like sand flies, gnats, and midges, as well as arachnids such as ticks; the beauty of the region's myriad butterflies hardly seemed just compensation. And although there was also an abundance of those stunning flowers that had prompted Juan Ponce de Leon to give La Florida its name, there were also eerie beds of red-veined, carnivorous pitcher plants that nonetheless seemed useless in reducing the insect population.

But the deadliest of the region's mortal threats came from tiny insects at that time unrecognized as a disease source: female mosquitoes of the genus *Anopheles*. They were the carriers of what would become widely known as malaria although at the time the usual diagnosis was simply fever—intermittent or otherwise.

As to the fever's cause, for decades "physicians still listed such factors as poor ventilation, lack of exercise, exposure, a hot dry climate, and boredom as contributing factors." For treatment of what were actually mosquito-borne fevers, the use of quinine was becoming more frequent, but the dosage remained uncertain, and army physicians varied in their opinions of the effectiveness of the drug, as opposed to various tonics.

In any case, malaria would ultimately kill many more soldiers than would the Seminoles: final statistics would show that while over 1400 officers and men perished during the Florida War, more than 1100 of them died of sickness, with exceptionally high numbers of maladies consistent with malaria. The invisible agents of ravaging dysentery provided the closest rival.

Commanders clearly recognized that the hotter months in the Floridas were more exhausting to troops, and that the same period was justly called the "sick season." Consequently, most campaigns were restricted to the fall and winter when possible.

The continued need for campaigning had begun to seem unnecessary in fall 1837, however. Although Craig had arrived at Fort Mellon during preparations for an attack to the southeast, some officers and men stationed at the fort felt that peace might actually be at hand. It was an unusually hopeful time in the war, bounded by the capture on October 21, 1837, of Osceola, a major architect of the war, and his death in captivity a little over three months later at South Carolina's Fort Moultrie on January 30, 1838.

In early 1837 General Thomas Jesup, the fourth general to fight the Seminoles, had arrived in Florida after winning the Creek War of 1836 along the lower Chattahoochee River in Alabama and Georgia. He had also achieved considerable success in persuading some of the Seminoles to leave for Indian territory, and in fall 1837 had seized Osceola, the major figure of the Indian resistance, near Fort Peyton, below St. Augustine.

Osceola's capture had provoked public outrage. General Jesup's critics in press and politics accused him of capturing Osceola under a flag of truce, a somewhat misleading description of what had really happened. Craig's commander has been so thoroughly vilified by historians over the capture of Osceola "under a flag of truce" that it seems appropriate to include Jesup's own explanation regarding the events below St. Augustine on October 21, 1837:

> As I had informed the chiefs at Fort King [in August 1837] that I would hold no communication with the Seminoles, unless they should determine to emigrate; as I had permitted no Indian to come in for any other purpose but to remain; as they were all prisoners of war, or hostages who had violated their paroles [pledges not to take up arms in return for freedom]; as many of them had violated the truce entered into at Fort King...and as the white flag had been allowed for no other purpose than to enable them to communicate and come in without danger to attack from our parties, it became my duty to secure them, on being satisfied of the fact they intended to return to their fastnesses. I accordingly required General [Joseph] Hernandez to seize them, and take them to St. Augustine; but, notwithstanding their character as prisoners of war and hostages who had violated their parole, and who, according to the laws of war, as recognized by civilized nations, had forfeited their lives, I directed that they should be treated with every kindness, and have every accommodation consistent with their security.

In addition, the Seminoles had attempted to arrange this meeting with the U. S. officer involved not being allowed an escort (though an adequate force was prudently sent) and the chiefs had brought mainly warriors to the talk, and very few women and children, often an indication of a plan to renew hostilities. The soldiers involved later discovered that the Seminoles had brought loaded muskets to the meeting ground, which they had concealed under deerskins.

Nonetheless, Osceola—whose initial act in the war had been to kill a government agent from ambush and then slice the man's scalp into enough pieces to provide trophies for his fellow assassins—would, finally and ironically, emerge as the only heroic, lionized figure of the Florida War, bound for lasting honor and fame.

General Jesup, however—already the most successful of the generals who commanded in Florida, where Seminole removal was concerned—felt that either his current peace initiative or a well-planned winter campaign would quiet the scoffers and critics. Soon, he thought, he would win the laurels he deserved. His latest attempts at bringing in the Seminoles for removal seemed to be prospering, and ongoing peace talks appeared to have an excellent chance of success.

If removal could not be accomplished peacefully, he had readied several well-supplied columns for a winter offensive. Meanwhile, Jesup had also allowed a truce to admit emissaries of Cherokee Chief John Ross to travel to Fort Mellon and, ostensibly, to go persuade the Florida Indians who were camped nearby to honor their treaty obligations to emigrate.

Jesup himself had seen enough of Seminole bad faith to have no illusions about the possible success of the Cherokee emissaries. The previous June, Osceola himself had brought his people to Fort Brooke at Tampa Bay and been treated hospitably by Jesup, to the extent of having the chief share his own tent. Then, having gained as much information as possible about U.S. strength and plans, having had his people subsisted for the duration with U.S. provisions, and having surreptitiously gathered war materiel and other goods, Osceola and the Seminoles had suddenly vanished back into the wilderness.

This time, Jesup felt that, with the Cherokees having summoned the Seminoles to receive John Ross's message, the usually "much dispersed" Florida Indians, would at least be concentrated to be "more readily attacked." Such being the case, Jesup felt positive that either the Cherokees would succeed and a "large portion of Indians" would emigrate at last, or his planned winter campaign would strike them heavily while they were concentrated and effectively "close the war" before spring.

When the Cherokees returned unsuccessful on December 14, Jesup declared the truce ended and prepared to send his columns moving toward the Seminole camps, in both the region above Lake Okeechobee and the area of Jupiter Inlet on the Atlantic. Another streak of bad luck, however, had already begun for Jesup. Coacoochee (Wild Cat), a young Seminole firebrand and charismatic war leader, though captured with Osceola, had escaped from the Castillo de San Marcos at St. Augustine and already returned to the front to lead his warriors against Jesup's troops.

As Craig and the other officers and men of Jesup's army would soon learn, the general had at least correctly assumed that the Seminoles would concentrate their forces. They certainly had time to do so. Although the Seminoles were seemingly able to dart like quicksilver through the wilderness, the U.S. Army—without roads, but with wheeled artillery, wagons of munitions and supplies, and columns of mounted and marching men—moved ponderously.

It would take almost three weeks for the column, including Craig and the Dragoons, to approach the coast near the Loxahatchee River's junction with the sea at Jupiter Inlet, a point chosen so that the troops could be reinforced and resupplied by water from St. Augustine. Arriving earlier via the coastal waters, a small detachment of some eighty sailors, soldiers, and artillerists under Navy Lt. Levi Powell arrived somewhat sooner. Meanwhile, to the west near Lake Okeechobee, the column of Virginian Col. Zachary Taylor had arrived ready for battle and became the first to fight.

In all three engagements the Seminoles quietly awaited the U.S. forces in carefully chosen positions that made maximum use of natural obstacles—streams, bogs, stands of saw grass, and thickly wooded cypress hammocks. Taylor's battle, on Christmas 1837, ended as a costly victory against some 400 Indians, among them Coacoochee. In this "largest battle of the war," Taylor's force of some 1,000 men, mostly regulars, suffered casualties of 26 killed and 112 wounded.

Along the coast, Lt. Powell's detachment, after several skirmishes, encountered a numerically superior Seminole force near Jupiter Inlet. An immediate charge against the Seminole position quickly fell backward as a rout; five men were killed and fifteen (including Powell) were wounded. Volunteer topographical engineer Joseph E. Johnston of Virginia prevented total disaster by directing an artillery-supported rear-guard action, during which his hat and clothes were torn by several bullets.

Finally in late January 1838, Jesup's column—the largest of all, comprising over 1500 men, including 600 Dragoons, 400 artillerists, and over 500 volunteers from Tennessee and Alabama—met the enemy. An army surgeon, eyewitness to what was to be called the Battle of the Loxahatchee River, provided a detailed after-action account, including a description of the charge of Craig and the Dragoons:

> On the 24th [of January] we renewed our march, as usual, at daylight; and continued to overcome the same obstacles we had to overcome for the previous week; cutting roads through dense hammocks; passing innumerable cypress swamps, and pine flats, interspersed with an almost impassable growth of saw-palmetto; and wading in water nearly up to the men's waists; many of whom were barefooted, and their clothes torn off, and flesh badly lacerated by the saw-palmetto.
>
> About 12 o'clock word was brought...that the enemy were strongly posted in a dense hammock....Gen. Jesup immediately gave orders for the Dragoons and volunteers to move forward with all speed, and attack the enemy....
>
> We quickly arrived in sight of the hammock where the Indians had posted themselves, and were awaiting us. In front was an almost impassable cypress slough, nearly half a mile wide; in passing through which we were up to our saddle girths in mud and water, our horses constantly stumbling over the cypress knees.
>
> The disposition for battle was immediately made; the Dragoons dismounting, and leaving their horses in the care of one man to every seven horses, charged the hammock in gallant style....The Indians yelled and shrieked; the rifles cracked, and their balls whistled; the musketry rattled; the Congreve rockets whizzed; the artillery bellowed; the shells burst; and take it all in all there was created no small racket for awhile.
>
> On gaining the centre of the hammock, we found a rapid stream flowing between us and the Indians, who were delivering a deadly fire from behind trees on the opposite bank. The stream was about thirty yards in width; but nothing daunted, our men hesitated not a moment, but plunged into the swift torrent, and crossed in the face of a shower of balls which whistled about their ears. The stream proved deeper than anticipated; and many could only reach the opposite side by swimming. Such unexpected conduct in direct

> opposition to their own mode of procedure so astonished the savages that they...scattered up and down the hammock in greatest alarm; and ceasing their yells soon disappeared altogether.

Jesup's force had suffered casualties of nine killed and around two dozen wounded, including the general himself. As Jesup turned to urge the volunteers to advance, a rifle ball ripped through his face below his left eye and crashed through his spectacles, carrying them away. Fortune favoring the bold, the Dragoons had none killed and only one wounded, with plaudits directed to lieutenants Lewis Craig and Charles May by Lt. Col. Harney for having penetrated farthest into the Seminole position. Seminole numbers were estimated at as many as three hundred; Jesup thought no more than one hundred but considered that they had abandoned an "impregnable" position. In any case, the Florida War's last major battle had now been fought, although a grinding war of attrition would continue for several more years.

It would be Jesup's last battle of the war. His certainty of triumph had been shattered along with his spectacles. And other subordinates, including the aggressive Twiggs, now agreed that it would be futile to continue to chase the Seminoles through the swamps. During a truce following the battle, five hundred Seminoles (including 150 warriors and several chiefs) parleyed with Jesup. The general afterward wrote to Secretary of War Joel Poinsett to request that the government allow these gathered Seminoles—at the suggestion of those who had parleyed with him—be allowed to stay in southernmost Florida on a reservation, where there was no immediate push for white settlement.

When the secretary's negative response finally arrived on St. Patrick's Day, 1838, Jesup ordered Colonel Twiggs and his Dragoons to disarm the waiting Seminoles and prepare them for their trip to Indian Territory. As usual, Jesup was subjected to complaints from Congress and ill-informed attacks from the press for following his orders. With the five hundred just captured, Jesup would be credited for having sent almost 2400 Seminoles west, about half of what had been calculated as their original population.

Despite his critics, Jesup considered that his success in the Floridas compared favorably to that of General Anthony Wayne in the Northwest Territory. After Fallen Timbers in 1794, the Indians had been moved west to reservations and white settlement had rapidly followed. By 1838, the

Ohio portion of that territory had not only achieved statehood but also grown to a population of 1.5 million that commanded twenty-one electoral votes, far outstripping all Southern states except Virginia.

Such could be the political dimensions of military choices, as politicians in the South noted. To the north of the Floridas, the state of Georgia, with an 1838 population of around 700,000, had only recently been allowed to expand into those Indian lands beyond the Flint and Chattahoochee rivers, long ago promised in the Georgia Compact of 1803.

The price of the advance from Fort Mellon had been steep, "marked by much suffering and fatigue to officer and soldiers." The cost to the Dragoons' horses had been even higher—one Dragoon officer later described it as "a great destruction of the finest horses that I have ever seen." Given Craig's noted love of horses, which remained a subject of comment fifteen years later, this circumstance must have been quite disturbing.

After resting briefly at newly built Fort Jupiter near the Loxahatchee battlefield, Craig's company was ordered on February 4 toward Lake Okeechobee to build another of the string of small forts that been constructed all along the road cut from Fort Mellon. This new fort was called Fort Van Swearingen in memory of a captain of the Sixth Regiment who had been killed in action during General Taylor's recent battle.

Since he routinely explored the environs of the places he was posted, Craig probably took this opportunity to see Lake Okeechobee, a vast sheet of water that could easily cover the square mileage of both Spotsylvania and Henrico counties. Despite its size, the lake had only recently passed from myth. As an indication of the lack of general knowledge of the Floridas at the time of the war, the Okeechobee had been "regarded by some as legendary as late as the early nineteenth century."

At Fort Van Swearingen, as would be the case throughout his career, Craig sought to improve his chances of promotion. Talking with survivors of the Sixth Regiment, he calculated that moving to that regiment would benefit his hopes of advancement, especially following his recent acclaim. Writing to the Secretary of War on March 12, 1838, he asked for a transfer, if he could be "placed next on the list of 2nd lieutenants to Lt. [Henry W.] Wharton, who is fourth."

If anything, Craig's chances of early promotion were even worse than he dreamed, as he long continued to occupy the lowest rung on the officers' ladder. Moreover, unknown to Craig, in 1836 Adjutant General Roger

Jones of Virginia had presented the Secretary of War with a bleak prediction on the promotion possibilities for newly minted 2nd lieutenants in the U.S. Army. Jones calculated that it would take eight years for such a young officer to reach 1st lieutenant, ten more to advance to captain, another twenty to become a major, ten more to be raised to lieutenant colonel, and an additional decade to attain a full colonelcy, in the faraway year of 1894.

Worse for Craig, Adj. Gen. Jones was speaking of West Point cadets who had become 2nd lieutenants upon graduating, normally during their early twenties. Craig was thirty. Yet war often rapidly promotes the brave, and within ten years Craig would be brevetted lieutenant colonel.

It would be a long time before Craig received a response to his transfer request, and during the interval he almost died from disease, as had so many others. Given his malady's slow onset and increasing severity, it must have been malaria that prostrated him. He was first sent to garrison duty in St. Augustine, then, progressively sicker, to Fort Heilman on Black Creek, until Zachary Taylor ordered Craig home to Fredericksburg on sick leave in June 1838.

Cognizant of these developments, Adj. Gen. Jones sent a belated, though enlightened, response to Craig's transfer request on the last day of July 1838. "If agreeable to Col. Twiggs and accomplished without prejudice to anyone," Adj. Gen. Jones wrote, Craig's "proper place," given his lengthy illness, would instead be in one of the vacancies in the Third Infantry at Fort Jesup, Louisiana.

The Third Regiment would certainly be Craig's appropriate place in many ways—in fact, the "Old Third" would ultimately command his love and allegiance for the remainder of his life. Nonetheless, even after his departure from the Dragoons, Twiggs and Harney would continue to figure largely in Craig's future. Raised to general and colonel respectively, both would serve among Craig's commanders in the approaching Mexican War.

Craig's slow recuperation in Fredericksburg alarmed his physician, Dr. Edward Carmichael, who supported Craig's request for an extension of medical leave. Dr. Carmichael thought Craig's "return to the Floridas would endanger his life and would certainly bring on a relapse," and prescribed "the use of the Virginia springs to restore his health"—meaning White Sulphur Springs in Greenbrier County, Virginia; in the late nineteenth century it would be noted that the springs had for decades enjoyed "a high reputation for the cure of malarial diseases."

Nonetheless, it would be December 1838 before Craig could report for duty at Fort Jesup, where he would continue on the sick list until February. Thereafter, however, he finally regained such robust health that he felt a return to the Floridas would not compromise it. It was perhaps at about this time that he copied out the following lines from *Tristram Shandy*: "O Blessed Health! Thou art above all gold and treasure; 'tis thou who enlarges the soul,—and openest all its powers to receive instruction and to relish virtue.—He that has thee has little more to wish for...."

As Lewis Craig's full recovery proved, Fort Jesup's location made it more healthful than almost anywhere in the Floridas. An unwalled military compound in western Louisiana, it occupied a forested, breeze-swept ridge, underlain by limestone. Located between the Red River port of Natchitoches (pronounced "Nackadish") and the Sabine River, western border of the United States, it had been a flashpoint since the days of the old plotter James Wilkinson. At that time, American presence at Natchitoches had been matched by Spanish forces at the Texas town of Nacogdoches (pronounced "Nacka-dochis"), separated by one hundred miles and the Sabine River.

Across the Sabine now lay the Republic of Texas, which had won its independence from Mexico in May 1836, after a war against Mexican dictator Antonio Lopez de Santa Anna. The conflict had been marked by Mexican slaughters of the Texans at Goliad and the Alamo in March, followed by complete victory over the Mexicans at San Jacinto in April.

In March 1837, President Andrew Jackson had acknowledged the independence of the new republic. Foreseeing the coming fight in Congress over the annexation of Texas, Jackson advised the Texans to claim the area from the Sabine to the Pacific, so that California could serve as a mammoth consolation prize for the Northern anti-annexationists.

Even after U.S. recognition, sporadic conflict continued between the Mexico and Texas, and the Third Regiment had twice moved briefly into the Lone Star Republic to protect American interests. Nonetheless, reduction of the number of troops in Fort Jesup's garrison began later in 1838, and, upon the Third Regiment's return to Florida in 1840, only a single Fourth Infantry company remained at the fort.

Fort Jesup, to be Craig's duty station more than once, had been founded back in 1822 by Virginians Lt. Col. Zachary Taylor and Major General Edmund Gaines, and named for their fellow Virginian, Quartermaster General Thomas Jesup. The fort's site possessed "a constant running spring of water (a thing seldom found in this country)." And its location was excellent. Near the U.S. frontier with what was then Mexico's Texas province, it occupied high ground twenty-five miles west of the Red River and within an eighteen-mile march of the Sabine.

Through the post passed the road to San Antonio, some four hundred miles distant, an avenue for the numerous travelers going to and from Texas. Earlier, it had been used by many groups of emigrants as well, drawn by the invitation of the Mexican government to become Texas colonists.

Almost from its beginning Fort Jesup had been associated with James B. Many (pronounced "Manny"), later colonel of the Third Regiment, which frequently formed part of its garrison. Colonel Many embodied the long-standing lack of a retirement policy for career U.S. Army officers—a situation that prompted Craig and many fellow officers to petition Congress (unsuccessfully). Born in Delaware before the signing of the Declaration of Independence, Many would spend his last decades on leave before dying in 1852, long too old and ill for active command, but still in dire need of his officer's salary and perquisites.

The year before Craig arrived at Fort Jesup, an officer stationed there described it as "one of the healthiest and most pleasant posts in the county":

> We are situated in the midst of a dense forest, on an eminence, which alone has been cleared of its timber. The loftiest and most ornamental trees (chiefly oak) have been left standing, scattered here and there, around the buildings and about the parade ground. The houses of the post are arranged in a rectangle, almost a square. They are painted white, are ornamented with balconies, piazzas, and pillars, and all face toward the grand parade ground.

Also at or adjacent to the post were "a large store, a post office, and, on the opposite side of the road, a well-ordered, quiet hotel." The Fort Jesup Hotel, offered among its amenities, "in addition to the comforts of a well-regulated house," the guests' privilege of being regaled "at night and morning by the delightful music of the well-known *Military Band* at the fort, to listen to, which is a treat, which will doubtless be an inducement for many to call."

To the post's describer, one of its finest attractions was a ground floor reading room in the officers' quarters, containing "an extensive, well-selected library, with newspapers from every part of the United States." Upstairs on the second floor, were "four neat, well-furnished rooms, with doors opening on galleries, both in front and rear," to accommodate bachelor officers such as Craig.

Craig would be stationed at Fort Jesup with the Third Regiment until fall 1840, mastering additional military arcana and becoming more accomplished at drill. When his health unquestionably returned in March 1840, he requested to be sent to the Floridas as part of a rumored 1500-man force; his allegiance to the Third Regiment had not yet solidified.

Gratifyingly, on June 1, 1840, Craig was promoted to 1st lieutenant, less than three years after joining the army. Continuing to watch carefully the effect of resignations on the promotion list and for the possibility of various opportunities for transfer to other posts, Craig requested and was granted the staff position of regimental assistant commissary of subsistence, a post which he kept from August 1840 until the following April.

By November 1840, when Craig and his regiment disembarked from the steamship *Caddo* at Fort Brooke near Tampa, much had happened in the seemingly unending Florida War. Most importantly to Craig and the Third Regiment, General Zachary Taylor, successor to General Jesup, had decided to deal with the dispersed Seminole bands by dividing Middle Florida and much of northern East Florida into twenty-mile squares, each containing a fort with its garrison charged with patrolling its square—protecting the settlements by detecting and moving against any Seminole war parties. Taylor's successor, yet another Virginian, General Walker Armistead, continued Taylor's strategy while also sending part of the army south in an attempt to confine the Seminoles to the lower peninsula.

Among the troops sent to South Florida was Craig's former regiment, the Second Dragoons. In 1839, another truce had been declared at Fort King and an attempt had been made to keep the peace by serving the Seminoles with a trading post on the west coast's largest river, the Caloosahatchee. Colonel William Harney had been sent in July 1839 to construct a fort fifteen miles upriver and to open trade with the Indians, who appeared friendly and grateful. But, as was so often the case, a band of hostile

Seminoles soon attacked the post in the night, and Harney had to escape barefooted, dressed only in his shirt and underwear.

Miraculously surviving to gather reinforcements, Harney returned to the camp to "find buzzards roosting in the trees above the bodies of six soldiers and two civilians," including the man Harney had given charge of the trading post. A search brought the number of the dead to sixteen, including three men who had been taken away to be tortured and killed at leisure.

"Our humane efforts to save a portion of the Indians from extermination have only led to another exhibition...of malice and disregard of their pledges," Harney wrote. "There must be no more talking—they must be hunted down as so many wild beasts."

Eventually fitting his words to action, Harney in December 1840 tracked the Indians responsible for the trading post attack to their island stronghold in the Everglades, where his force killed or captured all of them. Two of them Harney hanged, along with the corpse of Chief Chakaika, the leader of the attack on the Caloosahatchee trading post, killed early in Harney's attack. Both General Armistead and the Secretary of War were pleased with this outcome, and in St. Augustine Harney was extensively celebrated.

There were years of war to come, but the number of soldiers killed in the conflict was almost complete. Ultimately, around 270 officers and men would be killed (dwarfed by the over one thousand dead from disease—and also, no doubt, by the uncalculated numbers of volunteers and militiamen dead from all causes, during or after the war). Almost half of the deaths of U.S. Army officers and men had taken place during three actions: the Dade Massacre, the Battle of Okeechobee, and the Caloosahatchee Massacre. Seminole casualties, for a variety of reasons, are "impossible to estimate."

For Craig and his fellow officers, there was to be no more battle action. Instead, there was mainly garrison life, punctuated by scouting missions that made occasional contacts with parties of the Seminoles, who now confined most of their activities to the south, as planned by Armistead's strategy.

Meanwhile, starting from Fort Brooke on Tampa Bay, the various companies of the Third Regiment began to be deployed ever northward, often singly. In 1841 Craig himself, now commanding Company "D," was ordered from Fort Brooke to a succession of forts (usually separated by a day's march), including Fort Fanning, Fort Wacassassa, Fort Macomb, and Fort Pleasant.

Finally, over two hundred miles from Tampa Bay, Craig was placed in command of his own stockade fort in Middle Florida's Madison County, just below the Georgia line. Apparently named for Second Dragoons lieutenant James W. Hamilton, who had died in St. Augustine in late 1837, the fort stood beside the sandy, oak-lined St. Augustine-Tallahassee-Pensacola Road, five miles east of the sluggish Aucilla River and around forty miles west of the state capital.

Craig was justifiably proud of his isolated position of responsibility, and soon prepared it (and kept it) ready for inspection, while also fulfilling his principal task of ensuring that local settlers were protected and that travelers could pass safely between Tallahassee and St. Augustine.

Craig now also had various administrative duties, such as the submission of monthly muster rolls to the War Department. From this point, he would begin to feel strong resentment at a chronic Army problem—desertion, particularly galling to someone with his strong concept of military discipline and duty.

With Craig's command responsibilities came the perquisite of double rations, convertible to currency, which, though not generous, constituted reasonable compensation. No doubt quite sensitive to his rights in light of his earlier decade of costly litigation, Craig was astonished when his additional pay was denied. Consequently, he began a years-long and contentious correspondence with the War Department, in the person of Adjutant General Roger Jones, who often gave Craig the rough edge of his pen.

The year 1842 brought many changes to the Florida War. In January Lt. Col. Josiah H. Vose, who had commanded the Third Regiment since 1830 during Col. Many's perpetual absence, selected Craig and some of his men for detached service. They marched to Deadman Bay on the coast to investigate Seminole activity along the lower Steinhatchee River, earlier General Jackson's furthest point of penetration during the First Seminole War.

Lt. Col. Vose well represented the vagaries of U.S. Army promotion. A veteran of the War of 1812, he had not made lieutenant colonel until 1830, at which grade he had spent a dozen years. He could obviously never make colonel in the Third Regiment while Many lived.

In March 1842, however, transfers and promotions suddenly created a new world for Craig's regiment: the Many conundrum was neatly sidestepped by transferring Vose to the Fourth Regiment, where he was promoted to colonel to fill a vacancy there. Col. Vose would soon find himself in charge of the Florida War during the temporary absence of the new commander, Col. William Worth.

At the same time, Lt. Col. Ethan Allen Hitchcock was likewise transferred and took Vose's place in active command of Craig's regiment. This was a quite fortunate development. With Colonel Many continuing on extended leave, Hitchcock would soon transform the Third Regiment, by bringing it to a high level of efficiency and professionalism.

The greatest change, however, would occur in August 1842 when the increasingly unpopular Florida War was declared over. Finally, the beginning lines of a long-popular piece of doggerel could be dismissed: "Ever since the creation / By the best calculation / The Florida war has been raging…."

When Col. William J. Worth had replaced General Armistead in command in May 1841, he had continued Armistead's strategy of pushing the war southward into ever-more remote Seminole strongholds—even campaigning during summer—and he had also enjoyed success through bribing various chiefs and warriors to travel to Indian Territory. This policy enabled Worth to transport most of the remaining Seminoles, including the recalcitrant Coacoochee, who in 1849 would ultimately lead a group of his people from Indian Territory to freedom in Mexico. Also in August, as a final buttress to peace, the U.S. Congress finally began to lure sufficient numbers of settlers into the Florida territory with the Armed Occupation Act of 1842, which gave free land to those willing to occupy and defend it.

The most adamant Seminoles, numbering around three hundred—some one hundred of them warriors—were provided a reservation in far southwest Florida. As the war-ender, Col. Worth was widely celebrated and brevetted Brigadier General. This was "humbug," thought Col. Hitchcock, who had been ignored when he had suggested a policy similar to Worth's two years earlier.

As Hitchcock began his transformation of the Third Regiment, Craig's former comrades in the Second Dragoons also underwent a drastic change. As the U.S. Congress searched for ways to cut costs and economize after the seven-year war, the House attempted to disband the regiment entirely. The U.S. Senate intervened, however, cost-cutting instead by taking away the Dragoons' expensive horses and transforming the mounted infantry into riflemen. But in time, the Second Dragoons would ride again.

Although the war was officially over, various operations continued, the last of which involved the Third Regiment and its new commander, Lt. Col. Hitchcock. The regiment's officers and men continued to be scattered at their various forts in Middle Florida for a time, but a concentration of companies would soon be ordered at Fort Stansbury, thirty miles south of Tallahassee. From there, Hitchcock would attempt to capture the Florida War's final holdouts—not Seminoles, but a band of Creeks under Chief Pascofa.

Hitchcock arrived in Florida in October 1842 and soon joined his regiment at Fort Stansbury. The fort's location impressed him. "There is something solemn and grand in the moaning of the winds through the tall pines among which my post is situated," he wrote. As a note of the picturesque, the fort also had a large pond adjacent to it, formed by one of the territory's many sinkholes.

Arranged in a parallelogram, Fort Stansbury boasted a spacious parade ground which Hitchcock immediately put into use. A paragon of a drillmaster, he noted with pleasure that he had not lost his edge while on a recent diplomatic assignment: "I would tomorrow drill a regiment with any field officer in service. My voice is clear and my manner entirely free from impatience." A visiting officer concurred: "It is a delight to see Hitchcock handle his men." Hitchcock's diligence in putting the Third Regiment through it evolutions was such that during its coming deployment to Mexico, the unit "was so perfected in drill as to attract much attention."

Hitchcock was much more than a drillmaster, however. As one of his biographers noted of the transformation of Craig's regiment, "Though stationed amid pine barrens, under [Hitchcock's] careful instruction and guided by his scholarly influence, the Third became the crack regiment of infantry, not only in drill and discipline, but in high mental culture."

Hitchcock was surely one of the most remarkable officers in the U.S. Army. Although neither Twiggs nor Harney could be accused of being intellectuals, Hitchcock was probably the foremost savant in the service. One of the few officers with whom he could converse at his own level was

Zachary Taylor's longtime staff officer and future son-in-law, William W. S. "Perfect" Bliss, with whom Hitchcock "sympathetically discussed Hegel and Kant, Iamblichus, Goethe, and Carlyle, Locke, Glanville, and the philosophy of modern thinkers, especially of Germany."

When not on duty, Hitchcock read and wrote constantly and would publish books on Christianity, Spinoza, Swedenborg, Shakespeare, Spenser, Dante, and, one of his particular interests, alchemy. He was also deeply interested in American literature and in 1831 dined with Washington Irving, now the most famous man of American letters after publishing *The Sketch Book* and other works. Hitchcock found Irving "like his portraits,—mild, amiable, benevolent." At about the same time, as commandant of cadets at West Point, Hitchcock briefly had charge of a younger author, the soon-to-be-dismissed cadet E. A. Poe, who had already privately published a volume of poems.

On November 28, 1842, Hitchcock received an order to "reopen the war" just concluded, by attacking Chief Pascofa and his band of Creeks. Instead, he decided to make his "expedition a test of peaceful methods." He was successful. During December 1842 and early January 1843, Hitchcock located and captured Pascofa and his band without firing a shot, through his "skillful and energetic steps...seconded by the zealous exertions of the officers of his regiment."

Hitchcock used a variety of blandishments to attract Pascofa and his few warriors to him, so that he could use his powers of persuasion through an interpreter. An important qualification for Hitchcock during these negotiations was his recent mission to investigate government mismanagement and corruption in Indian Territory. At the least, this put him in the position of being able to answer pertinent questions about the land where Pascofa and his people were bound. But his genuine kindness, his sympathy, and his concern for the Indians and their lot featured quite conspicuously.

Pascofa and his people were ready for peace, or, as the chief expressed it, for "sunshine after years of rain." Given blankets and rations, they soon went back into the wilderness, with a promise to assemble soon near the Ochlockonee River's mouth for steamship transportation to Indian Territory.

Over a week passed without a sign from the Indians, and it appeared that Hitchcock had failed, as had so many before him. But the delay had been entirely due to Pascofa's difficulty in gathering his scattered band. When Pascofa's people appeared in obedience to Hitchcock—calling him "The Controlling Spirit"—it became obvious that years of war had reduced them to a ragged and starving remnant. They numbered fifty-one, only twenty-nine of them warriors. Hitchcock noted the absence among them of any children younger than four, which lent credence to the rumor that, during their years of being hunted, the Indians had routinely killed their newborn infants to prevent their cries from alerting searching soldiers.

In Tallahassee, the news of Hitchcock's success was greeted with jubilation by Territorial Governor Richard Call and the Florida legislature. Later in March a letter reached Fort Stansbury: an invitation to attend "a party and a dinner" in the capital on March 7–8, 1843, "in honor of Colonel Hitchcock and his gallant officers." Hitchcock at once replied that he would be there with all those officers who with "propriety could be absent from the post."

It seems probable that among those officers attending were Lieutenant Lewis Craig and his friend Capt. L. N. Morris. The latter had for over a year been posted at Fort Gamble, west across the Aucilla from Craig's Fort Hamilton. Morris's fort was named for the planter Robert Grattan Gamble—a native Virginian (a Richmonder, in fact) and a Whig like many of the area planters—on whose Welaunee Plantation the fort was located.

Although the fort was well suited for sending out scouting parties, the plantation itself was long rumored to be considered by the Indians inviolable because of the Gamble family's long friendship with the powerful Seminole leader Tiger Tail, who had grown up in the vicinity. In November 1842, Tiger Tail had been captured, but had died aboard ship halfway between Florida and New Orleans.

There were also many plantations near Welaunsee owned by prominent members of Middle Florida society who were friends of the Gambles. Probably most interesting to Craig and other officers was Lipona Plantation, owned by Achille Murat, "nephew of Napoleon and son of one of his marshals"; he was said to have been "born on the steps to throne of Naples," where his warrior father had been king.

Unassuming rather than pretentious, Murat (husband to a Virginia beauty) was not known to any of his friends by royal titles. The American army officers' attraction to his proximity must have been strong, however, given the contribution of the Napoleonic era to the United States army, everything from tactics and uniforms to even the sobriquet "the Old Guard," by which Napoleon's Imperial Guard was known, but soon to be bestowed on the Third Regiment.

Another friend of the Gambles was Col. Hitchcock himself, who had visited Welaunee on his arrival in Florida the previous October and had been "dined and entertained by old friends." Capt. Morris and his fellow officer Lt. Philip Barbour had also enjoyed the Gambles' hospitality, given their proximity to the plantation house, and Craig himself seems to have met his wife-to-be at Welaunee. In later years Craig recalled that he had first heard Elizabeth Church sing to her own piano accompaniment when he was in the company of Captain Morris and Ann Selden ("Nannie") Gamble, Robert Gamble's daughter.

An accomplished young lady, aged twenty, Elizabeth Church was the daughter of Dr. Alonzo Church. From the time she was six, her father had been president of the University of Georgia (interchangeably known as Franklin College). A Vermonter like Col. Hitchcock, Dr. Church had been among that legion of Northerners who had come South for health reasons and had stayed. His father, a Revolutionary War veteran, "styled Gentleman" in his militia lieutenant's commission, had seen his son educated at Middlebury College. During Church's first job as a schoolmaster in Putnam County, Georgia, he had met Sarah Trippe, daughter of a local planter, and in 1817 had married her. By 1843 she had given birth to seven daughters (two of whom died in infancy) and four sons.

As the daughter of a university president, Elizabeth's unusual semi-public upbringing had left her quite comfortable in society and very fluent in conversation. Her family lived at the center of the college campus (and campus life) in the President's House, near the university's first major building, now called Old College. Near the corner where the famous Arch would rise in the 1850s, the Presbyterian church stood, emblematic of the Presbyterians' great power on campus during the antebellum period.

Elizabeth's parents' social duties as hosts (assisted by their children) were wide and varied. They involved both education and religion, for Dr. Church had not only been university president since 1829 but also performed ministerial duties within the Presbyterian Synod of Georgia since the 1820s.

Where politics were concerned, Dr. Church hosted an important conclave that met annually at the university until 1859. This was the Senatus Academicus—"a bicameral body...composed of a Board of Trustees for the university and a Board of Visitors comprised of the governor and other high officials," including the judges of Georgia's superior courts—over which Dr. Church sometimes presided.

Georgia's major politicians in particular looked forward to these yearly face-to-face meetings, where open discussion and confidentiality were much better assured than by letter. Although Dr. Church practiced a rigid political neutrality, his university had long been considered a bailiwick of the Troupites, opponents of a rival faction, the Clarkites, each originally followers of either George M. Troup or John Clark. The heyday of these factions had been the 1820s, before the Troupites generally evolved into Whigs and the Clarkites into Democrats.

Since Elizabeth had been, from an early age, accustomed to Georgia's political and social stratosphere, her comfort in social settings presents no mystery. As one of Dr. Church's eulogists would note, "surrounded by his wife, his daughters, and his sons, [Dr. Church] was the recognized leader in the social life of [the University]. Here were formed the manners, and here was stimulated the emulation of the men who, in almost every Southern State, have since adorned so many places in public and private life."

For several years Elizabeth had made winter visits Tallahassee and vicinity, visiting a sister who lived there with her husband, and enjoying the hospitality of nearby friends like the Gambles and the Calls. In February 1843, a second sister had married another Floridian. Consequently, it would not have been unusual for Elizabeth to have encountered Lewis Craig at any time after he became established at Fort Hamilton in August 1841, or for her to have attended the governor's ball for the regimental officers in March 1843. Even a brief social conversation would probably have revealed that Craig was a Virginian, as were two prominent members of the Athens gentry, both John Addison Cobb and his wife, Sarah, who was a native of Fredericksburg. Their U.S. congressman son, Howell, had been married to Elizabeth's friend Mary Ann since 1835.

In honor of Col. Hitchcock and his officers, Governor Call provided a sumptuous banquet for hundreds at his Tallahassee residence, The Grove. The governor's toast to his guests was "Beauty and Chivalry—the pride and glory of our country." Col. Hitchcock responded, "'Beauty—its defense and protection the noble privilege of Chivalry, whether with or without the button,' thus including citizens among the chivalrous"—the button mentioned was the gutta-percha cap used at the tips of gentlemen's foils for fencing practice, but removed by officers engaged in an actual duels.

It appears that at about the time of the banquet at The Grove, Lewis Craig asked Elizabeth Church (known to her friends as Lizzy) to marry him. In any case, their marriage followed in June 1843. Young bachelor Linton Stephens, half-brother of the more famous Alexander, visited the Churches in Athens soon after Elizabeth returned home, and noticed an appreciable change in her:

> Miss Lizzy has just returned from her winter visit to Florida, and truly the "land of flowers" with its southern sky and soft breezes, combined with the fact that she is the last of an illustrious galaxy, has imparted a new bloom to her cheek, a new elasticity to her step, and the finishing stroke to a form almost faultlessly round. She stands forth ripe in the glories of full-blown womanhood and oh! what a sight she is for a Christian! Perhaps too a consciousness of having arrived at the height of her charms...has vested her beautiful face a new facility of smiling and inspired her with a new desire of pleasing. At any rate I am sure I never had so exquisite a pressure of the hand or so smiling a welcome as last Saturday night; nor ever heard a voice so tremulously sweet as her, when she sang "Far Over the Deep Blue Sea" and "Rory O'More."

Since 1837 "Rory O'More" had been one of the most popular songs of Irish poet and composer Samuel Lover. It tells the musical tale of young Rory, "bold as a hawk," and his courtship of Kathleen Bawn, "soft as the dawn." After several amorous advances and retreats by Rory, the song concludes:

> Then Rory, the rogue, stole his arm round her neck
> So soft and so white, without freckle or speck,
> And he look'd in her eyes that were beaming with light,
> And he kissed her sweet lips—don't you think he was right?
> "Now, Rory, leave off, sir—you'll hug me no more,
> That's eight times to-day you have kiss'd me before."
> "Then here goes another," says he, "to make sure,
> For there's luck in odd numbers," says Rory O'More.

Elizabeth Church and Lewis Stevenson Craig were married in the President's House on the university campus on June 8, 1843, with Presbyterian minister Rev. Nathan Hoyt officiating. The sudden event provoked gossip—a mixture of fact, misinformation, and embellishment—that was preserved like a fly in amber in a letter from an Athens student of the time. In four pages mainly devoted to recent rampages by the university's famously rowdy students, Henry Hunt Jones (of the esteemed Jones family of coastal Liberty County, Georgia) wrote on June 27, 1845,

> Doctor Church's remaining marriageable daughter, Miss Elizabeth, was lately married to Lieutenant Craig of the United States army. The Lieutenant drinks wine *daily*, uses very profane language, and is *forty-one* years old. The Dr. and Mrs. Church were violently opposed to the match, but could not prevent the young lady from having her own way. They were married, and on this very morning left for St. Louis, Missouri.

This amusing letter also contains several references to the young Presbyterian Jones's own exceptionably decent behavior, and his principalship of a "sabbath school carried on in a neighboring factory by a number of pious young men connected with the College." To some, the letter might suggest the adjective "Pecksniffian," drawn from Seth Pecksniff, the holier-than-thou character from Charles Dickens's *Martin Chuzzlewit*, then appearing in serial form before its book publication in 1844.

As for the facts of the case, Craig actually was not 41, as charged, but 36. Jones's references to profanity might suggest that Twiggs and Harney had found an apt pupil in Craig, but, if so, Col. Hitchcock was working on that. And, as to his daily resort to alcohol, the Florida War may indeed have driven Craig to drink, but it was also then common for chronic malaria sufferers to mix quinine with wine, and Craig would later have the reputation of being only a moderate drinker. But, without a doubt, the newlyweds did leave Athens for St. Louis in late June 1843.

Regarding Dr. and Mrs. Church's violent opposition to the wedding, such resistance would not be surprising. Many parents of the time had little desire for a daughter to marry a man devoted to the dangerous, unpredictable life of a U.S. Army officer, a son-in-law who would by definition often be in harm's way. Indeed, General Zachary Taylor had in 1835 forbidden his daughter to marry Dragoon lieutenant Jefferson Davis. In any case, Taylor's opposition proved futile, as did the Churches', if opposition there was.

As a noted belle, Elizabeth Craig probably looked forward to St. Louis's famously "cosmopolitan society," which depended heavily on the bachelor officers, as well as the married officers and their wives, who resided nine miles below the city at Jefferson Barracks, the western headquarters of the U.S. Army since 1826. Moreover, bachelor officers often found wealthy wives in St. Louis, as had Edmund P. Gaines and William S. Harney and as Ulysses Grant would.

St. Louis, famously the departure point for the Lewis and Clark expedition, had been founded by the French on the west bank of the Mississippi in 1764. With an 1843 population of around 36,000 (twelve times that of Athens, Georgia), St. Louis was entering a "new period of growth and prosperity." A recent building boom had been crowned in 1841 by the opening of the magnificent Planters' Hotel. Its four stories, all accessed by a wide spiral staircase, occupied an entire city block. The hotel boasted a "classic limestone front," 150 bedrooms, "a huge dining room" with "a beam-paneled ceiling and classical pilasters," along with a vast second-floor grand ballroom, "with decorative details copied from the Temple of Erectheus." Jefferson Barracks, with its parade ground faced on three sides by Spartan two-story barracks and other buildings, no doubt provided a marked contrast.

Soon, however, the Craigs were bound for the even more minimal brand of society at remote Fort Jesup—accessible by steamer only as far as Natchitoches—then by carriage or wagon to the fort itself. There the couple occupied one of the small married officers' houses, and there on September 18, 1844, the Craigs' first and only child was born—a daughter named Sarah, after her Church grandmother, but always called "Sallie." She was headstrong like her mother, and as years passed there would be stormy times in their relationship. But Sallie's adoration of her officer father was unmixed, and she would always glory in the fact that she not only had been born the daughter of a border soldier but also had come into the world at one of his outposts.

As war with Mexico became more and more probable, Mrs. Craig and infant Sallie were soon bound for Athens, where they would reside with Dr. and Mrs. Church. It would be years before the family of three would again live together. But when that time came, Elizabeth would be pleased that the reunification would take place in a metropolis even more cosmopolitan than St. Louis—New York City.

Chapter 3

To the Sierra Madre Mountains

> We were not many—we who stood
> Before the iron sleet that day—
> Yet many a gallant spirit would
> Give half his years if he then could
> Have been with us at Monterrey.
> —Charles Fenno Hoffman, Moterrey

In March 1845, James Knox Polk, a Tennessee Democrat and protégé of Andrew Jackson, entered the Executive Mansion. He had foresworn any idea of serving more than one term but was determined that his administration would attain several goals. The most daunting were territorial ambitions that could be summarized as "Manifest Destiny." First, he wished to secure the Northwest coast and its interior for the United States—the territory to become Washington and Oregon. This would require war with the British Empire if diplomacy failed. Second, with the Northwest acquired, Polk wanted to continue the America's coastal acquisitions by buying the Province of California from the deeply indebted Republic of Mexico. In a rough-hewn way he would succeed in both aims though the war would be fought with Mexico, not the British. This conflict would be the making of Lewis Craig and many other U.S. army officers, most of them Whigs.

The Democrat who had from the first championed the addition of Texas to the Union, President Andrew Jackson, died at 78 of heart dropsy at The Hermitage near Nashville on June 8, 1845. He had recently rejoiced at the first step toward Manifest Destiny when annexation was offered to Texas in March, just as "Young Hickory," James Polk, was inaugurated. Almost exactly four years later, Polk, having expanded America beyond even Jackson's dreams, died of cholera at 53 in Nashville, having recently left the presidency, thoroughly exhausted by accomplishing the territorial tasks he had set for himself.

The month after Jackson's death, July 1845, found Lewis Craig leaving Fort Jesup for the last time, as the Third Regiment followed General Zachary Taylor from its old post near Texas's eastern border. A Virginian turned Louisiana planter, Taylor looked more like a farmer than a general and more than earned his nickname, "Old Rough and Ready." Taylor and his troops were headed toward that region of West Texas where the Nueces River emptied into the Gulf. In late July, off the Texas coast, Lewis Craig commenced his journal.

———

LSC*

Left New Orleans on Wednesday morning about 3 o'clock a.m. on the *25th of July 1845* for Aransas Pass (Texas). We arrived off the Pass on Friday night the 25th of July 1845. I did not suffer at all from sea sickness on my passage over.

On Saturday morning *July 26th* I was ordered by General Taylor to take eight men and a non-commissioned officer and proceed to Live Oak Point for the purpose of seeing if a sufficient quantity of wood and water could be procured for the troops, and how near a steam boat drawing four feet water could approach the shore.

I left the steamship *Alabama* on Saturday, *26th July*, at 10 o'clock a.m. for the Point, taking with me Lieutenant [John J. C.] Bibb, Sergeant Golder, Privates Anderson, Collins, [missing], Lightfoot, McNoe, McDonnell & Presley, all of Company "D," Third Infantry, and one man of "K" Company, Third Infantry, and one of the men of the band as an interpreter to our pilot, who was a Spaniard, and whose name was Thomas. We arrived a Live Oak Point at half past 5 o'clock of the same day.

Live Oak Point is situated in an area some twenty feet above Aransas Bay. The soil is very sandy. The point is covered with live oak. There are several fresh water lakes on the Point, and we found several good wells of water. The water of this place is of the best, I have no doubt, in all this section of country, & the distance from Aransas Pass to Live Oak Point is between 25 & 30 miles. Boats drawing 5 or 6 feet water can go in twenty yards of the shore at Live Oak Point.

---

* Within the narrative for chapters three through five, Craig's journal entries will be marked ***LSC***.

We returned on Sunday the *27th July, 1845*, leaving Live Oak Point about 10 o'clock in the morning, and, after a hard day's rowing, reached the steamboat *Undine* (which we found lying in the Bay) about 2 miles from the mouth of the Pass, having landed the Third Infantry on St. Joseph's Island. I remained that night on board of the *Undine*, and on the following morning (*Monday 28th*) I left in the *Undine* for the steamship *Alabama*, where I found General Taylor and Staff. I then reported to the General the result of my investigations at Live Oak Point.

On the same day that I left for Live Oak Point, Captain Van Horne was sent to Corpus Christi to make an examination of that part of the country. He returned on Monday the *28th* and reported favorably of that position, upon which the General determined to make that his Headquarters. On Monday evening the *28th*, the General and all his staff with the exception of Captain [W. W. S.] Bliss, his Assistant Adjutant General, left on the steamship *Alabama* for the Third Infantry encampment.

On Tuesday, *July 29th*, Adjutant General Bliss came over on the cutter. The General and his Staff, Colonel Hitchcock with "G" & "K" Companies, left on the evening of the *29th July* in the steamboat *Undine* for Corpus Christi this morning, *Thursday, 31st July*. They are still in sight, and I presume will have to return to this point. The steamship *Alabama left* for New Orleans on Tuesday night, *29th July*.

Monday, July 28th, 1845. Wrote to my dear wife. Sent the letter by the steamship *Alabama*. Was taken very sea sick while writing, owing to my being compelled to write in one of the state rooms on board of the *Alabama*.

Tuesday, July 29th, 1845. [St. Joseph's Island] Received an order to strike the tents of Companies "C" & "D" for the purpose of going to Corpus Christi. In a few moments after the order was issued, it was countermanded, and "G" & "K" Companies were ordered to go.

Wednesday, July 30th, 1845. [St. Joseph's Island] Commenced a letter to my dear wife. In the evening made a visit in Company with Captain [George P.] Field and Lieutenant [missing] to a Mr. O'Dougherty and a Mr. Jones.

We were treated with a great deal of kindness at the last mentioned house. They feasted us on melons. In speaking of Live Oak Point, Colonel James Power, who owns a greater part of the Point, we found absent, having gone to Austin as a member of the Convention [that voted to accept annexation to the United States and prepared a Texas state constitution]. The other family is named Fox. The wife of Colonel Power was very kind to us, insisted on our taking supper with them, and, on our return to our boats at night, sent us down several blankets and pillows, which was very acceptable. The nearest settlement to Live Oak Point by land is the Mission of Refugio, which is about 40 miles.

Thursday, July 31st, 1845. I have become very tired of this encampment. The water is so very bad that it is almost impossible for one to drink it. I hope that General Taylor will come this evening and take the command to Live Oak Point, and there let us remain until we can get a smaller boat, for we can never get the boat we now have across the flats between this point and Corpus Christi.

I have just given a party of my men permission to go a-fishing, with the understanding that they are not to bring back more fish than the Company can consume at one time, for on yesterday there were nearly two boatloads thrown away and floated onto the beach near our encampment. I am afraid that I shall become disgusted with fish and oysters before leaving this place, for it seems to me that every man I see has either fish or oysters in his hands.

The *Undine* returned about ten o'clock today with General Taylor and staff. The boat could not be gotten over the flats. Colonel Hitchcock with the two companies procured [two?] small boats to Corpus Christi, and it is thought by some that, should a squall come up while they are on the Bay, they will stand a very good chance of going to "Davy Jones's Locker," for the boats are very small and too much crowded.

General Taylor has gone to Live Oak Point in the *Undine*. The boat has gone there for water and is expected back early in the morning. "E" Company left this morning in a small sailboat for Corpus Christi. The Revenue Cutter has gone to Galveston for the purpose of seeing if a smaller steamboat can be engaged by the Government.

I have just returned from bathing and enjoyed it very much. I found Dr. Jones on the beach looking for a breast pin which he had lost while bathing on yesterday, but I believe he did not find it. Retreat has just beaten, and I must close for the day.

I thought I would not write any more today, but, having taken a nap this morning, I feel very little like sleeping and will therefore make a few remarks relative to our move.

Although I do not think it right for a junior to speak of the acts of his senior, I am compelled to say that our move has been very badly managed from the commencement, and, since our arrival at Aransas Pass, everything appears to have gone wrong. It would have been much better if, instead of landing the Third Infantry and all of its baggage on this island, they had been carried immediately to Live Oak Point, where they could have procured a plenty of good water and wood, and we could have remained there until the Commanding General could have sent to New Orleans for steamboats that would be able to run between St. Joseph's and Corpus Christi. As it is, we shall be compelled to remain on this island until we are taken off in small boats, which will detain us for some time to come.

Friday, August 1st, 1845. I am officer of the day. The steamboat *Undine* returned from Live Oak Point at Retreat this morning (with the Commanding General and staff, together with several *amateurs*) having gone there for water. Nothing of interest occurred today. We had one small sailboat to pay us a visit from Matagorda Bay, with chickens, and a quantity of fine water melons.

Saturday, August 2nd, 1845. The steamboat *Monmouth* arrived off the Pass sometime last night and landed today Companies "B" and "I" of the Third Infantry. They were then taken by the *Undine* and landed on the beach between this and Corpus Christi, from which point they will go to Corpus Christi in small boats. Two ships arrived about the same time with the 4th Infantry on board of them, convoyed by the U.S. ship *St. Mary's*. The steamboat *Monmouth* was very near being lost today, the pilot having run her up on shore; the *Undine* was sent to her relief and got her off.

I received a letter by the *Monmouth* from my dear, dear wife, in which she informs me that dear little Sallie was then sick with the whooping cough, dear little creature. I hope ere this she has recovered from it. Oh, what a pleasure it is to receive letters from one's dear wife, one who I love so much, and so devotedly. My heart is sad indeed, when I think that it will be three months, and *perhaps* longer ere I see her and my *dear* little *angel* Sallie.

Unfortunately, Craig would not be reunited with his family for almost three years, and he would find that his wife was not the thoughtful correspondent he wished her to be. Indeed, she later admitted that her friends often complained of how infrequently she would send letters and admitted that she had a "repugnance" to writing. This was quite a pity, since letters from home have always been one of a soldier's chief pleasures, and having no letters at mail call represented a major disappointment of camp life.

LSC

Sunday, August 3rd, 1845. All the 4th Infantry under the command of Captain [John] Page, excepting Captain [Gouverneur] Morris's Company "E," landed today about 11 o'clock a.m. A large number of the officers dined with us today. We gave them a hearty welcome and the best we had.

I neglected to state that Lieut. [Braxton] Bragg and his Company of the Third Artillery was also landed at the same time. There are four officers with that Company, viz. [namely], Lts. Bragg, [Francis J.] Thomas, [John F.] Reynolds, and [Daniel H.] Hill.

I understand that my friend L. T. Waller, Purser in the Navy, is on board the Sloop-of-War *St. Mary's*. I hope I shall have the pleasure of seeing him ere he leaves the Pass. The last time we met, I think, it was in old Williamsburg, Virginia, when I saw a great deal of him. We frequently met at a relative's of his, Dr. Robert Waller's, whose politeness and great kindness to me I shall never forget. Since that time a great many changes have taken place. Mr. Waller has entered the Navy and I the Army, and to think that we were so very near meeting on the borders of Mexico.

Monday, August 4th, 1845. Major [Andrew Jackson] Donelson arrived last night from Galveston. He appears to be very much indisposed. He brings little or no news. I saw a letter he received from a member of the Convention, saying that he had understood that there was a large number of troops collecting at Matamoros under the command of General [Mariano] Arista, supposed to be in number some 6,000 men. What their intentions are no one knows. Captain [Henry] Bainbridge left with his company for Shell Island, between this and Corpus Christi. He will take his company there by detachment to Corpus Christi in small sailboats.

Tuesday, August 5th, 1845. The U.S. Ship *Falmouth* arrived off the Pass sometime last night, Captain [J. R.] Sands in command. Lieutenant Gardner reported to General Taylor this morning with dispatches from the commanding officer of the *Falmouth*. I have just received orders to leave with my company for Corpus Christi in the morning. Captain Field will also leave with his Company. I finished my letter of the 30th July to my dear wife, and shall send it by Captain [Winslow] Foster of the Revenue Cutter *Woodbury* to New Orleans, as the ships that brought over the 4th Infantry will not leave for some days.

Wednesday, August 6th, 1845. Left St. Joseph's Island in the steamboat *Undine* with my Company for Corpus Christi. The steamboat landed us at Shell Island. I then left a part of my company under the command of Lieutenant [Douglas S.] Irwin, and, with Lieutenant [Henry B.] Schroeder and the rest of the company, left for Corpus Christi in a small boat called the *Montezuma* and arrived at Corpus Christi about ½ past 5 o'clock p.m. of the same evening. We were compelled to anchor our little boat nearly 200 yards from the shore, and land our men and property in small boats, the men being compelled to wade and push them ashore. Here our march ends for a time, and so ends my short *journal*. Having no table in camp, I was compelled to write on my knee, and I fear, should this fall in the hands of anyone, they will find it hard to decipher.

Having been in proximity to Gen. Taylor since Fort Jesup, Craig continued to be close to the general's headquarters. In the long line of tents that occupied the sandy campground, the Third Regiment was situated in the center, immediately to the left of Taylor's tent.

The U.S. army would at first love Corpus Christi. The settlement was small, just twenty or thirty structures, chief among them Pennsylvanian Henry L. Kinney's trading post; he would do brisk business as the local population was augmented by four thousand soldiers.

Later Kinney would join the march to Mexico as a colonel with the Texas Volunteers. The troops found the weather equable, the bay diverting, and the surrounding prairie charming. Spare time allowed saltwater seining by the men (who could bring back up to sixty bushels of fish), as others gathered oysters and green turtles. The officers went far afield shooting game. After one "three-day hunt," they brought back "fifty-one geese, ten deer, four bittern, two crane, sixty-nine snipe, eighteen ducks, four curlew, three turkeys, and one panther." Consequently, letters were sent home extolling the manifold virtues of the new duty station.

Then the weather changed. "Northers" would blow and electrical storms would strike regularly and with astonishing violence. During one storm two of Lt. Braxton Bragg's body servants were struck by lightning, one of them killed. The thunder so resembled artillery fire that the incoming Second Dragoons (probably delighted to have their horses restored) galloped headlong into Corpus Christi, thinking they would save the camp from a Mexican attack.

Craig's preoccupation with the water sources at Live Oak Point was vindicated when the brackish water at Corpus Christi came to contribute to disease in the camp. In the Mexican War, as in the Seminole War, disease would kill more men than enemy fire. The Corpus Christi encampment soon came to be described as a vast hospital, and Col. Hitchcock would suffer to the extent of ultimately having to take sick leave. Before continuing into Mexico the army would be described as "enfeebled," but the Corpus Christi contingent's resistance to disease in Mexico (compared to the freshly arriving volunteers) would suggest that they had at least been "seasoned" during their stay.

Various groups arrived to make money from the soldiers, including, as ever, those women "plying an ancient trade." But there were also vendors of food, blankets, jewelry, horses and other goods, as well as several photographers, happy to provide likenesses to be sent home.

Theatrical productions were presented in makeshift playhouses by members of the army, as well by professional actors. Craig perhaps saw the amateur *Othello*, in which Lt. Ulysses Grant of Ohio played the part of Desdemona, to the satisfaction of no one.

Whenever officers are gathered together and have abundant spare time, committees will often meet to prepare and present petitions. One such petition, signed by 155 officers—including Craig (who would himself later be brevetted twice)—had to do with the vexed question of brevet rank.

At a time in the service when medals for valor weren't commonly given, a brevet was an honorary promotion for exceptional gallantry, an advance in rank without an advance in pay or responsibility. Officers were also commonly addressed by their brevet rank. A brevet was not an empty honor, however, since it had to be proposed by the president and approved by the U.S. Senate—and in certain unusual cases an officer might actually be given a command commensurate with his brevet rank, but the subject of the officers' petition was not such a situation.

The Corpus Christi controversy saw Col. William Worth claiming that his earlier brevet rank of brigadier general made him the superior of Col. David Twiggs, who was by date of appointment Worth's "senior as a colonel in the regular line of the army." Craig and most officers supported Col. Hitchcock's conclusion (signed by the officers and sent to the president) that Twiggs outranked Worth, that line rank superseded brevet rank. The president agreed.

Worth left for Washington to resign, but soon decided against it and returned to duty. Having acted in such a way in the face of the enemy, however, Worth had lost the respect of Craig and many others, who subjected him to a certain amount of mockery in their journals and in their letters home.

Fortunately for Craig, Col. Hitchcock had ultimately become his champion in the continuing battle with the Adj. Gen. Jones over his back pay from Fort Hamilton. Hitchcock wrote Craig (for submission to Jones) that he felt that the claim for back pay was well founded, and that Craig was being penalized by "the absurd and injurious principle…that an officer on duty at a *distant frontier* post rarely visited by a paymaster would…be made to suffer a loss of perquisites allowed to officers more favorably situated where they could month by month receive their pay & allowances. The injustice done you is too manifest not to be finally acknowledged and remedied." As satisfying as this was to Craig, it would take several more years before the controversy would be settled by bringing political pressure against the Adjutant General.

As the stay at Corpus Christi grew longer, rowdiness increased. As a stern disciplinarian Col. Hitchcock found himself irritated by Craig's former Dragoon regiment—although on the other side of the Rio Grande the misbehavior of many volunteers would soon throw a better light on the

Dragoons' bumptious activities. For their part, the Dragoons famously took pride in being the "epitome of military impudence whether in the parlor, in the tavern, or on the field of battle".

As Hitchcock confided to his diary in October, "It is noteworthy that since the arrival of the 2nd Dragoons there have been several disgraceful brawls and quarrels, to say nothing of drunken frolics. The Dragoons have made themselves a public scandal. One captain has resigned to avoid trial, and two others have had a dirty brawl. Two others still are on trial for fighting over a low woman."

As described by Craig, the U.S. Army on March 11 began a march from Corpus Christi on the Nueces River to the east bank of the Rio Grande, a distance of some 175 miles.

LSC

Wednesday, March 11, 1846. Left Corpus Christi (Texas) for the Rio Grande on the 11th (Wednesday) of March 1846. After a pleasant march of 12 or 14 miles we encamped in a beautiful valley on the banks of the Nueces River. We left our encampment at Corpus Christi about 8 o'clock in the morning and halted for the night about 4 o'clock p.m. The day was a lovely one.

Thursday, March 12th, 1846. Rained last night very hard. Left our encampment at 8 o'clock in the morning. Found the road very bad across the Hog Wallow Prairie [a depression resembling a drained swamp]. Owing to the badness of the road, we were only able to march about 8 miles, and encamped 6 miles east of the Agua Dulce.

About 9 o'clock last night an express was sent out by Major Ewing of the 2nd Artillery with a mail. I received several letters, but not one from my dear wife. One was from Captain [N. C.] Macrae, one from my nephew Robert Stanard, one from the Adjutant General in relation to my claim for double rations, and one from Lieutenant [A. W.] Whipple of the 5th Infantry on Public Service.

Lieutenant [Mansfield] Lovell of the [4th] Artillery passed our encampment about 3 o'clock this morning with letters for General Taylor (who encamped about 3 miles west of us) from Commander Cameron of the Navy. We are all on *tiptoe* to hear the news from Vera Cruz. We encamped today at

5 minutes past 1 o'clock.

Because of the lengthy amount of time that it took messages to reach Washington City from Vera Cruz, President Polk was as much on tiptoe as Craig or anyone else in mid-March. Polk had remained focused on the purchase of California and believed Mexico would sell it. Ambassador John Slidell had been told "money would be no object," since there then seemed still to be a possibility of war with Britain over Oregon. But as Craig was writing, the Mexican government had already committed the belligerent act of refusing to meet with Slidell. Polk received word of this on April 7, and war became a certainty.

Another virtual certainty was the precarious nature of dealing with any Mexican government since administrations fell so frequently. In fifty-six years between 1789, when Washington's first term began, and 1845, the beginning of the Polk Administration, there had been eleven U.S. chief executives. In the two decades between independence in 1822 and 1845, there had been over two dozen administrations in Mexico, several of them led by Santa Anna. As a debtor nation with a history of numerous revolts and unstable government, Mexico would prove a dangerously weak neighbor and a risky partner in diplomacy.

Craig continued his March 12 entry:

LSC

Had quite a jollification in camp tonight. I had a large fire made in front of my tent, and a large number of officers gathered around it. Lieutenant [Don Carlos] Buell brought out his liquor case and *toddied* the gentlemen until some of them could scarcely find their own tents.

Buell wrote years later that in the service, he had "no more intimate friend" than Lewis Craig and none "whom [he] esteemed more highly."

LSC

I retired early in the action, leaving Captain Morris of the 3rd Infantry (and *President* of the *Juveniles*), Lieutenant [Theodoric H.] Porter of the 4th Infantry, Reynolds of the 3rd Artillery, Irwin of the 3rd Infantry, and Buell of the 3rd Infantry. Last thing I heard was from Porter, and he proposed the health of my little daughter and his two little *ones*. I regret to say that the party kept Colonel Hitchcock awake nearly the whole night, who was quite unwell.

———

Ironically, with Col. Hitchcock too unwell to lead the regiment's advance to the Mexico, his place was taken by the "President of the Juveniles" himself—Capt. Morris. Sadly, of those at the "jollification" with Craig, Lt. Porter would be killed April 19 near the Rio Grande by Mexican guerrillas. Morris and Irwin would die at Monterrey in September. Reynolds would survive the Mexican War to be killed on the first day of the Battle of Gettysburg in 1863 in which a then-inconceivable 175,000 American soldiers would fight each other over three days. Only Buell would die in his bed, age 80, in 1898.

———

LSC

Friday, March 13th, 1846. Left our encampment about 7 o'clock in the morning. Passed over a very pretty prairie. Found the greater part of the road a very good one. About 2 miles of it we found very wet. Our train met with no accident today. Met Lieutenant Lovell at a pond about two miles or little more from our last encampment, returning to Corpus Christi.

We marched about 9 miles today and encamped at the "Los Pintos" (the Ponds). Found the water very good, and an abundance of wood. The view this morning (the 14th) was lovely. The Prairies looking towards the west had the appearance of the Blue Ridge mountains, with a lake at the foot. The prairies are covered with flowers, and every one I saw reminded me of my dear, dear absent wife.

Saturday, March 14th, 1846. We left our encampment this morning about 7 o'clock. Had a pleasant march across the prairies. Saw a large number of mustangs and antelopes. Several of the officers gave chase to the mustangs. Lieutenant Irwin's horse fell with him and Lieutenant Irwin was very near being seriously injured.

Today we passed the San Fernando Hammock. The bed of the creek was perfectly dry. We arrived at Santa Gertrudis, at which place we had established a depot some two weeks before. Major [William] Graham with his Company of the 4th Infantry and Captain Field of the 3rd Infantry with his Company composed the guard for the Depot. We arrived at the Depot about 4 o'clock p.m.

Sunday, March 15th, 1846. Left Santa Gertrudis this morning at 6 o'clock, breaking up the Depot and taking all the forage and provisions with us. Today we marched over pretty much the same kind of country as we marched over for the last day or two and encamped at 12 o'clock p.m., after a march of about 14 miles, at the Santa Clara Motte. Just after arriving at our camp ground Captain [Charles H.] Larnard was arrested by Lt Col [John] Garland relative to the *division of some wood.*

Monday, March 16th, 1846. Left our encampment about 8 o'clock and intended to have encamped at the Santa Rosa, which is 8¼ miles from Santa Clara Motte. On our arrival at the last-named stream, we found the water so very brackish that we determined to go on to El Pista or Live Oak.

Just before reaching El Pista we met an express which had been sent back by General Taylor, informing Colonel [William] Whistler that Colonel Twiggs, who was 45 miles in advance of us, had met with the advance guard of the Mexican Army, and that the officer in command informed him that if he advanced any farther that he would meet with opposition. Colonel Whistler received instructions to push on, and leave a part of his train should it be necessary. I presume if we meet with any opposition, it will be at the Colorado [usually known as the Little Colorado], but I little expect to meet with a Mexican soldier between this and the Rio Grande.

One of Captain Morris's men was missing this morning when the roll was called. He had gone out the evening before in search of Captain Morris's horse, and it is supposed that he could not find his way back to camp (his name is Colby). Today we marched over a sandy prairie and found it very hard marching. Private Haggardies of my Company was so much fatigued that I was compelled to carry his gun for him for some distance.

Today my servant Willis was mounted on a mustang mare loaned to me by the Wagon Master (Bell). She, I am afraid, will foal ere we reach the Rio Grande, and, in that case, Willis will be compelled to *foot* it the rest of the march.

We reached El Pista or Live Oak about 12 o'clock and encamped between two ponds. Found the water very good, and an abundance of wood. The mesquite trees are just budding out, and look very green and beautiful. Some mile or so west of us is a large live oak hammock. The country about our encampment is certainly a lovely one. Tomorrow we expect to march 13 miles. The 2nd Brigade encamped at this place last night. We found their fires burning when we arrived.

Tuesday, March 17th, 1846. Started at daylight this morning. Marched over a very sandy prairie. Saw more timber today than we have seen since leaving Corpus Christi. We marched today over 20 miles. Suffered very much for water. Encamped at 4 o'clock at a place called Cavancho's.

Wednesday, March 18th, 1846. Left our encampment at 8 o'clock this morning. I was the Officer of the Guard today. We marched about 17 miles. The men suffered more today for water than they have since leaving Corpus Christi. Several of them gave out. It is thought that we are about ten miles from the Colorado. I *pray* that we may be in twenty.

I missed my ink stand this evening, and it has put me very much out of *sorts*, for it is almost impossible for me to do without it. We expect to leave at 8 o'clock in the morning. We passed a large number of salt ponds today, and not more than one fresh water pond on the whole march. This day's march was across the worst part of the desert. Captain Morris's man Colby came into camp about 10 o'clock tonight. We were all delighted to see him *again*.

Thursday, March 19th, 1846. Left our encampment a little before 8 o'clock. Our march today was over a very pretty country. Found a plenty of *good water*. Saw large groves of mesquite timber. We marched ten miles today, and we were informed by a citizen of Matamoros (who came into our camp on his way to Corpus Christi) that we were about *20* miles from the Colorado. We expect to join General Taylor with the rest of the Army day after tomorrow on the other side of the Colorado.

Friday, March 20th, 1846. First thing I heard this morning was that the mare that Willis was riding had produced a fine colt. I immediately hunted up a Mexican who encamped near us the evening before, and purchased from him a large mule, well broken. Paid for it $16. Willis was very much pleased to find that he had not to *foot* it. The mare was left, together with one belonging to the Government, which also had a colt on the same night at the encampment, to be brought on with the ox teams which were a short distance in our rear.

Captain Bainbridge was ordered back with his Company for the purpose of escorting the ox train. I neglected to state that Lieutenant [Andrew W.] Bowman of the 3rd Infantry was left in charge of the ox train on the morning of the 18th at Cavancho's, as the Quartermaster thought it would be better to let the oxen travel at night. We left our encampment this morning about 8 o'clock. We marched over a very pretty country. Found a plenty of water, and passed through a large number of groves of mesquite wood. We encamped a little before 3 o'clock. Our encampment is supposed to be about 5 miles north of the Colorado.

Saturday, March 21st, 1846. Left our encampment a little before 8 o'clock and arrived at the Colorado at 10 o'clock a.m. We found the road very good, and the country we marched over a beautiful one. The mesquite and a species of the acacia tree have just commenced putting out their leaves, and everything had a green and refreshing appearance.

The Colorado River is a very pretty stream. I should judge that it was about 125 yards wide. The depth when we crossed it was about 4 feet. We were four hours crossing our command and train.

It was very amusing to see the *capers* that the mules *cut* after getting a little way into the stream. We lost no mules in crossing. One died after reaching our encampment. We passed the camp of the Dragoons, 1st Brigade & 2nd Brigade, who were encamped about two miles south of the Colorado. We passed them and encamped a little more than a mile from them, on the road to Matamoros.

General Taylor with the Dragoons, 1st & 2nd Brigades, crossed the

Colorado on Friday the 21st. On his arrival at the river, a small Mexican force showed themselves on the opposite side of the river. After a short time they had an interview with General Taylor and informed him that if he attempted to cross the river, that he would meet with opposition. The General informed them that, if a *single* one of *their party* showed himself after he commenced crossing his army, he would fire into them. Only one man showed himself after the crossing commenced, and he was captured.

Just before reaching our encampment today Captain Morris's servant, Aggy, was thrown from a horse and had one of her legs fractured, poor creature. I fear that she has a great deal of suffering to undergo ere she can get into comfortable quarters.

Sunday, March 22, 1846. We remained in camp today awaiting the arrival of the ox train, which we expect will reach here tonight. We have a report in camp that we are to leave at 6 o'clock tomorrow morning for Point Isabel [Taylor's fortified supply depot on the Gulf, near the mouth of the Rio Grande]. We are about 27 miles from that place, and about the same distance from Matamoros. An order has *just* been issued to leave at 6 o'clock tomorrow morning. Captain Crossman, Quartermaster, with the ox train reached camp tonight.

Monday, March 23rd, 1846. Left our camp at 6 o'clock this morning and proceeded to join the rest of the Army. After marching about two miles we found the Army drawn up in order of march; the Dragoons on the right, the First Brigade with their Artillery, then the Second Brigade with their Artillery, then on the left came the Third Brigade with their Artillery. Each brigade was in column of companies, with their Artillery in the center. The train of each Brigade followed in their rear. It was certainly a beautiful sight to see the whole Army in motion.

We marched the whole day in that order and encamped a little before sundown. We marched about 8 or 9 miles today over a pretty prairie country, here and there interspersed with the mesquite and acacia tree. Owing to the high grass on the prairie, the marching was very fatiguing.

Tuesday, March 24th, 1846. Last evening the different Brigades encamped a short distance from each other. We left our camp this morning about 7 o'clock, the Dragoons in advance, then followed the 1st Brigade and the other in succession. We marched about two or three miles and then came into the road heading from Matamoros to Point Isabel. The Army was halted here for a few hours, and the greater part of the train was sent to Port Isabel for provisions, escorted by the Dragoons under the command of Colonel Twiggs.

General Taylor at this point turned over the command of the Army to General Worth, with instructions to proceed to a certain *point* on the Matamoros Road and there to await his arrival, until his return from Point Isabel. After the General (Taylor) left, we took up our line of march in the same manner we had marched the day before, and encamped at a pond on the Matamoros Road, supposed to be about 13 miles from the city of Matamoros. Here we shall remain until General Taylor comes up, and we shall then proceed to the Rio Grande and plant our flag opposite to Matamoros. The Mexicans from all we can learn are scared nearly to death. They are under the impression we intend marching into Matamoros.

Wednesday, March 25th, 1846. The country about our encampment is certainly a lovely one. I have just returned from a stroll through the mesquite and acacia trees out to the prairie, which is in a half a mile of the camp. I have been amusing myself looking at the horses and mules enjoying the mesquite grass and the wild pea vine which grows luxuriantly in this country.

An order was issued at 12 o'clock today to break up our encampment and to proceed 3 miles farther on the Matamoros Road in the direction of the city. We struck our tents at 3 o'clock p.m. and encamped about 9 miles from Matamoros. The place that we are now encamped at is one of great beauty. We shall remain here until General Taylor joins us, which will be some time tomorrow.

We have a report in camp that there is a probability that we shall be attacked tonight. An order has been issued for the men to sleep on their arms. I shall take good care and not sleep in my pantaloons, let *General Worth think as he may*. A mail was sent up from Point Isabel, but I received no letter from my dear, dear wife. I still hope that Bliss may bring me one when he arrives.

Thursday, March 26th, 1846. I am happy to find that we are all alive this morning. The Mexicans did not make their appearance, as it was thought they would. Captain Morris, I understand, slept in his pantaloons. I fear that we shall not see a Mexican soldier between this and the Rio Grande.

Friday, March 27th, 1846. General Taylor arrived about 12 o'clock today from Point Isabel. Brought up a load of mail with him but I did not receive a letter from my dear, dear wife. I have not been as well today as usual, and not receiving a letter from my dear wife made me feel much worse. I pray that Major Macrae of the Quartermaster's Department may have letters for me. He had not reached Point Isabel when General Taylor left.

The General found on his arrival at Point Isabel that several houses had been burnt, and some of them were on fire when he arrived, which he had put out. An order has been issued to take up our line of march at ½ past 6 o'clock in the morning, so we shall be at the end of our journey if nothing occurs to prevent [it] by tomorrow night.

Saturday, March 28th, 1846. Left this morning a little after 6 o'clock. Marched over pretty much the same kind of country as we marched over for the last three or four days, and arrived opposite to Matamoros, on the banks of the Rio Grande, a little after 10 o'clock, with our *colors* flying and drums beating "Hail, Columbia" and "Yankee *Doodle*."

We have encamped opposite to the city. Immediately after encamping a flag staff was erected, and our Flag was soon floating on the banks of the Rio Grande, much to the annoyance of the Mexicans. Just before reaching the river this morning, two Dragoons who were some distance in advance were made prisoners and are now in Matamoros. I presume General Taylor will demand them immediately.

General Worth soon today after we reached the river was sent over by General Taylor for the purpose of having an interview with General [Francisco] Mejia. On his reaching the opposite side of the river, he was met by a Mexican officer, and after a short interview was informed that General Mejia would not see him, but that he would hold a conference with General Taylor if he wished it.

As soon as our Flag went up, the English and French flags were seen to fly from the Quarters of the different Consuls. So ends my journal from Corpus Christi (Texas) to the Rio Grande. After one of the most delightful marches that ever was made by an army, the officers and men both improved in health, and we did not lose a man by death on the whole march, that I heard of.

Deaths would come soon enough. In early April, near their campsite, the American soldiers began construction of a bastioned earthen fort opposite Matamoros. In response, the Mexicans built two earthwork batteries commanding the American fort from both sides.

On April 24, General Mariano Arista arrived in Matamoros as commander of the Mexican Army of the North. He carried with him an April 4 order directing him to attack the Americans. He promptly sent a body of 1600 cavalrymen across the Rio Grande above the town. The same day, General Taylor reacted to reports of a Mexican troop movement by sending out an eighty-man reconnaissance squadron commanded by two of Craig's comrades from the Second Dragoons—Captain Seth Thornton (a Virginian who, like Craig, had been appointed from civilian life) and Captain William J. Hardee of Georgia, a West Point graduate. They met with disaster the next day. At Rancho de Carrecitos were captured, along with most of their force, with eleven men killed and six wounded.

On April 26 Taylor advised President Polk that "Hostilities may now be considered as commenced," and suggested it was time to raise volunteers. For his part, Taylor asked the states of Texas and Louisiana to send men at once. Sallying across the Rio Grande from Matamoros, the Mexican forces then besieged the new American fort.

In his war message on May 11, President Polk proclaimed that Mexico had "shed American blood on American soil." By May 13, both Houses had passed Polk's war bill and a call for war volunteers had been issued.

Before crossing the Rio Grande and being reinforced by the U.S. war volunteers, Taylor's army would fight its first two battles entirely with regular troops; Craig's Third Regiment participated in both engagements. These actions would be fought west of Point Isabel, Taylor's supply depot on the Gulf, ten miles north of the Rio Grande's mouth—the U.S. Army's point of resupply and reinforcement from New Orleans and Pensacola.

Having left a force in the American fort opposite Matamoros, Taylor went to bolster Point Isabel's defenses and to organize a supply train of food and munitions for the forces besieged at Matamoros. As Taylor retraced his route with the wagon train, he found the Mexican force of General Mariano Arista astride the Matamoros Road, mustering 3,300 men to Taylor's 2,200.

The Battle of Palo Alto that followed was essentially an artillery duel, with the Americans having twice the guns, together with advanced explosive projectiles (3000 of which were fired into the Mexicans' lines) against the Mexicans' solid shot (850 rounds fired). Moreover, the inferior Mexican gunpowder threw some balls so feebly that they struck the ground and rolled slowly enough into the U.S. lines to be dodged. Moreover, there was also the vital participation of Capt. Samuel Ringgold's "flying artillery," which deployed in the front line with the infantry and quickly moved where needed as needed.

At that point, it seemed that Taylor's infantry might not need to take part, but the Mexican horsemen, with their eight-foot lances, began attempting to turn Taylor's flanks with cavalry charges. Showing that Hitchcock's drilling had not been in vain, the Third Infantry performed the difficult maneuver of forming a hollow square near the supply train; other units performed similar movements during the battle. Despite never having faced battle together before, the disparate elements of the U.S. Army performed together with unusual precision.

Both armies slept on the battlefield that night. Taylor now needed to return to Matamoros to relieve the garrison at his now heavily besieged fort. Arista was determined to prevent him from doing so. In the opposing camps, the Mexicans counted a loss of 200, with some 100 killed in action. Taylor had lost forty-three men, four of them killed, with Capt. Ringgold mortally wounded and transported to Point Isabel to die.

For the next day's engagement, called the Battle of Resaca de la Palma, General Arista withdrew his troops from the previous day's open, prairie battleground to a more defensible position five miles south, within a "brushy wood." It hid a ravine or resaca—an old channel of the Rio Grande—"several hundred feet wide and three or four feet deep at the banks." This V-shaped ravine enclosed Taylor's approach route and stretched toward the U.S. Army like waiting arms.

Arista's artillery was well-posted where the approach road crossed the ravine, with his troops deployed in the brush on either side. With sharpshooters stationed in the chaparral across the ravine, and his lancers posted to the rear, Arista now waited with a force of 3,800 to fight Taylor's force, now reduced to 1,800 after soldiers were sent behind to protect the supply wagons.

Unlike the day before, there would be no coordinated troop movements during this battle. The organization of Taylor's troops disintegrated as it advanced into the rugged, wooded terrain. But its mass remained and moved to either side of the road, into conditions that often demanded hand-to-hand fighting. Although Arista had hoped that his new position would neutralize the American guns, the "flying artillery"—now under Capt. Randolph Ridgely, Ringgold's fellow Marylander—was soon firing against Arista's men north of the ravine.

Later in the action, Craig's regiment disentangled itself from the underbrush and struck Arista's left flank, as other regiments joined in the attack. Lt. Charles May, who had been paired with Craig at the Loxahatchee, led the Second Dragoons back and forth over Arista's artillery position and ultimately, with infantry support, cleared the remaining battery. With Arista's left and center crumbling, his right wing collapsed, and the Mexican army fell back into Matamoros.

Charles May did perform heroically at Resaca and thus became an early U.S. hero of the Mexican War. But the popular illustrations of the time that showed May—his blond locks flowing behind him as his steed charged—singlehandedly capturing Mexican field commander Romulo Diaz de la Vega, as he stood beside a cannon, were fiction. The general was captured by infantrymen.

The battle had been more costly to the Mexicans than the previous day's engagement; Arista suffered 160 troops killed and 228 wounded. He blamed his defeat on the weakened state of his troops and argued that they had been demoralized by the savage artillery pounding they had taken the day before.

Taylor's loss was 45 killed and 98 wounded, but Mexico's Army of the North was now defeated and dispersed, and the siege would soon be broken at the American fort, now called Fort Brown in honor the garrison's commander, Major Jacob Brown of Massachusetts, who had been killed during the siege. Taylor occupied Matamoros on May 17, to cries of "Amigos! Amigos!" from the citizenry. The U.S. army would rest in the town until early August when Craig, unscathed in the battles that had established U.S. control of the Nueces-Rio Grande sector, resumed his journal.

LSC

August 7th, 1846. Camp near Camargo, on the right bank of the San Juan River. Left Matamoros on board of the steamboat *Big Hatchee* the *29th July 1846* in the evening for Camargo, having on board Major [William W.] Lear, Lieutenants Craig, Irwin, and [George] Sykes of the Third Infantry; Captain [Robert C.] Buchanan, Lieutenants [Richard H.] Graham, [Jenks] Beaman, [Ulysses] Grant, and [James S.] Woods of the 4th Infantry, and Surgeon [Nathan Sturgis] Jarvis U.S.A.; one Company of the 3rd Infantry and two of the 4th Infantry, with the non-commissioned staff and band of the 3rd Infantry, together with a large number of women of both Regiments.

We arrived a mile and a half below the town of Camargo on Sunday the *2nd of August 1846* between 1 & 2 o'clock p.m. We passed the town of Reynoso on the morning of the *1st of August* about 8 o'clock in the morning. The steamboat, not having any troops or supplies for that place, did not stop. The town from the river had quite a neat appearance.

The houses are built generally of brick and whitewashed. The town is situated on an eminence, and when it rains all the filth is carried off, and, by that means, the streets are kept in good order. Our encampment is about one mile and a quarter from the town of Camargo on the right bank of the St. Juan River, and when we have finished it, it will be a very pretty camp. The ground is perfectly level, dotted here and there with fine shade trees.

The town of Camargo was visited a few weeks since with an awful calamity. The water rose to such a great height as to flood the whole town, and the houses, being built generally of brick dried in the sun, were nearly all washed away. The town before the flood contained some 3,000 inhabitants. At this time there are not more than a thousand souls in the place. Those who lost their homes were compelled to leave and settle in the country. The inhabitants of Camargo speak of building a town several miles higher up the river. The town of Camargo is about three miles from the mouth of the St. Juan River, which empties into the Rio Grande. The town is situated on the right bank of the river.

On our passage up the Rio Grande, we passed a large number of beautiful situations for farms. I saw some fine cotton growing on the banks of the river. I should think the land on the Rio Grande would produce fine cotton if well cultivated, and the seasons proved favorable. The St. Juan River is a very pretty little stream. It is about 100 yards wide and navigable for steamboats several miles above Camargo. The banks of the river are quite high.

August 8th, 1846. General Taylor and staff arrived about 8 o'clock p.m. today in the steamboat *Hatchee Eagle.* The boat brought us no mail, none having arrived since we left Matamoros. As soon as the boat passed up the river, I hurried to the town, expecting *certainly* a letter from my dear wife. But on my arrival at the Post Office, I was informed that the boat brought no mail, and I was compelled to retrace my steps to camp with a *heavy* heart.

August 15th, 1846. Colonel Garland arrived at our camp this morning about 8 o'clock in command of Companies "C" & "K" of the 3rd Infantry, commanded by Captains Morris and [William S.] Henry, and Companies "C" and "D" of the 4th Infantry, and a part of Lieutenant Bragg's battery, commanded by Lieutenant Bragg. Colonel Garland's command left Matamoros on Wednesday the 5th of August. They found the greater part of the road very good. The men suffered very much owing to the extreme heat.

August 22, 1846. Camp near Camargo. General Twiggs arrived here on the morning of the 21st in command of the Dragoons and two batteries of Horse Artillery. His command suffered very much from sickness, having on his arrival at this place seventy sick, *so reports Dr.* [Joseph K.] *Barnes.*

[There are no entries for August 23rd to August 31st, 1846.]

Tuesday, September 1, 1846. Camp on the left bank of the St. Juan, opposite to Camargo. We left our encampment on the right bank of the river on yesterday at 12 o'clock in the day, and expect to leave this camp sometime today en route for Monterrey. Left our encampment this evening at 3 o'clock p.m. and encamped for the night five miles from Camargo near the Rio Grande.

Wednesday September 2nd, 1846. Left our encampment this morning at 8 o'clock, and, after a *hot* march of eleven miles, encamped in a few hundred yards of the Rio Grande. Passed [Charles] May's camp at a Ranch called Ciudado Abajo, situated about 8 miles from Camargo.

Thursday, September 3rd, 1846. Left our encampment this morning about 5 o'clock. Passed the town of Mier about 9 o'clock in the morning, leaving it a little to our right. The town from the road has the appearance of being quite a pretty place. The road passes in about a mile of it. Just after passing Mier, we came in sight of the mountains, and the view from the point I first saw them reminded me of the view of the Blue Ridge from the Glebe in Culpepper County, Virginia, once the residence of the late John Woodville, the first boarding school I was sent to. The road today was more rolling than any we have marched over. We marched 11 ½ miles today and encamped opposite to La Casa Blanca.

Friday, September 4th, 1846. Left our encampment at ½ past 3 o'clock a.m. this morning. The road we marched over today was not as good as the first two days, having been cut up by the train that took up General Worth's command. Today we marched 11½ miles and encamped at Chicharron near the Rio de Agualeguas. Arrived at our camp ground about 9 o'clock a.m.

Saturday September 5th, 1846. Left our encampment at ½ past 2 o'clock a.m. this morning. The country we marched over today was quite a pretty one, having the mountains in sight nearly the whole way. We arrived at Puntiaguda, a small rancho, about 9 o'clock a.m., after a *hot* march of some 14 miles, and encamped near the river Puntiaguda. General [Persifor] Smith's command is here, but will leave tonight at 10 o'clock for Cerralvo. We will occupy their ground tomorrow. Today I dined with Captain [Albert Gallatin] Blanchard of the Louisiana Volunteers. He was at one time a Lieutenant in the 3rd Infantry and resigned in 1840.

Sunday, September 6th, 1846. Colonel [Henry] Wilson arrived today about 10 o'clock with the Fourth Brigade. How long they will remain here I cannot say, but I presume they will leave when we do.

Tuesday, September 8th, 1846. General Taylor and staff arrived here today about 10 o'clock and also General Twiggs with the Dragoons and Horse Artillery. Captain [Joseph H.] Eaton brought me a letter from *my dear wife*, and also my commission as a Captain in the 3rd Regiment of Infantry.

Craig recorded his receipt of commission matter-of-factly and acknowledged its receipt to Adjutant General Jones three days later from Cerralvo. The captaincy was, however, a quite significant promotion for an officer, and Craig, through his own wartime conduct and exertions, had been elevated in nine years to what Adjutant General Jones had calculated would take eighteen years in peacetime.

LSC

[The September 8 entry continues] Bliss dined with me today, and informed me of Colonel Harney's having been ordered to return to San Antonio, which place he had reached. General Taylor's order, I believe, overtook him ere he reached the Rio Grande, and I understand that he was arrested by General Wool immediately on his return to San Antonio.

Here Bliss and Craig discuss one of Harney's adventures, that, like all his exploits, had been watched with interest by the army. During the previous July, with Twiggs's section of Dragoons advancing with Gen. Taylor, Harney had been left behind with another section in San Antonio, chafing at his inactivity while awaiting the arrival of Gen. John Ellis Wool of New York.

Advising Gen. Taylor by courier that he was moving against Mexican troops said to be gathering at the Rio Grande, "some two hundred miles above the mouth of that stream," Harney had set out with some seven hundred men, including his Dragoons and some San Antonio volunteers. Crossing the river, he advanced to Presidio de Rio Grande without finding any Mexicans.

Meanwhile, in mid-August Gen. Wool had arrived in San Antonio and sent couriers out, one with an order for Harney to return, another ordering his arrest for abandoning his post without orders. At about the same time, an order reached Harney from Taylor forbidding the invasion he had just concluded. With Harney's timely return, Wool had substituted a "tongue-lashing" for the arrest, but Wool had made an enemy for life, and there would also be later repercussions for Harney. At the time that Bliss and Craig spoke, Harney had been notified of his promotion to colonel, and, with Twiggs advanced to Brigadier General at the same time, Harney would now command the Second Dragoons.

Also by this time, U.S. forces had occupied Los Angeles and Monterey in California, and Gen. Stephen Kearney had taken Santa Fe, then "an impoverished town of adobe houses" with a population of fewer than 5,000 souls. A few days later, General Santa Anna would enter Mexico City and take command of the army.

Craig's journal for September 8, 1846, continues:

LSC

The river runs in a few hundred yards of our camp, and just at the foot of this dam is the place to bathe. The depth of the water is about 4 feet. I certainly enjoyed bathing more in that place than I ever did before. We expect to leave here tomorrow morning for Cerralvo, and I presume we will remain only a few days at that place, ere we take up our line of march for Monterrey.

Wednesday, September 9th, 1846. We left our encampment this morning at daylight, and, after marching over a pretty country, arrived at the town of Cerralvo (which is situated just at the foot of the mountains) a little after 11 o'clock today; we would have had a very pleasant march today had we not have had so large a train of wagons, which caused our march to be much slower than it would otherwise have been. We would have made our march, had it not been for the train, by 8 o'clock a.m., and would not have suffered at all from the heat.

The country we passed over today was *very rich.* We passed through some of the finest grazing lands that I have seen since my arrival in the country. I have not visited the town as yet, but expect to do so tomorrow. Our whole force will be concentrated here in a few days, and we expect to leave here on Sunday next for Monterrey.

The town of Cerralvo is a very pretty one. The houses are generally built of stone, and whitewashed, which gives it a very neat appearance. There is a beautiful stream running through the center of the town. With this water the whole town can be irrigated. The town of Cerralvo, I presume, must contain some 2,000 inhabitants. Near the town there is a large number of beautiful springs, gushing out from the sides of the hills.

Saturday, September 12th, 1846. I received orders late last evening to leave early this morning in command of all the Pioneers of the Army to repair the road between Cerralvo and Marin. [Pioneers were soldiers detailed from different companies, under the command of an officer of officers, to cut or improve roads. They were equipped with "saws, felling axes, spades, mattocks, pickaxes, and billhooks," according to H. L. Scott's *Military Dictionary*, 1861.]

Captain [L. P.] Graham of the 2nd Dragoons received orders at the same time to proceed with me, with a squadron of Dragoons and Captain [Benjamin] McCulloch's Company of Texian [Texas] Rangers, for the purpose of covering the working party. Captain [William G.] Williams, Lieutenants [George G.] Meade, [Thomas J.] Wood, and [John] Pope of the Topographical Engineers also accompanied the command. Lieutenant [Thomas B.J. Weld of the Artillery, Lieutenant [Marcellus K.] Taylor of the Baltimore Volunteers, and Lieutenant [William] White of the Kentucky Volunteers were the officers attached to the Pioneers.

We left our encampment this morning but, owing to our not having a guide, on first leaving camp we missed the road and found ourselves at 9 o'clock a.m. not more than a ¼ mile from Cerralvo. Today the road required very little repairing. We passed Carrecitos, a small ranch, about 10 o'clock p.m., distant 7 miles from Cerralvo. We passed several running streams of pure water and encamped about 5 o'clock at the Arroyo Mojave, a large mountain stream. Today we marched 13 miles. We had a slight shower, just enough to wet us pretty well. The country we marched over today was certainly very picturesque.

Sunday, September 13th, 1846. Left our encampment this morning a little after sunrise. Today the road required a good deal of repairing, and we did not reach our encampment until near sundown. We encamped at Papagallos, a small ranch. Today we came in sight of the Sierra Madre

Mountains. They are certainly the highest mountains I have ever seen. The Blue Ridge is a mere mole hill when compared to them. We marched 15 miles today.

Late this evening Captain McCulloch came into camp and reported that the enemy was only a few miles in advance of us, he having driven in their picket guard. This report caused us to change our position, which we did after dark and encamped on a hill, where we could have put to flight 500 Mexicans, had they made their appearance. The country we marched over today was very much like that we passed over the day before.

Monday, September 14th, 1846. I took my command a little after light this morning a short distance back on the road we marched over yesterday, for the purpose of repairing a small portion of it that we were not able to finish the morning before, and returned to camp a little after breakfast time. As soon as we breakfasted, the whole command left about 9 o'clock. Today we had very little work to do.

General Taylor reached our encampment a short time after we left it, and is now encamped with the 1st Division five miles from us. Captain McCulloch today had a skirmish with the enemy's pickets, and it is thought he killed one of them, as he was seen to drop his escopette [carbine] and lance. We are now encamped at El Puerto (the pass), which is a mile and a half from Ramos, a small Mexican town, and if we are not all *scalped* between this and tomorrow morning, we expect to arrive at that place by 10 o'clock a.m.

Tuesday, September 15th, 1846. Left our encampment a little before 8 o'clock this morning The General and his staff came up before we got off. We passed the town of Ramos about 10 o'clock today. We had a good deal of work to do and arrived at Marin about 2 o'clock. The town is quite a pretty one, and is supposed to contain about 2,000 inhabitants. On our entering the town we saw only a few persons, nearly the whole of the inhabitants having left.

The town is situated on one of the most beautiful pieces of table land that the eye ever rested upon. In the town of Marin is a very handsome church, and from the cupola you have a view of the city of Monterrey and its lovely valley. We encamped today on the banks of the Rio de Santa Elena, a branch of the San Juan, about two miles from Marin.

Wednesday, September 16th, 1846. The 1st Division halted at this place for the purpose of awaiting the arrival of the rest of the Army. The 2nd Division under the command of General Worth arrived late today. The 3rd Division under the command of Major General [W. O.] Butler will reach this point sometime tomorrow, and then the whole Army will take up its line of march on Friday the 18th for the city of Monterrey.

Gen. Taylor now organized his army into three divisions: Gen. Twiggs, commanding the First Division (Regulars); Gen. Worth, commanding the Second Division (Regulars); and Gen. W. O. Butler, commanding the Third Division (Volunteers). The first and second divisions were accompanied by cavalry and artillery. Taylor's force numbered something over 6500 while General Ampudia had some 5,000 troops within well-fortified Monterrey. By this time the U.S. Volunteers had earned the disdain or hostility of the Regulars through misbehavior and worse in Matamoros and elsewhere. But as soldiers the volunteers were to prove they contained much good fighting stock, and they were to prove themselves on many a battlefield to come.

LSC

Thursday, September 17th, 1846. The citizens were visiting our camp in large numbers this morning, bringing us in eggs, chickens, and other marketing. [U.S. policy at this time was to purchase, rather than seize, food and fodder.]

The grazing about our camp is very fine, and if we were not in such a hurry to reach Monterrey, our animals would in a few days get in fine order. General Butler's Division arrived between 10 and 12 o'clock this morning. The Pioneer Advance under the command of Captain Craig was relieved late this evening, and the different detachments returned to their companies.

Friday, September 18th, 1846. Left our encampment this morning at 6 o'clock. The 1st Division marched at 6 o'clock, the 2nd Division at 7 o'clock, and the 3rd Division at 8 o'clock. We encamped today at San Francisco, a small town about 13 miles from the Rio de Santa Elena.

Today is the birthday of my dear little Sallie. What would I not give to see her and her dear mother this evening? It appears to me that I am becoming more anxious every moment of my life to see them both.

The country we marched over today was a lovely one. We are now in the Monterrey valley, and the land, I should think, was as rich as any on earth. Today I have seen corn growing as high as fifteen feet or more. This is the country for a man with a small capital. Here he can raise any quantity of corn and wheat, and nearly all of the tropical fruits. Today we passed the village of Agua Frio.

Saturday, September 19th, 1846. Left our encampment at 6 o'clock this morning. Passed through the village of San Domingo and encamped at the San Domingo Woods [also known as Walnut Springs], three miles from Monterrey.

This morning about 9 o'clock the Mexicans fired their first gun at our advanced guard. Several guns were fired through the day at our different reconnoitering parties, but no one was hurt. Today Major Bliss handed me a letter from my brother William, which I will answer as soon as the fight comes off, that is, if I am not *knocked* upon the head by a ball.

How much of Craig's inheritance was depleted in assisting his wastrel elder brother cannot be determined. As recently as 1843, however, as William was attempting to clear decades of debts, Lewis had conveyed to William's wife two hundred acres of land in Hickman County, Kentucky, which had been left him in Adam Craig's will.

LSC

Sunday, September 20th, 1846. General Worth left with the 2nd Division today about 10 o'clock p.m. for the purpose of attacking the Mexican forts on the heights which overlook the town. A little before sundown the 1st Division, commanded by General Twiggs, made a move in the direction of the city for the purpose of making a diversion, and also to plant our mortar, which we did in about 1800 yards of the Citadel [the largest fortification north of Monterrey]. We remained out until late at night and then returned to camp after having been well soaked with rain.

Monday, September 21st, 1846. Left camp this morning about sunrise and moved in the direction of the city. About 8 o'clock a.m. we received orders to form in line of battle, and to move in the direction of the enemy forts situated on the extreme right of the town.

Just before our line of battle was formed, Companies "C" & "H" of the 3rd Infantry, the first commanded by Lieutenant [Robert] Hazlitt, the second by Captain Field, were detached as skirmishers and sent in advance for the purpose of covering the Engineers who were reconnoitering the forts just in our front.

After marching some distance in line of battle under a heavy fire of Artillery and small arms from the enemy's forts, the command was given [the order] to march by the right flank, and in that way we entered the town. After getting into the city, our men covered themselves as well as they could from the destructive fire of the enemy's guns, and we kept up a continued fire of musketry for an hour, slaying the enemy right and left.

After some time, finding that we were fired upon from not less than three forts, and from almost every house near us, for every house appeared to be a fortification, and having lost several officers and a large number of men, the order was given to retire for the purpose of taking another position, and we fell back out of the range of the enemy's guns, and again formed our Regiment.

On this occasion we lost Brevet Major Barbour, Captain Field, and Lieutenant Irwin, the Adjutant of the Regiment. Major Lear received a severe wound from a musket ball, entering near the nose, and coming out the back of his neck. Several of my men were killed and wounded on this occasion.

The Regiment entered the town again about 10 o'clock, and, after a severe and bloody conflict, which lasted until late in the evening, and finding that it was impossible to effect anything, the order was given to retire in the direction of a fort [The Reboubt] which had been taken in the morning.

The fire from the enemy's guns at this time was very severe. The grape and musket shot flew about our heads as thick as hail in a hail storm. On this occasion we lost Captain Morris of the 3rd Infantry and Lieutenant Hazlitt. Captain Morris fell in a few feet of me [near the Purisima Bridge]. On this day I had five men of my Company killed and four wounded out of 52.

In Mexican War battles, the death-dealing projectiles included musket and pistol balls, buck and ball (a cartridge containing a musket ball and buck shot), grape shot (a number of cannon-fired cast-iron balls, up to six-pound weight, packed together in resemblance to a grape cluster), case shot or canister (a larger number of smaller balls, often musket balls, cannon-fired by means of a tin cylinder resembling a giant shotgun shell), solid shot (usually identified as cannon balls), and explosive shells (hollowed cannon balls, packed with powder and fitted with a fuse, designed to burst over a troop formation).

LSC

We remained in the fort [The Redoubt] (which I have just mentioned was taken early in the day) all night. Ridgely's Battery was placed in it, and a small breast work was thrown up in the gorge of the fort by our men. Our men were compelled to work until a late hour in the night, while the rain was falling in *torrents*. Neither the officers or men had eaten anything since early in the morning, and were compelled to spend the night in this fort without anything to protect us from the rain. I can truly say I never spent such a day and night before in all of my life.

Tuesday, September 22nd, 1846. A little after daylight this morning, the enemy opened their guns upon our fort [The Redoubt], throwing shells and round shot, but without doing any injury to anyone. About 1 o'clock in the day we received orders to return to camp for the purpose of getting provisions and to give our men some little rest.

As soon as the move was commenced, it was seen at the different forts of the enemy, and they opened a fire upon us from two forts [El Teneria and Diablo], and kept it up until we were out of the range of their guns. We lost no men out of our Regiment, but some three or four were killed out of the other Regiment that followed us out.

Our Regiment (the 3rd Infantry) was under fire from 8 o'clock on the 21st until dark, and from a little after daylight on the 22nd until near 2 o'clock of that day. On arriving at camp I had scarcely any use of my limbs, and when night came, I was so much fatigued that I could not sleep.

Wednesday, September 23d, 1846. This morning we again received orders to march in the direction of the town, as it was thought that the enemy was about retreating from the city. After getting out some distance from camp, the command was halted and the 3rd Regiment of Infantry was ordered to proceed with Captain Bragg's battery to the city for the purpose of supporting it, should it be found necessary.

On our arriving at the city, we found the enemy was retiring in the neighborhood of the plaza, which place was well-fortified in every way. General Taylor here ordered Captain Bragg to move into the town, and to *clear* the streets with his battery. The battery then moved down nearly opposite to the Cathedral. Our section under the command of Lieutenant [Francis J.] Thomas moved off some distance farther on the same street.

After remaining some time in the city, and finding that very little could be accomplished with the battery, we were ordered to retire. Our Regiment today had but one man wounded, and he belonged to my Company. We had to cross one street today where the bullets *flew* as thick as hail. Captain Bragg's orderly sergeant was killed today, while in the act of loading his piece, and a gallant soldier he was.

Thursday, September 24, 1846. This morning General [Pedro de] Ampudia sent in Colonel [J. M.] Moreno, his aide, with a proposition that he would surrender the town if he could be allowed to take off all the public property. The proposition was not acceded to by General Taylor, but the General informed General Ampudia that he would be at General Worth's camp at a certain hour, at which time he would receive any proposition that he might make.

In the course of the day all the preliminaries were settled. Three commissioners were appointed by each party. On our side we had General Worth, Colonel [Jefferson] Davis of Mississippi, and Governor [James P.] Henderson of Texas, and they agreed that the Mexicans should be allowed to march out with all of their small arms and six pieces of artillery, and that they were to retire beyond the confines of this province (Nueva Leon).

Today I was on duty with Colonel [William G.] Belknap cutting a road from our camp to the fort on the edge of the city, to avoid the guns at the Citadel.

General Pedro de Ampudia, the officer with whom the Americans met, had been called by Gen. Worth "the Culinary Knight," for having decapitated a rival and had his head fried to extend the time it could be publicly displayed. As one result of the Battle of Monterrey, Craig requested that his company be armed entirely with "the percussion musket" to replace their flintlocks. The request was approved.

LSC

Friday, September 25th, 1846. Today we remained in camp. Nothing of interest occurred worth recording. Captain Eaton left with despatches for Washington City this evening. I wrote to my dear wife by him.

Saturday, September 26th, 1846. Remained in camp today.

Sunday, September 27th, 1846. Visited the city this morning [and] called upon General Mejia with Captain [William J.] Hardee. The General appeared to be very much pleased to see us. I was introduced to several of his staff. After spending an hour with him, we rode through nearly the whole city.

The town is certainly a very handsome one, and, before they commenced fortifying it, I presume, it was a very neat one. We found the police [order and cleanliness] very bad. I saw some very handsome gardens, with a large number of orange trees in them, and other kinds of fruit. While in the city, I saw several Mexican regiments of infantry march out. They were a miserable set of poor devils. One of our men ought to whip six such men as I saw.

Sadly, Lt. Randolph Ridgely, one of the heroes of Resaca de la Palma, did not survive his own tour of Monterrey. He was an expert horseman, but his mount stumbled in the debris-strewn street and threw him onto his head. He soon died and was temporarily buried in the San Domingo Woods.

<u>LSC</u>

Friday, October 30th, 1846. Camp at the San Domingo Woods near Monterrey, Mexico. On the morning of the *27th October 1846*, a party of officers consisting of Lieutenants Buell and [William T. H.] Brooks of the 3rd Infantry, [William] Steele of the 2nd Dragoons, [Schuyler] Hamilton of the 1st Infantry and myself left our camp for the purpose of ascending the Saddle Mountain, which is situated about five miles from camp.

We passed though the small town of Guadalupe (which is distant about two miles from the foot of the mountain), at which place we procured two Mexican guides, and proceeded to the foot of the mountain. On arriving there we found that we could only ascend a short distance on horseback. We then left our horses in charge of some Dragoon soldiers and before 11 o'clock a.m. we commenced ascending the mountain.

After ascending about a mile, Lieutenant Brooks, who had just recovered from a severe attack of ague and fever, feeling very unwell, determined not to proceed any further, and returned to camp.

We continued ascending the mountain until 4 o'clock p.m., and finding that we could not reach the extreme summit of it until very late in the evening, we determined to retrace our steps. We regretted very much that we did not go prepared to remain all night, for in that case we would have had the pleasure of spending a night on the top of one among the highest mountains in this section of the country.

On our way up we halted frequently and surveyed the beautiful view presented to our sight. The whole valley of Monterrey had the appearance of a large number of beautiful gardens. The cane fields presented a lovely appearance, and reminded me very much of a luxuriant wheat field in the spring of the year. The city of Monterrey presented a beautiful view as we ascended the mountain, and at the point where we determined to retrace our steps the view was beyond all description. We had a fine view of the town of Marin, situated some thirty miles from us, and thirteen other smaller towns all in the Monterrey valley.

We commenced descending the mountain after 4 o'clock p.m., and, night coming on, we got out of our track and did not reach the foot of the mountain until 11 o'clock at night. Just before reaching the foot of the mountain, Lieutenant Steele, who had injured one of his legs, and Lieutenant Hamilton, who was so much fatigued, determined not to go any farther, but to kindle a fire and remain on the mountain until daylight. They insisted that Lieutenant Buell and myself should not remain on their account, so we left them and one Dragoon, taking with us the two Mexicans.

We wended our way to the foot of the mountain, which we reached about two o'clock at night, and found ourselves some three miles from our horses and were compelled to cross the river twice ere we reached them. On arriving at our horses we found that Sergeant Major Tree and a private of Dragoons, who had become fatigued while ascending the mountain, and had left us to return to the horses, had not reached them, so we mounted the two Mexicans on their horses, and turned our faces *campwards*.

On arriving at the town of Guadalupe we parted with our Mexican guides. Here the Sergeant and the private of Dragoons joined us, and we pushed on to camp through a hard rain and arrived there at 3 o'clock in the morning, *wet*, *hungry*, *and as much fatigued* as *two gentlemen would well wish to be*. We congratulated ourselves that we had been so fortunate as not to have some of our limbs broken, for we certainly passed over some of the roughest ground in the course of the night as any men did ever pass over. The view was certainly beyond all description, but I think we "paid dear for the whistle."

I neglected to state that the two Mexicans had promised Steele and Hamilton to return to them that night with water, as there was no water to be found anywhere near their encampment, but on our arriving at the river the Mexicans were so much fatigued that they declined returning, as it was so very late, and finding that it was going to rain, and that the party would be able to get a plenty of water ere the morning came, we determined not to insist upon the Mexicans' returning. Early the next morning the party came into camp very much refreshed after their night's *repose* in the gorge of the *Saddle Mountain*. [There are no entries from October 31–December 12, 1846.]

One of the few U.S. losses of the Mexican War occurred December 6–9, 1846, at the Battle of San Pasqual, California. There, Gen. Stephen Kearney, guided by frontiersman Kit Carson, neared the end of a grueling march from Santa Fe, New Mexico, to San Diego, California. Near starvation, Kearney's force of 160 Dragoons, many without mounts, was struck by an equal number of Californios (Hispanic Californians), who were resisting the U.S. military occupation that had begun the previous July. The Californios inflicted losses on Kearney of 19 killed and 15 wounded, including Kearney himself. Surrounded, Kearney held out until reinforcements arrived from San Diego. Kearney and the U.S. forces then campaigned against the Californios until their capitulation in January 1847, after which Kearney became military governor of U.S. California.

LSC

Sunday, December 13th, 1846. Left our encampment at the San Domingo Woods near Monterrey on Sunday the 13th of December 1846 at a little before 7 o'clock for Victoria, which town is situated on the road leading from Monterrey to Tampico, some 180 miles from the former place. [U.S. forces had occupied the Gulf port city of Tampico the previous November, after its abandonment by the Mexican forces. From Tampico, the U.S. Navy would transport the U.S. invasion force south to the port of Vera Cruz, from which the march to Mexico City would begin.]

The morning was quite a pleasant one, and our road today was quite a good one, with the exception of its being somewhat dusty, which rendered it more unpleasant than it otherwise would have been. We crossed the Monterrey River a short distance above the little town of Guadalupe.

As we passed through the town nearly all of the inhabitants crowded to the street through which the troops passed, and it struck me that they were under the impression that the troops intended leaving that section of country, not knowing that we had left as many more behind us, *poor devils*. I have no doubt but that they would be delighted to get rid of us.

Today we marched about 12 miles and encamped on the left bank of the Monterrey River. We crossed the river twice in the course of the day. We got into camp about 10 o'clock. My Company was for guard tonight.

Monday, December 14th, 1846. Left our encampment this morning at 15 minutes after 6 o'clock. The country we marched over today was quite a pretty one. Soon after we left our encampment we ascended on a beautiful piece of table land. Just at the foot of the table flowed the lovely river Monterrey, and the valley on the opposite side of the river presented the most beautiful view that the eye ever rested upon. The cane fields were just as green as anything could be, and off at a distance was to be seen the majestic Sierra Madre looming to the very heavens. The scenery today was certainly beyond all description.

We arrived at the beautiful town of Cadereyta at 12 o'clock noon precisely, for as we marched through the plaza the town bell struck the hour of 12 noon. I regretted very much that it was not in my power to see more of the town, as I only saw it as I marched through, but judging from what little I saw of it, I should say that it was one of the prettiest towns I have seen since my arrival in the country. I noticed that almost every yard and garden was filled with orange trees and many of them loaded with fruit.

The town, I understand, is very unhealthy. Dr. Barnes, U.S.A., informed me this evening that he was told that there had been a great deal of sickness this fall in the town and surrounding country. The country, after passing through the town going south, is certainly a very pretty piece of land, and is as rich as it is beautiful. We marched today nearly 20 miles, and encamped on the south side of the San Juan River, four miles south of Cadereyta.

Today has been quite a warm one, and our men were very much fatigued from the march. When looking at the Sierra Madre and beholding the tall pines that grow upon the very peaks of them, and whose tops appear to reach to the heavens, it brings to mind those *happy*, *happy days*, in which I was *wont* to sit and listen to my dear, dear wife while singing so sweetly that favorite song of mine, "The Mountain Pine." Oh, I can never forget the first time I heard my dear wife sing. On that day she had three visitors, Miss N. Gamble, Captain Morris, and myself. How melancholy it is to think that out of those three, two of them have paid the debt of nature.

Captain Morris had recently been killed at Monterrey; Nannie Gamble of Welaunee Plantation had died the previous November in her mid-

A short distance from Montemorelos we passed the camp of General Quitman's Brigade, and I had just time to give Dr. [Abram S.] Hill of the Georgia Regiment [from Athens, Georgia] a shake of the hand. The doctor was kind enough to bring me a letter which he found in the post office in Monterrey for me. It was from my sister Mrs. Mary Claiborne, dated the *16th of September*.

Saturday, December 19th, 1846. Left our encampment this morning a little after light. We found it quite cool early in the morning, but after the sun rose, it was quite pleasant, and, had it not been so *very dusty*, our day's march (although a very long one) would have been quite a pleasant one.

We passed through Cadereyta today about 12 o'clock noon, and encamped about 6 miles north of it at the San Antonio Ranch. We reached our camp ground about 2 o'clock. Today's march has been the longest one that we have made, being upwards of 20 miles.

Sunday, December 20th, 1846. We left our camp this morning at a little after daylight. My Company was the rear guard. We had not marched over four miles before one of the ammunition wagons broke down, and we were detained some hours, until another wagon could be sent back for the ammunition. We found the road very dusty.

We arrived in camp about 2 o'clock. The command encamped at Guadalupe, three miles from Monterrey. Tonight we were informed our command would not go to Saltillo, but return to our old encampment at the San Domingo Woods. I presume Santa Anna has declined the invitation given him by the inhabitants of Monterrey to take his *Christmas dinner with them*, is the cause of our not going to Saltillo. General Worth, it appears, was mistaken *this time*.

Monday, December 21st, 1846. Left our camp this morning a little after 7 o'clock and arrived at the San Domingo Woods about 11 o'clock. Our regiment encamped on the ground that the 1st regiment occupied ere leaving for Victoria. We had scarcely fixed ourselves comfortable, ere an order came out ordering us back to Victoria, and that we were to leave on the 23rd, so that there will be no rest for the wicked.

Colonel Harney has been relieved from the command of the 3rd Brigade, and will join General Worth at Saltillo. Colonel [Bennet] Riley of the 2nd Infantry is now in command of the Brigade.

Tuesday, December 22nd, 1846. The troops remained in camp today. I paid a short visit to Monterrey (perhaps the last I will ever pay) for the purpose of purchasing a few things, and returned to camp to dinner.

Wednesday, December 23rd, 1846. We again took up our line of march for Victoria. The morning was rather unpromising, and there were several orders issued *pro* and *con* by those in authority in the command left [behind]. We had a driving rain for a few hours, but before 12 o'clock noon it cleared off, and the day turned out to be a very pretty one.

Today we found a part of the road a little heavy, caused by the rain that fell the night before. We encamped on the left bank of the Monterrey River, at the same place we encamped going down. My Company was for guard tonight.

Thursday, December 24th, 1846. We left at daylight this morning. The road today was in fine order. It was somewhat cloudy in the early part of the morning, but the sun soon came out, and we had a delightful day's march. The scenery this morning was indeed lovely.

Looking in the direction of Monterrey, from the table land that overlooks Monterrey River, I discovered the clouds rising above the mountains in the vicinity of Monterrey, and the sun was just rising, and the mountains had the appearance of being bespangled with gold, while a few white clouds floated between the foot and the top of the majestic Sierra Madre. I must confess I have never before seen so lovely a sight, and indeed it was a scene worthy of the pencil of an artist.

We passed through Cadereyta again, and the more I see of the town, the more I am pleased with it. The streets are certainly very clean, and particularly so for a Mexican town, and the houses present a very neat appearance. We encamped tonight at the same place that we encamped at when going down before.

Friday, December 25th, 1846. Reveille beat this morning at 3 o'clock, and we started before it was light. Shortly after leaving camp the bells of Cadereyta commenced ringing, it being Christmas morning, I presume, was the cause of it. I presume some great church ceremony was about to be enacted.

We marched today upward of 20 miles, and a very hard march it was for our men. I think that our Regiment stood it better than any other, judging from the few men that fell out. We arrived at our camp ground about 2 o'clock, and encamped on the left bank of the Garrapatas River, and I regret to say we found the *ticks* very troublesome. Tonight I am invited to take egg nog at Sykes's tent and also at Dr. [Hamilton S.] Hawkins's, which invitations I will *certainly* accept.

Saturday, December 26th, 1846. We left our encampment this morning a short time after daylight. I do not remember ever beholding a more lovely morning. The sky was perfectly clear, not a cloud was to be seen, and the air was as balmy as that of a summer's morning. The road was a very good one. The rain we had the night before leaving our encampment at the San Domingo Woods had laid the dust and made the road very fine.

We arrived at the hill of hills about 8 o'clock, marched our command to the top of it, stacked our arms, and relieved our men of their knapsacks, etc., and then returned to the foot of it, and assisted our wagons to ascend, which we did in a very short space of time. We passed through Montemorelos about 10 o'clock a.m., and encamped on the opposite side of the river Pilon, about a mile and a half from the town. Since our arrival at this place, we hear that General Scott has arrived in the country. If so, I presume we will lose General Taylor. We encamped today about 11 o'clock.

Sunday, December 27th, 1846. Left our encampment this morning a little after light. The road today was quite hilly and dusty, and the country we passed over was very poor. We marched today about 17 miles and encamped on the bank of the river San Fernando. We arrived at our camp ground about 1 o'clock.

Monday, December 28th, 1846. Left our encampment a short time before light this morning. Our road today was through a very poor country until we arrived in a few miles of Linares, and there the face of the country entirely changed. The lands near the town of Linares were in a high state of cultivation, and I do not recollect of ever seeing finer cane growing on any land.

The town of Linares is certainly a very pretty place. There are two churches and a large number of very handsome buildings in it. The town and surrounding country are well watered, having irrigation ditches running in every direction. We encamped on the right bank of the San Fernando River about 12 o'clock noon, having marched about 16 miles. I received a letter from my dear wife today, dated the 21st of November, which made me quite sad.

Tuesday, December 29th, 1846. Left our encampment this morning about light. The country we marched over today was generally very good. We passed over several very pretty pieces of table land, covered with mesquite wood. We passed through one valley where the mesquite wood was larger than any I have seen since my arrival in this country.

We are now in a part of the country resembling somewhat the country about Camargo. We marched today about 16 miles, and encamped on a small stream of very good water. We have found no scarcity of water on any portion of our route so far, and the whole march up to this time has been a pleasant one. The weather has been very fine, and I hope it will continue so until we arrive at Victoria.

Wednesday, December 30th, 1846. We left our encampment this morning a short time after daylight. The early part of the morning was somewhat cloudy, but before 12 o'clock noon it cleared off, and the rest of the day was a bright and delightful one. About 9 o'clock a.m. we halted a short time at a river, and a very pretty stream it was. The valley through which it flowed was quite a rich one, but quite small. The growth on the right bank of the river reminded me very much of the Florida hammocks.

After crossing the river the road led through quite a rich piece of table land. This table extended some miles, and at the eastern edge of it we came to the town of Villa Grande, a small town situated on a very pretty stream, and very near the foot of the mountains. At this place we encamped for the night. We arrived here about 12 o'clock noon. Our road today was quite dusty, but a good one for footmen. We marched today about 16 miles. My Company tonight is detailed for guard.

Thursday, December 31st, 1846. We remained in camp today, owing to the arrival of the express from Lieutenant May of the 2nd Dragoons (who had been sent to the town of Labradores, which is situated at the extreme end of a pass in the mountains on a road leading in the direction of Saltillo) reporting that he had lost his rear guard and baggage, and that his horses were so much fatigued, that he would not be able to join the main body of the army for a day or two.

Today all of the troops were mustered. I strolled into the village of Villa Grande this morning and found it a filthy little place. The only tolerable house in the village was the church. The women were sitting at their doors entertaining themselves and neighbors with their *favorite amusement*: that of seeing what quantity of vermin can be taken from the head of a relation or friend in a *given* time.

Friday, January 1, 1847. We left our encampment at light this morning. Our road was quite a good one. Some parts of it we found quite dusty. I should judge that this was a fine grazing country. We passed through some bottom land on the river which was very rich and well wooded.

Today we passed through the town of Hidalgo, which was said to have contained at one time some 15,000 inhabitants. I should think at this time that it scarcely contained as many hundred. This place had a church in it which had the appearance of having been built in the *year one*. The town, like most of the Mexican towns, was a filthy hole.

We encamped about a mile beyond the town. At this place we procured some of the best and certainly some of the most delicious oranges that I have ever eaten. We marched today 18 or 21 miles.

Saturday, January 2nd, 1847. We left our encampment this morning about 4 o'clock. Our road was through pretty much such a country as we passed over yesterday. [Lieutenant] May joined us about 9 o'clock last night. He reports that on his return, in passing through a very narrow pass of the mountains, he was in a short advance of his pack mules and rear guard, and that his guard was attacked by a number of rancheros [guerrillas] from the top of a high precipice, by rolling immense stones on them, and firing at the same time, while a party of them was concealed, ready to carry off the plunder. It appears as soon as they commenced rolling stones upon the rear guard, they [the rear guard] fled to the rear, while the sergeant who was in command of the Guard continued in the direction of May and the rest of the command. May returned, but was not able to recover his pack mules.

The rear guard, it is supposed, returned in the direction of Labradores, and I presume will endeavor to return by the route that they went to that place. Lieutenant [Samuel D.] Sturgis, who had been ordered to take charge of the guard a short time before it was attacked, but who it appears did not reach it, was arrested by Lieutenant May for neglect of duty.

We encamped today at the sugar estate of a French gentleman. He was very polite and invited some of the officers to dine with him. He had one of the finest fruit gardens I have seen since my arrival in the country. Besides the large number of oranges, there were a great number of lemon and banana trees. In the garden was to be found the *sweet lemon*, a fruit I never heard of before, and a delicious fruit it was. This place is called Santa Gracia. We marched today about 20 miles or more.

Sunday, January 3rd, 1846. We left our encampment this morning about light. Our route was over pretty much such a country as we marched over yesterday. Near the river San Pedro we saw large numbers of parrots. They certainly had the prettiest plumage I have ever seen. We marched about 12 miles today. Some of the road we marched over today was rather miry, made so by someone's turning the water into the road.

We encamped at a hacienda about 12 miles north of Victoria. The proprietor of this place has a fine fruit garden, very much such a one as we saw yesterday. The country for the last day or two has been filled with game, such as turkeys, deer, partridges, and the Chaparral cock [roadrunner]. My Company was the advance today.

Monday, January 4th, 1847. Left our encampment this morning about light. We passed a large plantation belonging to the gentleman near whose house we encamped. The land appeared to be very fine. Indeed, we found the land very good all the way from this plantation to Victoria. The valley in which Victoria is situated is a rich and lovely one.

We arrived at Victoria about 1 o'clock, and passed through it, and encamped about two miles from the town. Victoria is quite a pretty little place. I presume it has some 2,000 inhabitants in it. While camped at Victoria, we experienced some very cold weather, and had several severe blows. On one occasion nearly all of our tents were blown down.

[No entries January 5–11, 13, 1847]

On the *12th of January, 1847*, an order was issued for us to take up our line of march in the direction of Tampico, the command to leave on the 14th.

Thursday, January 14th, 1847. We left our encampment this morning about light, with orders to proceed as far as Alamitos, a ranch about sixty miles north of Tampico, and then to halt until further orders. The road we marched over today was quite a good one, with now and then a hill, and a few rocks. The country, I would say, was a fine grazing one.

I noticed today a large number of ebony trees, some of them quite large. It is certainly a lovely tree, and would add very much to the appearance of the grounds about a handsome establishment in my *dear*, *dear*, *native* State.

The cactus appears to grow to a great height in this section of Mexico, than it does in any portion of the country that I have been. I saw some today that must have been 15 or 20 feet high, and its shape different from any that I have ever seen before.

We marched today about 12 miles and encamped at the ranch of Santa Rosa. The country over which we marched today was very well-watered. An express from General Taylor (who we left at Victoria) arrived at our camp a little after Tattoo, with an order for General Twiggs to proceed direct to Tampico with his Division, and also informing him that General Scott was at Matamoros, and had assumed command of the Army in Mexico.

Friday, January 15th, 1847. We left our encampment this morning about 6 o'clock. The road was somewhat hilly and rocky. We passed through several very pretty valleys covered with the finest kind of grass. When beholding these valleys from the heights, they frequently presented the appearance of a highly cultivated garden, the mesquite trees presenting the appearance of peach trees in many places.

We passed over a great deal of fine grazing land today. The grass was in many places higher than the knee. We marched today about 12 miles and encamped on a very pretty stream. Today we overtook the Pioneer party, which left Victoria the day before we did. This country abounds in game of all kinds. Captain [W. S.] Alexander of our regiment shot quite a large spotted tiger [jaguar] near our camp at Santa Rosa.

Saturday, January 16th, 1847. This morning reveille through mistake was beaten at 3 o'clock, instead of ½ past four. We did not get off until 6 o'clock. It put everyone in a *bad humor*. After a two and a half hours' march, we overtook the Pioneers again. The road today was pretty much through such a country as we marched over yesterday, but the road as was not as good and, of course, required a great deal more work on it.

Our march today was a short one, not more than 8 or 10 miles. We encamped about 12 o'clock noon. Today we passed through a valley in which there were a large number of palm trees, the first tree of this kind that I have seen in the country.

Sunday, January 17th, 1847. We left our encampment this morning about 6 o'clock. The road we marched over today was a good one, quite level and very few stones in it. The country we passed over was very much like that between Corpus Christi and the Rio Grande.

We are now encamped a short distance from a ranch called Fenelon. Our encampment is on the right bank of a very pretty stream, the Rio Panuco. The water is very good, and I have just returned from taking a delightful bath. We marched today about 12 miles. We found no water between our last night's encampment and this place.

Monday, January 18th, 1846. As we expected to make a long march today, we left our encampment at 5 o'clock, which was a little before day-light. Our road today was very much like the one we passed over yesterday, only a little more rocky. After marching about two hours we crossed the river we encamped upon the night before.

After leaving the river we came into a fine grazing country and passed through several groves of the palmetto tree, which reminded me very much of Florida. Our march was not as long a one as we expected it would have been, having been informed that we would have to march some twenty miles, ere we could find a sufficient quantity of water for our command. The distance we marched today was about 15 miles. We arrived at our encamping ground a little before 12 noon. Today I received a letter from my dear wife, and the President's message [regarding promotion] which was sent me by her.

Tuesday, January 19th, 1846. My Company was on the rear guard today. We did not leave our encampment until 7 o'clock. Our road today passed through very much such a country as we marched over yesterday. Today we passed through several groves of a kind of tree that I do not recollect of ever having seen before. The tree had somewhat the appearance of the walnut tree. We also saw groves of a species of locust. The trees were large and quite handsome.

We passed a little to the left of a large pond, and before arriving at our camp ground, crossed a small stream. Today we marched not more than 8 or 9 miles and encamped near the Rancho Alamitos. We heard today that General [Robert] Patterson's command was just behind us, supposed to have camped at the pond I have just mentioned that we passed today.

Wednesday, January 20th, 1847. We left our encampment this morning at 5 o'clock. Our road today was over a rolling country. Near Lastimas Ranch, we passed through a high and dry hammock. We came upon a large prairie, on which we saw large droves of horses and mules grazing. We passed a ranch a little to the right of the road called Tierras Blancas, and, after a march of some *25* or *28* miles, encamped a short time before sunset at a ranch called Chicor. This is the hardest day's march that we have made since leaving Monterrey.

Thursday, January 21st, 1847. Left our encampment about 6 o'clock this morning. The country we marched over today was very much like that we passed over yesterday, only that we passed through a much more extensive piece of low hammock land. This land, I should think, would produce the finest kind of sugar cane. The country that we are now in indicates very strongly that we are approaching the seaboard. We marched today about 12 miles and encamped about 12 o'clock noon at the Rancho Los Esteros.

Friday, January 22nd, 1847. Left our encampment this morning about ½ past 6 o'clock. The road was not as good as the one we marched over yesterday, having a large number of gulleys in it. We met Colonel Kinney today, just from Tampico on his way to General Patterson's command. Our command halted, and the colonel gave us all the news, and some very fine brandy.

The colonel informed us that Tampico was quite a pleasant place, and that we will be able to get everything we want in the way of delicacies, which information put us all in fine spirits. We marched about 14 miles and encamped near the town of Altamira. I cannot say much for the beauty of the town. It has quite a handsome church in it. The rest of the buildings are nearly all on the hut order. We arrived at our encamping ground a little after 10 o'clock.

Saturday, January 23rd, 1847. We left our encampment this morning a little before 7 o'clock. Our road today was through a live oak hammock. The land is as rich as any I have seen since leaving the country about Cadereyta. Just on the edge of the hammock is a lake which extends all the way to Tampico The road today was very sandy, which rendered the march a fatiguing one. We arrived in about two miles of Tampico a little after 12 o'clock, and here we intend encamping until we have *Vera Cruz* or some other *delightful* place.

The place to be taken would indeed be distant Vera Cruz, a hard march of over three hundred miles from Tampico. But Craig and the army would instead enjoy a smooth voyage across the western Gulf, courtesy of the U.S. Navy. Its warships would then silence the guns of the offshore island fortress of Vera Cruz, the "Castle of San Juan de Ulúa," begun by Spain in 1565, over a century before the Castillo de San Marcos in St. Augustine. The fort reduced, the army, including Craig, would be landed. Once Vera Cruz was taken, the U.S. Army would begin its march toward the fabled city that had so long glittered in American eyes.

Chapter 4

To the Valley of Mexico

Of iron wars....
Of sallies and retires, of trenches, tents,
Of palisadoes, frontiers, parapets,
Of basilisks, of cannon, culverin,
Of prisoners' ransom, and of soldiers slain,
And all the currents of a heady fight.
—Shakespeare, *Henry IV, Part One*

At the time Craig again began keeping his journal in late February 1847, Gen. Taylor's 5,000-man army was preparing to fight Gen. Santa Anna at Buena Vista, some seventy miles southwest of Monterrey. There Santa Anna had gathered an imposing force of 15,000 troops.

President Polk had now given Gen. Winfield Scott command of military operations in Mexico, so Craig and almost all the other regulars had been ordered to concentrate at the Gulf port of Tampico to take ship for the vicinity of Vera Cruz.

On February 22–23, fighting raged at Buena Vista. At battle's end, Taylor's outnumbered force—mostly volunteers, though supported by regular artillery and cavalry—had achieved a brilliant victory and kept Northern Mexico firmly in U.S. control. Meanwhile, Santa Anna began a 500-mile retreat south to Mexico City, recruiting soldiers along the way to fill out the ranks of his army, now reduced by some 3500 casualties, to Taylor's 650.

Craig's journal resumes:

<u>*LSC*</u>

A March from Tampico, Mexico, to Molino del Rey, Mexico
20 February 1847–8 September 1847

Left Camp Watson near Tampico on the *20th of February 1847* for the mouth of the River Panuco for the purpose of shipping for the Island of Lobos. We arrived at our encampment (near the mouth of the river) about 2 o'clock the same day. We remained at this point until the *24th of February*, when our Regiment embarked for Lobos. "C," "D," "H," and "I" Companies embarked on the schooner *Henry A. Basling*, and arrived at Lobos on the *26th of February*.

We left Lobos for the island [anchorage] of Anton Lizardo [several miles south of Vera Cruz] on the *2nd of March*, and we were the last of the whole fleet arriving at that point. We were so long out that our friends had given up all hope of ever seeing us again, thinking that we were "in the Ocean buried."

On the morning of the *4th of March, 1847*, the whole Army left for the island of Sacrificios on board of the different U.S. vessels forming the blockading squadron. The companies which were on board of the *Basling* went aboard of the U.S. vessel the *St. Mary's*.

On this vessel I met with an old friend, Purser Waller of Virginia. He was delighted to see me, and the officers of the *St. Mary's* treated us with the greatest kindness. The officers of the Navy are as hospitable and gallant [a] set of fellows as ever drew a sword, and the officers of the Army will ever recollect their great kindness to them on that occasion.

The troops commenced landing about 4 o'clock on the evening of the *9th of March*. General Worth commanded the first line, and his landing was certainly one of the most interesting sights that I have ever witnessed. The surfboats of every vessel were used by the first line in landing the troops, and when they were all ready to move, a signal was given, and they immediately got under way for the shore.

At this time the excitement on board of the different vessels was very great, and as soon as our boats touched the shore, and our men leaped out of the boats, the troops and sailors on board of the different vessels rent the air with their cheers. We expected that the Mexicans would have disputed our landing, but they did not.

As soon as the first line landed, the boats returned and took off the second line, commanded by General Patterson of the Volunteers, and then returned and landed the third line (which was designated as the reserve), commanded by General Twiggs. Our Regiment belonged to the third line, and it was near 12 o'clock at night ere we arrived on shore. All of the surf boats were manned by the Navy, and never did men acquit themselves with more credit than they did on that occasion. Had it not have been for the Navy, we would have had a great deal of trouble and hard work to have landed our troops.

Although to Craig the landing seemed almost a lark, he had actually just participated in the "largest amphibious assault" ever conducted in American history until that time, and the surf boats "were the first American craft built specifically for amphibious landings." The boats, "double-ended, flat-bottomed craft" could "carry 40 men and a crew of eight." In this operation "over 8,600 men were landed without a single loss in just over four hours."

LSC

The whole army encamped on the beach that night, and, a little before daylight, the enemy fired upon our pickets, and the whole Army in a few moments were under arms. Our pickets soon drove them off, with a loss to the enemy of some 18 or 20 wounded.

On the morning of the *10th of March*, General Worth took up his position on the south side of the City, his right resting near the sea shore. General Robert Patterson, with his Division, took up a position on the left of General Worth's lines. This command, before they got into position, had several skirmishes with the enemy pickets. General Twiggs' command moved on the *12th* for the purpose of occupying a position on the south side of the City, where the road from Jalapa to Vera Cruz passed. We arrived at the Jalapa road on the morning of the *14th of March*.

Our advance guard (composed of the Rifle Regiments) had a skirmish, on arriving at the road, with a small detachment of Lancers. They fled in the direction of the City after firing a few shots at our men. Our command having arrived at this point, the investment of the City was completed. On the evening of the *22nd of March*, about 4 o'clock, our batteries opened upon the City, and the firing was kept up until the morning of the *26th of March*, when the City capitulated by a complete surrender of the troops and public property, both in the City and Castle. There were five thousand prisoners and the same number of small arms, and four hundred pieces of cannon. The officers and men were allowed to leave on parole.

This swift reduction of Mexico's heavily fortified port city would prove a vindication for West Point, since this success, as well as many to follow on the way to Mexico City, would rest in large part on the reconnaissance and engineering genius of Robert E. Lee of Virginia, in particular, along with fellow Southerners Louisianan P. G. T. Beauregard and Kentuckian Gustavus W. Smith.

State-of-the-art American artillery also had once again proven decisive, since the fortifications had been built for the "sullen pounding" of more primitive cannon, not explosive shells. In 1838, however, the French had also taken Vera Cruz, mainly through bombardment by war ships. Santa Anna was at first thought supposed mortally wounded in this battle, but he was saved by amputation of his left leg. In Mexican eyes this grievous injury restored him to the heroic status he had lost at San Jacinto in 1836. The leg was buried with full military honors.

LSC

The City of Vera Cruz is surrounded by a wall of some twelve feet high and some three feet thick. The houses are generally built of a kind of cement, and the houses generally present a very ancient appearance. The country just around the City for some miles is nothing more than a succession of sand hills, and, while the investment was going on, we had several Northers that rendered us very uncomfortable. The clouds of sand were frequently so thick that one could scarcely distinguish an object twenty steps from him.

I visited the Castle of San Juan de Ulua and was perfectly astonished, after seeing the strength of the place, that any set of people could be such a set of cowards as to surrender such a place without making an effort to defend it. The armament of the Castle amounted to some 160 pieces of cannon, several of them sixty-eights [cannon that fired projectiles weighing sixty-eight pounds]. The same number of our troops in possession of the Castle could have held it against the whole Mexican Nation.

During the time that Craig and many other American officers and men occupied their time as martial tourists, Santa Anna was hastening to the supposedly impregnable pass of Cerro Gordo, some fifty miles west of Vera Cruz. He had by then raised more men to augment the force defeated by Taylor at Buena Vista in late February. At Cerro Gordo he posted 12,000 men and 42 artillery pieces. He had abundant time to do this, for, as historian Col. G. F. R. Henderson noted, although troops and guns and cavalry may be landed fairly quickly, the unloading of "stores, wagons, hospitals, ammunition, and transport animals…demand far more time."

Scott's plan to march against Mexico City astounded the Duke of Wellington, conqueror of Napoleon. He predicted disaster: "Scott is lost—he cannot capture the city and he cannot fall back upon his base [Vera Cruz]." In June 1847, unaware of the Iron Duke's opinion, conservative Mexican politician and historian Lucas Alaman wrote to a friend on the same subject. He differed strongly with those who shared Wellington's opinion and provided an accurate prediction of Scott's campaign:

> It seems reckless of Scott to march with such a small army (12,000 men) against a city of 180,000 inhabitants plus a very considerable garrison—which outnumbers the attacking army—and to have no communication with the coast; despite this, there is no doubt in my mind that he will take the city, because our army consists mainly of recruits under the command of generals who are renowned for how fast they can flee, and nothing will move the masses, who are watching all this as if it were happening in a foreign country. That is how weary they are after so many revolts. This will all be over very soon.

Alaman was correct. Gen. Scott's campaign was nearing its end. But there would be much fighting and many delays before Mexico City would fall the following September.

<u>*LSC*</u>

Thursday April 8th, 1847. Our Division under the command of General Twiggs left for Jalapa this morning at 8 o'clock. For the first six miles we found the road very sandy, which rendered the marching very fatiguing, many of our men having to fall out before they had marched six miles. We marched today about fifteen miles and encamped at Manga de Clavo, one of Santa Anna's haciendas. His house is situated some miles from the road, on a high eminence, and, from the road, has the appearance of being a lovely spot.

The manner in which this day's march has been conducted ought to cashier any Second Lieutenant in the Army, had one been in command of the troops, for when the command arrived at the encampment, many of the Regiments had not more than twenty or thirty men in them. They were scattered from near the encampment we left in the morning to Manga de Clavo. Had we have met the enemy, the few men that were in the advance would not have been able to have resisted an attack, owing to their being entirely overcome by the heat and the hard march.

We reached our encampment a little before sundown. The country we marched over today, after leaving the sea a few miles, was generally broken, and the road we found pretty good. We passed over two very handsome bridges today.

The historian Justin Smith agreed with Craig that for Twiggs's division the

> beginning of the march was terrible. After going three miles along the beach they struck off at a right angle...on a deep, sandy road...with a blazing sun overhead, not a breath of moving air, and Twiggs' horse for a pacemaker. Many threw away everything detachable, and the greater part of the division—at least four fifths, it was said—fell by the way. Some died, and many others did not rejoin the command for days.

Fortunately, the next day the paved National Road emerged from the coast's drifting sand—"a spacious, comfortable graded cement avenue…that penetrated a dark forest of palms, cactus, limes, and countless other trees."

LSC

Friday, April 9th, 1847. Left our encampment this morning a little after daylight. A short distance from our camp, we crossed a very handsome bridge over the stream which we had encamped on the night before. The bridges we have passed over would do credit to any country. Nowhere in the U.S. have I ever seen anything of the kind to compare with them. In the U.S. over such small streams you would generally find a *log bridge*, and that not a very good one.

The country we marched over today was very much like the country we marched over the day before. The country appears to be very little cultivated near the road. Now and then we passed a few miserable looking huts, many of them deserted. We marched today about 15 miles, and encamped about 12 o'clock on a stream called Paso de Ovejas. Over this stream was another splendid bridge. So far we have found the road a very good one, a greater part of it having been macadamized [paved with cemented broken stones on a convex roadbed].

Saturday, April 10th, 1847. Left our encampment this morning at daylight, and, after a short march of some eight miles, we arrived at the Puente Nacional (or the National Bridge). This is a splendid bridge over the small but beautiful river Antigua. The scenery at this place is not to be surpassed by any I have ever seen. It is equal to the scenery about Harpers Ferry in Virginia.

As you approach the bridge going from Vera Cruz to Jalapa, there is a small fort perched upon a cliff of an immense height on the left of the road. This work protects the bridge. On the opposite side of the river, on another height, is also a small work, which also protects the bridge and the road leading from Jalapa to Vera Cruz.

On the left bank of the river is a small village, and on a hill overlooking the village and the river, is one of Santa Anna's residences. The house is quite a handsome one, containing six large rooms and several smaller ones, which I did not enter. Three of the large rooms had marble floors. The doors were all of mahogany. The windows were all large, which rendered the rooms very cool and pleasant. A large portico extended nearly around the whole house. From all I saw, I have no doubt but that the General is a man of some taste. I was surprised to find that he had no flowers about his grounds. I presume he prefers his *game fowls* to handsome shrubbery.

There was no furniture in the house, excepting one mahogany bedstead, which was a very handsome one. The rest of the furniture, I presume, was in the rooms which were locked. The General's steward was a very respectable looking Mexican. He informed us that the General was at that time in Jalapa. The Mexicans had at one time determined to defend this point, but a few days before we arrived there, they thought better of it, and moved off all their cannon to Cerro Gordo.

———

It would transpire that Santa Anna, lately preoccupied with stifling a revolutionary movement in his own capital, still intended to make his stand at Cerro Gordo ("Fat Hill"). There he thought that he could delay the U.S. troops until the beginning of the yellow fever season, which was at its worst from east of Cerro Gordo to the sea. The yellow fever, he calculated, would considerably weaken the U.S. Army to his advantage.

———

LSC

Sunday, April 11th, 1847. We left our encampment this morning at 4 o'clock. The country we passed over was pretty much like the country we marched over the day before. We are now getting into the mountainous country, and the air is very pure and delightful.

We marched today about fifteen miles and encamped about 3 o'clock p.m. at Plan del Rio. Our Dragoons, who were in advance, came upon one of the enemy's pickets and drove them in. We are now encamped about four miles from the enemy's advance foot. Just beyond their first work is the *celebrated pass* of Cerro Gordo. This said to be one among the strongest positions in the whole of Mexico. Early tomorrow morning we expect to feel the enemy and endeavor to find out his exact position, and also his strength.

———

The enemy's defenses lay along a rough arc whose chord was the deep, rocky ravine carved by the Rio Del Plan. The arc's eastern end, from which the National Road ascended over broken pavement into the hills, was commanded by several Mexican batteries. As the key to the entire position, its western end was swept by several batteries atop a loaf-shaped hill called Cerro Gordo, along with other emplacements located toward the western end of the arc, where the National Road descended through Cerro Gordo Pass toward the Mexican camp.

———

LSC

Monday, April 12th, 1847. We started a little after daylight this morning for the enemy works. After getting a short distance from camp, Captain [Croghan] Ker of the 2nd Dragoons reported that a large body of the enemy was seen a short distance in our rear, on the *strength of which*, our Regiment was ordered to halt, and to bring up the rear. The rest of the command marched in a short distance of the enemy's first work, and halted, and sent out reconnoitering parties.

Captain Joseph E. Johnston of the Topographical Engineers, while reconnoitering very closely one of the enemy's works, was fired upon by one of their pickets, and, I regret to say, received two wounds, one in the upper part of his right thigh, and the other in one of his arms. It is thought by his surgeon that he will recover from them. He is a splendid fellow, and one among the best officers in the Army. His death would be felt by all of his Army friends.

About 12 o'clock the Army returned to their old encampment at Plan del Rio. General Patterson arrived with his Division at this place about 12 o'clock today. A portion of his command under General Quitman was left at Vera Cruz, for the purpose of allowing them a little rest, having just returned from Alvarado. They are expected to join us in a few days.

Tuesday, April 15th, 1847. We expected to have left here this morning at 4 o'clock, for the purpose of *driving* the enemy from their position, but, owing to the Volunteers being very much fatigued, having just arrived from a long march, the move was postponed.

I intended to have written to my *own, dear, dear wife* today, but I have come to the conclusion that it will be better to postpone it until after the fight, for I know that it would make her very unhappy to know that we were just on the eve of a fight, and not to hear for several days afterwards the result of it, and, as it has always been my wish to make my dear Liz as happy as possible, I have determined not to write until after the *fandango* is over, and then I will be enabled to give my dear wife all the particulars.

It is reported that Santa Anna is in command of the troops at the pass of Cerro Gordo, and that he has some fifteen thousand men with him. I think ere three days passes over his head, he will find us in Jalapa, although some of us may be missing when the roll is called at the gay and festive board. The Engineers left this morning for the purpose of making another reconnaissance and returned this evening, and report that we can readily turn the enemy's advanced work.

The order is out for us to move at ½ past 12 o'clock tonight. The regulars are to take the right of the road, and the Volunteers the left, and, after carrying the works, we are to form in line of battle on the Jalapa road, the Volunteers on our left.

Wednesday, April 14th, 1847. A few minutes after Tattoo last night an order was issued by General Patterson assuming command of the troops at this place, and, at the same time, countermanding the order in relation to our move against the enemy until the arrival of General Scott, or until further orders.

The whole Army appears to be disgusted at the course General Patterson has taken in this matter, and we are all disgusted at General Scott remaining behind, after having been informed that a *large force* was in position just in front of us, and commanded by one of Mexico's best Generals.

The General, I presume, remained behind for the purpose of writing *pretty letters* relative to the capture of Vera Cruz, when he should have been here. We would have been in Jalapa ere this. As it is, we cannot say at what time we will arrive there. My Company is detailed for picket service, and we will leave at ½ past four o'clock this evening. We are to take post about two miles (in advance of our main body) on the Jalapa road.

In reality, the arrival of Patterson had prevented Twiggs from throwing his division against the closest Mexican batteries in a frontal assault. At Scott's arrival, and with further investigation of the enemy's works by Robert Lee and other engineers, a much better plan was matured for the attacks of April 17–18.

LSC

Thursday, April 15th, 1847. We were relieved this evening a short time before sunset. We were not disturbed by the enemy while on picket, although they appeared to be very uneasy, judging from the number of guns they fired during the night.

Today a large command under Major [Edwin Vose] Sumner went in the direction of the enemy's works, for the purpose of reconnoitering and also to see if they could find a trail leading around the enemy's works into the Jalapa road. They returned late at night, without having gone around the pass. General Scott and staff arrived late last evening, and we expect to have something to do in a few days. General Worth's command is expected to arrive in a few days. He will bring up our battering trains.

Friday, April 16th, 1847. A command left this morning accompanied by several or our Engineers for the purpose of reconnoitering from the point they left off yesterday, around the enemy's works to the Jalapa road. It appears that the reconnaissance so far made is not altogether satisfactory, and it is generally thought very important that the enemy's line from this point of the road, around to the extreme left of their line, should be thoroughly reconnoitered.

We are looking every moment for the arrival of General Worth's command, and we are all anxious for its arrival, as we understand they have a large mail for us; and I feel confident that I will have at least three letters from my *own dear*, dear wife. No one knows how anxious I am to write to my dear, dear wife. I have been on the eve of writing to her for the last two or three days, but knowing as I do that if I inform her that I am anywhere in the neighborhood of the enemy, it will only cause her a great deal of uneasiness, and prevent her from enjoying herself while on her visit to her dear sister. This affair must come off in a day or two, and I will then be able to give her a full account of the battle.

Saturday, April 17th, 1847. Our Division left their encampment at Plan del Rio at 8 o'clock this morning for the purpose of taking up a position on a height near the enemy's advanced work. On arriving at the point at which our Division left the Jalapa road, our Regiment (the 3rd Infantry) was ordered to halt and await a section of Captain [William] Wall's Light Battery of [the Third Regiment] Artillery, and a 24-pounder under command of Lieutenant Hodges of the Ordnance Department, and to escort them to a position which would be selected for them in the course of the day.

The road that we had made led over some very steep cliffs, and we were compelled to take out the horses and drag the pieces up with our men. It was certainly a very fatiguing operation, and our friends the Mexicans hurried the operations some little by firing several rounds of grape at us while ascending the hill.

Today our advanced party had a skirmish with the enemy. We had a large number of our men wounded and several killed, but we drove them into their works. Our regiment did not get into camp until near 9 o'clock at night. We then bivouacked near the road, and a very uncomfortable time we had of it, for very few, if any, of the officers had blankets, and before morning we found it very cool. Our cannon were put in position that night by the Illinois Volunteers, and an order was issued for us to be in readiness to march at light in the morning.

Sunday, April 18th, 1847. We started a little after light this morning for the purpose of supporting the batteries which had been planted the night before. Shortly after reaching the height, our guns opened upon the enemy's works, and they returned our fire with grape, canister, and round shot.

My Company was on the left of the line, and very much exposed to the enemy's fire. I had one man wounded in the thigh with a grape shot, and I considered myself fortunate that I did not get half of my Company cut to pieces. There were several Regiments on this height. The Rifle Regiment was ordered to form on my left, and before they could get into position, they had some 8 or 10 men killed and wounded. Captain [Stevens T.] Mason of the Rifles had his leg shattered by a ball and was compelled to have it amputated* (*[later footnote:] died in Jalapa a few weeks after the battle).

Whoever ordered the move showed himself to be very little of a soldier, but it appears that no one would acknowledge having given the order. It is said that Colonel Harney gave the order, but he denied having done so. [It was indeed Harney who had ordered the Rifle Regiments forward, but he would soon redeem himself.]

After firing a few rounds at the enemy's works, with our howitzers and 24-pounders, we gave a cheer and charged down the steepest kind of a hill, and then up another, a little steeper than the first, if anything. Upon this height were the enemy's works.

The enemy fired at us with their cannon as we started, and on arriving at their works, met us with a great deal of firmness. After a short time we carried the height, and the poor devils fled in every direction, leaving a large number of their men dead on the field.

This was one of the most important works. Indeed, it was the key to all the other works on the different heights. Having taken this prevented the troops in front of it from escaping, and we captured some four thousand of them. General Santa Anna, whose camp was just at the foot of Cerro Gordo, had just time to make his escape, horse-back, leaving his carriage and wooden leg behind him, together with some $28,000. [Santa Anna's wooden leg, captured by Illinois troops, now reposes in the Illinois State Military Museum, despite continued Mexican government requests for its return.]

Colonel Harney of the 2nd Dragoons commanded the storming party. Our loss was not every great. Our Regiment (the 3rd Infantry) had only one officer wounded, and that a flesh wound, and some thirty men killed and wounded. The whole loss of our Army in killed and wounded was about 400. I had four men of my Company wounded. One died on the day after battle, or on the evening of the fight. I do not know which.

The Dragoons, some short time after the height was carried, were sent in pursuit of the enemy, who had fled with Santa Anna in the direction of Jalapa. Our Regiment this evening marched about six miles in the direction of Jalapa and encamped in a few yards of the road.

The Battle of Cerro Gordo, according to General Scott, left him "embarrassed with the results of victory—prisoners of war, heavy ordnance, field batteries, small arms, and accoutrements. About three thousand men laid down their arms, with the usual proportion of field and company officers, besides five generals, several of them of great distinction."

Craig's regiment had participated conspicuously in the storming of the fortified height of the Cerro Gordo hill, overwhelming the enemy in his works with the bayonet. This action would accord the Third Regiment the honor of being the only U.S. regiment "authorized to parade with fixed bayonets."

In the regimental commander's report of the battle, E. B. Alexander noted "the general good conduct of the regiment," together with "individual instances of gallantry which came under my observation. I cannot speak in too high terms of the gallant bearing, throughout the day, of Capt. L. S. Craig." He also mentioned Craig's friends 1st Lt. D. C. Buell and 2nd Lt. Barnard Bee.

Harney, who had led the daring charge, was justly praised by all his superior officers and was brevetted brigadier general. This was a change from recent months when he had been court-martialed over his unapproved invasion of Mexico and had briefly lost command of the Dragoons. As a Democrat, Harney had been rescued by President Polk, however, who thought Harney "had been treated unjustly because he was a Democrat and 'one of Gen'l Jackson's personal friends.'"

As Craig noted, the victory had in great part been the result of reconnoitering and road building, as well as the transportation of artillery by the troops themselves. Moreover, when Cerro Gordo had been taken, Craig's friend and fellow Virginian John Magruder and his men had seized the enemy's field pieces and turned them against the fleeing Mexicans, who at the Mexican camp below were met by a sweeping flanking movement by brigades of James Shields and Bennet Riley.

At the other end of the battle field, another miracle of manpower had occurred—Charlestonian Roswell Ripley and his fellow artillerists had moved by hand for two-and-one-half miles a one-ton siege howitzer onto the heights on the Rio del Plan's steep southern bank, together with its complement of 45-pound shells and 8-pound powder charges. This battery supported General Pillow's failed attack on the position that Twiggs had wished to assault many days before.

<u>*LSC*</u>

Monday, April 19th, 1847. Left our camp this morning at light and about 8 o'clock came up with the rest of our Division, which had encamped the night before at Encero, one of the many residences of Santa Anna. The General's residence at this place is a very handsome one, and the improvements around about the house appeared to be in a good deal of taste. I regretted very much that I had not the time to pay a visit to the establishment, but we were in such *hot* pursuit of the *owner*, that I could not think of halting for a moment.

We arrived at Jalapa between 12 and 1 o'clock, and our men are now quartered in the barracks of the City, and the officers in tents, but expect to get quarters in a day or two.

Tuesday, April 20th, 1847. General Worth left this evening with his Division for Perote. I presume some of our Division will follow in a few days.

[No entries from April 21–May 6, 1847.]

Our Regiment left Jalapa on *Friday the 7th of May* for the Puente Nacional (the National Bridge) [in the rear] at which place we expect to meet the train coming from Vera Cruz, and to escort it to Jalapa. Our command consists of the 3rd Infantry and three Companies of the 7th Infantry, all under the command of Colonel Riley of the 2nd Infantry, and also a part of the *Mountain Howitzers* battery.

The command left Jalapa about 10 o'clock and encamped that night at Encero, Santa Anna's hacienda, which place is some 8 or 10 miles from Jalapa. We arrived there early in the evening. Some of the officers in the course of the evening visited the hacienda of Santa Anna and found that the house had been pillaged of some of its furniture by some *Volunteers*, who had passed there a day or two before. The depredations were said to have been committed by either the Tennessee or Illinois Volunteers. The Georgia Regiment left this morning on their return to Georgia, their time being out early in June. They are now encamped in a short distance of us.

Saturday, May 8th, 1847. We left our encampment this morning about sunrise. We had a very hot march of it and encamped at Plan del Rio, which place we reached between 11 and 12 o'clock in the day.

I had the pleasure of seeing the old battle ground at Cerro Gordo. It is certainly one of the strongest natural positions for an Army to defend that I could conceive of, and the Mexicans ought to have prevented our small force from proceeding any farther in the direction of the City of Mexico. Had we have had the pass to defend, *fifty thousand* Mexicans could not have driven us from it.

This evening I supped with Dr. [A. S.] Hill of the Georgia Regiment. What would I not give if I could only accompany him to Athens? I have sent by the doctor some little toys for my dear little girl, which he has been kind enough to take charge of. The doctor is a worthy & excellent man, and I regret he could not remain with us.

Sunday, May 9th, 1847. Left our encampment this morning at daylight. The day was a very warm one, and a large number of our men suffered very much from the heat. We had to march 15 miles before we could get water. We arrived at the Puente Nacional about 11 o'clock in the day. The Georgia and Alabama Regiments only halted a few hours at this place, and then proceeded on about six miles and encamped for the night.

Today I was invited by Colonel [Henry Rootes] Jackson, Lieutenant Colonel [Thomas Y.] Redd, Captains [John E.] Davis, [John] Jones, and Lieutenant [Charles P.] Hervey [of the Georgia Regiment of Volunteers] to dine with them at a Mexican house, where they had ordered a dinner to be prepared.

When the hour arrived, I attended, and, to the astonishment of everyone, the dinner consisted of *only* a little rice and a few free holders [*frijoles*] (a kind of Mexican pea [refried beans]), and *no meat.* The only excuse the Mexican made for his dinner was that he had nothing better in his house to give us.

Tonight my Company is detailed for guard. I went in bathing this afternoon in the river Antigua, near the splendid bridge which is over this lovely little stream, and I enjoyed the bath very much after the hot march of fifteen miles.

Tuesday, May 11th, 1847. We will remain here today and await the arrival of the train, which is expected tonight. A short time before breakfast this morning, I paid a visit to the fort, which is perched on a high cliff, which overlooks the Antigua river. This fort commands the bridge and road which leads over it. This fort, I believe, was built by the old Spaniards. This little fort was armed with some four pieces of Artillery in its best days. The Mexicans, hearing that part of our command was at the town of Antigua, a short time before our Army left Vera Cruz, became somewhat alarmed, fearing that we might pay them a visit at this place, and removed the cannon that was in this work to Cerro Gordo.

Tuesday, May 11th, 1847. We remained at the Puente Nacional today, awaiting the arrival of the train, which arrived here about 11 o'clock today. We will leave tomorrow morning at light for Jalapa.

Wednesday, May 12th, 1847. Owing to some mismanagement, we not did leave until sunrise this morning. Our men suffered very much from the heat, it being one of the warmest days we have had since leaving Jalapa. We arrived at Plan del Rio about 11 o'clock. We are to have Reveille at ½ past 1 o'clock tomorrow morning and leave as soon afterwards as possible.

Thursday, May 13th, 1847. We left our encampment this morning a little before light, and after another very hot day's march, reached Encero about 11 o'clock a.m. A short time before Retreat this evening, it was reported by someone in the command that a party of Lancers was seen on a hill a short distance from our encampment, upon the strength of which Colonel Riley ordered George H. Talcott's battery (which was some distance in advance of us at Santa Anna's hacienda) to return and take up a position near our encampment. A short time after Retreat, some men who had been out for the purpose of hunting up beef returned and reported that they had not seen *any sign* of Lancers, so it turned out to be a false alarm.

Friday, May 14th, 1847. Left our encampment at daylight this morning. The day was not as warm as the day before. We arrived at Jalapa about 9 o'clock a.m. This evening I attended a bull fight, an amusement I have never witnessed before. The place in which the fight came off was very much like our Circus rings, perhaps somewhat larger, with a railing between the spectators and the ring.

The bulls are kept in a dark stall near the ring, and when the hour arrives for the sport to commence, one of the party who is to fight him, makes his appearance on horseback, followed by some four or five other persons, with different colored cloths on their heads, which are used for the purpose of enraging the bull, and also to divert his attention from the man on horseback, should it be necessary.

As soon as they make their appearance in the ring, a trap door is raised, and out rushes a bull, looking as fierce as a lion. The first pass he makes is generally at the man on horseback, who receives him with a spear, which is generally a long staff with a barb at the end of it. As soon as this pricks him [the bull], he becomes furious and rushes at the first one he comes in contact with. On this occasion, he made a pass at the man on horseback a second time, and upset both the man and horse. I thought the man would certainly have been killed, but he escaped with only a sprained arm. I must confess that I felt more for the poor horse than I did for his rider. The horseman now retired, and the other portion of the Company commenced on the bull. This party had a number of small staffs decorated with ribbons, and at the end of each is a sharp barb.

Whenever the bull makes a pass at them, they stick one of these in some portion of his body, and there they remain, which enrages him the more. After this they apply fire crackers to him, which renders him perfectly furious, and woe be to the man who is not active enough to get out of his way. After tormenting him in this way for some minutes, one of the Company makes his appearance armed with a small sword, and, after causing the bull to make several separate passes at him, he runs the sword up to the hilt in his breast, which causes instant death. Then in dash two horsemen, and each of them throws a lasso around the horns of the *poor wretch*, and dash out of the ring with him, and *I have no doubt*, but that he is sold the next morning in [the] market for beef.

As soon as the first bull is removed, another one is brought out, and the same scene enacted with him, as with the first. On this occasion they had five bulls. I only remained to see four tortured. Bull fighting and cock fighting are the most fashionable amusements in Mexico. The *Priests* are passionately fond of the *latter amusement*, and would prefer *any time* attending a cock fight to attending *high mass*.

[No entries from May 15–21, 1847.]

Left Jalapa for Puebla on *Saturday* evening at 3 p.m. on the *22nd of May 1847*, and marched out three miles, and encamped in a very pretty valley. It commenced raining today about 10 o'clock and cleared off a short time before we started. It rained a little in the course of the night, but not enough to render us uncomfortable. The country around Jalapa is certainly the loveliest I have seen.

Sunday, May 23rd, 1847. Left our encampment this morning a short time before sunrise. Our march today was through a very pretty country. We passed several fields of wheat, barley, and corn. The two first named crops were nearly ready for the scythe. The road today was a very fine one, passing over the mountain of [Cofre de] Perote. We marched today about 12 miles and encamped at the pass of La Hoya.

At this place is a small village. The houses are all built of pine logs, and covered with pine slabs, put on with pine pins. At this place the pine growth commenced, the first I have seen since my arrival in Mexico. At this place the Mexicans commenced fortifying. They erected several small works on the different heights commanding the road, but took good care not to remain *long enough* to defend them, but *vamosed* before our troops reached that point, leaving some ten or twelve pieces of cannon on the ground. This is a very strong pass, and five thousand *resolute* men could defend it against twenty thousand Mexicans.

Monday, May 24th, 1847. Left our encampment this morning a short time after daylight. Our march today was through a section of country not as good as the country we passed over the day before. We arrived at the village of Las Vigos (which is at the top of the mountain of Perote) about 8 o'clock. We halted at this place a short time for the purpose of allowing our men to procure water.

At this point we commenced descending the mountain, and before we arrived at our encampment at Rio Frio, we passed some very good land. We marched today about 12 miles and encamped at the foot of the mountain, on a small stream called Rio Frio. The water from this stream was the best and coldest that I have drunk since my arrival in Mexico. We encamped today about 12 o'clock.

Tuesday, May 25th, 1847. Left our encampment this morning a short time after daylight. Our march was through a lovely valley. On each side of the road were highly cultivated fields of wheat, barley, and corn. The soil in this valley appears to be of a light nature, and, if it was properly cultivated, I have no doubt but that it would produce the finest kind of crops.

We arrived at Perote about 9 o'clock a.m. and encamped just on the outside of the celebrated Castle of Perote. I visited the Castle today in Company with several officers. It is certainly one among the strongest fortifications that I have seen. It is a bastion work. The ditch is one of the largest that I have ever seen to a work of the kind. Had Santa Anna, instead of fighting us at Cerro Gordo, had fought us at this place, he would have stood a much better chance of stopping us for a time in our forward march to the Halls of the Montezumas.

The town of Perote is a small place and a very dirty one, but the country around it is certainly a lovely one. I forgot to mention in my notes of yesterday that I saw for the first time in my life mules working as oxen, that is, with yokes on, and without bridles. Poor wretches, they are used in every way in this country by their hard masters, the Mexicans. A Mexican has no feeling for a mule.

We expect to leave at daylight tomorrow morning, as we will have to march some 17 miles. On one side of the Fort of Perote, in the ditch, was a cross, with a large number of human bones lying around it. At this cross, I was informed, all malefactors were shot, and their bodies allowed to remain there. I have no doubt that a large number of *poor devils* have suffered death at this cross since the erection of this Fort. Our march today was not more than six or eight miles.

Wednesday, May 26th, 1847. Left our encampment at Perote this morning at light. The morning was a wet one, and it did not clear off until near 9 o'clock a.m. We halted a short time at the hacienda of San Antonio for the purpose of allowing our men to procure water. The water we found was not very good, being somewhat brackish. This hacienda is about nine miles from Perote.

The country we marched over today is a perfect barren, being entirely destitute of both wood and water. This morning the top of Perote mountain was covered with snow. We marched today about 17 miles and encamped at the village of Tepeyahualco, where we were compelled to use brackish water. Today has been a very cold one. I do not think that I ever felt as cold a day at this season of the year in any part of Virginia. The table land we marched over today is the poorest I have seen in Mexico.

Thursday, May 27th, 1847. My Company was on the rear guard today, and we did not leave camp for some time after the rest of the Army left. One Company of the Rifles under the command of Lieutenant [Andrew] Porter, one Company of the 7th Infantry under command of Captain [Richard H.] Ross, and my Company ("A") of the 3rd Infantry composed the rear guard, the whole under the command of Major [Harvey] Brown of the [Fourth] Artillery. For the first nine miles the country was perfectly barren. We found neither water or wood until we arrived at the hacienda of Viveys. There we found very excellent water, and the land very good.

At this place we watered our train, and halted near an hour. I neglected to put up a lunch this morning, and on arriving at this place, my servant, Willis, purchased some eggs and boiled them, which satisfied my appetite until night. At this place I saw a field of at least one thousand acres in corn. It was a beautiful sight, and brought to mind those beautiful fields of corn that are to be seen on the Rappahannock river in *old* Virginia. The country from the hacienda of Viveys to our encampment at Ojo de Agua was certainly a lovely one, and in a high state of cultivation.

Two miles from our encampment of tonight we passed a very handsome hacienda, at which place there was a very handsome little church. I was very much astonished today on looking into a wagon to see a *horse lying* in it. On inquiring the cause of having such a *load*, I was informed that it was a sick pony belonging to a circus Company which was going to Puebla under the protection of the Army. That is the way things are done in the Army. Our sick men are made to walk, *while sick horses* are *allowed to ride.*

At Retreat this evening we were requested to attend at the tent of Colonel Riley, for the purpose of hearing a letter read from General Worth to General Scott, informing the latter that he had heard from *undoubted* authority that 20,000 men were marching upon him, and that it was their intention to endeavor to *crush him* before General Scott could arrive to his aid, and advising General Scott to keep a sharp look out on his right, as three thousand cavalry had moved in that direction for the purpose of attacking the train and preventing us from arriving in time to his succor. The rear guard and train reached camp at 4 o'clock p.m. We marched today about 17 miles.

Friday, May 28th, 1847. We left our encampment this morning at light, and, after marching a few miles, we met several carriages with the Governor of Vera Cruz and his family. From them we learned that Jose Joaquin de Herrera was President and that Santa Anna was a prisoner in Mexico, and that one of his Generals had been put to death, and also that the peace party was rapidly gaining the ascendancy.

On arriving at Puebla, we found that the above information was not correct. We marched today about 12 miles and encamped at the hacienda of La Venton* ([Footnote, added later:] *This place is also known by the name of La Penar.) about 11 o'clock a.m. We passed through a very pretty village today (Nopaluca). In this place was a very handsome church. From this village you have a view of two mountains [the volcanoes Popocatépetl and Iztaccíhuatl] whose summits are covered with perpetual snows.

Saturday, May 29th, 1847. Left our encampment a short time before light this morning. Just after Reveille this morning, I found that my pony I had purchased the evening before had broken away. I was compelled to leave Willis behind for the purpose of looking for him. A short time after we reached the village of Amazoc* ([Footnote, added later:] *This town is the Manchester of Mexico. It is celebrated for its fine work in steel. In this place the finest steel spurs and bridle bits are manufactured. One of the finest bits I think I have ever seen was in this place. The owner of it asked *only* twelve dollars for it.) Willis came up with the pony, much to my delight, for I was somewhat afraid that I would never see him again, as the road from Jalapa to Puebla is infested with robbers.

The country we passed through today was generally very good. Today we passed several large fields of wheat, barley, and corn. In many places they were reaping their small grain. In this country they put up their wheat, and barley straw, with a good deal of taste. I never saw anywhere in *old Virginia* straw put up with so much neatness.

We arrived at Puebla about 4 o'clock in the afternoon. Just before leaving for the City, we heard that the enemy was in a short distance of the town, and that a fight was expected to come off sometime in the course of the evening. But, on getting into the city, we found that it was nothing more than a stampede of General Worth's. On arriving in the City, we were ordered to take up our Quarters in the Monastery of San Augustin. We were late in the night getting our men fixed. Such confusion I never saw before.

[No entries for May 30, 1847, through July 26, 1847.]

Tuesday, July 27th, 1847. Last night at 10 o'clock our Brigade received an order to be ready to move in the direction of Perote, at 7 o'clock this morning, owing to General Scott having received information that a large body of troops had passed to the North of Puebla, moving in the direction of Perote, with the intention, it was thought, of attacking General Franklin Pierce's command, which is now on its way from Vera Cruz to Puebla. Our Brigade, composed of the Rifles, 1st Artillery, and 3rd Infantry, with a part of [Capt. James] Duncan's battery[, Second Artillery], one Company of Dragoons, One Company of Mounted Riflemen, the Regiment of New York Volunteers, and one Company of our *Allies* (or better known as the Hitchcock Guards) left about 8 o'clock this morning and encamped at Amazoc. Today's march was a short one, being about nine miles.

Wednesday, July 28th, 1847. We left Amazoc a little after daylight this morning. The morning was quite cool, but before 12 o'clock it became quite warm, and, the road being very dusty, made our march a rather unpleasant one. Last night we had one of our men killed by the Mexicans. He belonged to "H" Company of the 3rd Infantry. He left the Regiment without permission, and no doubt became intoxicated and insulted some Mexicans, who sent him to his final roll call. We arrived at La Penal about 12 o'clock, where we encamped for the night.

We sent out our Allies (who act as our spies). They returned after a short time and reported no enemy in the vicinity. This Company of Mexicans is composed of *convicts*, who have lately been released from prison by the Commanding General. They are commanded by a Virginian by the name of Spooner. This man was born in Fredericksburg, Virginia, and his father owned at one time a small farm in a few miles of my plantation on the Rappahannock River. What brought him to this country I do not know.

The mysterious Spooner was one of the several sons of George W. B. Spooner, who lived near Elba Plantation. Hitchcock, who simply calls him "Mr. Spooner," identifies him as the interpreter for Manuel Dominguez, who was actually the leader of the "Allies," also known as "the Spy Company." Spooner and the others were notoriously robbers and brigands, explaining why a gentleman wouldn't engage Spooner in conversation relating to his presence in Mexico.

<u>*LSC*</u>

Thursday, July 29th, 1847. Left our encampment before sunrise this morning. Passed through the little town of Nopaluca. This town is situated upon a hill. On either side is a beautiful valley, in a high state of cultivation. We encamped today a little after 12 o'clock at Ojo de Agua, and it is rumored that we will not leave our encampment tomorrow, it having been reported that General Pierce is between this and Jalapa. Should that be the case, he ought to reach this point tomorrow or next day.

Friday, July 30th, 1847. We remained in camp today and hope to have the pleasure of remaining here until General Pierce's arrival. The only thing that has kept up our spirits on this march is that we have heard that General Smith was authorized by General Scott to open the mail as soon as we met General Pierce. Should that be the case, *I*, for one, will certainly not complain of the march, for I would agree to march to Vera Cruz through *Tierras Calientes* [the Infernal Regions] to hear from my dear, dear wife and dear little daughter.

We had a very sudden death in our Regiment last night. We lost our Sergeant Major in a fit of apoplexy. This morning we sent out a Company of Dragoons and the Company of Mounted Riflemen and our Allies to a town some thirteen miles from this on the road to Perote, and a short distance off of the main road, for the purpose of surprising a body of Guerrillas, who were said to have their headquarters in that place. Just before our party searched the town, they were discovered by some of the Guerrilla scouts, who immediately fled to the town, and by the time our command arrived there, they had barricaded the doors and were seen on the housetops, ready to give them a street fight.

The Company of Dragoons charged up into the streets and gave them a volley, and then dismounted. The Dragoons and Riflemen then broke into the houses and were soon on the housetops, and our Riflemen, many of them firing good shots, picked off the Mexicans as they were wont to do squirrels in their own native woods of the far West.

In a very short time the Mexicans retreated to their church, and Captain [Charles F.] Ruff of the Rifles, who was in command, sent back to camp for a piece of Artillery, supposing that the Mexicans would hold out for some time, having a strong position. A piece of Artillery and the Rifle Regiment was sent to reinforce him, but, before they reached there, Captain Ruff had driven them from the Church, and they had fled to the mountains.

We had one man wounded, none killed. The Mexicans are supposed to have lost some thirty killed and wounded. The number of Guerrillas was supposed to have been about fifty, but there were a large number of inhabitants also armed, and they took an active part in the affray. Our party brought in two Priests as prisoners of war, but I understand that they deny having anything to do with the affair. They say that they had not the power of preventing the Guerrillas and the inhabitants of the town from occupying the Church. I presume they will be allowed to *depart in peace*.

Our *Allies*, I understand, plundered to a very great extent. They are a *finished* set of scoundrels, and nothing pleases them more than to have a chance of plundering their own people. The best thing that has occurred for some time is a little circumstance that took place a few days since. It appears that a courier of General [Valentín] Canalizo's was captured a few days since, and, in his possession, was found an order from the General to a Guerilla Chief to take any horses that he might require for the [use] of his party. This *order* was turned over to the *Chief* of our Allies, and I have no doubt but that he will make *good use* of it. The planters are already complaining of the depredations committed by them (our Allies), and I have no doubt they have good reason for so doing, for they will not hesitate a moment to take anything that they may fancy, more particularly a fine horse.

Saturday, July 31st, 1847. Today I was ordered to take up a position with my Company at the Hacienda of Becencio, about two miles and a half from camp, for the purpose of preventing depredations from being committed on the establishment. I spent quite a pleasant day. It is a large hacienda, and I should judge the proprietor was a man of great wealth. On this plantation is a very neat Church, built, I presume, for the use of his servants. I also noticed a school room, in which were a large number of children. They were, I presume, the children of his peons.

Sunday, August 1st, 1847. We are still in camp and anxiously awaiting the arrival of General Pierce with his command. General Smith has sent down a squadron of Dragoons to Perote and a wagon for the mail, and we expect by tomorrow evening to receive letters from our dear wives and sweethearts. If only we can get our letters, it is all we care for.

Monday, August 2nd, 1847. A report came here last evening that General Pierce's command had *at last* reached Perote. We hope that he will reach our camp this evening so that we may leave for Puebla in the morning, for we are becoming *somewhat tired* of our camp. We are expecting every moment for the Dragoons to arrive with the mail. "Oh" what pleasure I anticipate in receiving letters from my beloved wife. Indeed, it is the only pleasure I have, separated as I am from all that are dear to me in this life.

But my spirits are kept up with the hope that my life has not been spared me through so many scenes of danger without having something good in store for me, and I hope that it may be that I am *once* more to see my dear, dear wife and my dear little daughter. If that is only granted me, I will consider all the fatigue and danger I have passed through in the last few years as a *mere nothing*.

I have learned in the last eight or ten months to bear the ills of this life with some little fortitude, and have come to the conclusion that whatever ill befalls me is intended for my good, and I have therefore determined to take the *ups* and *downs* of the life *coolly*, believing, as *I do*, that what is to *happen, will happen*, let us do as we will. The ends of Providence must and will be carried out, and we poor mortals cannot prevent it, let us fret and chafe as we may under our misfortunes.

The mail arrived at 4 o'clock this afternoon, and it is impossible to conceive the pleasure it gave me on receiving a letter from my beloved wife. "Oh," what a pleasure it is to learn that those who are dearer to you than all the world are well. It fills one's heart with joy and makes him feel like a *different* man. We leave tomorrow morning for Puebla. General Pierce will reach our present encampment tomorrow evening.

Tuesday, August 3rd, 1847. We left at 3 o'clock this morning and, after quite a pleasant march of twelve miles, encamped at La Penal, the same ground we encamped on as we marched down. We arrived at our encamping ground about 9 o'clock a.m.

Wednesday, August 4th, 1847. Reveille beat this morning at half past 1 o'clock, and the advance left at 3 o'clock. Our Regiment composed part of the rear guard and did not get off until near 4 o'clock. We marched today twenty-seven miles, and arrived at Puebla about 4 o'clock p.m. On our arrival we found that Lieutenant [John H.] Hill of the 2nd Dragoons had died while we were absent. He had been sick for some weeks, and, when we left Puebla, it was thought he would recover.

[No entry for Thursday, August 5th, 1847.]

Friday, August 6th, 1847. Tomorrow we are to leave Puebla for the *City* of *Mexico*, and I cannot think of leaving it without mentioning something about the beauties of the place.

The City of Puebla contains between sixty and eighty thousand souls. The first object that would strike a stranger upon his arrival in Puebla would be the Cathedral. This is a splendid building and does great credit to the City. I can never forget my feelings the first night I arrived in the City, when looking at this magnificent building by moonlight, and for the first time since my arrival in the country did I feel as if I was in a *land* where there was anything worth *traveling* so far to see. But, I must confess, that *I almost persuaded* myself that I had been pretty much repaid for my long march, in beholding so fine a piece of Architecture.

The inside of the Cathedral is really magnificent, and the organ is far superior to anything of the kind I have ever listened to. There is a tradition among the Mexicans that this church was built in a single night by Angels. There is a picture in the Palace representing two angels, descending with the Church, while two angels are measuring the foundation with a measuring tape, upon which the Church is to be placed.

In Puebla there are two Alamedas [tree-lined streets]. The one in the west part of the City is a lovely spot for promenading. Nearly every evening there are to be seen hundreds of citizens, both on foot and horseback, enjoying themselves among flowers, and a large number of beautiful fountains that are scattered over the whole ground.

There are a large number of fine buildings in Puebla, and many fine Churches independent of the Cathedral. The only things that the houses require to make them very comfortable are fireplaces.

The market at Puebla is a very fine one. In it you can purchase all kinds of vegetables, and those of the finest kind, and all of the tropical fruits. The meats are to be found in the meat shops and are generally very good. The country around Puebla is a lovely one, and very fertile, producing fine wheat, corn, barley, and Lucerne [alfalfa].

Our Regiment was quartered in the Concordia Convent. This Convent is under the charge of a Padre by the name of [Joaquin] Furlong, a very intelligent and, I have no doubt, a very pious man. He was very kind and polite to the officers of my Regiment, and the old gentleman appears to dislike parting with us very much. His kindness will be long remembered by us all.

Saturday, August 7th, 1847. The 2nd Division, composed of the Rifle Regiment, 1st Artillery, 3rd Infantry, 4th Artillery, 2nd Infantry, and 7th Infantry, under the command of General Twiggs, left this morning for the City of Mexico. The Division formed on the street on which General Scott was quartered, a little before 7 o'clock a.m., and, after giving three cheers, wheeled into sections and marched off, the bands and field music playing "*Yankee Doodle*."

After a march of some ten or eleven miles, we encamped at "Rio Prieto," about 10 o'clock p.m. The road today was a good one. The valley we are now in is certainly a lovely one. The road passes in a short distance of Popocatepetl and Iztaccihuatl mountains. It may have been my imagination, but I certainly thought that those two snow mountains looked more beautiful than I had seen them before.

Sunday, August 8th, 1847. We left our encampment this morning a short time after daylight. Our march today was through a lovely valley. We passed on either side of the road some of the finest estates I have seen since my arrival in the country. The crops of all kinds look well, and I have no doubt that this is among the finest farming land in this country.

We arrived at San Martin about 10 o'clock. Some of the troops were quartered in the town. Our regiment encamped just on the suburbs of it. San Martin contains some fifteen hundred inhabitants. There are several churches in it. The surrounding country is a lovely one.

Monday, August 9th, 1847. Started this morning about 5 o'clock and found it quite *cold*, but after the sun rose it became quite pleasant. Today we passed several large and pleasant plantations. On one of the farms, I saw some eighteen or twenty double ploughs at work, and it brought to mind some of those large farms on the Rappahannock River.

We commenced today ascending the mountains, and in a few days, I presume, we will have the pleasure of beholding the Valley in which the City of Mexico is situated. Our march today was a short one, not more than seven or eight miles. We encamped at the small village of Tesmeleos about 10 o'clock a.m.

Tuesday, August 10th, 1847. Left our encampment this morning shortly after daylight. Our road today was over the mountains, and a lovely mountain road it is. The growth of timber upon the mountains is generally pine, interspersed here and there with oak timber.

We passed Rio Frio early in the day. At this point the Mexicans had thrown up several breastworks on the heights commanding the road, but they had not the courage to defend them. This pass would be a difficult one to turn, if it was defended by a resolute army.

At this point we passed over a delightful stream of water, which flows from the foot of the snow mountains. At Rio Frio there is a ranch. The owner of it is a Dutchman. Some of the officers who stopped there a short time procured some very nice *butter* and other *little* delicacies.

At this place there had been sent cards by the different boarding-house keepers in the City of Mexico, to be distributed among the officers of the Army, stating in what part of the City their respective boarding-houses were situated. We marched today about seventeen miles and encamped a short distance from a Ranch called Cadova. Our encampment was situated on a ridge which overlooked the beautiful valley in which the City of Mexico is situated. We reached our encampment about 3 o'clock this evening.

Wednesday, August 11th, 1847. We did not leave our encampment this morning until 11 o'clock, as we did not intend marching more than five or six miles. Our march today was through a lovely piece of country. On either side of the road were to be seen fine crops of corn and other grain crops.

We encamped about 3 o'clock at the small village of Ayotla, where we expect to remain a day or two for the purpose of reconnoitering the pass of El Pinon, where, it is said, there are some *fifteen* thousand of the enemy. [El Pinon] is said to be eight miles from this village, and eight miles from the City of Mexico.

Thursday, August 12th, 1847. Today we remained in camp. Some of our Engineers (escorted by the 4th Artillery) left this morning for purpose of reconnoitering the pass of El Pinon. They returned late this evening, and the Engineers report it as being a *very strong* position. Generals Worth and Quitman have arrived with their respective commands and will be placed in position, I presume, in a few days.

Friday, August 13th, 1847. Our Brigade left his morning for the purpose of covering our Engineers while they reconnoiter the works at El Pinon. I did not accompany my Regiment, having been detailed on a commission for the trial of several men belonging to the Division, who had been charged with *stealing hogs*.

The command returned about 8 o'clock p.m. on the same evening. The pass of El Pinon is reported to be a *second Gibraltar. I presume* the Commanding General will have other points reconnoitered ere he determines at what point he will enter the City.

Saturday, August 14th, 1847. We are still in camp at Ayotla. No order yet has been issued in relation to a move. I presume in the course of the day something definite will be determined upon as to what point we will attack. We have just heard that Lieutenant Schuyler Hamilton of the 1st Infantry, who is an acting aide of General Scott's, while absent a short distance from Camp, on duty, was charged upon by a party of Guerillas and received a severe wound, the lance entering his body just under the shoulder blade. The wound is said to be a dangerous one. Lieutenant Hamilton had an escort of Dragoons with him. They soon put the Guerillas to flight, killing and wounding several of them.

I saw Major Bainbridge today, and he informed me that Major [John B.] Clark of the 1st Infantry had transferred with Major [William R.] Jowett of our Regiment which I was delighted to hear.* Bainbridge hopes to transfer with Major [Ephraim K.] Barnum. I hope the transfer will be made, for we will then have added to our Regiment two very interesting ladies. (*[Later footnote:] I regret to say that the transfers did not take place.)

Sunday, August 15th, 1847. We remained in camp today. General Scott has determined to leave with the whole Army early in the morning for the other side of the City, and from that point we expect to enter the City.

Monday, August 16th, 1847. We left our encampment at Ayotla early this morning and had not marched more than three miles, before we discovered a large body of Cavalry, a short distance from the road on our left. We immediately moved in the direction of them with our Division, and as soon as they discovered our movement, they commenced moving off in an opposite direction. We gave them a round or two from our Light Batteries, and they soon took to their *heels.* We killed one or two of them and several horses. We marched about seven miles and encamped about half past 12 o'clock at a small village called Chalco. The other Divisions of the Army had left that place the day before.

Tuesday, August 17th, 1847. We left Chalco this morning a short time after daylight. Last evening a short time after getting into camp, my Company was detailed to take up a position on the right of Captain [Frank] Taylor's Light Battery, for the purpose of supporting it, should it be necessary. The road today we found not very good. We passed through several *very fine* plantations. I saw some of the finest crops of corn today that I have seen since my arrival in this part of Mexico.

We marched today about eight miles and encamped in the small village of Teyahualco. Our encampment today was in a grove of olive trees. The trees were very large and are said to be very valuable. Some of them are said to be more than *two hundred years* old. We were told that many of the trees yielded as much as two hundred dollars a piece. We passed through two or three small villages today, all of which presented a miserable appearance. We did not get into camp today until near sundown.

Wednesday, August 18th, 1847. We started this morning a little after 7 o'clock. We had not marched over a mile or two before the rear of our column was fired upon by a small party of Guerillas. They took very good care, though, not to come near enough to do us any injury. Some of our Riflemen endeavored to get a shot at them, but I believe they proved rather too cunning for them.

The road today was a very bad one. It was as much as we could do to get our Artillery over it. We had quite a hard rain early in the day, which made the road much worse than it would otherwise have been. We arrived at the small village of [Xochimilco] about 4 o'clock p.m.

I was very much distressed upon my reaching there, to hear that my friend Captain [Seth] Thornton of the 2nd Dragoons had been killed early in the day by a cannon ball, while on a reconnoitering expedition in the neighborhood of San Antonio. He was a gallant and noble fellow, and his death will be mourned by all of his brother officers.

It is thought by many that we will have pretty hot work of it, ere we get into the City, as there are several works between this point and the City.

This prediction soon proved correct. In the center of the next day's battlefield would be an inhospitable waste called El Pedregal. Its appearance suggested that a three-by-five-mile stony disc had broken away from the moon and crashed into Central Mexico. The Pedregal had, however, come from within the earth: it comprised a vast area of "volcanic scroriae," cut with fissures and strewn with dark, honeycombed, igneous rocks.

To the Pedregal's east, the Acapulco Causeway ran north from the village of San Augustin to the strongly fortified towns of San Antonio and Churubusco before entering the Mexican capital. West from San Augustin a rough road lost itself in the Pedregal before reaching a better road that ran north along the western side of the Pedregal to the village of San Angel and Mexico City. South of San Angel this western road ended at a village called Contreras. To Craig and most other Americans, Contreras, though untouched by the fighting, would give its name to the coming battle; the Mexicans would more accurately call the battlefield Padierna, after a small ranch compound north of Contreras where the engagement would actually occur.

<u>*LSC*</u>

Thursday, August 19th, 1847. We left our encampment about 7 o'clock this morning, and after a short march came to the town of San Augustin. Here we were ordered to leave our wagons and take with us two days' provisions. General Pillow's Division was ordered to clear a road in the direction of San Angel, and our Division (Twiggs') was ordered to cover his working party. We left San Augustin a little after 12 o'clock, and a little after 2 o'clock the enemy opened a fire on us from their works at [Padierna].

The enemy's defensive works were beyond Padierna, which, according to the contemporary map based on surveys by Engineer Lee and others, was a small ranch composed of a rectangular fenced (or walled) area, such as a corral, with an adjacent structure, probably an adobe house (as Craig later suggests), and some type of shed or small stable. As described below, the cornfield occupied by the riflemen appears on the map, with thc ranch and the ravine beyond between it and the high ground where the enemy's fortified artillery positions were located. The infantry passed to the right of Magruder, unseen by the Mexicans because of the rugged terrain, and entered the church described in the village of San Geronimo, about a mile northwest of Magruder's position.

<u>*LSC*</u>

Soon after the enemy commenced firing, Captain Magruder was ordered to take up a position in about 800 or 900 yards from the enemy's works with his Light Battery. At the same time, the Rifle Regiment was deployed in a corn field in front of [Padierna] and engaged the enemy's light troops, while the other Regiments crossed a ravine which lay between us and [the Mexican works] and occupied a church in a short distance of the enemy's works. A short time after the firing commenced, I was ordered with three companies of the 3rd Infantry ("A," "E," and "I") to support Captain Magruder's battery.

On reaching the Battery, I found that it was very much cut up, Captain Magruder having lost one officer (Lieutenant Johnston) and several men and a large number of his horses. It is not necessary, in this journal, to enter into the particulars of what occurred through the day, as the different *reports will, I hope*, give a *true* and *correct* account of all that transpired.

———

LSC

[Excerpts from Craig's after-action report appear below:]

Agreeably to instructions received…on the morning of the 19th…, I repaired with three companies (A, E, and I), of the 3rd Infantry, numbering five officers and about one hundred men, to support Captain Magruder's light battery, which had taken position at about eight hundred yards from the enemy's works…. The captain…requested me to make such a disposition of my command as I thought best, for supporting him, which I did, by placing them a short distance in front. In this position we remained for the day, the enemies' batteries keeping up a constant fire upon Captain Magruder's battery, which was so cut up as to be as not to be able to do much execution, but fired through the day whenever an opportunity offered for annoying the enemy.

———

Thomas Jackson was among Magruder's subalterns. His biographer, G. F. R. Henderson, notes that in this case, "the Mexican artillery was far superior, both in number of pieces and weight of metal." Before Magruder's battery was withdrawn, "fifteen gunners and as many horses had been killed." Among the dead was John Preston Johnston (West Point, 1843), the nephew of Lt. Joseph E. Johnston; Johnston's gun was "taken and served" by Jackson after the young man fell.

General Franklin Pierce of the Volunteers was unhorsed at Padierna, and his mediocre war history later came to be a threat to his presidential ambitions in 1852. Some of his protégés came to his defense in print, but, more important, his good friend Nathanael Hawthorne wrote a dignified campaign biography of Pierce that placed his part in the battle in the most favorable light.

———

LSC

A short time after dark, Lieutenant [Edward H.] Fitzgerald, of the

6th Infantry, aid-de-camp of General [Franklin] Pierce, reported to me that a portion of that brigade were in a house a short distance in front of me, and surrounded by the enemy. I immediately consulted with Captain Magruder as to the propriety of taking a portion of my command to their relief; and, on being informed that one company would be sufficient to protect the battery, proceeded with two companies (A and E) to their relief.

On approaching the house, I discovered that it was occupied by Mexicans, who at first fire deserted it. After an examination of the premises, I found three wounded Americans, who were taken to the battery. On this occasion, one Mexican was killed.

After my return to the battery, Captain Magruder informed me that he had received order to retire with his battery out of range of the enemy's shot, and that he wished me to bring up the rear with my command. We left at a late hour, and owing to the darkness of the night and bad state of the road (it having rained all night) we progressed but a short distance before daylight overtook us.

A short timc after daylight, we met the 9th Regiment advancing, and I was informed by an officer, whom I took to be a field officer, that my command was to return and take up a position near the enemy's works, to make a diversion in support of the assaulting party.

Owing to the bad state of the road, many of my men were detached from their companies, assisting the batteries, and some time elapsed before the order to return was communicated....

I returned and took up my former position, and ordered my men to wipe out their guns and reload them. On reconnoitering, I found a large body of Mexicans occupying the same house I had driven them from the night before. I then determined, as soon as I found the storming army approaching the opposite side of the enemy's works, to open a fire upon those that occupied the house, thinking it might, in addition to driving them from it, draw the fire from their batteries, which I succeeded in doing. After firing a few rounds, we charged down upon the house, accompanied by a detachment of the rifles.

We drove the enemy from the house, pursued them down the ravine below the work, killing a great number and capturing some twenty-eight or thirty of them. After turning over the prisoners I had captured, I joined my regiment at San Angel.

Mexican after-action reports and memoirs would show that General Valencia, having disobeyed Santa Anna's orders to fall back closer to Churubusco, had satisfied himself that the fight of August 19 had been a great victory and that the Americans had withdrawn. Dreaming that he might replace Santa Anna, Valencia and his men (some of whom he promoted and decorated) spent the night carousing, as the Mexican band derisively played "Yankee Doodle" and "Hail, Columbia." They were thus quite unprepared when the American assault hit them the next morning and drove them in the direction that Santa Anna had earlier ordered them to go.

In his own report of the two battles, Craig's commanding officer, Capt. E. B. Alexander, confirmed Craig's account with some detail, and added a brief account of what happened at Churubusco:

On an intimation of General [Persifor] Smith, commanding the brigade, to bring the 3rd Infantry into action, it was moved forward, and occupied this [western] line, from which the regiment poured in a brisk and effective fire upon the enemy, who was not, until now, discovered to be strongly entrenched [before a fortified convent]. The regiment was hotly engaged for, I think, about an hour and a half, at the end of which time the enemy's position was carried by a charge. In this closing scene of the fight, it was the good fortune of my regiment to be the first to cross the enemy's lines and display its colors upon his walls.

Closing, Alexander wrote,

> [As] the regiment, during the greater part of the time was immediately under the eye of the general commanding the brigade, I feel sure that he will understand how difficult it is for me to discriminate in the conduct of my officers, when all were uniformly gallant. I cannot, however, omit to mention Captain Craig, an officer habitually gallant in action as he is zealous and untiring in the discharge of his public duties generally. He received a severe wound in the action at Churubusco.

In early September, Craig concluded his Mexico journal:

LSC

I will further state, though, that our troops carried [the Mexican position at Padierna] early on the morning of the *20th of August, 1847*, with very little loss to our troops, but killing and wounding a large number of the enemy. After routing the enemy at this point, we pursued them in the direction of the City, and, on arriving at Churubusco, we found the greater part of the Mexican Army occupying a Convent or Church, besides several works in this vicinity.

The fight commenced at this point about 2 o'clock p.m. and lasted for some hours, and, I can truly say, that I have never heard heavier firing in my life. At this fight our Army lost several of its finest officers, but Victory in the end "perched upon our Standard," and we drove the enemy from their different works, killing and wounding a large number of them and taking a large number of prisoners. In this fight, your humble servant received a severe wound. Sometime between the evening of the *20th* and morning of the *21st of August, 1847*, an Armistice was entered into between the two Armies, and hostilities ceased until the morning of the *8th of September, 1847*, when we made an attack upon Molino del Rey. At this fight we lost a large number of officers and men and killed, wounded, and captured a large number of the enemy, and drove the enemy into their works at Chapultepec.

Craig's Mexican War Journal ends here, and the war itself would soon conclude. The armistice mentioned by Craig was quite unpopular with many in the army, who rightly assumed that Santa Ann would use the time to rest his men and reinforce his positions, which he did. He also marched east and besieged the U.S. garrison at Puebla. The siege wasn't broken until mid-October when American reinforcements arrived from Vera Cruz. At Puebla the Mexican army would later defeat the French decisively on May 5, 1862.

Santa Anna had lost for the time being, but he would continue to be a major figure in Mexican history for decades to come. His many haciendas would pass out of his possession over the years, however, as his fortunes ebbed. In his last days "he resigned himself to waiting for death in anonymity, condemned to penury and oblivion." The republic whose army had defeated him in 1848 was preparing for its 100th birthday when Santa Anna died on June 21, 1876.

Mexico City fell to the U.S. army in mid-September 1848. The fortress of Chapultepec was bombarded September 12 and taken the next day. As the American flag was run up the mast over the captured citadel, thirty men of the San Patricio Battalion, captured at Churubusco, were hanged by Col. Harney on Gen. Scott's orders. These Catholic Irishmen, allies of the Mexicans, were U.S. army deserters who taken part against their former comrades in almost every battle of the war. After taking Chapultepec, the U.S. forces stormed the Belen Gate, a principal entry into Mexico City, and the capital was occupied September 14.

Early that day, after the "scruffy band of conquerors, bloodstained and ragged," filed into the Grand Plaza, the American flag was run up the mast of the National Palace. Gen. Scott, "astride a magnificent bay charger," and "resplendent in his full-dress uniform" appeared an hour later. According to tradition, this was the moment when, passing before the Third Regiment, he said to his staff escort, "Gentlemen, take off your hats to the Old Guard of the Army."

Sadly, the Old Guard was not allowed to rest on its laurels that night or the night of the September 15. On leaving the city, Santa Anna had loosed two thousand convicts into the city (possibly joined by as many former soldiers), and anarchy reigned for two days and nights. During that period the Third Regiment had a dozen men killed (or mortally wounded) and forty-eight men injured. Casualties for the "Old Guard" for the entire war had been fifty-two killed (including six officers) and 140 wounded (including seven officers). Totals for the regulars were 585 killed, 425 died of wounds, 4,899 dead of disease, and 2,745 wounded. Mexican army deaths alone "exceeded 10,000."

Among the wounded officers, Craig would remain in Mexico City until late March 1848, although he was able to move around the city to some extent. He took the opportunity to purchase gifts for his family, including a necklace with a beautiful silver cross for Elizabeth. Also, on October, 13, 1847, he became member number 36 of the 160 original members of the Aztec Club of 1847, an organization of Mexican War officers, with Gen. John A. Quitman, a former Whig governor of Mississippi, as president, and John B. Magruder as one of the vice-presidents.

Patterned after the Society of the Cincinnati, then in its sixty-fourth year, the Aztec Club adopted both the Cincinnati's principle of hereditary membership and a similar eagle badge. As noted by one historian, the members included "most of the major figures in the Mexican War army and a large group whose fame would come a decade and a half later as leaders of the Union and Confederate armies in the struggle of 1861–1865."

Craig would be reunited with his Elizabeth and Sallie in Athens in April 1848, during home leave that would last until mid-September of the same year. By this time, he had received news that he and his fellow Virginian officers and men had been honored by the Virginia General Assembly. According to the unanimous resolution, thanks were rendered to Gen. Taylor and his "officers and soldiers" of the commonwealth for their "skill, courage, gallantry, and patriotism." General Taylor and two field grade officers were also voted swords. Perhaps disagreeably to Craig and the U.S. army regulars, swords were also voted to the company officers of the Virginia volunteer regiment.

More important in terms of Craig's military career, his service in the Mexican War led to his being honored with two brevets: the first to major on May 12, 1848, "for gallant and meritorious conduct in the several conflicts at Monterrey," and the second to lieutenant colonel on August 25, 1848, "for gallant and meritorious conduct in the Battles of Contreras and Churubusco." Both commissions bore the signatures of President James Knox Polk and Secretary of War William L. Marcy. In the usage of the time, the second honor qualified him to sign himself as "Brevet Lieutenant Colonel" and to be addressed as "Colonel."

Even more personal honors were yet to come to Craig, along with one last adventure. Ironically, that adventure would be born of the peace that ended the war.

While Craig was spending his first Fourth of July back in the United States since 1845, President Polk was officiating at the cornerstone laying of the long-delayed Washington Monument. Shortly after Polk returned to the Executive Mansion, "an army surgeon, weary and disheveled, appeared…with dispatches from Mexico. In his pouch was the treaty of peace between the United States and Mexico, bearing the long-awaited ratification by the Mexican Congress."

The Treaty of Guadalupe Hidalgo ended the U.S.-Mexican War but entirely pleased no one in either country. Although through its terms Polk did decisively add Alta [Upper] California, Texas, and the territory between them to the United States, he and many other Democrats, mindful of the war's cost in blood and treasure, wanted more Mexican land to the south, perhaps to include Baja [lower] California and the territory southward to Monterrey. Some demanded "All of Mexico."

The Whigs, who had opposed the war (as well as the idea of Manifest Destiny), also opposed the U.S. acquiring any territory. Many Northern Whigs saw the conflict as a plot to expand slavery although few slaves were ever to enter the territory. Indeed, in 1848 Gen. Taylor, a slave-owner, would lead the Whigs to victory in the presidential election of 1848.

According to the treaty's terms, the U.S. also paid Mexico $15 million and dropped $3 million in claims by U.S. citizens against Mexico. The United States received over 500,000 sparsely populated square miles of Mexico's territory, containing "less than 1 percent of its citizens."

But two other treaty articles would have the greatest effect on the future of Lewis Craig: Article Five established that a Joint Mexican-American Commission would survey the new border between the two countries. And, adding quite a complication to the coming boundary survey, Article 11 made the United States responsible for protecting Mexico from the "savage tribes" inhabiting the ceded territory.

Chapter 5

To the Pacific

> They turned their tragic mounts to the west and they rode infatuate and half fond toward the red demise of that day, toward the evening lands and the distant pandemonium of the sun.
>
> —Cormac McCarthy, *Blood Meridian, or The Evening Redness in the West*

Unlucky from the start, Commissioner John Russell Bartlett's Mexican Boundary Survey began with a crippling misconception and proceeded through a series of desolating disappointments to tragedy and ultimate failure.

At the outset, however, heading the commission's military escort had seemed an enviable assignment to Lewis Craig. The two years preceding this 1850 posting had arguably been the most fulfilling and pleasant of his life, though he had spent the early months slowly regaining his health. He had continued to recuperate in Mexico City until early April 1848, when an army surgeon reported that his gunshot wound of August 1847 had again assumed "an unhealthy appearance" and threatened to reopen—he recommended a return "forthwith" to the "more salubrious climate of the United States," which might enable Craig to return to duty in five months. Consequently, Maj. Gen. William O. Butler ordered Craig's return to Athens, where he reported himself arrived in mid-May 1848. Although happily reunited with his wife and child, he saw his condition worsen.

Soon after his return to Athens, an august twenty-man committee of his "Fellow Citizens" expressed a wish to make "some suitable manifestations" of their "sense of [Craig's] gallantry and arduous military services" through a "public dinner." They were disappointed to find that his health would not permit him to join them.

Nonetheless, their exchange of letters was published in a local newspaper, along with Craig's regrets. His letter closed, "To have our conduct approved by our friends is at all times pleasing; but, situated as I am, to have so great an expression of good feeling evinced towards me, is, I assure you, one of the greatest compliments that could have been paid."

The editor of a Fredericksburg newspaper, reprinting this exchange, recalled that he had visited Florida during the war and seen Craig there. The young lieutenant had then "signalized himself as an active officer," the journalist wrote. Observing Craig in camp, he recalled, he "found him the same kind-hearted, noble, and generous fellow that he had ever shown himself when a plain citizen of this community"—a community, he noted, where "four-fifths of our readers" know him "personally."

Examined by an Athens doctor in June, the wound was little better: the "surface of the orifice" was "in a chronic state of inflammation," and the "skin of the cicatrice" was in such a "delicate condition" that "the slightest pressure from clothing" might "reawaken the diseased action." The doctor prescribed "exemption from duty for several months."

Nonetheless, Craig requested to rejoin his regiment on July 31, 1848, hoping "to be able to wear [his] uniform coat" by the end of the next month. He returned to duty first at Jefferson Barracks and then east of Biloxi at Camp Jefferson Davis, in East Pascagoula, Mississippi, before being ordered to recruiting service in mid-September 1848. He was to report after another leave in mid-October 1848 to New York City, where he would remain on recruiting service until November 1850.

During leave in early October 1848, Craig was finally able to accompany Elizabeth to Fredericksburg and introduce her to both friends and relatives and to show her the scenes of his youth. And there was also an invitation from twelve gentlemen of the town (including Hugh Mercer Patton, who had witnessed Craig's oath in 1837) to a public dinner in his honor. One tribute noted,

> It is with sincere gratification we welcome your return to this place, eleven years since you left us to engage in the hazardous conflict with the Florida Indians. The Mexican War succeeded, marked by deeds of prowess and gallantry unparalleled upon the page of history. The brilliant victories at Resaca, Palo Alto, Monterrey, Vera Cruz, Contreras and Churubusco thrilled every American heart....

When rumor reached us that these battles had been fought and won, the enquiry among your friends ever was, "What part did Craig have in them?" The reply was that "He was always in the post of danger, that, where duty called there he was, often in the foremost of the battle, reckless of any impulses save the success and glory of the American Army."

You bear upon your person the evidence of your gallantry; the severe wound you received at the hard-fought battle of Churubusco is an additional testimonial to that uncalculating courage which those who have known you since your boy-hood knew that you possessed.

Craig's appreciation of these words may only be imagined, but it is certain that he was able to translate his military experiences and unselfish service successfully into the responsibility of recruiting his shattered regiment back to full strength. In the Eastern Department of the Recruiting Service, which included the major eastern urban areas, Craig's station in Brooklyn, at the second Fort Hamilton in his career, routinely led the others in the number of men recruited per month.

Named for General Alexander Hamilton, the fort occupied someone hundred rugged acres on the southwestern shore of Long Island and commanded the Narrows with its artillery. In the early 1840s, Engineer Robert Lee had spent "five drab years" at the fort, involved in renovations there and at the cluster of other forts that guarded New York harbor.

Inside the fort, the quarters for the officers and men were located in the structure's stone casemates, although there were a few inferior one-story frame houses for the officers as well. As a recruiting officer, Craig presumably lived at the fort although, when his wife came to visit, they sometimes lived together at the Hotel Irving on Gramercy Park, about a mile from General Scott's residence, unless they took rooms somewhere in the village adjacent to the fort, also called Fort Hamilton, where Elizabeth made several friends.

While at Fort Hamilton, Craig, as a longtime reader of Richmond's *Southern Literary Messenger*, probably noted an article in the November 1849 issue regarding the "untimely death," as well as the genius and legacy, of Edgar Allan Poe. The previous October the multitalented author, who had contributed to the periodical's "earliest celebrity," had died in mysterious circumstances in Baltimore, Maryland.

Chosen for reprinting in the *Messenger* was Poe's "The Bells," with its troubling third stanza describing the brazen alarm bells, perhaps too evocative for fire-haunted Richmonders: "What a tale of terror, now, their turbulency tells! / In the startled ear of night / How they scream out their affright! / Too much horrified to speak, / They can only shriek, shriek, / Out of tune, / In a clamorous appealing to the mercy of the fire, / In a mad expostulation with the deaf and frantic fire, / Leaping higher, higher, higher…."

By December 1849, Craig seemed fully recovered from his wound. Returning from a visit south, Elizabeth was met by her husband in Philadelphia. She thought "he never looked in finer health" and had "a wondrous big moustache which gives him a very fierce appearance." She joked in a letter to a friend that in New York the couple had already become "very dissipated"—"last week we were invited out for every evening in the week, although we did not accept all of them."

One such invitation the Craigs would not be expected to decline. Gen. Winfield Scott, deploring Washington City and its politicians, had made New York his headquarters. In early 1849 at their hotel, the Craigs received a brief note from the general:

> My dear Colonel:
> Mrs. Scott joins me in requesting you and Mrs. Craig to dine with us, socially, tomorrow, at 5 o'clock.
> Yours truly,
> Winfield Scott

The officers no doubt enjoyed each other's company. And such occasions no doubt made Craig, as one of Gen. Scott's many admirers, feel honored. To Adj. Gen. Jones he would early the next year quote the compliment to Scott of preeminent Whig leader Henry Clay ("the greatest statesman now living," according to Craig), who had said that the general stood "unrivalled by Cortez himself, or any other commander in ancient or modern times." And Mrs. Scott was no doubt delighted with Mrs. Craig, who was well known for being excellent company. As for her own husband, Mrs. Scott had described "ennui" as "a tallow candle, a game of whist, and General Scott."

Having returned to full health in New York City and come near the end of his recruiting duties, Craig readied himself for a return to his regiment. Although he had earlier sent a leave request to Adj. Gen. Jones, he withdrew it in June 1850, because of the "probability that the Regiment would take the field against the Indians in the course of the year." Other regiments had already been engaged in the Indian War across the Mississippi; it had begun in 1848 and would continue for decades. Although no one could have expected it at the time, the Old Guard would be engaged in fighting the New Mexico Indians until 1860.

When another opportunity suddenly arose—the chance to head the military escort of the commission that was to run the boundary line between Mexico and the vast territory to the north just won in the war—Craig arranged instead to secure that appointment. It may be that Mrs. Craig had some influence on this decision, perhaps thinking that such a posting would be somewhat less dangerous for her husband than campaigning against the Indians. In any case, Craig requested that his political ally, William Crosby Dawson, help him get the assignment, and it was done.

Senator Dawson was among those Georgians that Craig had met through his wife and in-laws. Of Virginia ancestry, but a native of Greene County, Georgia—south of and adjacent to Clarke County, location of Athens—Dawson had graduated from the University of Georgia in 1816 and then gone to the famous law school at Litchfield, Connecticut, founded by Tapping Reeve. He had served in the Georgia state legislature, had fought in the Creek War of 1836 (and been given a command by Winfield Scott), and had been a Georgia Superior Court judge. He had also represented Georgia in the U.S. House from 1836 to 1841 (concentrating on military affairs), and, finally, had become nationally known as one Georgia's U.S. senators, serving from 1849 to 1855.

In politics, Dawson was a confirmed Whig, so prominent that he had brought his fractious state party together to support William Henry Harrison in his successful run for president in 1840 and had helped carry Georgia for Zachary Taylor in 1848. Unlike many Whigs during 1846–1848, Dawson had "favored the war and territorial indemnity." With his congressional colleagues—Whig Alexander Stephens and Democrat Howell Cobb—Dawson had also supported Henry Clay's Compromise of 1850.

Like Adam Craig, Dawson was a devoted Mason; unlike him, he was "eminently social in his nature and habits." One can see Lewis Craig appreciating Dawson as he was described by one of his sons: William Dawson "was remarkably fond of the chase,—always kept a fine pack of foxhounds....He was the best rider I ever saw, and surpassed all his companions in his exploits upon the field with his horse and hounds."

As Craig's friend, Dawson had in 1850 miraculously solved (through personal contact with Adj. Gen. Jones) the back-pay problem that had festered since 1842. And now he had arranged for Craig to prove again his leadership ability in filling a responsible and somewhat delicate position that involved more civilians than soldiers, an assignment that also promised to be an interesting adventure into almost unknown territory. Incidentally, it would give Dawson the benefit of having Craig's opinion of the land to be surveyed, an area which Dawson and other Southern Whigs hoped would form the roadbed of a new railroad: a "ribbon of steel" that would connect the Southeast with the "'untold wealth of the Orient,' the Southwest, and the Pacific coast."

Following a short boat ride to Fort Wood on Bedloe's Island, where their steamer was docked, Craig and his men bid farewell to New York City. This star-fort, constructed of granite and bristling with eleven points, could mount seventy-seven guns and garrison 350 men. Almost four decades later, Fort Wood would be converted into the base for a pedestal on which would be mounted a colossal copper statue, a gift to America from the Republic of France, in honor of the winning alliance that had been formed by the two countries during the War for Independence.

Tasked with commanding the military escort of the U.S. Boundary Commission, Colonel Craig almost immediately saw problems with some of the personnel of the commission party. It was a fateful omen for what would be an ill-starred proceeding and appeared early in his journal of his journey to El Paso.

LSC

Notes of a march form New York to El Paso, Texas

A detachment of recruits numbering in all eighty-one, and two commissioned officers, Brevet 2nd Lt. [Frederick M.] Follett of the 3d Infantry, and Assistant Surgeon White, U.S.A., left under my command from Fort Wood, New York, for El Paso, Texas, on the evening of the 3rd of August, 1850 in the steamer Galveston, bound for Indianola, Texas. On this steamer was also a large number of individuals belonging to the U.S. Boundary Commission on their way to El Paso.

The steamer arrived at Key West on Monday the 12th of August about 10 o'clock a.m. and left about 5 o'clock the same evening. A large number of the members of the U.S. commission visited the town, and while there became very much intoxicated, and on their return to the steamer conducted themselves in the most outrageous manner, so much so, that some of them were compelled to be tied hand and foot.

The steamer arrived at the barracks a few miles below New Orleans on the morning of the 16th of August, 1850 (Friday) and left again for Indianola, Texas, on Sunday the 18th of August, 1850. My men were landed at the Barracks, where they remained, until the steamer returned from New Orleans and took them off. While at the Barracks I visited the City and dined with my friends Dr. McCormick and Capt. and Brevet Major [Albemarle] Cady of the Army at the St. Charles Hotel.

The steamer arrived at the town of Galveston on Tuesday the 20th at a ¼ past 4 o'clock and left on Wednesday 21st at 3 o'clock p.m. and arrived at Indianola on Thursday 22nd at 10 o'clock a.m.

Indianola, eight miles northeast of Corpus Christi, had been a major port and depot for the U.S. Army since the Mexican War. Of its several wharves jutting into Matagorda Bay, the "Government Wharf" (where Craig and his party disembarked) extended 250 feet to reach water almost seven feet deep. From the wharf's end, a narrow rail line stretched to the port's government warehouses; there the line's mule-drawn flat cars transported supplies as they were unloaded. The port, however, was doomed for destruction. Within three decades, hurricanes would annihilate Indianola, and its commerce would shift to nearby Port Lavaca.

From the time that the California Gold Rush had begun in mid-1848, soldiers and civilians had followed the road from Indianola to San Antonio and then west to El Paso and beyond, as Craig and his party, along with their train of wagons, would soon do.

LSC

Left Indianola for San Antonio on Thursday evening the *22nd of August 1850* at 6 o'clock p.m. and arrived at Chocolate Bayou about 11 o'clock the same night, distance from Indianola about 12 miles. While at Indianola I met with Capt. [Joseph L.] Coburn, who was at one time a captain in my Regiment. I had not had the pleasure of seeing him since he resigned in 1846. He is now a Government agent at Indianola, and I have no doubt an excellent one.

We left our encampment on the Chocolate at 6 o'clock p.m. on the evening of the *23rd of August*, and, after a march of *near* 20 miles, we arrived at our encampment on Alligator Lake about 3 o'clock in the morning. Our march was pretty much like the one from Indianola to the Chocolate, through a *hog wallow* prairie, only that we passed through a better wooded country, the growth generally blackjack.

Saturday, 24th August, 1850. We remained in camp today. We find that our Northern men are not able to make long marches in this warm climate, the command generally (like recruits) suffering much from sore feet. Up to this time, my command has enjoyed excellent health. We have at this time one man with the dysentery.

Sunday, 25th August, 1850. Left our encampment about ½ past 2 o'clock a.m. Arrived at the River Guadeloupe at 7 o'clock a.m. We were detained here until 9 o'clock a.m. crossing our wagons, which had to be done in a ferry boat. Before reaching the river, we passed several fine farms.

We saw large numbers of grouse and partridges. I *wished several times* that I had had a good gun and pointers. I think I should have been able to have killed grouse enough for my *whole* command. From the river we had five miles to march to our camp ground. We marched two miles thorough a very rich bottom, heavily timbered with the pecan. I should think that this bottom land would produce fine sugar and cotton.

After passing through the bottom land we came into a prairie about 2½ miles long. In crossing this prairie our men suffered very much from the heat. Recruit John Hynes died from a stroke of the sun, and was buried after getting into camp.

We encamped on Wright's Creek in a handsome grove of *blackjacks*. I am delighted to say, that we have had no mosquitoes at this encampment. The whole command was nearly *eaten up by them* at Alligator Lake. We marched today about 15 miles.

Monday, 26th August, 1850. We shall remain in camp until about 6 o'clock this morning, and march in the night, as I find that our men are not able to stand the sun. We left our encampment this evening at ½ past 6 o'clock. Our march was through a scrub oak country.

About four miles from Wright's Creek we found water. After that we found no water until we arrived at our encampment on the lower Coleto Creek. Although the creek was not running, still, we found the water very good. Beyond this creek about a ½ mile is another. If anything, the water is better than where we encamped. We arrived at our encampment about 1 o'clock a.m. Our march today was about 15 miles.

Tuesday, 27th August, 1850. Left our encampment a few minutes after 4 o'clock p.m. and arrived at our encampment about ½ past 10 o'clock p.m. We encamped near the house of a Mr. Ring on Coleto Creek. We marched today 15 miles. Near Mr. Ring's across the creek was a *grog shop*, and I am pleased to say that my men showed *much good taste* in not patronizing it.

We passed a house about five miles from our last encampment (I think a Mr. Peters resided there), when we found an excellent well of water, the best we had drunk since our arrival in Texas. The country we passed through on this day's march was very much like the country we marched over for the last day or two.

Wednesday, 28th August, 1850. Left our encampment this morning about ½ past 5 o'clock. Our march today was over a prairie country. We reached our encampment about ½ past 11 o'clock p.m. At this place we found the water *very scarce*. We had to pay the man who resided here fifty cents a load to haul water for us, and that not very good. We marched today about 12 miles. A man by the name of McTenall resides at this place. I do not think that I could be induced to purchase land in this part of Texas if I could get it at *six* cents an acre.

Thursday, 29th August, 1850. Left our encampment at ½ past 2 o'clock a.m. and arrived at our encampment on the Clado about a ¼ before 5 o'clock a.m. Here we found a plenty of water, and very good. A man by the name of Wilkerson resides here. We marched today about 12 miles. There is a great deal of sameness in all of this country: a great deal of prairie, with now and then a grove of post oaks. Today we passed a quantity of mesquite growth. It commenced raining about 3 o'clock this evening, and such a storm I had not seen for some time. When it commenced raining I was some distance from my tent, and I had just time to save it from being blown down, with the assistance of one of my men. I held it up, but my tent was pretty well flooded, and I was wet to the *skin*.

Friday, 30th August, 1850. Left our encampment about 2 o'clock a.m. We had not marched more than eight miles when it commenced raining, and I had the misfortune to be well drenched again ere the cloud passed over. We met a train of some 25 wagons from San Antonio going to Indianola. We met them four miles east of the Satilla River. We reached our encampment on the Satilla River about ¼ before 7 o'clock a.m.

We encamped near the house of a Mr. [Creed] Taylor, who is said to be the greatest Indian hunter in this section of Texas, having followed but a short time since a number of Indians to the mountains, and before returning home killed one and brought off his bow as a trophy.

Today we passed through quite a grove of post oaks, and near the river there is to be found mesquite in abundance. We are now in two miles of a fine sulphur spring. The water is said to be very strong of sulphur. We shall pass near it in the morning, and I will endeavor to stop a few minutes so that I may have an opportunity of judging of the strength of the water.

We have been very much disappointed on our march up to this point to find so little marketing. We have found chickens and eggs *very scarce*. We have been able to get a little venison now and then, and milk enough for our coffee.

I must confess, that I dislike Texas as much as Gen. Zachary Taylor did. Would to God we could get Mexico to take the country back again, and let us have the Sabine River as the line.

At the house of Mr. Taylor I saw two pretty fawns, and I wished *again and again* that I could have transported one to my dear little Sallie, who is so very fond of *pets*. This country is filled with all kinds of game.

The land in this portion of Texas does not produce as I supposed it did. I was informed that from six to seven bushels of corn was considered an average crop to an acre. They plant their corn about the first of February, and the May rains make it.

Charles H. Clarke, one of my men was absent today. He was seen a short time before we encamped. I fear that some of the men belonging to the train we met induced him to return to Indianola with them.

Saturday, 31st August, 1850. Left our encampment this morning a little before 2 o'clock a.m. The country we marched over was pretty much such as one we passed over the day before. Our command watered about five miles from where we encamped. The road at this point passes near the River Satilla, and is the only water to be found between that point and the River Salado excepting in wet weather, and then very good water can be found at the Live Oaks, about four miles from the above mentioned place.

We encamped at the Live Oaks today, but found scarcely water enough for our command, and that not very good. We marched today about 14 miles, and reached our encampment about ½ past 7 o'clock a.m.

Sunday, 1st September, 1850. Left our encampment about 10 minutes after 2 o'clock a.m. We are now in four miles of San Antonio. The country we marched over yesterday was pretty much like the country we passed over for the last four days. We have now passed over the best country in Texas, and I would not give *ten millions of dollars* for *the whole of Texas.* The State of Texas will be fortunate, *I think*, if the United States gives her ten millions for the most indifferent portion of her Territory.

Craig refers here to another border adjustment, part of the Compromise of 1850, which involved a Texas Cession to accompany the Mexican Cession. Texas claimed territory that ran as far north as Denver, as well as land west to the upper Rio Grande, including both Santa Fe and Albuquerque. Texas was to receive ten million dollars for giving up its land claims, so that the state could retire its public debt. This was not paid to Texas directly, however, and holders of Texas securities and bonds complicated the matter, so that the matter was not resolved until 1856.

LSC

Monday, 2nd September, 1850. Remained in camp today. Will leave early in the morning for Camp Worth [named in honor of Bvt. Maj. Gen. William J. Worth, who had died of cholera in San Antonio in May 1849], situated three miles above the town of San Antonio upon the San Antonio River. Majors [Edwin] Babbitt and [James] Belger, U.S.A., and Major [L. G.] Capers, Sutler of the 8th Infantry paid me a visit this morning.

Tuesday, 3rd September, 1850. Left this morning for the purpose of visiting the different camp grounds in the neighborhood of San Antonio. Went first to the old encampment of the 3d Infantry, a few miles above us on the Salado, and was so much pleased with it, that I determined to move up immediately, and did so early on the morning of the 4th. After visiting the encampment, I went into town, and spent the day. I dined with Gen. [John] Garland, and visited several of the ladies of the Army, and returned to camp about dusk.

Wednesday, 4th September, 1850. Left our encampment this morning about sunrise, and after a march of about two miles, reached our present encampment, which I shall call Camp Fillmore in honor of our excellent President [Millard Fillmore, who had become president at Zachary Taylor's sudden death in July 1850]. In a few hours after our arrival we were all well *fixed*, and I hope, in a few days, to have the camp in nice order.

Thursday, 5th September, 1850. Made a short visit to town this evening. Called on my friend Mrs. Hardee. Was delighted to find her doing so well, having but a short time since given birth to a child.

Friday, 6th September, 1850. Visited San Antonio this morning to dine with Lt. R. B. Garnett, who is the nephew of Gen. G. M. Brooke and his aide. Saw several of the officers of the Garrison but could not find time to visit the ladies. On my return to camp in the evening I met Mrs. Reeve and her husband Col. [I.V.D.] Reeve of the 8th Infantry, and a Miss Dashiel, the daughter of Paymaster [Jeremiah] Dashiel. They had been out to pay me a visit. I regretted very much my absence, and they promised to visit me again.

Saturday, 7th September, 1850. Remained in camp today. It rained for a short time this morning, but cleared up about 11 o'clock a.m.

Sunday, 8th September, 1850. Remained in camp. Lt. Follett and the Doctor rode into town this morning.

Monday, 9th September, 1850. I rode into town this morning for the purpose of reporting to Gen. Brooke, who arrived last evening from

Austin, and also to dine with Major Capers. I met at Major Capers,' Gen. Brooke; Col. Joseph E. Johnston of the Engineers; Lt. Garnett, aide to Gen. Brooke; Brevet Major [James] Longstreet of the 8th Infantry; and Dr. [J. J. B.] Wright, U.S.A., who messes with Major Capers. We had a delightful dinner, and I returned to camp about sundown.

While in town I called on several ladies. Had the pleasure of seeing only Mrs. Babbitt. She appears to be a fine woman. Major Edwin B. Babbitt, her husband, was at one time a Lieutenant in my Regiment, and, of course, we had a great deal to say about the *Old Third.*

Tuesday, 10th September, 1850. Remained in camp today. Nothing of interest transpired.

Wednesday, 11th September, 1850. Visited San Antonio today with the hope that I might find a letter in the P.O. from my dear wife, but I regret to say I was disappointed. Dined with Major Capers *as usual*, where I met Colonel Hardee, who had the evening before returned from a long scout.

Thursday, 12th September, 1850. Remained in camp today. In the evening we had a visit from Col. [John J.] Abercrombie of the 5th Infantry, Major Babbitt, Quartermaster, and Major Capers, post Sutler in San Antonio.

Friday, 13th September, 1850. Did not leave camp today. Wrote to my father-in-law, Dr. Alonzo Church, of Athens, Georgia, a long letter. I was quite surprised this evening to see Brevet Major W. S. Henry of my Regiment. He came through from El Paso in seventeen days, which is considered a very *quick* trip. I was under the impression that he would not be detailed for the recruiting service, owing to charges having been preferred against him. The court by which he was tried sentenced him to be suspended from rank and pay for six months, and to be reprimanded in General Orders; but the court recommended that so much of the sentence as related to six months' suspension be remitted. [William Seaton Henry (1816–1851) had published *Campaign Sketches of the War with Mexico* in 1847, one of a flood of memoirs that had followed the war. His rapid trip from El Paso to San Antonio ("the quickest trip ever made with wagons") was much celebrated.]

Saturday, 14th September, 1850. Visited San Antonio today. Just before reaching town, I met with Lt. [George C.] Barber of the 8th Infantry, who had arrived the evening before with a detachment of Recruits belonging to my command. He had encamped a few miles beyond me on the Salado and was on his way to report his arrival to Gen. Brooke. During the day they moved up to Camp Fillmore.

Sunday, 15th September, 1850. Today Lt. Barber turned over all the Recruits of the 3rd Infantry, making my command 132 strong.

[Craig did not make another entry in his journal between these dates.]

Saturday, 21st September, 1850. This evening we had a visit from several ladies residing in San Antonio; viz., Mrs. Col Reeve, Mrs. Major [J. L.] Smith, Mrs. Major Longstreet, Mrs. Major Babbitt of the Quartermaster Department, Mrs. Major [J. H.] Belcher, Quartermaster Department, and her mother, Mrs. Col Abercrombie, and Mrs. Lt. [Clinton W.] Lear, both of the 5th Infantry, and Miss Dashiel daughter of Paymaster Dashiel, and a *number* of other ladies (citizens) from San Antonio were also of the party. We had a large number of the officers from San Antonio in attendance. The Adjutant of the 8th Infantry brought out the band of that Regiment, and, with the band of the 1st Infantry (which came out with the detachment of Recruits under command of Lt. Barber), we had delightful music, and we danced under the trees by *moonlight* until a late hour.

[Craig did not make another entry in his journal between these dates.]

Wednesday, 9th October, 1850. It rained off and on throughout the day. It was more like a Spring day, than a fall one. I rode into San Antonio, and extended my ride as far as the camp of the U.S. Boundary Commission. The Commissioner, Mr. John R. Bartlett, expects to leave for El Paso tomorrow the 10th. He will take a small escort and go the northern route. The rest of the Commission expect to leave in the course of ten days.

[Craig did not make another entry in his journal between these dates.]

Saturday, 12th October, 1850. It commenced raining shortly after Reveille this morning, cleared off before 8 o'clock, and commenced raining again a little before 2 o'clock p.m., and continued for an hour or more. I regret to say that my tent was very near being *flooded*, the ditch around the tent not being sufficiently deep to carry the water off. Gen. Brooke, Gen. Garland, Col. Johnston, Major [George] Deas, and Lt. Barber paid us a visit this evening. They report little or no rain in and about San Antonio.

Left Camp Fillmore on *Thursday the 17th of October 1850* for El Paso, Texas, at ½ past 8 o'clock a.m. Just before leaving we carried into execution the sentence of a General Court Martial, by flogging two of our men in presence of the command, who deserted some days ago and were apprehended. On the night of the 15th one of our camp women (a Mrs. Hart) gave birth to a fine son. She was the wife of one of my Sergeants, and I was compelled to leave him with her in San Antonio. He was an excellent man, and I shall miss him very much.

I received a letter from my dear wife on yesterday. In it was a *tooth* of my dear little daughter, the first one she ever had drawn. Dear, dear little creature, may her sufferings through life never be greater than what she suffered on that occasion. We marched today about 12 miles and encamped on a small stream called Leon. We arrived at our encampment today at 2 o'clock.

Friday, 18th October, 1850. Left our encampment about 8 o'clock a.m. Our men rode in the wagons today and were quite *fresh* on reaching camp. The country we marched over today was quite a pretty one. We saw quantities of mesquite, and small live oaks. We reached our encampment on the River Medina, opposite to Castroville, a small village, a little after 2 o'clock.

About daylight this morning it commenced blowing, and I was very much afraid that we were going to have a "Norther," but it cleared off, and we had a lovely day for our march. The distance from our last encampment is some 13 miles. A man by the name of Watts deserted from my command last night.

Saturday, 19th October, 1850. Left our encampment at 6 o'clock this morning. The country over which we passed today was quite a pretty one. The growth was generally of live oak, hackberry, and post oak, more generally known as *blackjack*.

The country after passing Castroville begins to rise, and we are now in sight of a small chain of mountains. Between San Antonio and

Castroville, in dry weather, water is only to be found in three places: the Leon, El Medio, and Medina. We marched today about 10 miles, and encamped at ½ past 10 o'clock a.m. on the Qhihi Creek.

Sunday, 20th October, 1850. Left our encampment a little after day break this morning. Last night was quite a cool one, and this morning felt something like those one frequently experiences much further south. Mr. Augustus de Vaudricourt and Mr. [Alexander A.] Camp of the U.S. Boundary Commission spent the night with us, their party having left our encampment a short time ere we reached it.

We arrived at our encampment on the Rio Sico about 12 o'clock noon. At this point there is a Military Post, garrisoned by two Companies, one of Dragoons and one of Infantry, Major [Charles F.] Morris of the 8th Infantry in Command. The Major has his family with him. I was very much pleased to see them, we having been stationed together for nearly two years at Jefferson Barracks, Missouri. I took tea with them the evening I arrived, and we talked over the many hours we had passed together so pleasantly while at Jefferson Barracks, and the many changes which had taken place since our departure from that Post, their family having suffered from death, having lost two children and one son-in-law, Lt. [Thaddeus] Higgins of the 4th Infantry. The country we passed over today was not so pretty a one as the one we passed over between the Medina and the Quihi. We marched 18 miles today.

Monday, 21st October, 1850. We left our encampment this morning shortly after daylight. The country we marched over was pretty much like the one we passed over yesterday. Eight miles from Sico we passed the Rancheros Creek, where we found very good water. I neglected to state in my notes of yesterday that we found water on the Arroyo Hondo, which is about 10 miles west of Quihi.

We reached our encampment today about 11 o'clock a.m. We had just pitched our tents when the alarm of fire was given. It was caused by the negligence of one of the teamsters, and had it not been for the *great exertion* made by the *Military*, *Uncle Sam* would have been *minus* some several thousand dollars. As it was, we only lost a few sets of mule harness, which I hope the Quartermaster will be able to replace on our arrival at Leona. We marched today eleven miles and encamped on the river

Sabinal.

Tuesday, 22nd October, 1850. Left our encampment this morning soon after it was light, and after a march of some five miles, we came to Comanche Creek, where we found water enough to water a large number of animals. The face of the country we marched over today is very much like that of the last day or two. I would not give *five cents* per acre for the *whole of it.*

We marched today about 14 miles and encamped on the Rio Frio. We reached our encampment about 11 o'clock a.m. We now have two of the Boundary Commission party, and one *outsider* belonging to it, with us. Mr. de Vaudricourt and Mr. Camp, and a Dr. [Harvey] Nott of Texas *the outsider*. They, *I presume*, will join their party tomorrow at Leona. Our encampment today is not as convenient to the river as we would wish it, the river having very little water in it, and that only to be found in holes. The grazing is tolerable.

Wednesday, 23rd October, 1850. Left our encampment this morning a few minutes after 5 o'clock. The country we marched over to day was *anything* but interesting. Just before reaching the Leona the country improves a *little*. We reached our encampment at the head of the Leona about ½ past 9 o'clock a.m. Today we marched 8 miles. The water here is very fine. We expect to remain here until Friday morning, then we bid farewell to the *white settlements*. There is a Military post about four miles below this on the river, Brevet Lt. Col. Hardee of the 2nd Dragoons in command of it.

Thursday, 24th October, 1850. Our command remained in camp today. I rode down to Col. Hardee's post today and dined with him and his interesting wife. He has quite a pretty situation for his post, it being in a few yards of the river. The mail from San Antonio came in while I was there, but I *regret* to say, it brought me no letters. We will leave our encampment tomorrow at daylight.

Friday, 25th October, 1850. The mule train left camp this morning at daylight. The ox train started about 10 o'clock a.m. The country we marched over today appears to be a fine *grazing* one, but *I should say*, it was fit for nothing else. Col. [John] McClellan, U.S.A., encamped today some ten miles west of us. He took with him his mule train, and left the ox train with my command. I remained with the ox train and reached camp about ½ past 2 o'clock. We marched today nine miles, and encamped on the Nueces River. Col. McClellan will encamp on Turkey Creek tonight. We expect to reach that point tomorrow.

Our train reached camp this morning as early as 8 o'clock. I regret very much that the Commissioner, Mr. Bartlett, attempted to get an ox train from San Antonio to El Paso, for I fear that they will not stand the march like our mules, and they will be a great *drawback* on our making anything like good marches. (A) Company the rear guard today.

Saturday, 26th October, 1850. Left our encampment this morning at daylight. The country we marched over today was quite broken, more so than any we have passed over. The valley of the Nueces appears to be very rich. There is quite a large quantity of timber in this valley. The mule train reached camp about 10 o'clock a.m. The ox train arrived about 2 o'clock p.m. We marched today upwards of ten miles.

Although the evidence suggests that Lewis Craig kept a journal covering the period from October 26, 1850, to November 16, 1851, it has not been found. Other members of the party, however, particularly Commissioner Bartlett, kept detailed records of the journey to the Pacific. Craig had met Bartlett only briefly in New York and had found him intelligent and interesting, as did most people. Bartlett had traveled to Texas separately from most of the commission members; it would not be the last time that he would go his own way, without the commission.

Bartlett's suitability for this enterprise was questionable. Born in Providence, Rhode Island, two years before Craig's birth, Bartlett was a fellow Whig, but, for this critical assignment, he "had no qualifications beyond his enthusiasm for travel and travel books"; critically, however, he had friends in the Whig administration in Washington City, including President Millard Fillmore. Consequently, part of Craig's mission would be attempting to protect a man who had previously been known mainly as "a bibliophile and a bookstore proprietor"—"the very epitome of visionary impracticality."

Bartlett's survival during his wilderness wanderings rested mainly with Craig, but also with other seasoned veterans of demanding marches such as Bartlett's interpreter, John C. Cremony. At the beginning of the journey, Cremony had looked at Bartlett's traveling vehicle with a "wild surmise"; it was "a close carriage drawn by four fleet and powerful mules," with its interior "well supplied with Colt's and Sharp's rifles, Colt's pistols, a double-barreled shotgun, lots of ammunition, and a number of small but useful tools."

The point of departure for surveying was the tiny settlement of El Paso, Texas, almost six hundred miles from San Antonio. Craig's duties were to begin there, so between the two towns, he traveled by the most-used route. Bartlett traveled by another lesser-known route. There followed a "series of misadventures, which included three murders committed by his men, habitual drunkenness, insubordination, mutiny, and an attempted quartermaster's fraud."

From El Paso, Craig would have immediate authority over the men of his "A" Company of the Third Regiment who were to form the military escort, but he also took responsibility for insuring that the wagons were sound (and that their contents of food and other supplies did not disappear), that the draft and burden animals were adequately fed, along with the sheep and cattle that were to provide fresh meat. In the desert, missteps or problems with any of these responsibilities could lead to injury, starvation, or death.

Craig was taking charge of the protection of something like a moving village of around three hundred people, a daunting task. There were not only the surveyors and the astronomical observers but also engineers, botanists, and draughtsman, along with blacksmiths, tailors, shoemakers, wheelwrights, stonecutters, and various teamsters and other laborers.

Fortunately, although Craig was entering a desert, it was neither entirely trackless nor totally unknown. Now taking place among his books was William Emory's *Notes of a Military Reconnaissance from Fort Leavenworth to San Diego* (1848), which contained a good deal of information on much of the route the commission would travel. Emory had accompanied General Kearny on his march to San Diego, so much of his information could be considered vital, instead of mainly providing the amusement that Scott's officers had gotten from reading William H. Prescott's *History of the Conquest of Mexico* (1843) on their way to the Halls of the Montezumas.

Craig had by this time become even more sensitive to the chronic problem of desertion, which had become epidemic since the California Gold Rush had begun. He had lately intervened in the case of his first deserter, who had been returned by a civilian for the $30 paid by the U.S. Army for such apprehensions. Craig suggested that in lieu of trial, the man, a promising recruit, be allowed to pay the $30 and be returned to duty without trial. Craig's suggestion was approved. Since it was peacetime, desertion was not a capital offense, but a deserter could be sentenced to be flogged.

The U. S.-Mexican Boundary Commissioners were to have their first conference on the Mexican side of the Rio Grande at the town of El Paso del Norte (present-day Ciudad Juarez). This was approximately where the southern border of the New Mexico territory met the Rio Grande, and the surveyors were to measure west to establish the line between the territory now belonging to the U.S. and the adjacent Mexican state of Chihuahua. Therein lay a tremendous problem. The joint commission had been set up through the Treaty of Guadalupe Hidalgo, hammered out in a villa of that name north of Mexico City in 1848. As a reference document for the boundary line to be drawn, John Disturnell's inaccurate *Map of Mexico* (1847) was appended to the treaty.

At the meeting in December 1850 in El Paso del Norte, Bartlett first met General Pedro Garcia-Conde, the Mexican commissioner. He had previously been his country's representative in the survey of the boundary from San Diego to the junction of the Colorado and Gila Rivers, which had been accomplished during the Polk administration. One of Bartlett's military surveyors, Lt. Amiel Weeks Whipple of Massachusetts, had also been employed on the original survey. He and Craig would find themselves kindred spirits, unlike surveyor A. B. Gray, who was a born controversialist.

Bartlett and Garcia-Conde ("a trained engineer") soon discovered that the Distrunell map was error-ridden: its faulty latitude and longitude placed El Paso too far north and too far east, deep into Texas. Nonetheless, Garcia-Conde, more experienced in these matters than Bartlett and a proud Mexican nationalist as well, demanded that the incorrect latitude and longitude be followed for the survey.

Following protests from Bartlett, Garcia-Conde accepted the "actual" Rio Grande as the eastern boundary, but persuaded Bartlett to agree to a "compromise" that shifted the border north of El Paso del Norte to the vicinity of Dona Ana on the Rio Grande, thus allowing Mexico to acquire an additional six thousand square miles. Significantly, this area was crossed by the famous Cooke's Wagon Road, cut in late 1846 and early 1847 by Gen. Philip St. George Cooke and the Mormon Battalion. It began on the Rio Grande south of Santa Fe, later followed Kearney's route to San Diego, and happened to approximate the proposed line of the Southern Pacific Railroad.

To some Southern critics, this seemed "a case of a New England Yankee blithely disregarding the needs of Texas and the South for a way to California." There were also angry protests against Bartlett's agreement from the commission's actual surveyors, but the survey would proceed to its illogical conclusion.

Bartlett had decided that Santa Rita del Cobre, an area generally known as the Copper Mines, would be the best depot for the commission's supplies as well as a central area for sending out surveying parties. It had been determined to survey the area to the west first and to leave for later the area of the Rio Grande below Dona Ana.

Somc 150 miles northwest of El Paso and 300 miles south of Santa Fe, Santa Rita del Cobre had much to recommend it. It lay between the Rio Grande and the Gila River, and was around fifty miles above the agreed Bartlett-Conde line, in a well-timbered valley with good grazing nearby. There was also plentiful water from a dependable stream that ran through the area and created a pool near the site Craig chose as headquarters on Craig's arrival late in January 1851.

There were some fifty adobe buildings at Santa Rita, in various states of repair. Chief among them was a triangular adobe fort, "with towers of the Martello-type at each corner, loop-holed not only in the towers but in the connecting walls as well." Built in the early 1800s by an owner of the copper mines as protection from the Apaches, the complex had been deserted since Apache attacks had shut down the mining works down in 1838.

Although abandoned for years, Bartlett noted that the fort "was in so good a state of preservation" that Col. Craig "in a few weeks...built up such walls as had fallen, restored the roof, and made the whole tenantable for himself and his command, furnishing besides storerooms for all his provisions." Craig called the post Cantonment Dawson, after William C. Dawson.

The presence of the fort suggests the worst feature of Santa Rita: it was within a network of Apache plunder trails into Northern Mexico that had been in use for decades. The American presence would soon prove to be a magnet to the Indians, with three hundred Apaches setting up camp within four miles, a like number eighteen miles away, and four hundred Navajos on the Gila River within thirty miles.

Bartlett and his party arrived May 2, with the commissioner having just been injured by falling from his mule, who then fractured Bartlett's left shoulder with a kick. Continuing in his carriage, the commissioner was welcomed by Craig, who assisted him to a cot in his own quarters. Bartlett was watched carefully by Craig during his two-week recuperation; during the first week Craig carefully turned him in his bed when he could hardly move, insuring his recovery.

Craig by this time had for months been plagued by even more desertions and was now willing to use draconian measures to deal with thieving deserters—many of them were drawn four hundred miles southward by the mining and marketing center of Chihuahua, a city of twelve thousand which had long been the source of supplies for Santa Rita.

As Craig wrote to Adj. Gen. Jones in early March 1851,

> As I am in the heart of the Apache country…[I wish] respectfully to bring to the notice of…the Commanding General of the Army…[and] the Secretary of War, the frequent desertions from the army in this department owing to the post being so near the Mexican line; and the large amount of public property stolen by the men who desert…. the *seven* men who deserted from my camp took with them six muskets; they also stole *six mules* belonging to the Quartermaster's Department. Two of the men who deserted were *members of the Guard*.

Craig had sent a sergeant and twelve men in pursuit, who followed their trail toward the Mexican border, but turned back after encountering "a large body of Apaches."

Craig suggested that the punishment for deserters be radically increased ("particularly where men desert while members of a Guard and take with them government property"). He suggested "*one hundred lashes* on the bare back, and be branded on the *forehead* with the letter (D), and also that *one* hundred dollars…be paid for any soldier apprehended out of the U.S." and delivered to any U.S. military post. Craig added that he had lately been informed that six Dragoons had recently deserted from another post, taking with them "*eight* Dragoon horses."

Craig closed, "Let me assure the Adjutant General that what I have recommended, I have been induced to do from the very *great interest* that I feel in the Service; I confess that I am *perfectly in love* with my profession, and wish to see the discipline of the Army *perfect*."

On June 23, 1851, a little over a month after Bartlett had his party arrived at Santa Rita, a party of Apaches finally appeared there to meet the Commissioner, along with their chief, Mangus Colorado ("Red Sleeves," also spelled "Mangas Coloradas"), a relative giant at well over six feet tall. Portraying himself as a friend to the Americans, he welcomed them as allies in his fight against the Mexicans. Mangus had similarly welcomed General Stephen Kearny and his men to the Copper Mines back in October 1846, at which time Kearny had given him the obligatory presents, while the scout Kit Carson noted with a wink, "I would not trust a one of them." Fortunately, Kearny and his men were only passing through.

Bartlett and Craig attempted to live peacefully with their Indian neighbors, Apache and Navajo alike, hoping that kindness and generosity would bring good treatment in return. Mangus was welcomed, and he and his party left laden with presents from the commission. The chief promised to bother neither the U.S. nor the nearby Mexican Commission, and to return any stock that might "be taken by his young men."

The Apaches continued to visit the commission's camp at Santa Rita for several weeks while the Americans still numbered some thee hundred. They "made their first calls on Col. Craig, who treated them with the greatest kindness." At other times, they paid calls to Bartlett, and often dined with him, but their favorite visiting place was the tent of the interpreter John Cremony, the only person with whom they could converse in their own tongue.

Wishing to emphasize the Americans' friendliness to Mangus Colorado, Bartlett had caused a military uniform especially made for him, since he had admired those worn by Craig and his men. The gift, as described by Bartlett, was "a full suit of blue broadcloth, consisting of a frock coat lined with scarlet and ornamented with gilt buttons. His pantaloons, at his request, were open from the knee downwards, after the fashion of the Mexicans, with a row of small buttons on one side, and broad strip of scarlet cloth on the outer side from the hip downwards."

Cremony, who had dressed him in this finery, recalled that Mangus for the rest of the day "strutted about the camp, the envied of all beholders, and as vain of his new dress as a peacock of his feathers." In less than a week, however, the "coat, shirt, pants, and epaulettes were sported by another Indian"—"Mangus had gambled them away."

It would be a very active summer at Copper Mines. On the evening of June 27, John Cremony noticed a campfire at the perimeter of the commission's compound, where the Indians were not allowed to camp. Going to investigate, he spotted "a young and handsome girl, clothed in a tattered chemise, with a buckskin skirt, and another skin thrown over her shoulders." She was preparing supper for a group of Apaches and Mexicans. Discovering she was a captive, Cremony reported to Bartlett, and Craig and several of his men rescued the girl.

Her name was Inez Gonzalez. Nine months earlier, she had left her home in Santa Cruz, Sonora, some 250 miles to the southwest, to attend a religious festival with a group of relatives. They had been attacked by Apaches, who had killed her uncle and the eight soldiers guarding the cavalcade, and she was to be traded to the Mexicans for "powder and arms." After Craig and a few of his men rescued the girl, they drove the Mexicans and Indians from their camp.

A more dangerous situation developed on July 6, when word was brought to Bartlett that Jesus had shot one of the Apaches. (Bartlett noted, "This name is so common among Mexicans, particularly the lower classes, that one can seldom get half a dozen of them together without finding a Jesus in the company.") The shooter in this incident was Jesus Ortiz, a teamster, and his action created immediate chaos, as Bartlett recorded:

> The Indians, of which there were many about us at the time, were screaming and running in all directions, as though fearful of a general rising and massacre of their people. Our own party too were in great alarm, and every man ran for his arms, not knowing but that the Indians…might at once attack us, to be revenged for the loss of their companion. Mangus Colorado, Delgadito and Coletto Amarillo, who were in our camp, seized their arms, and, mounting animals, retreated to a small hill a few hundred yards from the fort, where they stopped to see what was to follow, and make their escape in case of necessity.

Taking the interpreter John Cremony with him, "Colonel Craig saved the situation by courageously walking unarmed toward them alone, reaffirming the friendship of all the Americans, and inviting them to the questioning" of Ortiz, the guilty Mexican teamster. This persuaded the Apaches that "the shooting was a personal affair in which the Americans were not involved." When the wounded Apache later died, the Indians agreed to let the teamster live, as long as payment was given of the teamster's "monthly wages to the murdered man's wife," along with the promise that the murderer would be "kept in captivity indefinitely."

Beginning in late July 1851, the commission party began to lose stock through theft by the Indians. With the escorts' mules having disappeared from the grazing area, Craig immediately took thirty soldiers and visited the Apaches at their camp on the Mimbres River. The Indians told Craig they had not stolen the animals, and Craig and his men returned to the fort.

During the first two weeks of August, more stock disappeared. On August 11, Indians "made a descent on the mules belonging to Colonel Craig's command," and stole "twenty-five together with some valuable horses." This was done a mile from the fort in the face of several men guarding the animals; one man disappeared. Bartlett noted that "whether he was killed or taken away prisoner" they never knew—"He was never seen or heard of after."

From that time, the Indians ceased visiting the camp. They had learned that the commission was preparing to head west on the survey with its stock and began rustling extravagantly. On August 17, the men guarding the grazing stock six miles from the fort had "fifty of the best mules" run off by the Indians, although the guards saved around eighty by driving them into a corral.

Reduced by horse theft to riding on mules, Col. Craig and around twenty soldiers set off in pursuit of the Apache stock thieves and tracked them past the Gila River. Surprising and scattering two camps of them, the soldiers found "mule meat and corn half roasted," abandoned at the fires.

When Dragoon reinforcements arrived on August 23, Craig and the others set off again. While they were gone, some of the escort's other mules were stolen, along with eighteen mules belonging to the Dragoons. During the same raid, an attempt was made to drive off the commission's one hundred cattle.

The Indians did steal cattle belonging to a Mr. Hay, who was working a gold mine near Santa Rita; he arrived at about this time, bringing his family to the protection of the fort. He could identify the thieves as Apaches, for he had briefly parleyed with Delgadito himself, prudently from just outside rifle range. As Bartlett later commented, it had become obvious that most of the robberies had been "committed by the very Indians who had been fed by us, and had received every kindness at our hands."

Lt. A. W. Whipple immediately chased the Indians into a hilly pine forest with a party of volunteers, including Mr. Hay and John Cremony. The Apaches, numbering about fifty and led by Delgadito, dispersed into the trees to fire some warning shots as their comrades drove the stolen stock toward their camp.

As the Indians prepared to rejoin their raiding party, Delgadito "kept at a safe distance and poured out torrents of the vilest abuse upon the Americans." Cremony was armed with a new government-issue rifle, "which could throw their balls with fair accuracy a distance of four hundred yards" and had been fitted for him "with new and fine sights."

As Delgadito, preparing to depart, defied the party by turning and "slapping his buttocks"—"a favorite taunt among the Apaches"—Cremony handed the rifle to the commission's "crack shot," who went from tree to tree until he was within something less than three hundred yards from Delgadito. He then fired while Delgadito was "exhibiting his posterior."

Delgadito immediately "gave an unearthly yell" and began "a series of dances and capers," then "rushed frantically through a thick copse, followed by his band." Cremony later learned that the bullet had "gouged a neat streak across that portion of Delgadito's person denominated in school parlance as the 'seat of honor,'" and that he was thus "spoiled for several weeks" from "riding and general activity." What was more, Whipple's party then pressed the retreating band so closely that they succeeded in recovering two dozen stolen animals, plus two more belonging to the Indians.

From this time, Santa Rita was "in a state of siege." Until then, the several hundred men comprising the escort and the commission employees had camped at varying distances from the fort. All now returned. Supplies would need to arrive from El Paso before the survey could continue.

In late August the U.S. Commission finally left the Copper Mines. Since the Mexican Commission was heading south to Santa Cruz for supplies, Bartlett decided to accompany Garcia-Conde to that town, to restore Inez Gonzales to her family personally, and to gather supplies for his party. Col. Craig and the escort would go west with the party surveying along the Gila.

Lt. Whipple, running low on rations, voiced what was probably also Craig's opinion of this trip to take Inez Gonzales to her home:

> Instead of delivering her to the Mexican authorities, by them to be returned to her home...Mr. Bartlett retained her at his house, passed the camp of General Conde...and determined himself to carry her to Santa Cruz....No one is sent back to hasten the provisions for us, but the Commissioner & party...are all seeking the home of the captive....One naturally enquires, what is the great object to be acquired by wasting the time of the Commission in this prolonged search after a Mexican village?

Even worse, Bartlett's trip developed into a lengthy private escapade. Finally comleting his errand in Santa Cruz (after having spent much time lost during the trip), Bartlett continued southwest to the Sonoran port of Guayamas with Cremony and others of his party. He did not send them back toward the Gila until December, as he continued to conduct private business along with some related to the commission. Ultimately, Bartlett fell ill with typhoid fever, apparently the same malady that would kill Gen. Garcia-Conde on December 19, 1851.

In early February 1852 when the commission party next saw the commissioner, he had gone from Guaymas to Acapulco, a 1300-mile voyage. He then took ship from Acapulco and traveled another 2000 miles to San Diego. There he found that the commission had already arrived. Bartlett wrote that he "was first met by [his] excellent friend Colonel Craig, commander of our escort." No doubt with some understatement, Bartlett recalled that Craig told him "they had felt much anxiety on [his] account," since they had not heard anything from the commissioner since the previous October.

Since Bartlett's disappearance months before, Craig had continued to be harried by the Indians. In a letter to Gen. Scott of September 4, 1851, Craig recorded the first several months of his activities, writing from Cantonment Dawson as the Gila survey continued without Bartlett. His summary report of his activities in 1851, with his conclusions regarding the Indians, began in January, and would seem to have been gleaned from his missing journal:

<u>*LSC*</u>

The Commissioner, John R. Bartlett, Esquire, determined early in *January* last to establish a depot at this point for the provisions, etc., for the escort and the Boundary Commission. The escort arrived here on the *25th of January*. The day before reaching the Copper Mines, we met several Apache Indians, among them a sub-chief (Delgadito). They appeared be very much pleased to see us. The chief said that he would visit us in a few days at the mines, which he did, & I treated him and his people with a great deal of kindness. I told him that I was very anxious to see his chief, Mangus Colorado, that I had understood that he was very friendly disposed toward the Americans, and for that reason I was very anxious to make his acquaintance.

On the *2nd of February* Mangus Colorado made his first visit to this cantonment. I expressed great pleasure on meeting with him, and informed him that I had always understood that he was a friend to the Americans, that the country which he and his people resided in had lately been purchased from the Mexican Government by the Americans, and that he and his people *as long as they conducted themselves in a proper manner* would meet with the kindest treatment from the American Government, that we were about to run the line between the two countries, and expected to be among his people for eighteen months or more, and that I hoped he would see that his young men did not interfere with our animals while grazing in the neighborhood of the cantonment.

To all this he replied that he had a great hatred for the Mexicans, but that he looked upon the Americans as his friends, and that instead of interfering with our animals, should any by accident go astray, he would see that they were brought to us.

Mangus Colorado and his people continued to visit us almost daily, up to the last five weeks, and we were as kind to them as we could be. I frequently gave the chiefs corn, and many other things they desired, and they always appeared to be very much pleased with the treatment they received while here.

About some two weeks ago [in mid-August], Mangus Colorado with several of his band, and a number of Navajos, paid a visit here. That morning I had made an engagement to visit the gold mines some four miles from this, with one of the gentlemen of the Commission.

Just before leaving I had an interview with Mangus Colorado and informed him that I did not much like the Navajos visiting my cantonment. That I had understood they were not very honest and that I was somewhat fearful that they would make an effort to run off some of our animals. He replied to me that I might make myself perfectly easy on that subject, that he would hold himself responsible for *every animal that I lost.*

Some few days after this the herders reported at Retreat that several of the mules were missing, and that they believed they had been driven off by the Indians although they had not seen an Indian. Early next morning I went in pursuit of them with eight men mounted on mules (eight saddles being all I could raise). I pursued them some eighty miles. At this point they scattered, and I was unable to follow them any farther.

The Indians that drove off the mules I am certain were Navajos. I had scarcely returned before they ran off a number of mules belonging to the commission. This occurred a short time before sundown, and by 2 o'clock that night, with the saddles belonging to the commission, I was able to mount some twenty-odd men on mules and started in pursuit of them. We struck thc trail at daylight some nine miles from the cantonment and followed it for two days, some distance beyond the Rio Gila, but finding, I presume, that we were pursuing them, they scattered and we were not able to follow up the trail.

Just before leaving in pursuit of this last party, I sent off an express to Dona Ana, requesting Major [Oliver] Shepherd [Third Infantry] to send Captain [Abraham] Buford with his troop [H Co., First Dragoons] to this point, so that I might be enabled to make a visit to the Navajo camp, said to be some four or five days march from here.

Captain Buford arrived here on the *22nd of August*, and we started early the next morning, and took the direction which I was informed by Mangus Colorado that the Navajo camp was situated. After crossing the Gila, which is some forty odd miles from this, we struck into a large trail, which after following a day and better, we came upon a small encampment of Indians who fled into the mountains as soon as they discovered us.

After some short time two Indians showed themselves on a hill, and requested that I would send *one* man to talk with them. I requested the person I sent to endeavour to persuade them to come in to me, but they said they first must go and hunt up their women, who had hid themselves in the mountains upon our approach.

These two Indians stated that they were Apaches, and that they were the last of their tribe between that point and the Gila—that beyond them the Navajos resided. These Indians stated that the Navajos had passed them some few days before with a number of mules, and a very large number of sheep, going north.

The day after leaving this encampment we came to a beautiful stream running about South West, which we supposed to be the Rio Prieto. After following this stream up some fifteen miles or more, we came upon an Indian encampment with quite a large corn field attached to it. They had also a quantity of snap beans and pumpkins.

This party discovered us a short time before reaching their encampment and they fled to the mountains. We saw three warriors. We were only able to overtake one of them, which we shot.

The next morning we left this encampment, and, after scouting around in the neighborhood of the corn field, with the hope we might find their families and stock, we struck a large trail leading up the river. Upon this trail there had been a large number of mules and sheep. We followed it up until late that day.

Captain Buford's horses being in very bad condition, a large number of them without shoes, the Captain reported to me that he did not think they were able to go any farther, that if they did, he would be compelled to leave a large number of them on the road. The condition of the horses therefore compelled me to give up the pursuit.

The day after I left here with Captain Buford's troop the *Apache Indians* ran off several of our mules, and a number of mules belonging to Captain Buford's command, which had been left at this place. They were in charge of the herders and some of Captain Buford's men, grazing in a quarter mile of the post.

The Indians in this country are well-mounted and whenever they commit depredations they are mounted on their best horses, and they can charge into a caballada [a herd] of animals grazing before you are aware that an Indian is in a mile of you, and stampede the whole caballada. We are all well convinced at this cantonment that the Apache Indians are just as much interested in the robberies which have been committed here as the Navajos, and we will know how *to treat them hereafter.*

The fact of it is, General, that these Indians must be *well flogged*, and be made to return all the property which they have stolen, or this country can never be settled.

The whole army knows, General, that you have done everything in your power to have a sufficient force (and that a mounted one) sent to this country. Our excellent President and yourself recommended to Congress last session that a large mounted force should be raised for this frontier, but it appears that no attention was paid to the recommendation.

My opinion is that the Government ought either to send out two mounted regiments to this country, independent of the troops now here, or they ought to withdraw what they have here and let the Indians have the country.

At this point there ought to be at least five companies of mounted men, one company to remain in garrison, while the other four ought to be kept in the field until these Indians have not *one animal left, take their stock, and their women and children* from them, and then you can do what you please with them.

At this point there is the best of grazing, plenty of wood, and some very fine timber for building, and the water is not surpassed by any in New Mexico. There is no dependence to be placed in what an Indian says, *no treaty* ought to be entered into either with the *Apaches* or the *Navajos*, until every animal which they have stolen from the Government and citizens of the country is returned.

The Mexicans who have had an opportunity of seeing a great deal of the Apache Indians represent them as being a lazy, roguish race, not to be depended upon at all, and that they would much prefer stealing in preference to cultivating the soil.

The Apaches have large droves of horses. Mangus Colorado, I think, has some as fine horses as I have seen since I have come to this country. Now if we can rid them of their horses, I have no doubt but that they could soon be persuaded to turn their attention to agriculture.

In relation to the escort for the U.S. B. Commission, Mr. Bartlett addressed a letter to Colonel [John] Munroe, then commanding the 9th Military Department, requesting that one company more might be added to the escort, which request Colonel Munroe refused to grant.

A few weeks since, Mr. Bartlett made the same request of Colonel Edwin V. Sumner, now in command of this Department, *who* also refused to grant his request.

I think the General will agree with me, that there ought to be two companies comprising this escort, one of Infantry and one of Dragoons. Since the Indians have assumed a hostile attitude toward us, Mr. Bartlett has determined to change his plans in relation to the distribution of the escort, requiring one portion to accompany him down the Gila, and the other portion to accompany Colonel Graham down the Rio Grande, and he therefore determined to remove our supplies to some point on the Rio Grande.

When this point was first established as a depot the Commissioner expected to be some eighteen months to two years engaged in running the line between the Rio Grande and the junction of the Colorado, but, since the Surveyor Mr. Gray has objected to the initial point fixed upon by the U.S. and Mexican Commissioners, he, Mr. Bartlett, has determined only to trace the Gila down to its junction with the Rio Colorado, and leave the line between the Rio Grande and the Gila to be run as soon as the two Governments settle the point where the line shall commence on the Rio Grande.

As soon as I was informed by Mr. Bartlett, that this point would be no longer required as a depot, I addressed a letter to Colonel Sumner, commanding the 9th Department, and stated to him that I thought it would be wise to have a Regiment sent to this point immediately as my leaving here at this time might give confidence to the Indians, and as there were some fifteen or twenty citizens settled in a few miles of the cantonment, engaged in working the gold mines, they would be compelled to leave at the same time I did, unless troops were sent here.

———

By December 5, 1851, Cantonment Dawson had been renamed Fort Webster [after Secretary of State Daniel Webster], and Col. Edwin Vose Sumner had sent Maj. Gouveneur Morris a letter to that point: "On your arrival there you will take possession of the quarters vacated by Bvt. Lieut. Col. Craig and immediately make such repairs, as will make them habitable for the winter. If the Apache Indians should express a desire for peace, let them understand, distinctly, that they must pledge to abstain, at once, from all depredations upon the Mexicans." As it happened, the Apache Wars would continue until the surrender of Geronimo in 1886. But Mangus Colorado would be captured and killed in early 1863 at Fort McLane, a new post established fifteen miles south of the Santa Rita copper mines.

Craig's letter to Gen. Scott continues:

<u>LSC</u>

The General knows that it is *perfectly preposterous* to think for a moment that one company of Infantry, and that not full, is a sufficient escort for an expedition of this kind, where we have some eight hundred sheep, one hundred beeves, and, at one time, nearly two hundred mules, all of which are compelled to be grazed, and scarcely men to protect the others, provisions, etc.

I have been informed that on the Pacific side the [1849–1850] U.S. B. Commission [to which Lt. Whipple had been attached] had one company of Dragoons and one of Infantry as an escort, and that in a country where you seldom ever hear of an Indian, but *in the heart* of a tribe of the most *roguish* and *deceitful* Indians, a portion of an Infantry company is supposed to be a sufficient escort by the officers lately in command of the Department.

It is generally conceded by all intelligent military men "that an escort should be of sufficient strength to beat off any presumed force that the enemy can bring against it. A *weak escort* will only hold out a temptation to the enemy to attack it." I have frequently so many men detached with different parties that I can only mount a guard of one non-commissioned officer and three privates, and they go on guard every other day, and out of those three men composing the guard, I send out *one* to assist the sheep herders.

Craig had obviously become exasperated with the "skulking way of war," particularly when compounded by the desertions that had whittled away what was already a "weak escort." Col. George Archibald McCall had earlier shown himself to be much of Craig's opinion when he visited New Mexico to prepare a report for Secretary of War George W. Crawford of Georgia, except that he recommended execution, rather than flogging, for some Apaches. McCall doubted that the other New Mexico tribes would ever be able to reach the cultural pinnacle of the Pueblo Indians, who were considered the gold standard of the Southwest aborigines.

As McCall completed his report at Santa Fe on July 15, 1850, he added a final paragraph: "Within the last hour, information of a perfectly reliable character has been received that...about seventy miles south of Santa Fe, seven thousand sheep were driven off by Navajos a few days since, and a few miles lower on the river six hundred, the shepherd of the last flock being pierced with fourteen arrows."

As noted above, the U.S. Army occupied Cantonment Dawson after Craig's departure, with its commander instructed to inform the Apaches of the necessity of pledging themselves to abstain, at once, from all depredations upon the Mexicans before any truce can be granted." This was rather beside the point, as a dispatch from Craig's friend Abraham Buford indicated two weeks later; he then reported himself "in pursuit of a party of Indians that had stampeded and run off 44 mules and 3 horses of a government train of seven wagons."

Six months after Craig wrote General Scott, a New Mexico Indian agent described the situation in the territory in quite similar terms to Craig's, with the addition of daunting statistics: "There are 92,000 Indians (estimated) in this Territory. Many of them are at war. We have not 1,000 troops here...to manage them."

Until mid-November, when the survey approached that Gila River landmark, the Pima Villages, Craig's days were marked by the monotony of the trail: "Arrived at the Pima villages on *Wednesday, 12th of November 1851.* Left the villages on *Friday, November 14th* for an encampment some nine miles above, where we had a plenty of water, wood & grass." In his journal, Lt. Whipple recorded his visit with Craig to extensive adobe ruins, unrecorded by the colonel.

> *Sunday, November 16th, 1851.*Started with guide for the Casa Blanca [actually Casa Grande], Col. Craig [and others] accompanying. Ten miles east brought it in view, a ruin worthy of note. The main building is about 40 by 60 feet at the base and from 25 to 40 feet in height.... The walls are four feet thick built of adobe composed of a light, straw-colored clay, from which originates the name Casa Blanca.... For miles the earth is a barren prairie.

Casa Blanca was the name given the district where these ancient Indian ruins were located. Bartlett described them more minutely in his journal. Craig's journal for the march to the Pima Villages has not survived. Following the general summary above, he resumed his journal:

<u>*LSC*</u>

Monday, November 17th, 1851. Remained in camp today and spent the time in writing to my *dearest* wife.

Tuesday, November 18th, 1851. Nothing of interest has occurred in camp today worth noting. I am happy to say that our animals are improving daily.

Wednesday, November 19th, 1851. As we expect to remain at this encampment for three or four days more. I sent one of my wagons to the village for corn, where my sutler, Mr. Smart, has encamped for the purpose of purchasing a sufficient quantity of corn to serve me to the mouth of the Gila.

Thursday, November 20th, 1851. The surveying parties left this encampment yesterday, for the purpose of continuing their work down the Gila. I shall leave with the rest of the party in a few days. I am getting tired of remaining in one spot so long and am anxious to reach the mouth of the Gila.

Friday, November 21st, 1851. We had quite an excitement in camp last night, on the herders reporting that our sheep had strayed off and that they could not be found high or low. I immediately started out several men of the company to look them up, but it being very dark, and the mesquite bushes very thick, they were unable to find them.

This morning I started a party mounted on mules, and after a search of several hours they found them some miles from camp. If we lose our sheep, we shall be without fresh provisions, which would not be very agreeable.

Saturday, November 22nd, 1851. Mr. A. B. Gray, U.S. Boundary Survey, and his party all left this encampment today. Mr. Gray expects to be detained two or three days near the village of the Pimas ere he will be enabled to continue his work down the river. I shall leave with my command on Monday morning, and will encamp some short distance below the Pimas. Last night was one of the coldest that we have had since our arrival in the Rio Gila valley.

Sunday, November 23rd, 1851. Inspected my command this morning, and then spent a portion of the day writing to my better half. Today has been quite cold.

Monday, November 24th, 1851. Left our encampment this morning a short time after sunrise, and, after a march of some 12 miles, encamped near the Pima village, near the point at which a monument has been erected for the purpose of marking the boundary line between the United States and Mexico. We encamped about 12 o'clock noon. I shall leave early in the morning for Lt. A. W. Whipple's camp, which is some 15 miles below this on the river, and near the point where the road leaves the river to cross the jornada. ["Jornada," according to Bartlett, "literally means a day's journey; but it does not seem to be used, except there is a long reach of desert country without water. It is therefore applied to one or two days' journey." The *Jornada del Muerto*, between El Paso and Santa Fe, Bartlett says is "90 miles across, without water, and of the most desert-like character."]

Tuesday, November 25th, 1851. (New Moon). Left our encampment this morning a short time after sunrise, and, after a march of some 15 miles, encamped a short distance below the Maricopa village, near the point where the road leaves the river to cross the jornada. Where we are now encamped we have sufficient water, grass, and wood.

I expect to remain at this encampment for two or three days, so as to give the surveying party a day or two the start of us, as it will take them some four or five days to get to the point on the river where the road across the jornada strikes it, and it will not take more than a day and little better to cross the jornada. We arrived here today about 12 o'clock noon. I dined with Lt. Whipple today.

Wednesday, November 26th, 1851. Our camp today has been overrun with Indians. The Maricopas who reside in this village have not had an opportunity of disposing of their corn and vegetables, as our encampments have been some distance above them. We shall be able to purchase as much corn as we have transportation for.

Thursday, November 27th, 1851. Lt. Whipple and his party left for the mouth of Salt River [Rio Salinas], which empties into the Gila some nine miles below this. I sent a part of my command with him as an escort. Mr. Gray will leave in the morning for the same point. The weather is very pleasant. The days are warm, but we find the nights rather cool for tents.

Friday, November 28th, 1851. Mr. Gray and party left this morning for Salt River. My command will leave this encampment tomorrow morning for an encampment two miles below this, where we will have more grass than we have at this point.

Saturday, November 29th, 1851. Left our encampment a short time after sunrise this morning, and we are now encamped about two miles in advance of our last encampment. There is very little wood at this new encampment, but we have very good water, and the grazing is much better than at our last encampment.

Sunday, November 30th, 1851. Today has been a lovely one, more like a day in June than the last day of November. Although the days are very warm, the nights are very cold. Last evening I felt very unwell, and at one time I thought I should have an ague. I took a Dover's Powder and went to bed, and this morning I felt much better. [Dover's Powder, a medicine developed by the British physician Dr. Thomas Dover (1660–1702), was used to treat malaria and its aftereffects (such as the chills and fever of ague), among other maladies. A general formula called for 10 grains of calomel, 1 grain of pulverized opium, 1 grain of pulverized ipecac, and 16 grains of sulphate quinia.]

Monday, December 1st, 1851. We shall take up our line of march tomorrow at 9 o'clock a.m. and expect to reach the Gila again in one day and a half's march from this encampment.

Tuesday, December 2nd, 1851. Left our encampment this morning a few minutes before 9 o'clock, and marched until a few minutes before 4 o'clock p.m. We encamped on the jornada after a march of some 18 miles. When we encamped we found a small patch of grama grass [a tall forage grass usually found in clumps], which proved very grateful to our mules. [Postscript:] The Republic of France transformed into a monarchy by Louis Napoleon on the 2nd December.

Wednesday, December 3rd, 1851. Started this morning a few minutes before sunrise, and arrived at the Gila a few minutes before 3 o'clock p.m. The road across the jornada, with the exception of a few miles, is an excellent one. After leaving the encampment, which is a short distance below the Maricopa village, you find no water until you arrive at the Gila, some forty miles. There is very little grass to be found on this jornada. Now and then a small patch of grama grass is to be seen.

There is a sufficient quantity of wood to be found the whole way across the jornada. On our arrival at this point we found the Mexican boundary party encamped on the river, where they have been for some days. As our party have not yet reached this point with their survey, we will not leave here tomorrow.

Thursday, December 4th, 1851. Capt. Edmund Barry of the U.S. Border Commission and myself rode several miles down the river today for the purpose of seeing if an encampment could be found where there was more grass than where we are now encamped.

The road as far as we followed it ran parallel with the river, and nearly a mile from it. We only saw one small patch of grass and that some distance from the river. I am very much afraid that our animals will suffer very much ere we reach the mouth of the river, on account of the scarcity of grass. If they survive the march, they will be fortunate.

Friday, December 5th, 1851. We are still encamped where the road across the jornada strikes the Rio Gila, and I presume we will remain here for two or three days longer, as the surveying parties have not yet arrived.

I neglected to state in my *notes* of yesterday, that Capt. Barry and myself, while riding down the Gila, found in the *road two water melons*. The one that we cut was more like a *water melon* than any I tasted while among the Maricopa & Pima Indians. If we had have passed along here some six weeks sooner, I have no doubt but that we would have found it a delicious melon.

I presume the seed must have been dropped there last fall or this spring, and the rainy season brought it to perfection. It proves conclusively to my mind what I have been very anxious to find out, which was at what time the rainy season commenced in this valley. I have no doubt but that the rainy season commences here about the same time it does at the Santa Rita del Cobre Copper Mines.

Saturday, December 6th, 1851. Our surveying party is still up the river. I presume though, as their rations are out tomorrow, they will reach this point tomorrow night or early next morning. We had quite a blustering day yesterday. The wind blew very hard from the southwest, and, during last night, it rained quite hard, which was an improvement to our encampment, as it laid the dust.

Sunday, December 7th, 1851. The sun has set and not one of our surveying party has yet arrived. If they do not arrive here very soon, their rations will not last them until they can reach the mouth of the river. (*Note.* Mr. Conde [of the Mexican Commission] and his party left today.)

Monday, December 8th, 1851. Lt. Whipple arrived last evening a few minutes after writing the above. Some of his party did not reach camp until 8 o'clock p.m. It commenced raining early this morning, and continued until near sundown. It has every appearance of clearing off, and our camp is very much improved from the rain, as it had become quite dusty. Mr. Gray has not yet arrived, and I fear he will not be here for some days.

Tuesday, December 9th, 1851. This morning at daylight it was quite foggy, but, as soon as the sun rose, the fog disappeared, and we have had a very pleasant day. I should think, judging from what I have seen, that this must be a delightful winter climate.

Wednesday, December 10th, 1851. Lt. Whipple and his party left this morning for the mouth of the river. He expects to reach there in ten days. Mr. Gray sent in a party of men for provisions. They arrived here this morning about 8 o'clock, and left as soon as the provisions could be packed. The party reported that Mr. Gray was some 20 miles or more from this point, and that his provisions were *entirely out*. I am very much afraid that his party will suffer yet, ere they reach the mouth of the river, for the want of provisions, as he has not more than some *six* days flour on hand, and it will take him *eight* days from this encampment to reach the mouth of the river, supposing him to travel at the rate of 15 miles a day.

Thursday, December 11th, 1851. This day two months ago we left Cantonment Dawson, and, had it not been for the long delay in the neighborhood of the Pima villages, we would have been at the mouth of the river long ere this. Mr. Gray and his party reached here today. It appears that he is determined to carry on the survey, provisions *or no* provisions.

Tomorrow morning the wagons will leave for the mouth of the river, for the purpose of procuring provisions for the party remaining behind. A large number of Mr. Gray's men will leave him for the want of provisions. I am surprised that any of them should remain with him, for he appears to have very little idea of management about him.

Friday, December 12th, 1851. We left our encampment on the Gila (where we have been ever since the 3rd of the month) a few minutes before 10 o'clock and made a march of some 18 miles. We encamped some two miles from the river. Just at this point the road leaves the river, and when we shall see it again is rather as the Mexicans would say a "quien sabe" ["who knows?"] case. I left an escort of one non-commissioned officer and 8 men with Mr. Gray, owing to several of his laborers refusing to remain with him any longer.

We encamped this evening a few minutes before sunset. Today has been a lovely one, not a cloud has made its appearance in the heavens. This is certainly a delightful climate. This month has been more like the month of May in the States than a winter month.

Saturday, December 13th, 1851. Left our encampment this morning a few minutes before 7 o'clock. Our road today, a greater part of it, was very bad. We had a great deal of heavy sand to pull through, and one very bad hill.

We passed today the spot upon which the *Yuma Indians* it is said murdered several Americans. We saw the bones and hair scattered about, and several papers, among them a part of a letter to a Miss Crane. The party, I should suppose from the scraps of paper found near the spot where they were murdered, were from Illinois. [This was the site of the infamous "Oatman Massacre" of the previous February.]

We passed Lt. Whipple today. He encamped tonight a few miles above us on the river. We marched today some twenty-four miles, and are now encamped near the river. We have seen no grass since early yesterday, and our mules tonight are *endeavoring* to make a supper on the leaves of the cotton wood and willow.

Sunday, December 14th, 1851. Left camp this morning a short time before sunrise, and, after going about seven or eight miles, we came to a small *patch* of grass, where we halted and grazed our animals for about two hours. After watering of them, we started again and encamped near the river, having made a march of some 27 miles.

The morning was quite a cool one, but before the sun went down, it was *hot enough* to *cook* an egg. A person who has not been in this country can form no idea of the difference of temperature between the days and nights. Our wagons reached camp about sunset.

Lt. Whipple joined [us] this evening. His provisions not being sufficient to take him to the mouth of the river, like a man of *good sense*, he determined to go down with me, and as soon as he can procure supplies, to return and finish his work. Had Mr. Gray been a man of *as good judgment*, he would have done likewise.

Monday, December 15th, 1851. Left camp this morning about 9 o'clock. We would have left earlier but having little corn for our animals we were compelled to graze them before starting. Our road today was not quite as good as the one of yesterday, owing to its being more sandy. Just at our encampment the road leaves the river and passes over the plain, and strikes it again in about 7 or 8 miles. On this plain we saw a good deal of coarse grama grass scattered about in spots: and could we have reached it last night, our animals would have *feasted* upon it.

I neglected to state in my remarks of yesterday that the road left the river and passed over a plain of some 8 or 10 miles of very good road. There was also on this plain a great deal of the same kind of grass which I have mentioned above. Our march today was some 17 or 18 miles. We encamped in about a mile of the river and drove our mules to water. At this encampment is very little grass. We shall, in the morning, drive our mules out on the hills to graze.

I do think, that the *whole* of the Gila country is the most Godforsaken part of the world that I have ever seen. I would not give *three cents* for the *whole of* it. We encamped a short time before sun set.

Tuesday, December 16th, 1851. Owing to several of Lt. Whipple's mules having strayed from the herd, and not found until a late hour, the last wagon did not leave camp until 10 o'clock. We made but a short march of it to day, not more than 12 or 14 miles, *if* that.

We encamped a short time after 4 o'clock. We are now about the point where General Stephen Kearny's horse gave out and he was compelled to mount his mule. I should judge from Major W. H. Emory's report of the general's [1847] march down the Gila, that his mule was in nearly as bad condition as his horse.

Wednesday, December 17th, 1851. Left camp this morning about 9 o'clock. Our road today was a very sandy one, which made it very hard pulling for our mules. We marched some 15 or 16 miles and encamped near the river. Our encampment tonight is not a very pleasant one on account of the brush, which is very thick, but it was getting late, and we were compelled to "*drop down*" in this place.

There is said to be very good grazing in a short distance of the camp, and, as it is too late to graze our animals tonight, we shall send them out at daylight in the morning. It is supposed that we are now in about 18 miles of the mouth of the Gila. It commenced raining about 3 o'clock this evening, and we had quite a refreshing shower. It cleared off ere the sun went down.

Thursday, December 18th, 1851. Left camp this morning about 9 o'clock, and had marched but a short distance when we met Mr. Conde and his party returning, having completed his work as far as the mouth of the Gila. He gave us the sad intelligence that the post at the mouth of the river [Camp Yuma] had been evacuated. [The camp had been all but abandoned in June "because of the expense and difficulty of maintenance," and totally abandoned on December 6 because "the provisions at the post were almost exhausted." It would not be reoccupied until February 29, 1852, at which time it was named Fort Yuma.]

I immediately requested Lt. Whipple to write a note to Mr. Gray informing him that there was no post at the mouth of the river, and advising him to push for San Diego with all *speed*, as I should do *that thing myself*. Had Mr. Gray taken my advice, he would now have been with us, and there would have been a sufficient number of rations to have taken us to San Diego. I fear very much that we will lose some of our mules ere we reach San Diego, as our corn is all gone, and there is little or no grass to be found between this and that place. We are now encamped some 3 or 4 miles down the Colorado River.

No one can form the *least* idea of the dreariness of this Godforsaken country, unless they see it, and having seen it *once*, they will never wish to see it again. Having seen nearly the whole of the Gila country, I can truly say that I would not give *one* farm on the James River in *Virginia* for the *whole country*. We marched some 12 or 14 miles since reaching the Colorado. We have found the road very sandy, which makes it very hard on our mules.

Friday, December 19th, 1851. Started from camp this morning about 9 o'clock. After marching some 6 or 8 miles, we determined to cross the river. From the appearance of the river at the point where we halted, we thought it might be forded, but after trying it, we found it too deep, and determined to make a raft and cross it.

Just as we were commencing the raft, several Indians made their appearance on the opposite bank, and, after a short conversation with them, all of them *boldly* dashed into the river and swam over to us, their horses swimming by their sides.

On their reaching the shore, they appeared very much pleased to see us and informed us that there was a ferry some few miles below us, where we could cross without any difficulty. On receiving that information, we abandoned the idea of making a raft, and will leave early in the morning for the ferry. We had quite a sad accident to happen to us today. A young man by the name of Lt. Thomas Harper, in the employment of the U.S. Boundary Commission, soon after arriving in camp, went into the river to bathe, and I presume was taken with the cramp and was drowned. His father is a respectable farmer in the neighborhood of, I believe,

Georgetown, Kentucky. [The difficult Yuma Crossing became legendary, particularly in the annals of outlawry, when John Glanton and his murderous gang of scalp-hunters took over one of the Yuma ferries in 1849—sometimes ferrying travelers, other times robbing and killing them. Glanton and his men had also attempted to interfere with a competing ferry of the Yuma Indians, who in April 1850 had exterminated them.]

Saturday, December 20th, 1851. Left our camp a short time after daylight this morning and, instead of finding a ferry in a few miles, we marched some ten miles, over the most sandy country I have very seen, without a road. We are now encamped in a short distance, (*so says an Indian*), of the point where we will find a boat. We shall start early tomorrow morning and hope to find a boat, and be enabled to encamp on the other bank of the river.

Sunday, December 21st, 1851. Left our encampment a short time after sunrise, and, after going some two or three miles, came to where the boat was, and, after waiting some two hours, the Indians made out to get it across the river. We then took charge of it, and about sundown we had all of our *goods* and *chattels* across the river.

These Yuma Indians are certainly the greatest beggars I have ever met with. I do not believe they would be satisfied if you were to give them the last piece of clothing on your person. Santiago, the chief of the Yumas, is the greatest *beggar* of all his tribe. These Indians, *so far*, appear to be very friendly, but I put very little dependence in either an Indian or Mexican; they both require *constant* watching.

There were several Mexicans from Sonora with their families arrived at our encampment this evening. They have requested me to allow them to accompany my command, as they are somewhat doubtful about the friendly feelings of the Indians to persons passing through *their* country to California. One of them states that he passed here on his way from California about two months since, and that he understood that the Indians and troops stationed at the mouth of the Gila were not on very good terms, and that he is under the impression that the garrison was broken up owing to the small number of troops that were stationed in this neighborhood.

Monday, December 22nd, 1851. Left our encampment on the bank of the Rio Colorado a short time after sunrise, and, after a few hours' march, we struck the main road, much to the delight of everyone. We were guided to the road by an Indian who we promised to give a pair of pantaloons to if he would take us to the road over a good route. On our arrival at the road we gave him *the pantaloons*, and a piece of bread, and bid him adieu with the hope that we will not have the pleasure of seeing another Indian between this and San Diego.

We marched today some 12 miles and encamped at a place known as the wells. At this place we found just water enough for all of our animals, but not a sprig of grass. We brought a quantity of *willow boughs* from the river for our animals, which we will give them tonight. So far we have found the road sandy and very hard work for our *poor half*-starved mules to get the wagons along.

Tuesday, December 23rd, 1851. Left our encampment this morning a short time before sunrise. We found the road a very sandy one, and after a march of some 7 miles we came to water, where we halted some three hours and grazed our mules upon *mesquite leaves*. We then started and marched until near 8 o'clock p.m. and halted where there was neither grass nor water. We marched today some 15 or 16 miles.

Wednesday, December 24th, 1851. Left our encampment a short time after sunrise, and marched some 6 or 9 miles, and halted about 10 o'clock a.m., and grazed our animals on *mesquite leaves* until near 3 o'clock p.m., and started again and marched until 10 o'clock p.m. and halted near a salt lake, the water of which our animals would not touch.

That celebrated *New River*, which was said to have made its appearance, all of a sudden, has entirely disappeared. It was never anything more than rain water pools, and I presume will make its appearance again after a very hard rain. [As Craig presumed, the New River was simply an overflow channel from the Colorado that filled only after heavy rains.]

Thursday, December 25th, 1851. This is Xmas day, and I hope my friends in the States are enjoying themselves *rather* more than I am, marching over *such* a country as I am, without a *sprig* of grass or a *drop* of water for our poor famished animals.

We left our encampment a short time after sunrise, and, after a march of some 15 or 16 miles, came to a place known as the Coyotes or Sackett's Wells where it was said water could be found. On our arrival at this point, we found water enough in a hole for some three or four animals, and from the sign, we had great hope of getting water enough for all of our animals by digging, but I regret to say, that we were disappointed, and only made out to get enough for the *two-legged animals.*

We have found grass (a thing the mules have not seen for nearly a week, having dined upon willow and mesquite leaves for that length of time) a short distance from this point on the left of the road, and intend grazing our animals there all night, and early in the morning send them ahead some fifteen miles or more to water, and after watering of them, return for the wagons.

Friday, December 26th, 1851. Remained in camp today and sent our mules to water. We expect to leave here tomorrow night. The road from this point to the next water is said to be as sandy as the portion we have passed over. Our next water where we have sent our animals is known as Carrizo Creek or [illegible].

I wish I had the means of informing every citizen of the United States the difficulty of getting from Santa Fe in New Mexico to San Diego by this route. I should think any person fit for the lunatic asylum who would prefer this route to crossing the isthmus.

Ten miles south-southwest of the wells there is a plenty of fine *green* grass, which extends up and down the arroyo.

Saturday, December 27th, 1851. Left our camp this morning about 9 o'clock. The road was not as sandy as I had expected to find it. We arrived at Carrizo Creek about dusk. At this encampment there is very little wood, and no grass. The wind has been blowing hard nearly the whole day, and my eyes are quite sore from the sand, which has been beating in our faces nearly the whole way. We marched today some 18 miles.

I noticed this evening after reaching this creek a large number of carcasses of sheep. I think in one place I must have seen at least twenty. What could have caused their death I cannot imagine, unless it was the water of the creek, which I understand is at times very offensive to man and *beast.*

Sunday, December 28th, 1851. Left our encampment a short time before sunrise, and found the road a very sandy one. Today has been as hard a one on our poor mules, as they have had, (I mean in the way of hard pulling), since they left Cantonment Dawson.

We arrived at Vallecito a short time before sundown. At this place we have very good water, and a plenty of grass, but wood very scarce. We found a house at this place unoccupied. The Pueblo Indians residing here have informed us that it had been used by the troops as a depot for provisions &c., I presume while a post was at the mouth of the Gila. We are all delighted at having crossed the *desert* without the loss of many animals. I myself was fortunate, not having to leave a *single* mule.

I had no idea that a mule could survive *70* hours without water, and a greater portion of that time without anything to eat. Today the wind blew a perfect hurricane, and about sundown it was very cold. We all suffered very much from the sand blowing into our eyes. [In upper left margin: Distance 18 miles]

Monday, December 29th, 1851. We remained in camp today for the purpose of giving our poor mules the benefit of the grass. We will leave early tomorrow morning. The Indians inform us that we will find no one at Warner's Ranch, he having been compelled to leave on account of the Indians. This morning the crest of the mountain in front of our camp was covered with snow.

Tuesday, December 29th, 1851. Left camp as soon as it was light enough to see the road. Our road today was a good one, with the exception of two or three hills which we had to ascend in crossing the divide. We marched some 17 or 18 miles and encamped at San Felipe. At this place there is good grass and water, but no wood. We arrived at this place a short time before 4 o'clock p.m.

Wednesday, December 31st, 1851. Left our encampment about 8 o'clock this morning. We found the road today a very good one. Some 8 miles from where we encamped, just at the head of the valley, we passed through a beautiful grove of live oaks, and through this grove ran a beautiful mountain stream of delightful water. After a march of some 12 or 14 miles we came to Warner's Ranch. At this place the wagons encamped for the night.

Capt. J. W. Davidson, in command of the depot at Santa Isabella, having sent me word that he would leave early the next morning for San Diego, and that if I had any letters to send by the steamer, which would leave on the 4th of January, he would take them down with him, and invited me to come in and spend the night with him and Lt. Edward Murray of his Regiment (2nd Infantry).

After dining, Lt. Whipple, Topographical Engineers, and myself rode in, and reached the depot a little before 8 o'clock. From Capt. Davidson we learned, that Mr. Warner had been driven from his rancho by the Indians, who had destroyed his house and driven off his cattle. Major S. P. Heintzelman of the 2nd Infantry, with a command, left a few days since for the purpose of visiting the Indians residing in a short distance of this place, in company with the Indian Commissioner. We arrived at Warner's Ranch about 2 o'clock p.m.

Thursday, January 1st, 1852. Capt. Davidson did not leave today as he expected, but sent in an express with the mail. I wrote to my dear wife, who I presume will be astonished to learn of my being in California.

I shall remain here a few days to recruit my mules, and then proceed to New San Diego, where I expect to be for some time. Our wagons arrived here early today, having only 8 or 9 miles to travel.

Friday, January 2nd, 1852. Lt. H. B. Hendershott of the 2nd Infantry came in today from the party that left here some days ago to meet the Indians in council. He reports everything quiet, and the Indian Commissioner, Dr. O. M. Wozencraft, is expected to return to this place in a few days.

Saturday, January 3rd, 1852. Today has been a very pleasant one. Our mules have not improved as rapidly as I supposed they would have done. The grass I think is rather too young to do them much good, and they appear to care very little about the oats given them.

Sunday, January 4th, 1852. The express sent to San Diego by Capt. Davidson returned last night. The steamer had not arrived when he left. We had hoped to hear that Mr. John R. Bartlett and party had arrived in San Diego, and also Mr. Gray and the rest of my men, as Lt. Whipple thought he (Mr. Gray) would take the trail across the mountain to San Diego. But it appears nothing has been heard from either party by the good people in San Diego.

We will leave early tomorrow morning for the same place. The wind commenced blowing early last night, and is at this time blowing *nearly* a hurricane. It is as much as we can do to keep up our tents. I am happy to say, that it is a *dry wind* and not a very cold one.

Monday, January 5th, 1852. Left Santa Isabella this morning a short time after day light. Our road today a *portion* of it we found very good, but we had to *ascend* and descend some awful hills. Should we return this way I fear that we will have hard work to get up *some of* them, with a full load. We are now encamped at San Pasqual, Gen. Kearny's battle ground. At this place we lost several among the finest officers of the Army. Gen. Kearny himself received a severe wound.

Our march today was some 20 miles. The water here is very fine. There is not much grass, and *no* wood. I presume in a month or so the grass will be very fine. This is quite a pretty valley. There is an Indian settlement at this place. They have some fine cattle, and some few sheep. We arrived here a little before 4 o'clock p.m.

Tuesday, January 6th, 1852. Left our encampment this morning a short time before sunrise. Our road today was not quite as hilly as the one of yesterday. A few minutes after 12 o' clock noon, I saw the Pacific Ocean for the first time. Little did I think a few years ago that I would ever have that pleasure. We marched some 20-odd miles and encamped at a place known as the Soledad. Here we found the water very brackish.

We passed a rancho some six miles in reaching this place, where I presume the water was good, and I would therefore advise travelers to halt at that point, as it is not more than some 16 miles to San Diego. We arrived in camp a short time before sunset.

Wednesday, January 7th, 1852. Left our encampment a short time before sunrise this morning. We had to pass over a very steep hill. I had hoped after getting over those hills in the neighborhood of San Pasqual, we would have no more such hills, but the one we passed over this morning is a match to any we have yet seen.

I encamped my wagons six miles from San Diego, where we found pretty good grass, wood, and water. Lt. Whipple and myself rode in to New San Diego and dined, I with Major Justus McKinstry, where we met several other officers. We returned to camp this evening, and I will take my command into New San Diego in the morning.

Thursday, January 8th, 1852. Left camp this morning a short time after sunrise, and arrived at New San Diego early in the day. Here I presume we will remain until something is heard from Mr. Bartlett.

Friday, January 9th, 1852. I left this morning for the Playa [a fishing village], which is a short distance from Old San Diego [the original town, north of New San Diego], and at which place there are several camps of the 1st Infantry stationed, under command of Major Heintzelman, 2nd Infantry. On my arrival at Old San Diego I met Dr. Summers and wife, and several other acquaintances, and I was detained until I found it too late to pay the visit, and return the same evening, so I determined to postpone it until another day.

Saturday, January 10th, 1852. One of my men deserted last night, and this morning I found a mule missing, which I presume he *stole*. [Later] Saturday 10th The missing mule was found, but my man is still *missing*. This is a bad country for soldiers. There are so many vagabonds to be found in every portion of it, that it is a hard matter to keep up anything like discipline among the soldiers.

Sunday, January 11th, 1852. Here I will close my notes for a time, at least while I am in this place, as there is nothing of interest to note.

Monday, February 9th, 1852. John R. Bartlett, the U.S. Commissioner, arrived today from Acapulco, Mexico, much to the delight of his party, which had given up all idea of seeing him in this country. Mr. Bartlett's arrival will enable us to leave for the Rio Grande early in March.

Thursday, February 19th, 1852. Today, in company with Mr. Bartlett and several other gentlemen, I paid a visit to the initial point [from which the boundary was surveyed to the junction of the Colorado and the Gila in 1849–1850], some 14 miles from this, where there is quite a pretty marble monument to designate the point.

The morning was rather an unpromising one, it having rained in the early part of it, but before 12 o'clock noon it cleared off and we had quite a pleasant day. The weather has been anything but pleasant for the last few days. It has been raining off and on constantly, with now and then a heavy blow. I fear that it will be some days ere it clears off. Living in tents in wet weather is *anything* but pleasant, and wood being very scarce here makes it still more uncomfortable.

Friday, February 20th, 1852. This has been a very disagreeable day. It has been raining off and on the whole day, accompanied by stormy winds.

Saturday, February 21st, 1852. Today has been one of the most disagreeable days that I have ever seen. It has *rained*, *hailed*, and *snowed* off and on nearly the whole day, and being in a tent in such weather is indeed *disgusting*.

Sunday, February 22nd, 1852. The sun rose bright and clear this morning, and today has been just the opposite of yesterday. I hope we shall have no more bad weather this winter. If we can only have such weather as we have today until we reach the Rio Grande, we will be very fortunate.

Sunday, March 7th, 1852. It commenced raining about 9 o'clock this morning, and continued off and on through the day, and the greater portion of the night.

Monday, March 8th, 1852. Today has been very pleasant, and I hope we will continue to have just such weather, for I must confess I do not like rainy weather while in *tents*.

Wednesday, March 10th, 1852. It rained quite hard during last night, but by 8 o'clock this morning it cleared off, and the wind blew very hard through the day. The steamer *Sea Bird* arrived early this morning and will leave for San Francisco again this evening. Col. John B. Magruder, Majors McKinstry & G. W. Patten, and Lt. A. S. Bond of the Army will take passage in her for the *City of Gold*.

Thursday, March 11th, 1852. During last night we had quite a *shower*, and, from present appearances, we are likely to have a rainy day of it.

Sunday, March 28th, 1852. This has been one among the most disagreeable days that I have spent *for months*. It has been raining and blowing nearly the whole day, and I have found my tent anything but pleasant, owing to the want of fire, for this has been one of the coldest days that we have had for some weeks. This is *said to be* a *delightful* climate. Perhaps it is, in comparison with the country north of it, but so far as I have been able to judge of it, I think it is *only tolerable*.

Friday, April 2nd, 1852. We had quite an April shower last evening, and it continued to rain off and on through the night, but from present appearances I think we will have a clear day. I should think from all that I can learn, that the rainy season is nearly over in this portion of California.

Friday, April 23rd, 1852. This has been a very disagreeable day, *blowing* and raining since early this morning. It is now near 8 o'clock p.m., and there is every appearance of a wet night. The weather is *uncommonly cold* for April. Today has been as cold a one as any we had in January. This *is said* to be a very *uncommon season* in this part of California.

Saturday, April 24th, 1852. Mr. Bartlett arrived here this morning, having been absent from this place since the latter part of February. There is *some little prospect* of our leaving for the Rio Grande in the course of a few weeks.

Bartlett's latest excursion had taken him to San Francisco, which under Mexican rule had been a port town of some thousand souls. American occupation and the Gold Rush had changed that. Bartlett found himself in a city bursting with 35,000 individuals, most of them male. His and Craig's previous request for reinforcements having been ignored, Bartlett called on now-General Ethan Allen Hitchcock at the Headquarters of the Pacific Division of the U.S. Army.

The Commission could not afford to go back eastward without additional soldiers. By the time Craig had reached San Diego, Craig's small command had dwindled to twenty-five. Twenty then deserted, leaving only five, three of whom were non-commissioned officers. Hitchcock gave Bartlett orders to give to the officers commanding at San Diego and Fort Yuma to give Bartlett "such a force as they deemed necessary," which amounted to twenty-five men, a number that satisfied Bartlett.

Craig's journal resumes.

<u>*LSC*</u>

Thursday, April 29th, 1852. Left New San Diego for the purpose of encamping in the Mission Valley between Old San Diego and the Mission of San Diego, at which place Col. Magruder's Company of Artillery is stationed. I am now encamped in a very pleasant spot. The river of San Diego flows in a few yards of my encampment, and the valley furnishes fine grazing for my mules.

I shall remain here for some ten days. By that time, I hope, Mr. Bartlett will be ready to leave for New Mexico. Before my arrival at San Diego, I had heard a great deal said in praise of the fine climate of this portion of California, but I regret to say that since my arrival here about the 8th of January, I have seen very little of the *Italian* climate I heard so much of. We have not had *ten pleasant* days in the whole of this month.

Thursday, May 13th, 1852. It rained early this morning, and before 8 o'clock cleared off, and it commenced again about 8 o'clock p.m., and from present appearances, I would not be surprised if we should have a wet night of it.

Wednesday, May 14th, 1852. I am delighted to say that I have at last made a start for the Rio Grande. I am now encamped at Panasquitas, about 18 miles from San Diego. I left my encampment in the Mission Valley a short time after sunrise this morning and arrived at this place about 10 o'clock p.m. Mr. Bartlett and party will be here tomorrow evening.

Thursday, May 20th, 1852. Remained in camp today. Mr. Bartlett did not arrive as I expected. I suppose he will be along in the course of a few days. He does not appear to be in a *hurry* to return to the Rio Grande.

Friday, May 21st, 1852. Mr. Bartlett has not arrived. What detains him I cannot conceive. I fear very much he will be out of provisions ere he arrives at the Pima villages.

Saturday, May 22nd, 1852. Still in camp, awaiting the arrival of the Commissioner. If he does not arrive tomorrow, I shall begin to think that he has determined to spend the summer at San Diego. I presume he would as soon be there as anywhere else, so long as the Government pays him for doing nothing, for the little that has been done could have been performed by Lt. Whipple in six months, and would not have cost the Government one third of the expense.

Sunday, May 23rd, 1852. Doctors Summers and Abbott spent the day with me, and returned in the evening to the Mission of San Diego. Col. Magruder came out in the evening and will spend the night with me. I learn from the Doctors that Mr. Bartlett was quite unwell and would not be able to leave for some days. Lt. Whipple and party left the day before, and ought to be here tonight, but I fear they will not reach this place until tomorrow sometime.

Monday, May 24th, 1852. Col. Magruder left this evening for the mission. I presume it will be *many* months, *perhaps years*, ere we meet again. Not *one* of the Commission party has yet arrived. I have determined to send to San Diego tomorrow for more provisions and forage, as there is no telling when I shall get off.

Tuesday, May 25th, 1852. I received a note from Lt. Whipple this morning, informing me that owing to one of the Commission wagons having broken down, he would not reach here until tomorrow. I fear that we will not arrive at the Rio Colorado until about the 6th or 9th of next month. Some three or four wagons passed here today from the Colorado on their way to San Diego—one of the teamsters reported, that a detachment sent out from Fort Yuma [which had just been reoccupied February 29] had met with a party of Indians up the river, and killed four of them, and wounded two, all of which I hope may be true.

Wednesday, May 26th, 1852. Lt. Whipple and party arrived this evening, and we will take up our line of march early tomorrow morning.

Thursday, May 27th, 1852. Left our encampment at Panasquitas about 6 o'clock this morning and encamped in the Valley of San Pasqual about 11 o'clock. Very shortly after our camp was pitched, Major Brown of the Pay Department drove up, just returning from Fort Yuma, where he had been on a *paying expedition*.

The Major spent the day and night with me. The Major intended to have gone out with me, but Mr. Bartlett appeared to be so very uncertain at what time he would get off, that the Major determined not to wait any longer, and I therefore lost the pleasure of his company.

Friday, May 28th, 1852. Left our encampment this morning a short time after daylight. The road we passed over today is the worst portion of the whole route from San Diego to the commencement of the desert. We were compelled to double our teams at a hill today some three miles long, and although we have not marched over ten miles, our mules are as much fatigued as if they had traveled 25. We are now encamped in the Valley of St. Maria. We reached here a few minutes before 10 o'clock p.m.

Saturday, May 29th, 1852. Left camp this morning a short time after daylight. Our road today was a *hilly one*, and our mules were somewhat fatigued when we encamped. We marched some fifteen miles today, and are now encamped at Santa Isabel. We arrived today 25 minutes before 12 o'clock noon.

Sunday, May 30th, 1852. Mr. Bartlett reached here late last evening. We shall not leave this encampment until the arrival of Antoine Leroux, who was sent by Mr. Bartlett to San Bernardino for the purpose of purchasing a wagon, and it is presumed he will be here tomorrow evening. If so, we will get off the next evening. [Leroux had been a guide of Colonel Cooke and had just arrived in San Diego from another exploration. Wanting to return to New Mexico, he offered "the services of himself and two men, together with several pack and riding mules, for a moderate compensation" from Commissioner Bartlett.]

Monday, May 31st, 1852. The wagon that was sent for by Mr. Bartlett arrived today, and we expect to leave this encampment tomorrow evening at 5 o'clock.

Tuesday June 1st, 1852. Left our encampment at Santa Isabel today at a few minutes before 6 o'clock p.m. and arrived at San Felipe a few minutes before daylight, after a night march of some twenty odd miles. I do not think I ever saw a more beautiful moonlight night. The moon was just full, and it was nearly as light as day. Our teamsters had no difficulty in passing over the road.

Wednesday June 2nd, 1852. Left our encampment this evening a few minutes before 6 o'clock and arrived at Vallecito a short time before daylight, distance about 26 miles.

Thursday June 3rd, 1852. Left our encampment about 6 o'clock this evening, and arrived at Carrizo Creek about 2 o'clock a.m. Distance about 18 miles.

Friday June 4th, 1852. Left our encampment about 10 o'clock p.m. this evening, and had not gone more than some six or eight miles, when one of my teamsters in ascending a hill, upset his wagon, precipitating wagon & mules down a precipice of some fifty or sixty feet deep and, much to the astonishment of all hands, neither the wagon or mules were at all injured. This accident detained us an hour or two, and we did not arrive at Sackett's Wells until a little after 7 o'clock a.m. Distance marched today some twenty miles. The heat has been oppressive for the last few days. The Thermometer in the shade about 111.

In this brutally hot weather, the sudden pressure of unexpected events would make this June 4 entry Craig's last one, and it would be left to his companions to record his final days. On June 5, Lt. Thomas B. Sweeny arrived from Fort Yuma at the commission's encampment at Sackett's Wells. He was pursuing two deserters from the fort, and remained with

Bartlett's party during the day, since the temperatures had forced the wagons to move only at night.

Bartlett recalled that as the wagon train resumed its journey at 7 p.m., Colonel Craig at first accompanied him at the head of the train, riding a mule. "After keeping with me for an hour and a half," Bartlett wrote,

> [T]the Colonel left me, saying he would ride back and see to the wagons, as some of them were dropping behind. This course was usual with him. He felt a heavy responsibility upon his shoulders and deemed it his duty to watch every part of the train. He considered his post to be in the advance; but during every march, whether at night or by day, he rode around the train, to see that all was all right, and that his men observed proper vigilance.

Spotting the two Fort Yuma deserters making their way northwest, presumably toward the gold fields, Craig left most of his men with the train and set out in pursuit of them, ordering Sergeant [James M.] Bales, First Artillery, and Sergeant [Edward] Quinn, Third Infantry, to accompany him. One of the commission surveyors, Malcolm Seaton, rode with them for a while, as the wagon train continued toward the next encampment.

At seven on the morning of June 6, having journeyed forty-five miles, the commission's wagon train made camp at the Alamo wells. This site was often inaccurately called by the alluring name "Alamo Mucho," meaning "many cotton woods"—a certain promise of less arid conditions. Instead, the actual name, "Alamo Mocho," signified a more accurate description: "cottonwood stump," since the "wells" (often merely dry, sandy cavities) occupied a vast crater where, as Bartlett observed, "water is obtained by digging." The crater's floor was strewn with assorted wreckage and the withered carcasses of dead animals.

There had been no word from Craig and his party, except from surveyor Seaton, who had arrived at camp to report that Craig seemed to be making progress by following the deserters closely, as he continued to try to persuade them to surrender, wearing them down with talk as their continued walking exhausted them.

Then, at noon, Sergeant Quinn rode excitedly into camp saying that disaster had befallen Craig's party. Exactly what had happened would be told in various ways, with a good deal of self-contradiction, but what probably transpired was as follows.

Craig had long been troubled by the many army desertions that had plagued campaigning from the time of the Florida and Mexican Wars. After his recruiting duties, such desertions gnawed at him as personal failures because some of the deserters were men whom he had persuaded to enlist. Now, embarked on another laborious journey, his force had already been so weakened by desertion that the local commands had been ordered to supplement Craig's force. Craig had no intention of allowing the Fort Yuma deserters to escape.

These two, Acting Corporal William Hays and Private John Condon, both of Company D, Second U.S. Infantry, were Irish-born Catholics who had been recruited in Boston shortly after arriving in America. After identifying himself and learning their names and ranks, Craig used all his powers of persuasion in attempting to convince them to give themselves up. He promised them rations and transportation back to Fort Yuma, or, since they swore they would rather die than return there (a place quite well known as a miserable duty station for both officers and men), he offered to let them join his regiment and return to El Paso with the commission.

As the walking and the talking continued, Craig discerned that Condon was the better-natured of the two—he had an "honest face," as Craig told him. Craig used most of his arguments on Condon, hoping to split him from Hays. But Craig soon realized (and later declared) that Hays not only wasn't amenable to reason, but that he had been "thirsting" for Craig's blood from the start.

For Condon to continue to support and consort with Hays, Craig argued, would result in Condon becoming an accomplice to murder and end with his being hanged along with his comrade. All this time, it transpired, Hays was only biding his time, waiting for an opportunity for the two to use their rifles on Craig's party and then continue their journey on mule-back.

Apparently deciding on a brave, dramatic gesture, similar to Napoleon's at Grenoble, Craig dismounted, gave his revolver to Sergeant Bales, put his sword aside, and approached the two unarmed, as he had done successfully with the Apaches at Santa Rita. Again addressing Condon, he told him that to kill him would be murdering a man with a wife and child. Additionally, opening his uniform shirt, Craig exposed to both the welter of scars from his Churubusco wounds, showing them they would be killing an officer who had been gravely wounded fighting honorably for his country.

But, as Craig did so, his mule moved away from him, and he ordered Sergeant Quinn to catch him. Hays exclaimed, "While there is now only two of them here, now is our only chance," and shot Col. Craig from only six paces with buck and ball. As Quinn returned with Colonel Craig's mule, he saw Hays fire and the colonel fall. Condon then fired at Bales, wounding him and mortally wounding his horse—though, as his mount faltered, Bales fired a shot at each deserter with Col. Craig's six-shooter. Almost simultaneously, however, the horse fell dead and pinned Bales to the ground. Both deserters then directed their fire at Quinn, hoping to kill him and get the two mounts in his possession. Quinn, however, escaped, and "pushed on to camp to give information of the melancholy affair."

Epilogue

Posterity

But strew his ashes to the wind
Whose sword or voice has served mankind…
To live in hearts we leave behind
Is not to die.
—Thomas Campbell, "Hallowed Ground"

I.

The note of condolence from Winfield Scott, Commanding General of the United States Army, would be carefully preserved by Craig's widow:

> To Mrs. Lieutenant Colonel Craig:
>
> Scarcely had the army time to be proud of the bride of a distinguished brother, before we were called upon to mourn her great loss, & our own, in his untimely death—caused by a noble confidence in man's better nature. The young widow & her child have thus become the objects of the prayers of the whole service.

Earlier, the first to hear of Col. Craig's murder had been those anxiously awaiting news of him in the camp he had left that morning. When Sgt. Quinn returned and reported the recent catastrophe, Dr. Thomas H. Webb immediately organized a search party and readied an ambulance wagon. He set out not only as "surgeon to the escort," but as "a friend to Colonel Craig," whom he highly respected "for his military promptness and efficiency, and the humane feelings and sympathy" the doctor had often seen Craig "manifest for his men when sick or injured." Dr. Webb took with him his hospital steward and two others who insisted on going with him—the colonel's "faithful attendant," Willis, of course, who had been with Craig for fifteen years, and Lt. Whipple, "as a particular friend of the colonel's." Whipple's participation Dr. Webb welcomed as a "gentleman so well qualified to afford important aid in case of an emergency."

The search proved long and harrowing, partly conducted by

moonlight. Dr. Webb's party left camp at 1:00 p.m. and did not arrive in the vicinity of the shooting until 10:00 p.m. At last the searchers discovered a trail leading away from the rough road into the desert; there they found, first, "the colonel's loose riding coat," then his hat, and finally "about one mile off the road," Colonel Craig's body, lying beneath a blanket. Because Craig's remains were covered, Lt. Whipple hoped that Sgt. Bales might have survived. As Whipple noted accurately, the murderers would not "have paid such respect to the dead."

Whipple was struck with awe as the blanket was removed. "We uncovered him and his manly person never appeared more noble," wrote Whipple, "nor had his features ever worn more dignity of expression. His arms were nicely folded upon his breast, and he looked like a warrior taking his rest after a victory won." But examination of the mortal wound itself, Dr. Webb wrote, "produced a strong sensation upon all present," particularly on Willis.

After discussion, it was determined that, despite their wishes, the heat would not allow the body to be carried to Fort Yuma for a full military funeral; instead, there would have to be a temporary burial at Alamo Mocho. After traveling ten miles in that direction, the party came upon Sergeant Bales, "wounded and wearied out," having "given up hope of proceeding further."

The party reached camp at 2:00 p.m., and the commission train prepared to continue the march at sunset, with Craig's burial to be conducted just before departure, in a "deep grave," dug in the desert "a few rods from the margin of the great basin."

Bartlett described Col. Craig's burial rites:

> At sunset, when the mules had received their packs, the wagons had been loaded, and the party were ready to move, a procession was formed, and the mortal remains of our excellent and much beloved friend, borne upon a cot by four soldiers, were consigned to his lonely grave. I read on the occasion the burial service of the Church of England. There was neither mound, nor rock, nor tree to mark the spot: a dreary solitude reigned around us, uninterrupted by a single object, save the animals and men belonging to the party. Even the wind had died away; and in the silence that accompanied our sad and solemn rites, Wolfe's beautiful lines on the burial of Sir John Moore involuntarily suggested themselves…

Col. Craig would have appreciated this reference, an allusion to a British hero of the Napoleonic Wars. In 1809 at the Battle of Corunna on the northwestern tip of Spain, Gen. Sir John Moore had achieved a tactical victory that had enabled the British army to embark safely from the Spanish coast. Nonetheless, he had suffered a terrible wound similar to Craig's and, according to his wish, had been buried on the battlefield. His body, "wrapped in blankets and a military cloak," as in Craig's case, "was lowered into the grave by the red sashes of his staff." The Irish poet Charles Wolfe had commemorated the event in his most popular poem, "The Burial of Sir John Moore after Corunna." As Bartlett noted (though without quoting them), several of the lines resonated with the circumstances of Craig's burial at Alamo Mocho:

> Not a drum was heard, not a funeral note,
> As his corse to the rampart we hurried;
> Not a soldier discharged his farewell shot
> O'er the grave where our hero we buried.
> ...
> Slowly and sadly we laid him down,
> From the field of his fame fresh and gory;
> We carved not a line, and we raised not a stone,
> But we left him alone with his glory.

In the case of Col. Craig's temporary burial, however, Dr. Webb noted that a marker was carefully prepared: "a wooden cross was erected at the head of the grave, whereon was inscribed, 'Bvt. Lt. Col. L. S. Craig, U.S.A.; died June 6, 1852.'"

Bartlett, who had known Craig well during the last years of his life, recorded his considered opinion of the colonel, evaluating him as an officer and a gentleman:

> Colonel Craig was an officer of whom the army and the nation had just cause to feel proud. He entered the army from the love he felt for a soldier's life, and without the advantages which a military education at West Point is supposed to confer. Yet such was his devotion to his profession, such the skill he acquired in it, and such the bravery shown by him when called to serve his country, that he soon attained the rank of captain, and was brevetted Lieutenant

> Colonel for gallant service....
>
> His whole soul was absorbed in his profession, and he spared no pains to render his command skillful in the use of their arms. He was always most punctilious in the discharge of duty; and however much his command was reduced by sickness or absence, he kept up his daily drills and parades with as much rigor and discipline as though an entire regiment were under his charge. Towards his men he manifested the interest of a father as well as that of a commander, and was greatly beloved by them in return....
>
> It was a source of deep mortification to him, that men who had followed him through the severe campaigns of the Mexican War should desert him here, for the sake of pecuniary advantage. His genuine kindness of heart, honesty of purpose, and rigid adherence to duty, had won for him a large circle of devoted friends among civilians, as well as among his brother officers.

With John Magruder commanding in the region where his friend's killing had occurred, there was no doubt that a full and immediate manhunt would be ordered. Couriers hurried out with detailed information on the fugitives, and the murderers were soon captured.

Hays and Condon had traveled on foot as far as the adobe rancho of the Luiseño Chief Pablo Apis near Temecula, some two hundred miles from Fort Yuma, but still four hundred miles distant from the gold fields. The chief alerted Louis Rouen—a former mountain man and a local ranch foreman—that two travelers were stopping with him, whom he suspected were the wanted men.

After arriving and establishing that the Irishmen knew no Spanish, Rouen and the chief briefly made a plan of action in that language. Rouen persuaded the men they would not need their rifles on the trip and purchased the firearms from them. They refused to sell Craig's revolver, but when Rouen asked if he could examine the weapon, it was handed over and then turned on them. Several of the chief's men then rushed in and bound Hays and Condon hand and foot. Soon, the two were awaiting their court-martial in chains, in an adobe cell at the old San Diego mission that was Magruder's headquarters.

In late June, Col. Magruder and several Craig's fellow officers sent Mrs. Craig a condolence letter including appropriate resolutions, the type of sympathetic communication of sorrow that Craig himself had too often subscribed in the past. It noted that Craig, "our esteemed friend and companion in service," had enjoyed a "just reputation as a soldier, and high tone as a gentlemen" that "had endeared him to all who had known him." It assured Mrs. Craig that the colonel's "remains should be brought from their present lonely resting place" to be "interred by the side of similar noble spirits, who fell in the Battle of San Pasqual."

At the murderers' court-martial in late July and early August, all the grim and gruesome details of the murder were recounted, with graphic descriptions of the mortal abdominal wound, which had been inflicted at very short range by a load containing buck shot and a musket ball. During the proceeding, Condon was argumentative, especially because he felt that, since he had not personally killed Craig, he did not deserve death. (Since he had not succeeded in killing Bales, he argued that he had only meant to wound him.)

In his own testimony, Bales revealed the chilling detail that Hayes had paused in the murderers' escape to ask, "Has the old fellow got any brandy about him?" Despite being told that Craig "didn't carry liquor with him," Hayes still searched the colonel's body.

Hays, "being called upon to state anything in his defense" was said to have delivered "quite an eloquent speech." He stated that he had not killed the colonel out of "animosity," but because he was determined "to escape at all hazards." Having admitted to the murder, he asked only for "spiritual consolation, and the death of a soldier. He wished to be shot, not hung." The sentence of the court was that both men were guilty, and both were sentenced to be hanged.

But before the sentence could be carried out, the records of the courts-martial had to be sent up the chain of command, first to headquarters, Pacific division, in San Francisco. There they were endorsed and sent to President Millard Fillmore in Washington City by the commanding officer, Ethan Allen Hitchcock.

Reflecting on Craig's meeting such a sad fate, after surviving the Seminole and Mexican wars, the scholarly Hitchcock probably found a number of appropriate allusions to the Roman classics coming to mind. Among them perhaps was the warning line from Seneca's Fourth Letter to Lucilius: "He is lord of your life who scorns his own."

On January 31, 1853, the death sentences, having been approved by the president, were solemnly carried out. A wagon took Hays and Condon to the place of execution, seated on their coffins. Witnessed by a throng of soldiers and Indians, the convicted murderers were soon standing at the foot of the gallows in their shrouds, being shriven and blessed by a Roman Catholic priest.

With his final words, Condon continued to declare his innocence. But Hays seems to have at least come near redemption, presumably through the "spiritual consolation" he had been afforded by the local priest. In his own last words, Hays addressed his fellow soldiers, saying, in part, "I shot Colonel Craig. I should not have done it. I should have obeyed his orders. Let no man pattern after me."

Then, with the murderers hooded and standing atop the gallows' trap door, Magruder reported that the executioner took his axe and "severed at a blow" the rope that restrained the trap; thus, the murderers were "launched into eternity." The next day, Magruder further recorded, Col. Craig's remains "arrived from the desert," to be buried "with the honors of war."

In 1879 a new cemetery was created south of New Town San Diego "on the crest" of the peninsula called Point Loma; ultimately, it would become known as the Fort Rosecrans National Cemetery. There a stone enclosure was constructed to receive the remains of the dead of San Pasqual, their names recorded on a bronze plaque affixed to "a granite boulder from the battlefield."

Still beside them was the resting place of Col. Craig, now final, and marked with a standard marble military tombstone, as ordered by the Secretary of War for soldiers' graves in 1873—"4 inches thick, 10 inches wide, and 12 inches above the ground," rounded at the top, with a shield in relief—and, on this particular marker, in raised letters, "LT. COL. L.S. CRAIG, 3RD U.S. INF."

By that time, an outpost named Fort Craig had risen in the desert, 175 miles southwest of Santa Fe on the west bank of the Rio Grande. It was lastingly constructed in 1854 of adobe and stone, with "many interior squares enfolded by an almost continuous quadrangle of buildings." Its namesake would have been pleased that it served both as a site guarding the approach to Santa Fe and as a base for launching attacks against marauding Apaches.

No doubt Craig would also have been proud that the fort named for him was considered a good duty station, and, in particular, that during its existence both the Third Infantry and the Second Dragoons would constitute part of its garrison. Unlike most Florida forts, long disappeared, the extensive ruins of Fort Craig yet remain, despite the post's abandonment in 1885, only five years before the U.S. Census Bureau declared the end of the American frontier. The site was added to the National Register of Historic Places in 1970. The Bureau of Land Management took possession of the area in 1981 and now operates it as the Fort Craig Historic Site.

In February 1862, ten years after Craig's death, Fort Craig would also become a battlefield in the War Between the States. Confederate General Henry H. Sibley (of Natchitoches, Louisiana) and his force of some 2500 would win the notable Battle of Valverde near Fort Craig, defeating its U.S. garrison of some 3500 under Union general Edward Canby of Kentucky.

On the Union side at Valverde was a notable survivor of the Battle of San Pasqual, Kit Carson. Born two years after Craig, this more famous figure of southwest exploration was, after the New Mexico battle, brevetted brigadier general, U.S. Volunteers. To some readers, this might prompt the question of Craig's presumable allegiance during the Civil War, had he lived to serve. The simplest response would probably be another question. Late in 1862, would one expect Lewis Craig to have been with Mexican War artillerist Ambrose Burnside of Indiana, east of the Rappahannock, shelling Fredericksburg, or with fellow Virginians Robert E. Lee and Thomas J. Jackson, defending the town?

II.

As will be seen, there can be no question of the wartime allegiance of Craig's widow and daughter. But, for years after Craig's death, Elizabeth would face numerous challenges, prominent among them securing her husband's back pay and other money owed him by the government. The process would be long and exasperating and would echo Craig's fight for his inheritance as well as his controversy with Adjutant General Jones. Her fight began in early 1853 and would not conclude until 1859.

Unlike Col. Craig, his widow would not be immersed in litigation from a family will, for he died intestate. Although this would leave complications enough, Lewis's administered estate left provision for his survivors until the government paid Elizabeth and Sallie what they were owed.

For much of the 1850s, Elizabeth and Sallie remained in Athens, where Alonzo Church was moving toward retirement from his still unmatched thirty-year presidency of the University of Georgia. After Dr. Church's retirement, Elizabeth would see him and her mother comfortably settled outside town at Homewood, a farmstead that Elizabeth would always associate with her parents' enjoyment of its fields and flowers. She would particularly love seeing Dr. Church enjoying gardening and staying outside, in contrast to a professional life spent at desk or lectern.

Dr. Church's last years on the campus had brought no exemption from turbulent students, but the mid-1850s brought as well notable conflicts with fractious faculty members, in particular the brothers Le Conte—John (chemistry and natural philosophy) and Joseph (natural history)—who would not, as Dr. Church required, "visit the rooms of the students or…suppress disorder on the campus," among other duties.

The LeContes resigned and left Athens, but not before a quite unusual aspect of the controversy arose. This, according to Augustus Longstreet Hull's *Annals of Athens, Georgia*, revolved around Mrs. John LeConte and Mrs. Lewis Stevenson Craig, "both women of extraordinary beauty and the reigning belles of Athens society. They gathered around them each a coterie of admirers who vied with each other in devotion to their queen. The rivalry between the two came near splitting the town into factions." In the end, however, it was Mrs. Craig who stayed in Athens, and Mrs. LeConte who removed to California with her husband, ending the controversy.

After her husband's death, Elizabeth was until 1859 periodically in Washington City, where she ultimately received justice from the U.S. Congress in the matter of Lewis Craig's pension and "the settlement of the accounts" dating from his service during the boundary survey. Her champion in these matters was Senator Dawson, until his death in 1853, and Senator Alexander Stephens afterward. But Elizabeth's time in Washington would not be totally occupied with business. Usually the guest of Secretary of the Treasury Howell Cobb and his wife, the "sprightly young widow" was warmly welcomed by Washington society, where she soon became a noted belle.

At a reception for three thousand given by the Cobbs, Elizabeth

Craig helped Mrs. Cobb welcome guests, attired in "white silk with rich pink trimming." She impressed one who saw her as "beautiful, sunny-tempered, unselfish, warm-hearted, unaffected, sincere." A reporter from New York provided an additional reason for her charm: the "fascination of such a lady's conversation makes one forget externals, however elegant."

Attracting such attention in capital society, Elizabeth soon acquired a large autograph book, to which the capital's luminaries, political and otherwise, contributed—though seldom with only an autograph. More regularly Mrs. Craig's many admirers contributed letters, poems, essays, and sketches.

As one of Mrs. Craig's visits approached, Howell Cobb, who enjoyed teasing Mrs. Craig, had his wife to write to her for him, asking her "to stay away from the Treasury Department," so that she wouldn't "bedazzle the poor clerks, make their heads giddy, render them unfit for work, and thus disrupt the operations of the Treasury." Elizabeth responded, "Tell him I will not interfere with his Clerks. I shall aim at larger game, nothing short of the first man in office will answer." She referred to the bachelor president of the United States, James Buchanan of Pennsylvania.

The Cobbs were probably as surprised as anyone, when Elizabeth, remarkably enough, later moved into the Executive Mansion. She resided there, however, not as First Lady, but as the guest of her close friend Harriet Lane, President Buchanan's niece and hostess. Perhaps even more remarkably, Elizabeth received from the president jewelry and, apparently, a proposal of marriage. A love-struck Buchanan even told an amused Howell Cobb that he had begun to spend "restless nights dreaming of [Elizabeth]."

Having been in the peculiar old bachelor's company too long to harbor any illusions about him, Elizabeth satirically described the president to friends as "the Grand Turk." She found herself drawn instead to one of her chief champions in Congress, Alexander H. Stephens of Georgia. Her fond memories of him extended back to her girlhood, when he was the only student boarder of the Churches who had never pulled her pigtails.

Stephens appears to have been attracted to Elizabeth, as well, and she also received a gift of jewelry from him. But, although Stephens visited with Elizabeth and the Churches in Athens, his "pride" apparently persuaded him to break off the relationship. He seems to have felt that Elizabeth was too beautiful and accomplished a lady to waste herself as the nurse of a semi-invalid.

Meanwhile, New Orleans millionaire James Robb had laid romantic siege to Mrs. Craig. He had already won and lost more than one fortune as a banker, railroad magnate, and gas works builder in Cuba. His mansion in New Orleans occupied an entire block and housed a personal art gallery, complete with its own catalog. Famously, in the 1840s he had briefly owned a copy of the statue *The Greek Slave*, Hiram Powers's marble study of a classical female nude, which, according to the eye of the beholder, was either exquisite art or shocking pornography.

Although attracted to Robb, Elizabeth would not consent to be his wife; she feared she would be seen as mercenary. But Robb ultimately wore down her resistance, and Dr. Church married the couple in Athens on March 6, 1860.

Sallie Craig, now sixteen, having always worshipped her father, became unhappy with her mother's second marriage, as did Robb's Northern family by his first wife. Although Elizabeth had apparently been schooled privately at home, Sallie was soon sent to the Moravian Female Seminary in Bethlehem, Pennsylvania.

While mother and daughter remained in Athens, Sallie's most valued link with her father was Willis, who had crossed swamps and deserts with Colonel Craig and knew more about the colonel and his exploits than anyone else. When Willis was briefly sent to the Churches to assist with some project, Sallie feared he had been sold and had to be assured by her mother that his absence would only be temporary.

Nonetheless, until Sallie reached twenty-one years of age in 1866, she necessarily had guardians, in and out of her family. The last of these was Ferdinand Phinizy, a wealthy and prominent Athens merchant and banker, who, as required, took charge of his ward's financial interests. In summer 1863, Phinizy petitioned the ordinary of Clarke County to allow the sale of Willis, who was "becoming old and…of an ungovernable disposition, thereby giving your petitioner much trouble & likely to deteriorate in value." The petition succeeded, and Willis was sold that fall in nearby Watkinsville whether he lived to claim his freedom in 1865 is unknown.

When the war came in 1861, the strains between the Robb family and Mr. Robb's new wife and stepdaughter increased. Sallie and Elizabeth were both ardently pro-Confederate. Elizabeth's two brothers were both in Confederate service, one a West Point graduate; Sallie also vividly displayed her devotion to the cause of the Southern Confederacy.

While at school at Bethlehem during summer 1861, Sallie rushed in front of a platoon of Union soldiers. Brandishing a self-made Confederate flag, she dared them to shoot her. This they declined to do, and Sallie soon found herself back in Athens. She could not have been inspired by Barbara Frietchie's purported similar action at Frederick, Maryland, since it supposedly occurred in September 1862. In any case, John Greenleaf Whittier was not likely to write a poem about Sallie Craig.

At least one person was impressed by Sallie's action and determined to pay her tribute. This was twenty-one-year old Middleton Pope Barrow, whose father David owned a large plantation in the Wolfskin District of Oglethorpe County, Georgia, southeast of Athens. Recently a University of Georgia student and a graduate of its law school, young Barrow in 1861 became an officer of a C.S.A. artillery company. In admiration, he named one of the battery's guns "Sallie Craig." There were perhaps some young ladies in Athens who would have been insulted at having a howitzer named after them, but Sallie Craig was emphatically not one of them. Eventually, in March 1867, she would become Mrs. Pope Barrow.

Elizabeth, meanwhile, residing with the Robb family in Chicago, grew appalled at the mistreatment of Confederate prisoners at Camp Douglas. She spent much of the war visiting the camp and performing all the functions of a friend and nurse for the young Southern men, imprisoned so far away from home, and in such unhealthy precincts. When the Robbs moved to New York, Elizabeth assisted at prison camps in that vicinity and sent needed contributions to others.

III.

Both of Elizabeth's parents died early in the war; Mrs. Church died a few days after the firing on Fort Sumter, and Dr. Church a year later. Also in 1861, one of Elizabeth's brothers died in Columbia, South Carolina, in Confederate service, apparently of disease. Another brother became one of the heroes of the Battle of Brandy Station, and Pope Barrow served in both Northern Virginia and in the Georgia-Florida Theatre.

Lewis Craig's superiors and friends in the Old Army met a variety of fates. Adj. Gen. Jones barely outlived Craig, dying in July 1852. "Perfect"

Bliss died the next year of yellow fever, only thirty-seven. Winfield Scott remained with the U.S. Army to die after the Civil War's conclusion. Twiggs died a Confederate in 1862, acclaimed in the South for having turned Texas over to the Confederacy. Harney, accused of colluding with the Confederacy, sat out the war, and retired in 1865, brevetted to major general. Ironically, he engaged in much-praised Indian diplomacy rather than warfare after 1865. Ultimately, Harney lived, first on the Mississippi coast, where he often visited with his old comrade-in-arms Jefferson Davis, and then returned to Florida, where he lived out his days at Orlando, dying in 1889, having almost reached ninety.

Born in Vermont like Dr. Church, like him Hitchcock died in Georgia. He had lived out his days with a new wife in the stately Glen Mary plantation house near Sparta, Georgia, which had been east of Sherman's destructive path. His burial would take place at West Point.

Of those Craig had known well in Florida and Mexico, Joseph Johnston and William Hardee became Confederate generals who served most prominently in Elizabeth Craig's native Georgia. John Magruder also became a general, but of the three he was judged to have least lived up to early promise. Failing entirely to win fame after the Mexican War, Charles May resigned his commission as brevet colonel in April 1861 and sat out the war. Becoming a railroad official in New York, he died there in 1864 of heart problems.

Early in the war, Amiel Weeks Whipple served in many positions of trust and responsibility in the Union army, rising to major general. In May 1862 he was mortally wounded by a Confederate sharpshooter near the Rappahannock. He had probably heard Craig speak of Elba Plantation; it was near there that Whipple received his death wound. President Abraham Lincoln, one among Whipple's many friends and admirers, rode in an open carriage in Whipple's Washington City funeral cortege, having also arranged posthumous brevets for him.

John Russell Bartlett, having failed to run an acceptable boundary line between the United States and Mexico, saw others (including Lt. Whipple) complete the project to the satisfaction of the U.S. Congress. The area involved would be expanded in 1853 by the Gadsden Purchase to allow construction of a railroad to the Pacific over the most feasible route. Happily, the terms of the purchase would also relieve the U.S. of the responsibility of protecting Mexico from Indian raids. Bartlett would live and work productively into the 1880s, happily ensconced as the librarian of John Carter Brown's library in Providence.

In Virginia, Lewis's nephew Robert Craig Stanard, now a politician-lawyer like his father, had suffered the loss of his father, Robert Stanard, in 1846. The revered Judge Standard, Lewis's brother-in-law, had died, pen in hand, writing a last opinion; it was considered valuable though unfinished. Beside Jane Stanard's memorial stone, Rob would raise an impressive monument to his father, incised with his many achievements, together with a line of Latin on the reverse, expressing his great loss: "Alas! How much less it is to mix with those who remain than to remember thee!"

Rob Stanard married a Kentucky belle, Martha Pearce, who in the 1850s famously used their splendid mansion (later a private club) as "a notable *salon*, where the *beaux esprits* of the South gathered." And not of the South alone: Washington Irving was an eminent admirer of Mrs. Stanard, and the Stanards in 1856 would host British author William Makepeace Thackeray. During a dinner honoring Thackeray, "Mrs. Stanard was enlarging on the delightful republican simplicity of [America], as compared with the customs of Europe; Thackeray, in a theatrical manner, threw himself back in his chair, gazed at the beautiful, artistic frescoes on the ceiling, worthy of a royal palace, and with arms extended exclaimed, 'Oh! Mrs. Stanard, I do admire this republican simplicity.'"

Although Mrs. Stanard would live until 1894, Rob would die in 1857 at forty-three, younger at his death than his Uncle Lewis. And with the passage of eight years Old Richmond would be memory.

IV.

After the war that devastated Richmond ended, Mr. and Mrs. James Robb were among those friends who visited Alexander H. Stephens during his imprisonment at Fort Warren in Boston Harbor. He would be the last Confederate prisoner of war she would visit. Her work at Camp Douglas and elsewhere had been strenuous, and it would have been remarkable not to have affected her health, particularly since she had been diagnosed with ovarian cancer in early 1863, a fact known to very few.

Elizabeth had been comforted that her doctor had given her what he called "unpleasant information" as a "friend and as a Christian." At that time he thought it doubtful that she could withstand a risky, probably useless operation. He advised her, instead, as long as "her general health [was] not seriously impaired," to treat with palliatives "such painful symptoms as [would] from time to time arise." Her doctor apparently did not imagine Elizabeth would long survive, but she fought her illness for several more years.

Despite all, Elizabeth continued her work with the Confederate prisoners throughout the war. To an inquiring friend, Sallie wrote in late 1864 that her mother's health had improved but "would be still better had she not *prisoners* on the brain, she works all the time for them and when she is not doing actual work, she is worrying because she cannot give each of the 50,000 prisoners a blanket, hat, shoes, etc., and have them exchanged in the bargain. Poor sufferers, they do suffer so much."

Sallie herself, still necessarily in the North, "this *hateful* land," worried about the plight of her mother's native state during the March to Sea in late 1864. She confessed she could not "bear to think of loved Georgia, with all its recollections endeared by so many ties and hallowed by the graves of my sainted grandparents, being desecrated by the *Vandals* on her soil." An aunt in Athens, she hoped, would preserve and house what had been left behind: her "Father's portrait and Mother's pictures and books." Happily, these were saved.

In her last months, Elizabeth made final visits to her family members in Florida and Georgia and was honored to receive for her work with Confederate prisoners a tribute from the local veterans of the war in Athens, who compared her to the Crimean War's Florence Nightingale.

When Elizabeth died on January 6, 1868, she was first buried in New York City, but soon enough her remains were returned to Georgia, to the cemetery where her parents lay near the Cobb plot. James Robb purchased a tall stone obelisk to mark her hilltop resting place, and the local Confederate veterans bestowed all honors possible at her interment, led by Irish-born Confederate Colonel William M. Browne.

Writing to Mrs. Cobb in early July 1868, confessing herself "deeply affected" by Mrs. Robb's death, Mrs. Jefferson Davis asked, "How is dear little Sallie Barrow? Has she a child?" It was that year that the Barrows' first child was born, and by 1876 four others had come to the marriage. Of the five, only one was a girl and was named Elizabeth. One of the boys was named Craig in honor of Sallie's father. To all of the children, Lewis Stevenson Craig became a tangible presence through his portrait, his journals, and various relics associated with him, including his officer's sash (still a rich crimson) and a handsome diplomatic sword of the Republic of Texas, a souvenir of his time in the Southwest.

Craig Barrow, in particular, found the military career of his namesake an absorbing subject, and, like Col. Craig, was much interested in history in general. Like his father, Barrow graduated from the University of Georgia, but he went on to receive a medical degree from the University of Maryland. During the Great War, to his Hippocratic Oath he added the oath of an officer, as he served at the rank of captain in the U.S. Army Medical Corps.

Moving to Savannah (where his father had located in the 1890s to practice law and would die in 1903), Craig Barrow soon became known as a valuable, civic-minded citizen as his professional prominence as a surgeon grew. On his death in 1945, a eulogy also noted that "Georgians knew him also in connection with the preservation of the history" of Georgia. With his wife, Elfrida, daughter of the founder of the Wymberley Jones De Renne Georgia Library, Dr. Barrow had revitalized her family home, Wormsloe Plantation near Savannah, where both are buried.

As one of the linkages in what Mrs. Craig Barrow called "the round of time," the portrait of the Virginian U.S. Army officer grandson of James Craig of London had come to be displayed in a place of honor, within the residence located on the coastal Georgia plantation founded in the 1730s by Noble Jones of London.

Craig Barrow was only five in 1881 when his mother, Sallie, was struck with typhoid fever. By this time Pope's legal career had not only prospered, he had also entered politics; at the time he was serving in the Georgia House of Representatives, and he would be named the following year to complete the U.S. Senate term of the late Benjamin H. Hill. Such prominence made his wife's mortal illness newsworthy in the Atlanta papers, which printed lengthy obituaries. She died in Athens three days after Christmas 1881.

Knowledge of her father and his antebellum military career appears to have been unknown to one eulogist, though he mentioned that the name of her grandfather, "the late Alonzo Church," would "long be loved and revered" throughout Georgia, as well as that of her mother, "that noble woman who made herself so dear to the Southern heart by her great kindness to the suffering Confederate soldiers during the Civil War."

At Sallie's direction, the monumental slab placed over her own grave proudly displayed her lineage as the "Daughter of Lieut. Col. Lewis Stevenson Craig and Elizabeth Church, His Wife," and it noted as well her birth at Fort Jesup near the Sabine frontier.

Over two thousand miles west, Sallie's father's simple marker still stands among those of the dead of San Pasqual, joined now by the remains of thousands of other U.S. soldiers of several wars. The promontory where they lie is washed on its western edge by the Pacific. Across that ocean, beyond Lewis Craig's imagining, the soldiers of the Third Regiment were destined to fight, and they would battle across the Atlantic as well, in both Europe and Africa. Indeed, the officers and men of the Old Guard would campaign anywhere their oath called them, as had Lewis Stevenson Craig.

Acknowledgments

This book has been underway (in one form or another) for much longer than seems possible and has encountered all possible delays. Consequently, the institutions and individuals who have helped make this book are quite numerous. First, however—although tradition strangely dictates that appreciation directed to spouses be reserved until last—I wish here to express my grateful thanks to my wife, Wanda. She certainly deserves first place (and much more) as the vital, incredibly patient supporter of this book, as well as all the other scholarly work I have published. A fellow history major, she has always taken a sincere interest in my historical projects, happily accompanied me on research trips, and always given expert help as sounding board and proofreader. *Sine qua non*, as the old Romans put it.

Without that remarkable officer and gentleman Lewis Stevenson Craig, there would, of course, be no book. And, in particular, there would be none without the journals preserved by his family for over a century and a half. For entrusting me with these valuable documents and patiently awaiting completion of the research necessary for their interpretation and presentation, I will forever be indebted to Craig Barrow III, a worthy inheritor of proud traditions. My wife and I are also indebted to him and to Mrs. Barrow for the memorable hospitality of their home on several occasions.

Additional materials were generously shared by other descendants of Col. Craig, particularly the late Muriel Barrow Bell. She and her late husband, Malcolm Bell, Jr., both quite remarkable individuals, had a keen interest in the story of Lewis Craig, and they helped in several ways to bring this biography to completion. Their son Malcolm Bell III also offered valuable assistance with images and information, as did other of Col. Craig's descendants.

Elizabeth Church was less well represented in family materials, but some of her correspondence as Mrs. Lewis Craig and as Mrs. James Robb is held by a few repositories. Fortunately, a gifted history graduate student, Annelle Brunson, was embarking on a study of Elizabeth near the time this book was approaching completion. The materials and insights on her subject that she shared with me were most valuable and much appreciated.

That she has developed the judgment and values of a traditional historian was heartening to me at a time when much academic history has become so subjective and so politicized.

Annelle pleasantly reminded me of my own college students (graduate and otherwise) who always brought a spark to historical discussions in and out of class (and otherwise): John Belflower, Trey Bernard, Ashley Brown, Jason Childers, Ben Faulkner, Kyle Gore, Kate Hunter, John Hurley, Stephanie Lewis, Sarah McCook, Ian McMullen, Chris Miller, Nicole Mitchell, Gideon Norris, Angie Pitts, Justin Reeves, Nick Reonas, Rotonya Rhodes, Elizabeth Stephens, Donnie Summerlin, Deitrah Taylor, Jessica Thompson, Andrew Tweedy, Andy Veazey, Russell Wall, Jeffery Wells, and Daniel Wilkinson.

Similarly, the fact that this book has been finished shortly after I passed life's three-score-and-ten mark has put me in mind of those historians who taught me in college and set me a lofty example during their long and productive careers, in the classroom and otherwise. Among them were Drs. James C. Bonner, Helen I. Greene, Martin Abbott, and William I. Hair.

Heir to Dr. E. Merton Coulter's title of "Dean of Georgia Historians," Edward J. Cashin (1927-2007) left a sterling body of work in his field and a lofty example for all his fellow historians. One had no need to attend one of his classes to be his grateful student.

Dr. Frank B. Vinson, who thankfully remains as one of the "Old Guard" of Georgia historians, has served as a continuing inspiration, and over the years much of this book was profitably discussed with him and his wife, Ann, at convivial dinners. Both were present in 1989 at what served (to me and my wife) as my "debut" as a professional historian, in the presence of many actual historians, at the annual meeting in Savannah of the Georgia Historical Society. There, my first scholarly article received the E. Merton Coulter Award for Excellence in the Writing of Georgia History for an essay in *The Georgia Historical Quarterly*, still the honor of which I am most proud.

The Coulter Award, sadly, has been "retired" by the powers at the Society, and they have also reduced Dr. Coulter's impressive achievements and his decades of productive work in Georgia history to one ugly word. Ironically, the *Quarterly* is now edited from Ohio, which perhaps helps explain its campaign against Confederate memorials. Moreover, one of the delays in completing this book was using scarce time to defend one of my previous books, after it was subjected to a jaundiced attack by a nonhistorian in the Society's journal. Serious errors and misinterpretations were duly pointed out, without any real hope of correction. Indeed, the response was that it had been approved for publication by several historians, which, alas, was no doubt true.

On a much more pleasant note, I am particularly grateful that this book is the product of Mercer University Press, which published my first book long ago in 1987. This marks my fifth collaboration with a publisher that has gone from strength to strength since its establishment in 1979, bringing into print numerous books on a wide and true diversity of subjects. Director Marc Jolley has shepherded my books though the process during most of that time and has been ever patient and always thoughtful. He is ably assisted by a friendly and professional staff: Marsha Luttrell, Jenny Toole, and Mary Beth Kosowski. Jim and Mary Frances Burt have contributed beautiful art and design for most of my Mercer University Press books, most thankfully for this one. One of Mercer's editors gave this book a close going over and saved me from much mortification; whatever is left, I deserve. A talented cartographer, Brad Sanders, patiently and painstakingly produced the handsome maps that complement the text.

The late Tom Watson Brown was a treasured friend and fellow history lover although he preferred, when being introduced as a speaker, to be described as a "wit, raconteur, and bon vivant." All these were accurate descriptions. Thankfully, Tom was from the first an invaluable supporter of my work. His love for Mercer University and Mercer University Press will continue to find expression for many years to come. His vast, well-chosen library is held intact by the Mercer University Library, and visiting it puts you in touch with an intellect both wide and deep.

The other libraries and archives where this book was researched will be found among the citations, and their staffs provided uniform help and courtesy. I must mention particularly, however, the old Hargrett Library, where the earliest research was done, back on the third floor of the main library, with its stunning view of the old campus. It was then the domain of Mary Ellen Brooks, who helped me through this and many other projects, as did Nelson Morgan, then master of the library's treasury of images.

Closer to home, the Genealogical & Historical Room of Washington

Memorial Library is the finest facility of its kind in the state, ably and efficiently run by Muriel Jackson and her pleasant and knowledgeable staff.

One of the most pleasant phases of research into Lewis Craig's life was visiting (in company with my wife and, often, with my aunt, Dot Bragg) the localities Craig knew best, in Virginia and elsewhere. Most kind and helpful among those in charge of such places was Carrie L. Miller, the Superintendent at Louisiana's Fort Jesup Historic Site, perhaps the most evocative of those places where the three Craigs once lived.

Lewis Craig would be heartened and proud of the existence of The Old Guard Museum at Fort Myer, Virginia. There Director/Curator Kirk M. Heflin discussed with me the Third U. S. Infantry Regiment's storied past and provided valuable suggestions and materials.

Finally, for American war fighters like Lewis Stevenson Craig, in the past and to come, acknowledgement, appreciation, and honor will always be richly merited.

Abbreviations

AC	Adam Craig
AGLR	Adjutant General, Letters Received, NARA
CCSL	Papers of the Cazenove, Craig, Stanard, and Lee Families
ECC	Elizabeth Church Craig
Hargrett	Hargrett Rare Book and Manuscript Library, University of Georgia.
JCBL	John Carter Brown Library, Providence, Rhode Island
JRB	John Russell Bartlett
JRBC	John Russell Bartlett Collection, JCBL
LSC	Lewis Stevenson Craig
MBCC	Mexican Boundary Commission Correspondence, JRBC, JCBL
NAMP	National Archive Microfilm Publications
NARA	National Archives and Records Administration
PC	Private Collections of LSC's descendants
SC	Sallie Craig
VHS	Virginia Historical Society, Richmond, Virginia

Notes

PREFACE

O'Sullivan, "Annexation," 5; Bartlett, *Personal Narrative*, 2:146.

PROLOGUE: PORTENTS

For antebellum Richmond, see Duke and Jordan *A Richmond Reader*, 13; Dabney, *Richmond*, 74–98.

For the Burr conspiracy and trial, see Lewis, *Burr Conspiracy*, 296–330 (the definitive account); Abernethy, *Burr Conspiracy*, 25, 54; Lomask, *Aaron Burr*, 222–82.

For Washington's statue in Richmond and his influence on Washington City, including the Executive Mansion, see Hallam, "Houdon's Washington in Richmond"; Harris, "Washington's Gamble"; Hamlin, "The Birth of American Architecture"; and Morales-Vázquez, "George Washington, The President's House, and the Projection of Executive Power." The Executive Mansion would not be officially designated the White House until 1901 (Seale, *President's House*, 2:654).

For the War Department, see Ingersoll, *A History of the War Department*, 109–10. The War Department did not become the Department of Defense until 1947.

For comparative military power, see E. Upton, *Military Policy*, 65, 137; Jones, *Later Roman Empire* 1:679–86; Bruce et al., *Fighting Techniques of the Napoleonic Age*, 103; Bender, "The Soldier in the Far West," 159.

For Thomas Jefferson, see Peterson, *Thomas Jefferson and the New Nation*, 867–74; Malone, *Jefferson the President*, 330–39.

For John Marshall, see Paul, *Without Precedent*, 282–96.

For Valley Forge and Addison's play, see Kennedy, *Burr, Hamilton, and Jefferson*, 53–55; and Addison, *Cato*, viii–x, 84. The last words traditionally attributed to Nathan Hale before his execution also show a debt to Cato.

For the Cincinnati, see Thomas, *Society of the Cincinnati*, 24–32. For the Virginia membership, see Virginia Historical Society, "The Virginia Society of the Cincinnati," 22–29.

The best source for the attempts of the Federalists and the Democrats to fashion the U.S. Army into their own partisan image is Crackel, *Mr. Jefferson's Army*.

For officers' need for political patrons, see Skelton, *An American Profession of Arms*, 288–89.

For Kentucky, New Orleans, and the Louisiana Purchase, see Kukla, *A Wilderness So Immense*, 127–33, 232–34, 333–40.

For Alexander Hamilton and Spanish America, see Coleman, "'A Second Bounaparty?'" 205.

For James Wilkinson, see Linklater, *An Artist in Treason*, 207, 216–17, 220, 236, 246, 292; Narrett, "Geopolitics and Intrigue," 120–21.

For Commodore Truxtun, see DeConde, *Quasi-War*, 209–210.

For William Eaton, see Lambert, *Barbary Wars*, 150–55; Morgan, "General William Eaton," 586–614, 697–713. St. Clair's Defeat remains the U.S. Army's most devastating loss to an Indian force (637 killed, 263 wounded). Custer's Last Stand (1876) was a loss of 230 killed (his entire force) (Matloff, *American Military History*, 112–317).

For Anthony Wayne, see Weigley, *History of the United States Army*, 92–93.

For the 3rd Infantry Regiment and its lineage, see Mahon and Danysh, *Army Lineage Series*, 159–62; Wensyel, "The Old Guard," 38–45; Dept. of the U.S. Army, *Old Guard*, 3–18. A present-day member of The Old Guard, U.S. Senator Tim Cotton delves into the history of the regiment in his *Sacred Duty: A Soldier's Tour at Arlington National Cemetery*. The book is dedicated to "The soldiers of The Old Guard—past, present, and future."

For Washington Irving, see Burstein, *Original Knickerbocker*, 59–60.

For Andrew Jackson, see Remini, *Andrew Jackson and the Course of American Empire*, 157–58; Beveridge, *Life of John Marshall*, 3:404–405.

For Winfield Scott, see Peskin, *Winfield Scott*, 3–4.

For Scott, Jackson, and lieutenant general, see Johnson, *Winfield Scott*, 64.

CHAPTER 1: FROM THE OLD DOMINION

For the source of Virginia's being called "The Old Dominion," see Dent, "Virginia—The Founder of States," 286–87. Dent traces the term to the use of "the Queen's Dominion," for North America, as claimed after the Cabot explorations, when North America and Virginia were considered the same. Around 1736, William Byrd concurs in his *History of the Dividing Line* when he writes that "the other British colonies on the Main have, one after another, been carved out of Virginia, by grants from his Majesty's Royal Predecessors. All that part of the Northern American Continent now under the Dominion of the King of Great Britain, and Stretching quite as far as the Cape of Florida, went at first under the General Name of Virginia" (Byrd, *History of the Dividing Line*, 1:1).

For Virginia as "Mother of Presidents" and "Mother of Generals," see Hastings, *Ancient American Politics*, 51; Bonner, "The Historical Basis of Southern Military Tradition," 74.

For Virginia as a continent and its possible expansion to California, see [Waterhouse,] *A Declaration of the State of the Colony and Affaires in Virginia*, title page; Beverley, *History and Present State of Virginia*, 2:1–3.

For James Craig's Atlantic voyage and his life in Virginia, see Duffy, "The Passage to the Colonies"; for a detailed view of Colonial Virginia, see Fischer, *Albion's Seed*, 207–418. For London, Virginia, and tobacco, see Atton and Holland, *King's Customs*, 389; Breen, *Tobacco Culture*, 57; Ripley, *Financial History of Virginia*, 150–53; Einzig, *Primitive Money*, 281–82.

The best single source on James Craig is Hollan, *Virginia Silversmiths, Jewelers, Watch- and Clockmakers*, 195–99. Also valuable is Kopper, *Colonial Williamsburg*, 18, 109, 186, 276, 286. A great deal of primary source material on James Craig and the Golden Ball, including James Craig's will, may be found online at the Colonial Williamsburg Digital Library, especially the two overlapping reports: McWilliams, "Golden Ball Historical Report" (1942) and Stephenson, "Golden Ball Historical Report" (1946). All details of the life of James Craig are drawn from the above sources.

For John Norton and others, see Olson, "The Virginia Merchants of London"; Price, "Who Was John Norton?" For the "Association," see Schlesinger, *Colonial Merchants and the American Revolution*, 136–37.

For Adam Craig's profession, see Hoffer, *Law and People in Colonial America*, 33, 38; Whiffen, *Public Buildings of Williamsburg*, 130–34; Olmert, *Official Guide to Colonial Williamsburg*, 59, 119; and Hening, *Statutes at Large of Virginia*, 9:145–46.

For "gentleman," see Gilliam, "'Mr.' in Virginia Records before 1776," 144; Coss, "The Formation of the English Gentry," 38–64. For a detailed view, see Rozbicki, *Complete Colonial Gentleman: Cultural Legitimacy in Plantation America*.

For AC's seal, see *Richmond Times-Dispatch*, November 29, 1959, 32-A.

For "esquire" and "armiger," see Coss, "Knights, Esquires, and the Origins of Social Gradation in England," 155–78.

For the Craig house, see Mordecai, *Richmond in By-Gone Days*, 104–105; M. Scott, *Houses of Old Richmond*, 16–19.

For clerkships, see W. Porter, *County Government in Virginia*, 31–34, 117–18, 122–23, 186–89, 346–47; Johnston, *Memorials of Old Virginia Clerks*, 211, 228, 329; Nuckols, *A History of the Government of the City of Richmond, Virginia*, 72, 75.

For slavery in Richmond, see Sheldon, "Black-White Relations in Richmond, Virginia, 1782–1820," 29–33; J. C. Miller, *Wolf by the Ears*, 128–29; Egerton, *Gabriel's Rebellion*, 90, 111.

For the Anglican/Protestant Episcopal Church in Virginia, see H. Adams, *History of the United States of America during the First Administration of Thomas Jefferson*, 1:135–36; Posey, "The Protestant Episcopal Church: An American Adaptation," 3–30; D. Upton, *Holy Things and Profane*; Nelson, *A Blessed Company*; Brydon, "The Antiecclesiastical Laws of Virginia," 259–85.

For Masonry see "Williamsburg Lodge of Masons," 1, 15, 19; Walthall,

History of Richmond Lodge, No. 10, A.F.& A.M, 11–12, 14, 31; Moore, *History and By-Laws of Richmond Royal Arch Chapter*, 32–33, 66, 98; Brethren of Prince Edwin's Lodge, *Free-Masons' Melody*, 161.

For Andrew Stevenson, see Wayland, *Andrew Stevenson.*

For Lewis Littlepage, see Davis, *King's Chevalier*; [Douglas Southall Freeman], "Virginia Adventurers," *Richmond News Leader*, November 30, 1933.

Mrs. Craig's difficult pregnancy is mentioned in a letter from Elizabeth Stevenson to Jane Craig, April 26, 1807, Folder 3a, Papers of the Cazenove, Craig, Stanard, & Lee Families (cited as CCSL). Details on family members and events are found throughout this collection, with much detailed information regarding the Craig family ranging from 1782 to 1843, including AC's land purchases in Kentucky.

For Adam Craig's death and will, see *Richmond Enquirer*, May 14, 1808; Friend, "Craig," 159–60; and Deed Book E, Folios 176–179, Register of Deeds Office, Overton County, Tennessee.

Oddly, AC's will is not to be found in Richmond (where it was perhaps lost in the fire of 1865), but was entered in a Tennessee county where AC owned property.

For the Richmond Theatre Fire and the Monumental Church, see Shockley, *Richmond Stage, 1784–1812*, 360–82; Fisher, *History and Reminiscences of the Monumental Church*; and "Letters of John Tyler," 75.

For the painting of the Craig house and Jane Stanard's protracted stay at Richmond, see William Craig to Jane Stanard, October 3, 1812, and Robert Stanard to Jane Stanard, February 27, 1813, CCSL. Jane had apparently traveled too soon after a November 1812 miscarriage.

The description of the James River is from Charles Dickens, who visited Richmond in 1842 (Dickens, *American Notes*, 151).

For LSC's childhood fascination with reading and books, see Robert Stanard to Jane Stanard, May 16, 1813, CCSL.

For Winfield Scott and Sir Walter Scott's novels, see Peskin, *Winfield Scott*, 3.

For LSC's schooling at St. Mark's Parish Glebe School, see Meade, *Old Churches, Ministers, and Families of Virginia*, 1:81–82; Woodville diary, 166; Eckenrode, "The Glebes," in *Separation of Church and State in Virginia*, 130–51; Buckley, "Evangelicals Triumphant," 32–69.

For William Craig's letter regarding Lewis's homesickness and aptitude as a classical scholar, see William Craig to Jane Stanard, December 2, 1820, CCSL.

For LSC's schooling at Llangollen, see E. Smith, "The Llangollen School for Boys," 3–14; Kamieniak, *Fredericksburg, Virginia*, 67–73, 153; and J. Lewis, Llangollen School for Boys, Account Books, 1811–1818, MSS 3L 7702, VHS.

For the Jubilee, see Burstein, *America's Jubilee*, 5, 16–19.

For Jane Stanard's worries about her husband being drafted into the militia, see Jane Stanard to Mary Craig, August 23, 1815, CCSL.

For the Virginia Militia in the War of 1812, see Bonin, *Virginia in the War of 1812*, 55–57; Butler, *Defending the Old Dominion*, xiv.

For the marriage of James Craig, see James Craig to Mary Craig, July 12, 1814; and Jane Stanard to Mary Craig, August 8, 1814, CCSL.

For Jane Craig's estrangement from her mother, see Jane Stanard to Mary Mallory Craig, July 12, 1817, and Jane Stanard to Mary Mallory Craig, January 12, 1818, CCSL.

For the deaths of Mary Craig Paine and Samuel Paine, see *Richmond Enquirer*, November 26, 1819, and *Richmond Daily Mail & Advertiser*, May 5, 1821.

For Elizabeth Stevenson, see E. L. Stevenson to Jane Craig, undated, and Jane Stanard to Mary Craig, October 11, 1817, CCSL.

For Jane Stanard and Edgar Allan Poe, see Silverman, *Edgar A. Poe*, 8, 360; Thompson, ed., *Selected Writings of Edgar Allan Poe*, 47, 47n.1; Quinn, *Edgar Allan Poe*, 85–87. A portrait of a beautiful woman said to be Jane Stanard was published in Quinn's book (opposite 86), but is now considered to be misidentified. A plaque at the Stanard plot in Shockoe Cemetery, Richmond, includes part of the lyric beneath the heading "Poe's Helen," and another plaque at the Adam Craig house identifies it as "Birthplace of Poe's Helen."

The deaths of Jane Craig Stanard and her daughter Jane are reported in the *Richmond Enquirer*, April 30, 1824, and in the *Fredericksburg Arena*, October 21, 1828. Marriages, births, and deaths in the Stanard family are recorded in the family Bible, MSS 6:4 St243:1, VHS.

The most inclusive of the many records of *Craig v. Fox*, etc., is *Craig et ux vs. Fox*, 1830, Collection CR-SC-H, Record ID 48–4, Fredericksburg, Va., Circuit Court, Fredericksburg, VA. Capt. John Fox's pungent description of LSC's brother William is in an affidavit found in the above collection, dated July 22, 1830.

The history of the sale of re-sale of Elba Plantation is the subject of numerous indentures, one of the most important of which is Deed Book CC, 1828–1831, ff. 144–45, Spotsylvania County, Virginia, Land Records, microfilm reel no. 53, Library of Virginia.

The voluminous records related to LSC's court battles are found in the Archives of the Fredericksburg, Virginia, Circuit Court, ranging from 1833 to 1838, which include the filings beginning in April 1828, when LSC reached his majority, and cover as well earlier events, such as Elijah Fox's purchase of Elba in 1824. The *Bank of Virginia v. Craig*, decided in May 1835, is found at 6 Leigh 399, Virginia Reports Annotated, along with an appeal by one of the sureties, denied in April 1836, which effectively marked the end of the litigation.

For Andrew Jackson's effect on the banking system, see McGrane, *Panic of 1837*, 113–14, 171; McFaul, *Politics of Jacksonian Finance*, 39–41, 98–101.

On Henry Clay and the Whigs, see Remini, *Henry Clay*, 459–60; Holt,

Rise and Fall of the American Whig Party, 116–19.

LSC's Recommendation for Appointment, October 3, 1837, is found in Records of the Registers of Secretary of War, Letters Received, August 7–Nov. 30, 1837, Roll 43, No. 22, NARA.

For the Dragoons, see Rodenbough, 17-30, and Karnes, 29, 43.

CHAPTER 2: TO THE FLORIDAS

For LSC's first battle, see *Army and Navy Chronicle*, March 22, 1838, 177; and Rodenbough 29–31, 502. Rodenbough's book is the standard source on the Second Dragoons. See also Stubbs and Connor, *Armor-Cavalry, Part I*, 9–10, 113–16.

LSC's commission, October 24, 1837, is found in AGLR, 1822–1860, C553, NA.

For Hugh Mercer Patton, see Goolrick, *Life of General Hugh Mercer*, 107, 109–10, 114–15.

Details of steamer traffic from the upper South to Florida are found in E. A. Mueller, "East Coast Florida Steamboating, 1831–1861," 241–60; and E. A. Mueller, "Steamboat Activity in Florida during the Second Seminole War," 407–31. Florida visitors' impressions are found in Rogers, "Florida Seen through the Eyes of Nineteenth Century Travelers," 177–81.

For the Floridas, see Darby and Dwight, *Gazetteer of the United States of America*, 163–66; Finley, "Florida, 1831," 31; Cox, *West Florida Controversy*, map facing page 2, 661–68.

For the First Seminole War, see Watson, *Jackson's Sword*, 141–53; Field, *Seminole Wars, 1818–58*, 4–7; Remini, *Andrew Jackson and His Indian Wars*, 143–62.

For Cow Ford and Jacksonville, see Cutler, *History of Florida*, 1:267.

Statistics on the Seminole Indians are found in Krogman, "Vital Data on the Population of the Seminole Indians," 335–38.

For General Scott's manuals, see W. Scott, *Infantry-Tactics*, 73; *General Regulations for the Army of the United States*, 62.

For U.S. Army officers' body servants, see Callan, *Military Laws of the United States*, 247–48; May, "Invisible Men," 466–67.

For the inventory of LSC property, June 6, 1852, see Whipple Journal.

For the Indian Removal Policy, see Prucha, *Sword of the Republic*, 249–68; Upton, *Military Policy*, 173; Sprague, *Origin, Progress, and Conclusion* (2000), 252, 403–417.

For the Virginia Indians from the early 1600s to the 1800s, see Tyler, *Narratives of Early Virginia*, 10; and Egloff and Woodward, *First People*, 55–68; Wood, "The Changing Population of the Colonial South," 60, 62–66.

For slavery among the Southeastern Indians, see Doran, "Negro Slaves of the Five Civilized Tribes," 335–50.

For the Black Seminoles, see K. Porter, *Black Seminoles*, 5–7, 31–36, 98–105. For slavery in Virginia and resistance to it, see Filler, *Crusade Against Slavery*, 22, 53–54, 60; Hunt, *Haiti's Influence on Antebellum America*, 148–49. The most expansive study is Taylor, *Internal Enemy*.

For Fort Heilman, Garey's Ferry, and Black Creek, see Motte, *Journey into Wilderness*, 95. Heilman (given thus in most records, but actually spelled "Heileman") was a West Point graduate from Massachusetts.

For military forces and settlers in Florida, see Denham, "'Some Prefer The Seminoles,'" 38–54 and Denham, "The Florida Crackers before the Civil War as Seen through Travelers' Accounts," 453–68; Missall and Missall, *Seminole Wars*, 101–102; Mahon, *History of the Second Seminole War*, 241–42, 268–70, 297

For Wheelock and Lane, see Mahon, *History of the Second Seminole War*, 174–75, 182.

For Reveille, etc., see *General Regulations for the Army of the United States*, 24–25.

For regimental organization, see Robinson, *An Account of the Organization of the Army of the United States*, 1:28–29.

For Twiggs and Harney, see Heidler, "The Military Career of David Emanuel Twiggs," 1–10; Brown, "An Old Woman with a Broomstick," 58; and G. Adams, *Harney*, 8, 47, 80–81.

For Uncle Toby Shandy's eighteenth-century oath, see Sterne, *Life and Opinions of Tristram Shandy, Gentleman*, 383; for nineteenth-century cursing, see Montagu, *Anatomy of Swearing*, 224–38.

For Fort Mellon, see Francke, Jr., *Fort Mellon, 1837–1842*.

For Florida forts, see Dibble, "Giveaway Forts," 207–33; Reid, *Osceola the Seminole*, 129–31; Knetsch, *Fear and Anxiety on the Florida Frontier*, 128–40.

For campaigning in Florida, see F. L. White, ed., "The Journals of Lieutenant John Pickell, 1836–1837," 166; Heidler, "Twiggs," 35–36; Potter, *War in Florida*, 139; Mahon, *History of the Second Seminole War*, 129; Alden et al., *National Audubon Society Field Guide to Florida*, 24–35; and J. L. Williams, *Territory of Florida*.

For military bands, see W. C. White, *A History of Military Music in America*, 39, 84, 269, 272; and Murray, "Weeping and Mourning," 287–88.

For early nineteenth-century descriptions of Florida flora and fauna, see J. L. Williams, *Territory of Florida*, 62–75. For a comprehensive modern inventory of Florida's plant and animal life, see Alden et al., *National Audubon Society Field Guide to Florida*, 78–377.

For diseases of the Floridas, see Gillet, *Army Medical Department*, 62, 63, 135; Missal and Missal, *Seminole Wars*, 204; Coolidge, comp., "Florida," in *Statistical Report of Sickness and Mortality in the Army of the United States*, 329–30.

For Jesup's campaign, see Mahon, *History of the Second Seminole War*, 228–32; Sprague, *Origin, Progress, and Conclusion*, 89, 203; Procyk, *Guns across the Loxahatchee*, 76–78, 83; Motte, *Journey into Wilderness*, 182, 194–98; Kieffer,

Maligned General, 184–207; G. Adams, *Harney*, 66; Mahon, *History of the Second Seminole War*, 235–37. Kieffer's *Maligned General*, which does not idolize Jesup, nevertheless give a thoughtful presentation of Jesup's point of view where Osceola and the Seminoles were concerned. For details of Jesup's defense of the capture of Osceola, see Kieffer, *Maligned General*, 185–88.

For a Georgia governor's view of the Indian situation from 1803 to removal, see Lumpkin, *The Removal of the Cherokee Indians from Georgia*, 1:57–102, 224–28, 304–307.

On young officers' chances of promotion, see Coffman, *Old Army*, 49; United States Military Academy, *Centennial of the United States Military Academy*, 2:92.

On treating malaria, see Bibber, "The Therapeutic Value of the Mineral Waters of the United States upon Malarial Diseases," 10.

For Jackson on California, see McElroy, *Winning of the Far West*, 49.

For Jackson and Texas, see Remini, *Andrew Jackson and the Course of American Democracy*, 368.

For Fort Jesup, see Nardini, *No Man's Land*, 120; Hardin, "Fort Jesup" [parts 1–4]. For Harney and Chakaika, see G. Adams, *Harney*, 72, 77. For the battles most costly in American lives and for factors making Seminole casualties incalculable, see Missall and Missall, *Seminole Wars*, 204–206.

For the end of the Florida War, see Field, *Seminole Wars*, 17–19; Mahon, *History of the Second Seminole War*, 303, 312, 313, 316.

For the doggerel quoted, see full quotation in Rodenbough, *From Everglade to Canyon*, 27.

For Ethan Allen Hitchcock and the 3rd Regiment, see Hitchcock, *Fifty Years in Camp and Field*, 63, 159, 163 ("humbug"), 166–67; Cullum, *Biographical Register*, 1:170; Russell, *Edgar Allan Poe*, 4, 9, 11.

For Col. Many and Hitchcock's path to command of the 3rd Infantry, see Heitman, *Historical Register*, 451; Foreman, *A Traveler in Indian Territory*, 180, 180n.101; McRae, "The Third Regiment of Infantry," 434–35.

For Middle Florida planters, including Murat, see Paisley, *Red Hills of Florida*, 82–86. Two combinations of memoir and historical novel relating to the area and its people are Ellen Call Long, *Florida Breezes* (1883; repr., Gainesville: University of Florida Press, 1962); and Reinette Gamble Long, *Welaunee: A Sketch of Seminole Days,* serialized in 1915 in *The Tropic Magazine.*

For Napoleonic influences on the U.S. Army, see Bonura, "A French-Inspired Way of War," 6–22.

For the capture of Pascofa and the Tallahassee banquet, see Hitchcock, *Fifty Years in Camp and Field*, 168–75; Sprague, *Origin, Progress, and Conclusion* (2000), 501.

For Elizabeth Church, Dr. Church, and the University of Georgia, see Coulter, "The University of Georgia—Old and New," 12–21; Dyer, *University of Georgia*, 9; Knight, *Georgia's Landmarks*, 1:141; "Obituary: Rev. Alonzo

Church, D. D.," undated, unidentified newspaper clipping, PC; Linton Stephens to A. H. Stephens, April 17, 1843, in Rabun, "Alexander H. Stephens, 1812–61," 546; Lover, *Songs and Ballads*, 19–20.

For the marriage of LSC and Elizabeth Church, see *Athens Banner*, June 9, 1843; *Tallahassee Star of Florida*, June 22, 1843; Henry H. Jones to "My dear Sister," June 27, 1843, in C. C. Jones Collection; Bauer, *Zachary Taylor*, 69–70.

For LSC and Elizabeth Craig at Jefferson Barracks and Fort Jesup, see Ravenswaay, *Saint Louis*, 19, 243, 246, 324–25.

CHAPTER 3: TO THE SIERRA MADRE MOUNTAINS

LSC's account of his Mexican War experiences is found in four separate journals in private possession of LSC's descendants, written in ink on unbound sheets of paper. LSC titled them "First Part—A March from New Orleans, Louisiana, to Corpus Christi, Texas: 25 July 1845–6 August 1845"; "Next Part: A March from Corpus Christi, Texas, to the Rio Grande:11 March 1846–28 March 1846"; "Second Part—A March across Mexico from Matamoros to Tampico:7 August 1846–23 January 1847"; and "Third Part—A March from Tampico, Mexico, to Molino del Rey, Mexico: 20 February 1847–8 September 1847." No journals have been found that cover the lengthy encampment at Corpus Christi or the battles of Palo Alto and Resaca de la Palma. LSC's letters to his wife perhaps covered those events. Neither they, nor any other letters to or from ECC, have been found.

For President James Knox Polk's territorial aims, see Pletcher, *Diplomacy of Annexation*; Hietala, *Manifest Design*; and Merk, *Manifest Destiny and Mission in American History*.

For the goals and deaths of Jackson and Polk, see Remini, *Andrew Jackson and the Course of American Democracy*, 511, 524–25; Borneman, *Polk*, 344–48.

Among the best general secondary sources on the Mexican War, are two of the oldest: Rives, *United States and Mexico*, and J. Smith, *War with Mexico*. A brief account, featuring an analytical bibliography is Connor and Faulk, *North America Divided*. Bauer, *Mexican War*, has stood the test of time. Eisenhower's *So Far from God* features good military detail. Most distinguished among recent histories of the war is Clary, *Eagles and Empire*. The best primary sources are found in the bibliographies of the above titles. Osprey Publishing continues to do an excellent job of producing military (rather than political) histories, such as Meed, *Mexican War*, and their books on the Mexican War in both the Elite and Men-at-Arms series, which provide the period detail often missing in general histories.

Best among reference books on the Mexican War are Frazier, ed., *United States and Mexico at War*, and, with briefer compass, Moseley and Clark, *Historical Dictionary of the United States-Mexican War*.

For the U.S. Army's seven months at Corpus Christi, see Baker, "Seth

Eastman's Drawing of Corpus Christi," 179 (Corpus Christi's structures); Payne, "Camp Life in the Army of Occupation," 329 (fishing and hunting); 331 (storms); 332–33, 341–42 (sickness); 335–36, 340–41 (commerce); 337–38 (playhouses); Patch, *Concentration of General Zachary Taylor's Army at Corpus Christi, Texas*, 11 (campsite details). For Hitchcock and the 2nd Dragoons, see Hitchcock, *Fifty Years in Camp and Field*, 203, and Rodenbough, *From Everglade to Canyon*, 93–94.

For Mrs. Craig's "repugnance" to writing letters, see her letter to "My dear Friend," September 13, 1858, folder 317, James Robb Collection.

For the brevet controversy, see Hitchcock, *Fifty Years in Camp and Field*, 204–206; Henry, *Story of the Mexican War*, 45; Petition of United States Officers at Corpus Christi, Dec. 12, 1845, in *Senate Miscellaneous Documents*, Special Session, 1851, 8–19.

During the army's time at Puebla, Mexico, another even more important petition emerged, also signed by LSC and most officers, asking for "a law providing for the retirement of old and disabled officers." It would be many years, however, before such legislation would be passed (see Petition of United States Officers in Mexico, in *U. S. Senate Executive Documents*, Special Session (1851), vol. 1, document 1, 8-18.

For anxiety over U.S.-Mexican diplomacy, see Pletcher, *Diplomacy of Annexation*, 371, 378, 378n.63, 379; Hicks, "Diplomatic Relations with Mexico," 15–16; Rives, *United States and Mexico*, 2:121–24.

For the Mexican government's refusal to meet with Slidell, see Clary, *Eagles and Empire*, 77–78.

For the number of Mexican administrations, see Bancroft, *History of Mexico*, 573.

Don Carlos Buell's estimation of LSC is in Don Carlos Buell to Mrs. James Robb, November 25, 1861, PC.

For the march to the Rio Grande, see Thonhoff, "Taylor's Trail in Texas," 7–22, which matches Craig's account and follows mainly W. S. Henry's *Campaign Sketches of the War with Mexico*, also by a member of the 3rd Regiment.

For the war's first hostilities, see N. C. Hughes, Jr., *General William J. Hardee*, 25–30; Bauer, *Mexican War*, 47–50; Smith, *War with Mexico*, 1:148–50; Haynes, *James K. Polk*, 145; Henry, *Story of the Mexican War*, 400.

For the battles of Palo Alto and Resaca de la Palma, see Haecker and Mauck, *On the Prairie of Palo Alto*, 15, 87; Murphy, *Two Armies on the Rio Grande*, 198–99, 218–28, 222–25 & 297n.46 (Lt. May); Smith, *War with Mexico*, 1:170–76.

For LSC's promotion to captain, see LSC to AG, September 11, 1846, RG 94, AGLR.

For Harney's freelance adventure, see Reavis, *Life and Services of Gen. William Selby Harney*, 154–55, 159–160; G. Adams, *Harney*, 87–91.

For Santa Anna taking command of the Mexican Army, the capture of

Monterey, California, and the Capture of Santa Fe, New Mexico, see Dufour, *Mexican War*, 109, 135, 138.

For Santa Fe, see Chudacoff, *Evolution of American Urban History*, 47.

For Taylor's organization of his army, see Wilson, *Maneuver and Fire Power*, 10.

For the Battle of Monterrey, see Dishman, *Perfect Gibraltar*, 92–199.

For "death-dealing projectiles," see H. L. Scott, *Military Dictionary*, 64–70, 145, 151–54, 325–26, 470–77, 551, 563–64, and U.S. Ordnance Department, *Ordnance Manual* (1850), 248.

For William Craig, see Deed of Trust, February 25, 1843, in Clerk's Loose Papers, Prince William County, Virginia, 1808–1860, Circuit Court Clerk's Office, Manassas, Va.

For "The Culinary Knight," see Smith, *War with Mexico*, 1:241

For LSC's request for percussion muskets, see LSC to AG October 4, 1846, RG 94, AGLR.

For Ridgely's death, see Eisenhower, *So Far from God*, 154.

For the Battle of San Pasqual, California, see Groom, *Kearney's March*, 202–12.

For "The Mountain Pine," see Breed, *History and Use of Hymns*, 182–85.

CHAPTER 4: TO THE VALLEY OF MEXICO

For the Battle of Buena Vista, see Bauer, *Zachary Taylor*, 196–206.

For "largest amphibious assault," see Johnson, *Gallant Little Army*, 9.

For the surfboats at Vera Cruz, see Paulus, "Pack Mules and Surf Boats," 34–40.

For the vital contribution of the engineers during the Mexican War, see Winders, *Mr. Polk's Army*, 54–55; Traas, *From the Golden Gate to Mexico City*, 184–85.

For the comments of Wellington and Alaman on Scott's march, see Wright, *General Scott*, 195–96; Krause, *Mexico*, 143.

For the march to Cerro Gordo, see Henderson, *Stonewall Jackson*, 1:30; Smith, *War with Mexico*, 1:45–46.

For Twiggs at Cerro Gordo, see Johnson, *Gallant Little Army*, 68–72.

For the Battle of Cerro Gordo, see Heidler, "The Military Career of David Emanuel Twiggs," 121; Rives, *United States and Mexico*, 2:395; McWhiney and Jamieson, *Attack and Die*, 30; Wensyel, "The Old Guard," 41; S.Ex.Doc., 1st Sess., 30th Congress, vol. 1, doc. 2, 257, 293 (from reports of Scott and Alexander); G. Adams, *Harney*, 100–101; Smith, *The War with Mexico*, 2:55, 57–58; R. S. Ripley, *War with Mexico*, 2:66–67.

For Spooner and the Spy Company, see Hitchcock, *Fifty Years in Camp and Field*, 264, 330–31. A Fredericksburg guardianship bond of 1810 indicates that Spooner the spy was a son of George W. B. Spooner of Spotsylvania

County, but it was not possible to determine which son: Gustavus Wallace Spooner, George Wilson Spooner, William Alexander Spooner, Jacob Kuhn Spooner, Edward B. Spooner, or Horatio Spooner?

For the Pedregal below Churubusco, see Henderson, *Stonewall Jackson*, 1:35–36.

For the battlefield of Padierna/Contreras, see "Plan of the Battleground of Contreras and Its Defenses" (NARA). At the same repository, a similar manuscript map dated January 19, 1848, shows the three companies of the 3rd Infantry to the left of a field road leading to Padierna and the riflemen to the right of the road, below the U.S. batteries For Magruder's battery; see Henderson, *Stonewall Jackson*, 1:36–37; and R. M. Hughes, "Joseph Eggleston Johnston," 64.

For Hawthorne's Franklin Pierce at Contreras, see *Life of Franklin Pierce*, 91–105.

For Craig's and Alexander's full reports, see Senate Executive Document, vol. 1, doc. 1, 30th Congress, 1st Session (1848), 79–84.

For R. E. Lee's Description of LSC at Padierna, see Senate Executive Document, vol. 8, no. 65, 30th Congress, 1st Session, 75–76.

For Santa Anna's fate, see Fowler, *Santa Anna of Mexico*, 345.

For the final battles at Mexico City and the San Patricio execution, see Henry, *Story of the Mexican War*, 362–68.

For Scott in the Grand Plaza, see Peskin, *Winfield Scott*, 193.

For Scott, the "Old Guard," anarchy, and statistics, see McRae, "The Third Regiment of Infantry," 440, and Wensyel, "The Old Guard," 41. For total U.S. army losses, see Bauer, *Mexican War*, 397. For Mexican army losses, see Clary, *Eagles and Empire*, 412.

For the Aztec Club, see Breithaupt, *Aztec Club*, 1–7; and Aztec Club of 1847, *Report of a Committee*, 20. Craig and the officers who joined (and those who did not) were listed in an unusual imprint: [W. Scott,] *Official List of Officers Who Marched…with Major General Winfield Scott from Puebla upon the City of Mexico…and Who Were Engaged in the Battles of Mexico* (Mexico City: American Star Print, 1848). The publication lists the officers by regiments and notes LSC's presence at the August battles and the severe wound that rendered him "disabled" for the September battles.

For the honors voted to Virginia's Mexican War veterans, see *Acts of the General Assembly of Virginia*, 229. Gen. Scott was voted a gold medal the following year. The Virginia House had passed a resolution voting the surviving Virginia officers swords and listing them by name, but the resolution was tabled by the Virginia Senate (House Journal [1848], 558–59; Senate Journal [1848], 272).

For LSC's promotions, see Records of the Divisions of the Adjutant General's Office: Appointment, Commission, and Personal Branch, 1783–1917, 2:79, 3:162, NARA.

For Polk and the Washington Monument, see Johannsen, *To the Halls of the Montezumas*, 5–6.

For the Treaty of Guadalupe Hidalgo, including the text of the treaty, see Castillo, *Treaty of Guadalupe Hidalgo*; for a condensed version of the treaty, see Crawford, *Encyclopedia of the Mexican-American War*, 128.

For Whigs, Democrats, the treaty, and the election of Zachary Taylor, see Sibley, *Party over Section*, 30–32, 57.

CHAPTER 5: TO THE PACIFIC

Lewis S. Craig's journals of his experiences with the U.S. Boundary Commission are incomplete. The first, composed of unbound papers like the preceding journals, is "Notes of a march from New York to El Paso, Texas, of a detachment of Recruits under command of Brevet Lieutenant Colonel Craig, U.S.A." The next (and last) is a small black-bound notebook, a product of the Wall Street stationer William W. Rose. It measures 0.5 inch thick and 7.5 inches tall by 5 inches wide and is titled on page 1 "Continuation of a March from Cantonment Dawson, New Mexico, to the Mouth of the Gila River," covering November 17, 1851, to June 4, 1852.

The journal or journals that either have not been found or have not survived cover a sizeable gap: October 27, 1850–November 16, 1851.

For Craig's wound and his reception in Athens, see Surgeon Keeney to LSC, April 5, 1848; SO No. 35, April 10, 1848; LSC to AG, May 18, 1848, RG 94, AGLR, 1822–1860; *Athens Southern Banner*, May 25, 1848; undated, unidentified Fredericksburg newspaper clipping, PC; Dr. A. S. Hill to LSC June 30, 1848; LSC to AG July 31, 1848—both AGLR. Craig's banquet in Fredericksburg is found in "Manuscript Remarks in Honor of Lt. Col. Lewis S. Craig, Fredericksburg, October 9, 1848," PC.

For Fort Hamilton and recruiting, see Freeman, *R. E. Lee*, 1:184–93; Ms. Registers of Numbers of Recruits (1814–1882), Vol. 6:49, 50; Records of the Adjutant General's Office (1780–1917), Recruiting Division (1814–1913), NARA; Billings, *Report on Barracks and Hospitals*, 33–37; Coffman, *Old Army*, 139.

For the death of Poe, see [Thompson], "The Late Edgar A. Poe," 694–97.

For the Craigs in New York City, see ECC to "My Dear Friend," December 3, 1849, Nathaniel Wyche and Sarah R. Hunter Papers, box 3, file 14, Hargrett; Winfield Scott to LSC, January 23, 1849, Autograph Book, PC; LSC to Adj. Gen. Jones, February 16, 1850, (Roll #425) AGLR; and Peskin, *Winfield Scott*, 70.

For LSC and Dawson, see LSC to JRB, July 31, 1850, MBCC, 2:16; Northen, *Men of Mark*, 2:248–52, S. F. Miller, *Bench and Bar of Georgia*, 299, 314, 317; McCrary, "Georgia Politics and the Mexican War," 222; and Roberson, "South and the Pacific Railroad, 1845–1855," 163, 178.

For the 3rd Regiment in New Mexico, see McRae, "Third Regiment of Infantry," 441–42.

For New York City's harbor forts, see Billings, *Report on Barracks and Hospitals*, 33–39.

For the relinquishment of Texas's claims to western and northern lands, see Hamilton, "Texas Bonds and Northern Profits," 579–94.

For Craig, Bartlett, and the Boundary Commission, see LSC to Bvt Major Van Horne, December 19, 1850, and endorsement; Cremony, *Life among the Apaches*, 18–19; Castillo, *The Treaty of Guadalupe Hidalgo*, 56–57; J. E. Mueller, ed., *Autobiography of John Russell Bartlett*, xv–xvii; Goetzmann, *Exploration and Empire*, 261–62; Faulk, *Too Far North*, 58–65; Wallace, *The Great Reconnaissance*, 26–27. For the most comprehensive account of U.S. activities in the border region, see Couchman, *Cook's Peak*, 51–87.

For Santa Rita del Cobre and environs, see Sully, "Story of the Santa Rita Copper Mine," 135–38; Bartlett, *Personal Narrative*, 1: 226-36; DeLay, *War of a Thousand Deserts*, 294–95; Hutton, *Apache Wars*, 17–20. *U. S. Senate Executive Documents*, 32nd Congress, 1st Session, vol. 14, 398.

For LSC's letter regarding deserters, see LSC to Adj. Gen. Jones, March 1, 1851, RG 94, AGLR, NARA.

For Mangus Colorado (now usually given as "Mangas Coloradas"), see After Cremony—(Sweeney, 214-15, 227-40.) Cremony, *Life among the Apaches*, 30, 47–48, 52; Hutton, *Apache Wars*, 17, 23–24; Bartlett, *Personal Narrative*, 1:300–302, 319–20; Wellman, *Death in the Desert*, 6, 10–13, 49–54. For the death of Mangus, see Hutton, *Apache Wars*, 100–102. *U. S. Senate Executive Documents*, 32nd Congress, 1st Session, vol. 14, 398.

For LSC's incident with the Apaches, see Bartlett, *Personal Narrative*, 1:262, 331–39; Cremony, *Life among the Apaches*, 67; Wallace, *The Great Reconnaissance*, 36–37.

On the "state of siege" at Cantonment Dawson, see Bartlett, *Personal Narrative*, 1:343–53; Cremony 52–55, 82–84; Bartlett, *Personal Narrative*, 1:437, 455, 505.

For Craig's suggestions on Indian policy, see LSC to Winfield Scott, September 4, 1851, Letters Received, 9th Military Department, 1848–1853, RG 393.3, Roll 6, NARA Microfilm Publication M1102; Wadsworth, *Forgotten Fortress*, 57 (Sumner's orders to Morris, December 1851); McCall, *New Mexico in 1850*, 100, 105, 108, 109, 182n3, 187–88n4.

For the continuation of the war with the Apaches, see Hutton, *Apache Wars*, 364–67.

For Whipple's visit to Casa Grande, see his journal for November 16, 1851. For JRB's account of Casa Grande, see Bartlett, *Personal Narrative*, 2:271–83, with image opposite 274 and elevation and ground plan on 276.

For "jornada," see Bartlett, *Personal Narrative*, 1:215 and note.

For Dover's Powder (incidentally listed among the medicines at St. Mark's

Glebe School) see Sturdivant, "Dover's Powder and Its Modifications," 215.

For the Oatman Massacre, see Martin, *Yuma Crossing*, 160–67. On her eventual rescue, the surviving Oatman daughter was found to have been subjected to extensive blue facial tattooing on her lower lip and chin.

For Glanton see, Martin, *Yuma Crossing*, 139–51. The fact of LSC's fearlessness makes his journey across the desert seem matter of fact. On the other hand, the terrible combination of a hostile environment and vicious humans, graphically described, makes Cormac McCarthy's *Blood Meridian* (1985) one of the most horrifying historical novels ever written. Significantly, *Blood Meridian* shares three sites with Craig's experiences with the U.S. Boundary Commission: Santa Rita del Cobre, Alamo Mocho, and the Yuma Crossing.

Also significantly, Craig was posted in the three antebellum territories and states that had the highest homicide rates: Florida, Texas, and California. See Denham and Roth, "Why Was Antebellum Florida Murderous?" 216, 216n.1.

For Bartlett in San Francisco, see Bartlett, *Personal Narrative*, 2:13–14, 107; Chudacoff, *Urban History*, 16–19.

For the deadly incident near Alamo Mocho, see Bartlett, *Personal Narrative*, 2:136–45.

For Napoleon at Grenoble, see Sir Walter Scott, *The Life of Napoleon Buonaparte*:

> As Napoleon approached Grenoble, he came into contact with the outposts of the garrison, who drew out, but seemed irresolute. Buonaparte halted his own little party, and advanced, almost alone, exposing his breast, as he exclaimed, "He who will kill his Emperor, let him now work his pleasure." The appeal was irresistible—the soldiers threw down their arms, crowded round the General…and shouted *Vive l'Empereur!*"(3:202)

EPILOGUE: POSTERITY

Winfield Scott's letter [undated] to Elizabeth C. Craig, PC. Lt. Whipple's account of the aftermath of Colonel Craig's murder, Whipple Journal, ibid; Craig's burial: Bartlett, *Personal Narrative*, 2:145; Whipple Journal, ibid.; Dr. Webb's account, June 7, 1852 (printed), box 6, file 40, JRB Papers, JCBL; Faulk, "A Letter from John R. Bartlett," 207–209; Wolfe, "The Burial of Sir John Moore after Corunna," 712–13; Hibbert, *Corunna*, 140, 146–47.

For Bartlett's tribute to LSC, see Bartlett, *Personal Narrative*, 2:146–47.

The original manuscript copy of the Resolutions of Magruder and the other officers, June 26, 1852, PC. The officers requested specially that the resolutions be printed in the newspapers of Virginia and Georgia.

Transcripts of the courts martial of Col. Craig's murderers are in RG 153 (Manuscripts)—Office of the Judge Advocate General (1808–1942), Court Martial Case Files (1809–1894), File HH212, NARA.

Hays's speech is found in the *Daily Alta California*, August 9, 1852.

The news of Craig's murder and of the murderers' trial was widely covered in newspapers from California to New York, including the *New York Times*, which also excerpted the notice from the Fredericksburg newspaper. Noting the colonel's kinship to Robert Craig Stanard and Andrew Stevenson, it ended "He leaves a widow and one child in Athens, Georgia, to whom, may God temper the sad intelligence, as he does 'the winds to the shorn lamb!'" (*New York Times*, July 23, 1852).

In Georgia, news of Craig's death appeared in the *Macon Georgia Journal and Messenger*, July 28, 1852, and the *Athens Southern Banner* for July 29, 1852.

The best and most detailed periodical account of the murder, the manhunt, the trial, and the execution is Coyer's "Let No Man Pattern After Me," 10–19, which includes the story of Louis Rouen.

For Pablo Apis, see Bibb, "Pablo Apis and Temecula," 256–71.

The fullest account of the execution appeared in the short-lived *Illustrated News* (New York), April 8, 1853.

For Fort Rosecrans National Cemetery and related information, see Ruhlen, "Fort Rosecrans, California," 60–69, and D. W. Holt, *American Military Cemeteries*, 377.

For Fort Craig, see Grinstead, *Life and Death of a Frontier Fort: Fort Craig, New Mexico, 1854–1885*; Frazer, *Forts of the West*, 98; Horgan, *Great River*, 810; Josephy, *The Civil War*, 61–73.

The documents relating to LSC's estate are found in Guardian Bonds (Vol. C-E) and Journals (P, etc.) and loose materials in the Records Center of the Probate Court of Athens-Clarke County, Georgia.

For the beginning and end of the ultimately successful attempts to have Congress settle LSC's accounts are found in William C. Dawson to ECC, 1 February 1852, PC, and *Statutes at Large of the United States of America*, 11:558.

ECC's thoughts on her parents' life at their country home, Homewood, are found in ECR to SC, December 11, 1862 (PC).

For the LeConte-Craig controversy and related matters, see Hull, *Annals of Athens, Georgia*, 184–86.

For Elizabeth's business before Congress, see Senator Dawson's successful bill, passed in the U.S. Senate on February 1, 1853, providing the widow a pension "at the rate of one-half the pay her husband was receiving at the time of his death…to continue during her widowhood; and should she marry again, or die, while her daughter, now living, shall be a minor, the same allowance shall be made to said daughter during her minority" (*Statutes at Large*, 10:764–65). Senator Dawson's February 1, 1853, letter to Mrs. Craig, advising her of his bill's passage in the Senate, and its imminent passage in the House, with the support of Reps. Stephens and Junius Hillyer of Georgia, PC. For Rep. Stephens' Act, passed January 21, 1859, settling Col. Craig's boundary survey accounts, see (*Statutes at Large*, 11:558). Stephens's letter announcing his success in the

House, addressed to "Mrs. Craig, Executive Mansion," is also located in PC. The bill received full approval on February 5, 1859.

For Elizabeth Craig and others in Washington City, see Rabun, "Alexander H. Stephens," 547–49; Schott, *Alexander H. Stephens of Georgia*, 260, 261–63; Klein, *President James Buchanan*, 277 ("sprightly young widow"), 285, 333, 348, 426.

Cook's *The Gates of Trevalyan* embeds the relationship of ECC and Alexander Stephens within a historical novel that makes effective use of their correspondence and is the product of a good deal of research in the appropriate sources.

An amazing treasury of materials from antebellum Washington City society is Elizabeth Craig's scrapbook, PC.

The piece of jewelry President Buchanan gave Mrs. Craig was a gold bracelet with black trim and five dangling jet beads. It is inscribed using her initials "From James Buchanan to ECC, Dec. 24, 1858," PC.

Pope Barrow's account of Sallie Craig and the Union regiment, including his intention to name one of Troup Artillery's howitzers after her, is found in Pope Barrow to Mrs. [Mary Ann] Cobb, June 19, 1861, Folder 6, Box 62, Howell Cobb Manuscripts, Number 1376, Hargrett.

Mrs. Robb's illness is the topic of ECR to JR, January 11, 1863, MSS 265, folder 418, James Robb Collection.

For Sallie's remarks on her mother and the war in 1864, see her letter to "Aunt Janie," November 27, 1864, in the Sanders, Lee, and Sargent Families Papers, Ms. 574, Special Collections Department, Mississippi State University Libraries.

For the tributes to and obsequies for ECR, see Coulter, *William Montague Browne*, 142. As late as 1898 she was remembered in Athens as the "Guardian Angel of the Prisoners" (see *Athens Weekly Banner*, March 18, 1898).

For Mrs. Davis's letter, see Phillips, ed., *Correspondence of Robert Toombs*, 700.

For one of the reports of Sallie's final illness and death, see *Atlanta Weekly*, January 3, 1882.

For the Barrow family, see Hull, *Annals of Athens*, 424–25, 442; Hutcherson, "Barrows," 15–19; obituaries of Dr. Craig Barrow, *Savannah Evening Press*, August 31, 1945, and *Savannah Morning News*, September 1, 1945. The lives of Dr. and Mrs. Barrow are described in Bragg, *De Renne*, 286–396.

Bibliography

A Note on National Archives Sources

A book whose subject served as an officer in the U. S. Army will necessary involve research at the National Archives in Washington, D.C. (where some must be consulted in actual manuscript), or at one of its state facilities, such as the National Archives at Atlanta, located in Morrow, Georgia. Research for this study was conducted several times at both these places, as well as online, with the work at the Morrow branch generously facilitated by Nathan Jordan.

Those sources most helpful (both manuscript and microcopy), particularly as to related correspondence and to the posts where Lewis Craig served, are listed below, but are seldom cited in the notes. In general, within any group, the records appear chronologically, in regard to units or posts, and are thereafter arranged chronologically by surname.

Record Group 77: Office of the Chief of Engineers, 1789–1999

"Plan of the Battleground of Contreras and Its Defenses, August 19th and 20th 1847…Surveyed by Capt. R. E. Lee…of the Corps of Engineers. Drawn by Lt. Z. B. Tower," Drawer 112, Sheet 57, National Archives, College Park, Maryland.

Record Group 94: Office of Adjutant General

Adjutant General. Letters Received, 1822-1860.

"Records of the Divisions of the Adjutant General's Office: Appointment, Commission, and Personal Branch, 1783-1917. Registers of Brevet Commissions, 1825–1899," 6 vols. [Bound mss.], II:79, III:162. National Archives, Washington, D.C.

Returns from Regular Army Infantry Regiments, June 1821–December 1916. M665, Rolls 30–32. 3rd Infantry.

Returns from Military Posts, 1800–1916. M617, Rolls 351, 408, 514, 546, 555, 715, 941, 1083, 1202, 1514, 1516; M665, Rolls 30–32.

Record Group 107. Office of the Secretary of War

General Orders and Circulars of the War Department and Headquarters of the Army, 1809–1860.

Secretary of War Letters Received, 1801–1870

Secretary of War, Letters Sent, 1800–1889.

Record Group 153. Office of the Judge Advocate General (Army)

Court-Martial Case Files, 1809–1894, file HH212 (Hayes & Condon).

Record Group 391.3.2. Returns from Regular Cavalry Regiments, 1833–1916 M744, Roll 14, 2nd Cavalry/2nd Dragoons, December 1836–December 1845.

Printed Documents

U. S. Adjutant General. *Official List of Officers Who Marched…with Major General Winfield Scott from Puebla upon the City of Mexico…and Who Were Engaged in the Battles of Mexico* (Mexico: American Star Print, 1848).

U.S. Ordnance Department. *Ordnance Manual for the Use of the United States Army*. 2nd ed. Washington: Gideon & Co., Printers, 1850.

U.S. Paymaster General of the Army. *A Compendium of the Pay of the Army from 1785 to 1888* by Thomas M. Exley. Washington: Government Printing Office, 1888.

U.S. Senate Executive Documents, 30th Congress, 1st Session, Vol. 1, doc. 1.

U.S. Senate Executive Documents, 32nd Congress, 1st Session, Vol. 14, doc. 119.

U.S. Senate Miscellaneous Documents, 30th Congress, 1st Session, document 1.

U. S. Senate Miscellaneous Documents, Special Session 1851, Document 11.

Other Archival Sources

Clerk's Loose Papers. Prince William County, Virginia, 1808–1860. Circuit Court Clerk's Office, Manassas, VA.

Court Records, Fredericksburg, Va., Circuit Court, Fredericksburg, VA.

Deed Book CC. 1828–1831. ff. 144–45, Spotsylvania County, Virginia, Land Records, Microfilm Reel No. 53. Library of Virginia, Richmond, VA.

Guardian Bonds (Vol. C-E) and Journals (P, etc.) and loose materials in the Records Center of the Probate Court of Athens-Clarke County, GA.

Jones, C. C. Collection. Box 6, folder 4. Special Collections. Tulane University, New Orleans, LA.

Lewis, John. Llangollen School for Boys Account Books, 1811–1818. MSS 3L 7702, Virginia Historical Society, Richmond, VA.

"Papers of the Cazenove, Craig, Stanard & Lee families, chiefly of Alexandria, Va., 1786–1897 (1930)." Accession #9039-a, Special Collections, University of Virginia Library, University of Virginia, Charlottesville, VA. Abbreviated as CCSL.

Robb, James. Collection. MSS 265. Historical New Orleans Collection, Williams Research Center, New Orleans, LA. Cited as James Robb Collection.

Sanders, Lee, and Sargent Families Papers, Special Collections Department, Mississippi State University Libraries, Mississippi St., MS.

Stanard Family Bible. MSS 6:4 St243:1, Virginia Historical Society, Richmond,

VA.
United States. *The Statutes at Large and Treaties of the United States of America... / by Authority of Congress*. Vol. 9 (December 1, 1845, to March 3, 1851)–Vol. 11 (December 3, 1855, to March 3, 1859). Boston: C.C. Little and J. Brown, 1851–1859.
Whipple, Lt. A. W. Journal. 1849–1853. Amiel Weeks Whipple Collection. Microfilm AMD 1. Oklahoma Historical Society, Oklahoma City, OK.
Woodville, John Walker. Diary. 1801–1851. Accession #4055 to 4055-a, Special Collections Library, University of Virginia, Charlottesville, VA.

Nonarchival Sources
Abernethy, Thomas Perkins. *The Burr Conspiracy*. New York: Oxford University Press, 1954.
Acts of the General Assembly of Virginia. Richmond: Samuel Shepherd, 1847.
Adams, George Rollie. *William S. Harney, Prince of Dragoons*. Lincoln: University of Nebraska Press, 2001.
Adams, Henry. *History of the United States of America during the First Administration of Thomas Jefferson*. 2 vols. New York: Charles Scribner's Sons, 1909.
Addison, Joseph. *Cato: A Tragedy and Selected Essays*. Edited by Christine Dunn Henderson and Mark E. Yellin; foreword by Forrest McDonald. Indianapolis: Liberty Fund, 2004.
Alden, Peter, et al. *National Audubon Society Field Guide to Florida*. New York: Alfred A. Knopf, 1998.
Atton, Henry, and Henry Hurst Holland. *The King's Customs*. New York: E. P. Dutton & Co., 1908.
Aztec Club of 1847. *Report of a Committee*. Washington DC: Judd & Detweiler, 1890.
Baker, James Graham. "Seth Eastman's Drawing of Corpus Christi: A Military Man's Representation of the South Texas Frontier Settlement, Circa 1849." *The Southwestern Historical Quarterly* 116/2 (2012): 168–81.
Bancroft, Hubert Howe. *History of Mexico*. New York: The Bancroft Co., 1914.
Bartlett, John Russell. *Personal Narrative of Explorations and Incidents in Texas, New Mexico, California, Sonora, and Chihuahua, Connected with the United States and Mexico Boundary Commission, during the Years 1850, '51, '52, and '53*. 2 vols. New York: D. Appleton & Co., 1854.
Bauer, K. Jack. *The Mexican War: 1846–1848 (MWUS)*. New York: Macmillan Publishing Co., 1974.
Bauer, K. Jack. *Zachary Taylor: Soldier, Planters, Statesman of the Old Southwest*. Baton Rouge: Louisiana State University Press, 1985.
Bender, A. B. "The Soldier in the Far West, 1848–1860." *Pacific Historical Review* 8/2 (June 1939): 159–78.
Beveridge, Albert. *The Life of John Marshall*. 4 vols. New York: Houghton Mifflin, 1916.

Beverley, Robert. *The History and Present State of Virginia.* 4 parts. London: R. Parker, 1705.

Bibb, Leland E. "Pablo Apis and Temecula." *San Diego Historical Quarterly* 37/4 (Fall 1991): 256–71.

Bibber, W. C. "The Therapeutic Value of the Mineral Waters of the United States upon Malarial Diseases: With Rules for Their Use." *Medical Bulletin* 11/1 (January 1889): 8–12.

Billings, John S. *A Report on Barracks and Hospitals, with Descriptions of Military Posts*, Washington: Government Printing Office, 1870.

Bonin, Christopher M. *Virginia in the War of 1812.* Jefferson, NC: McFarland & Co., 2018.

Bonner, James C. "The Historical Basis of Southern Military Tradition." *The Georgia Review* 9/1 (Spring 1955): 74–85.

Bonura, Michael A. "A French-Inspired Way of War: French Influence on the U.S. Army from 1812 to the Mexican War." *Army History* 90 (Winter 2014): 6–22.

Borneman, Walter R. *Polk: The Man Who Transformed the Presidency and America.* New York: Random House, 2008.

Bragg, William Harris. *De Renne: Three Generations of a Georgia Family*. Athens: University of Georgia Press, 1999.

Breed, David R. *The History and Use of Hymns and Hymn-Tunes.* New York: Fleming H. Revell Co., 1903.

Breen, T. H. *Tobacco Culture: The Mentality of the Great Tidewater Planters on the Eve of Revolution.* Princeton: Princeton University Press, 1985.

Breithaupt, Richard Hoag, Jr. *Aztec Club of 1847 Military Society of the Mexican War Sesquicentennial History, 1847–1997.* Los Angeles: The Aztec Club Society, 1998.

Brethren of Prince Edwin's Lodge. *The Free-Masons' Melody, Being a General Collection of Masonic Songs.* Lancashire: Hellawell, 1818.

Brown, Russell K. "An Old Woman with a Broomstick: General David E. Twiggs and the U.S. Surrender in Texas, 1861." *Military Affairs* 48/2 (April 1984): 57–61.

Bruce Robert B., et al. *Fighting Techniques of the Napoleonic Age, 1792–1815.* New York: St. Martin's Press, 2008.

Brydon, G. MacLaren. "The Antiecclesiastical Laws of Virginia." *Virginia Magazine of History and Biography* 64/3 (July 1956): 259–85.

Buckley, Thomas E., S. J. "Evangelicals Triumphant: The Baptists' Assault on the Virginia Glebes, 1786–1801." *William and Mary Quarterly* 45/1 (January 1988): 32–69.

Burstein, Andrew. *America's Jubilee: How in 1826 a Generation Remembered Fifty Years of Independence.* New York: Alfred A. Knopf, 2001.

Burstein, Andrew. *The Original Knickerbocker: The Life of Washington Irving.* New York: Basic Books, 2007.

Butler, Stuart L. *Defending the Old Dominion: Virginia and Its Militia in the War of 1812*. New York: University Press of America, 2012.

Byrd, William, of Westover. *History of the Dividing Line and Other Tracts*. 2 vols. Richmond: n.p., 1866.

Callan, John F., ed. *The Military Laws of the United States*. Baltimore: John Murphy & Co., 1858.

Castillo, Richard Griswold del. *The Treaty of Guadalupe Hidalgo: A Legacy of Conflict*. Norman: University of Oklahoma Press, 1990.

Chudacoff, Howard P., et al. *The Evolution of American Urban History*. New York: Routledge, 2014.

Clary, David A. *Eagles and Empire: The United States, Mexico, and the Struggle for a Continent*. New York: Bantam Books, 2009.

Coffman, Edward M. *The Old Army: A Portrait of the American Army in Peacetime, 1784–1898*. New York: Oxford University Press, 1986.

Coleman, Aaron N. "'A Second Bounaparty?' A Reexamination of Alexander Hamilton during the Franco-American Crisis, 1796–1801." *Journal of the Early Republic* 28/2 (Summer 2008): 183–214.

Connor, Seymour V., and Odie B. Faulk. *North America Divided: The Mexican War, 1846–1848*. New York: Oxford University Press, 1971.

Cook, Jacquelyn. *The Gates of Trevalyan*. Smyrna, GA: Belle Books, 2008.

Coolidge, R. H., comp. "Florida." In *Statistical Report of Sickness and Mortality in the Army of the United States* [January 1839–January 1855]. Prepared under the direction of Brevet Brigadier General Thomas Lawson, Surgeon General United States Army. 1839 to January 1855 issued as Senate ex. doc. 96, 34th Cong., 1st sess. Washington: A. G. P. Nicholson, Printer, 1856. Available at https://archive.org/details/statisticalrepor02unit/page/n5/mode/2up.

Coss, P. R. "The Formation of the English Gentry." *Past and Present* 147/1 (May 1995): 38–64.

Coss, Peter. "Knights, Esquires, and the Origins of Social Gradation in England." *Transactions of the Royal Historical Society* 5 (1995): 155–78.

Cotton, Tom. *Sacred Duty: A Soldier's Tour at Arlington National Cemetery*. New York: William Morrow, 2019.

Couchman, Donald Howard. *Cooke's Peak—Pasaron Por Aqui: A Focus on United States History in Southwestern New Mexico*. Las Cruces, NM: Bureau of Land Management, 1990.

Coulter, E. Merton. "The University of Georgia—Old and New." *The Georgia Review* 5/1 (Spring 1951): 12–21.

Coulter, E. Merton. *William Montague Browne: Versatile Anglo-Irish American, 1823–1883*. Athens: University of Georgia Press, 1967.

Cox, Isaac Joslin. *The West Florida Controversy, 1798–1813*. Baltimore: Johns Hopkins Press, 1918.

Coyer, Richard J. "Let No Man Pattern After Me." *True West* 28 (September

1981): 10–19.

Crackel, Theodore J. *Mr. Jefferson's Army: Political and Social Reform of the Military Establishment, 1801–1809*. New York: New York University Press, 1987.

Crawford, Mark. *Encyclopedia of the Mexican-American War*. Santa Barbara, CA: ABC-CLIO, 1999.

Cremony, John C. *Life among the Apaches*. 1868. Reprint, Lincoln: University of Nebraska Press, 1983.

Cullum, George W. *Biographical Register of the Officers and Graduates of the United States Military Academy*. 2 vols. Boston: Houghton Mifflin, 1891.

Cutler, Harry Gardner. *History of Florida: Past and Present*. 3 vols. New York: Lewis Publishing Co., 1923.

Dabney, Virginius. *Richmond: The Story of a City*. Garden City, NY: Doubleday & Co., 1976.

Darby, William, and Theodore Dwight, Jr. *Gazetteer of the United States of America...with the Population of 1830*. Hartford: Edward Hopkins, 1833.

Davis, Curtis Carroll. *The King's Chevalier*. New York: The Bobbs-Merrill Co., 1961.

DeConde, Alexander. *The Quasi-War: The Politics and Diplomacy of the Undeclared War with France, 1797–1801*. New York: Charles Scribner's Sons.

DeLay, Brian. *War of a Thousand Deserts: Indian Raids and the U.S.-Mexican War*. New Haven: Yale University Press, 2008.

Denham, James M. "'Some Prefer The Seminoles': Violence and Disorder among the Soldiers and Settlers in the Second Seminole War." *The Florida Historical Quarterly* 70/1 (July 1991): 38–54.

Denham, James M. "The Florida Crackers before the Civil War as Seen through Travelers' Accounts." *The Florida Historical Quarterly* 72/4 (April 1994): 453–68.

Denham, James M., and Randolph Roth. "Why Was Antebellum Florida Murderous? A Quantitative Analysis of Homicide in Florida, 1821–1861." *Florida Historical Quarterly* 86/2 (Fall 2007): 216–39.

Dent, Louis Addison. "Virginia—The Founder of States." *The Virginia Magazine of History and Biography* 54/4 (October 1946): 286–305.

Dept. of the U.S. Army. *The Old Guard: History of the Third Regiment*. Washington, DC: Government Printing Office, 1970.

Dibble, Ernest F. "Giveaway Forts: Territorial Forts and the Settlement of Florida." *Florida Historical Quarterly* 78/2 (Fall 1999): 207–33.

Dickens, Charles. *American Notes*. New York: Penguin Books, 2004.

Dishman, Christopher D. *A Perfect Gibraltar: The Battle for Monterrey, Mexico, 1846*. Norman: University of Oklahoma Press, 2010.

Doran, Michael F. "Negro Slaves of the Five Civilized Tribes." *Annals of the Association of American Geographers* 68/3 (September 1978): 335–50.

Duffy, John. "The Passage to the Colonies." *Mississippi Valley Historical Review*

38/1 (June 1951): 21–38.
Dufour, Charles L. *The Mexican War: A Compact History, 1846–1848*. New York, Hawthorn Books, 1968.
Duke, Maurice, and Daniel P. Jordan eds. *A Richmond Reader, 1733–1983*. Chapel Hill: University of North Carolina Press, 1983.
Dyer, Thomas G. *The University of Georgia: A Bicentennial History, 1785–1985*. Athens: University of Georgia Press, 1985.
Eckenrode, Hamilton James. *Separation of Church and State in Virginia: A Study of Development of the Revolution*. Special Report of the Department of Archives and History, H. J. Eckenrode, archivist. Richmond, VA: D. Bottom, Superintendent of Public Printing, 1910.
Egerton, Douglas R. *Gabriel's Rebellion: The Virginia Slave Conspiracies of 1800 and 1802*. Chapel Hill, University of North Carolina Press, 1993.
Egloff, Keith, and Deborah Woodward. *First People: The Early Indians of Virginia*. 2nd ed. Charlottesville: University of Virginia Press, 2006.
Einzig, Paul. *Primitive Money: In Its Ethnological, Historical, and Economic Aspects*. London: Pergamon Press, 1966.
Eisenhower, John S. D. *So Far from God: The U.S. War with Mexico, 1846–1848*. New York: Random House, 1989.
Faulk, Odie B. *Too Far North... Too Far South*. Los Angeles: Westernlore Press, 1967.
Faulk, Odie, ed. "A Letter from John R. Bartlett at Camp Yuma, 1852." *Journal of Arizona History* 6/4 (Winter 1965): 204–13.
Field, Ron. *The Seminole Wars, 1818–58*. New York: Osprey Publishing, 2009.
Filler, Lois. *The Crusade Against Slavery, 1830–1860*. New York: Harper & Row, 1960.
Finley, Anthony. "Florida, 1831." *A New General Atlas*. Philadelphia: Clark & Raser, 1831.
Fischer, David Hackett. *Albion's Seed: Four British Folkways in America*. New York: Oxford University Press, 1989.
Fisher, George D. *History and Reminiscences of the Monumental Church*. Richmond: Whittet & Shepperson, 1880.
Foreman, Grant, ed. *A Traveler in Indian Territory: The Journal of Ethan Allen Hitchcock, Late Major-General in the United States Army*. 1930. Norman: University of Oklahoma Press, 1996.
Fowler, Will. *Santa Anna of Mexico*. Lincoln: University of Nebraska Press, 2007.
Francke, Arthur E., Jr. *Fort Mellon, 1837–1842*. Miami: Banyan Books, 1977.
Frazer, Robert W. *Forts of the West*. Norman: University of Oklahoma Press, 1965.
Frazier, Donald S., ed. *The United States and Mexico at War*. New York: Simon & Schuster Macmillan, 1998.
Freeman, Douglas Southall. *R. E. Lee: A Biography*. 4 vols. New York: Charles

Scribner's Sons, 1947.

Friend, Mrs. C. E. "Craig." *William and Mary Quarterly* 11/2 (April 1931): 159–60.

General Regulations for the Army of the United States. Washington: The Globe Office, 1835.

Gillet, Mary C. *The Army Medical Department, 1818–1865*. Washington, DC: Center of Military History, 1987.

Gilliam, Charles Edgar. "'Mr.' in Virginia Records before 1776." *William and Mary Quarterly* 19/2 (April 1939): 142–45.

Goetzmann, William H. *Exploration and Empire: The Explorer and the Scientist in the Winning of the American West*. Austin: Texas State Historical Association, 1993.

Goolrick, John T. *The Life of General Hugh Mercer*. New York: The Neale Publishing Co., 1906.

Grinstead, Marion C. *Life and Death of a Frontier Fort: Fort Craig, New Mexico, 1854–1885*. Publications in History. Socorro, NM: Socorro County Historical Society, 1973.

Groom, Winston. *Kearney's March: The Epic Creation of the American West, 1846–1847*. New York: Alfred A. Knopf, 2011.

Haecker, Charles M., and Jeffrey G. Mauck. *On the Prairie of Palo Alto: Historical Archaeology of the U.S.-Mexican War Battlefield*. College Station: Texas A&M University Press, 1997.

Hallam, John S. "Houdon's Washington in Richmond: Some New Observations." *American Art Journal* 10 (November 1978): 72–80.

Hamilton, Holman. "Texas Bonds and Northern Profits: A Study in Compromise, Investment, and Lobby Influence." *Mississippi Valley Historical Review* 43/4 (March 1957): 579–94.

Hamlin, Talbot F. "The Birth of American Architecture." *Parnassus* 10/6 (November 1938): 8–12.

Hardin, J. Fair. "Fort Jesup, Fort Selden, Camp Sabine, Camp Salubrity: Four Forgotten Army Posts of Western Louisiana" (in 5 parts). *Louisiana Historical Quarterly* 16 (January 1933): 5–26; 16 (April 1933): 278–92; 16 (July 1933):441–453; 16 (October 1933): 670–80; 17 (January 1934): 139–68.

Harris, C. M. "Washington's Gamble, L'Enfant's Dream: Politics, Design, and the Founding of the National Capital." *William and Mary Quarterly* 56/3 (July 1999): 527–64.

Hastings, Hugh J. *Ancient American Politics*. Harper's Franklin Square Library 543. New York: Harpers and Brothers, 1881.

Hawthorne, Nathaniel. *Life of Franklin Pierce*. Boston: Ticknor, Reed, and Fields, 1852.

Haynes, Sam W. *James K. Polk and the Expansionist Impulse*. 3d ed. New York: Pearson Longman, 2006.

Heidler, Jeanne Twiggs. "The Military Career of David Emanuel Twiggs." Ph.

D. diss., Auburn University, 1988.
Heitman, Francis B. *Historical Register and Dictionary of the United States Army*. 2 vols. Washington: GPO, 1903.
Henderson, G. F. R. *Stonewall Jackson and the American Civil War*. 2 vols. London: Longmans, Green, and Co., 1919.
Hening, William Waller, ed. *Statutes at Large of Virginia*, vol. 9. Richmond: J. G. Cochran Printers, 1821.
Henry, Robert Selph. *The Story of the Mexican War*. New York: Bobbs-Merrill Co., 1950.
Henry, W. S. *Campaign Sketches of the War with Mexico*. New York: Harper and Brothers, 1847.
Hibbert, Christopher. *Corunna*. Whitney, England: Windrush Press, 1996.
Hicks, Robert S. "Diplomatic Relations with Mexico during the Administration of James K. Polk." *Annual Publication of the Historical Society of South California* 12/2 (1922): 5–17.
Hietala, Thomas R. *Manifest Design: American Exceptionalism and Empire*. 1985. Rev. ed., Ithaca: Cornell University Press, 2003.
Hitchcock, Ethan Allen. *Fifty Years in Camp and Field*. Edited by W. A. Croffut. New York: G. P. Putnam's Sons, 1909.
Hoffer, Peter Charles. *Law and People in Colonial America*. Baltimore: Johns Hopkins University Press, 1992.
Hollan, Catherine B. *Virginia Silversmiths, Jewelers, Watch- and Clockmakers, 1607–1860, Their Lives and Marks*. Marceline, MO: Hollan Press, 2010.
Holt, Dean W. *American Military Cemeteries*. 2nd ed. Jefferson, NC: McFarland & Co., 2010.
Holt, Michael F. *The Rise and Fall of the American Whig Party: Jacksonian Politics and the Onset of the Civil War*. New York: Oxford University Press, 1999.
Horgan, Paul. *Great River: The Rio Grande in North American History*. Hanover and London: Wesleyan University Press, 1984.
Hughes, Nathaniel Cheairs, Jr. *General William J. Hardee, Old Reliable*. Baton Rouge: Louisiana State University Press, 1965.
Hughes, Robert M. "Joseph Eggleston Johnston, Soldier and Man." *William and Mary Quarterly* 12/2 (April 1933): 63–84.
Hull, Augustus Longstreet. *Annals of Athens, Georgia, 1801–1901*. Athens: Banner Job Office, 1906.
Hunt, Alfred N. *Haiti's Influence on Antebellum America: Slumbering Volcano in the Caribbean*. Baton Rouge: Louisiana State University Press, 1988.
Hutcherson, Mary Denmark. "The Barrows." *Georgia Alumni Record* 49 (June 1970): 15–19.
Hutton, Paul Andrew. *The Apache Wars*. New York: Crown, 2016.
Ingersoll, L. D. *A History of the War Department of the United States*. Washington, DC: Francis B. Mohun, 1879.
Johannsen, Robert W. *To the Halls of the Montezumas: The Mexican War in*

American Imagination. New York: Oxford University Press, 1985.
Johnson, Timothy D. *A Gallant Little Army: The Mexico City Campaign*. Lawrence: University Press of Kansas, 2007.
Johnson, Timothy D. *Winfield Scott: The Quest for Military Glory*. Lawrence: University Press of Kansas, 1998.
Johnston, F. *Memorials of Old Virginia Clerks*. Lynchburg, VA: J. P. Bell Co., 1888.
Jones, A. H. M. *The Later Roman Empire, 284–602: A Social, Economic, and Administrative Survey*. 2 vols. Baltimore: Johns Hopkins Press, 1964.
Josephy, Alvin M., Jr. *The Civil War in the American West*. New York: Alfred A. Knopf, 1991.
Kamieniak, Ted. *Fredericksburg, Virginia: Eclectic Histories for the General Reader*. Charleston, SC: History Press, 2008.
Karnes, Thomas L. *William Gilpin, Western Nationalist*. Austin: University of Texas Press, 1970.
Kennedy, Roger G. *Burr, Hamilton, and Jefferson: A Study in Character*. New York: Oxford University Press, 2000.
Kieffer, Chester L. *Maligned General: The Biography of Thomas Sidney Jesup*. New York: Presidio Press, 1979.
Klein, Philip Shriver. *President James Buchanan: A Biography*. University Park: Pennsylvania State University Press, 1962.
Knetsch, Joe. *Fear and Anxiety on the Florida Frontier: Articles on the Second Seminole War, 1835–1842*. Dade City, FL: Seminole Wars Foundation Press, 2008.
Knight, Lucian Lamar. *Georgia's Landmarks, Memorials, and Legends*. 2 vols. Atlanta: The Byrd Printing Co., 1913.
Kopper, Philip. *Colonial Williamsburg*. New York: Harry N. Abrams, Inc., 1986.
Krause, Enrique. *Mexico: Biography of Power: A History of Modern Mexico, 1810–1996*. New York: HarperPerennial, 1997.
Krogman, Wilton Marion. "Vital Data on the Population of the Seminole Indians of Florida and Oklahoma." *Human Biology* 7/3 (September 1935): 335–49.
Kukla, Jon. *A Wilderness So Immense: The Louisiana Purchase and the Destiny of America*. New York: Alfred A. Knopf, 2003.
Lambert, Frank. *The Barbary Wars: American Independence in the Atlantic World*. New York: Hill and Wang, 2005.
"Letters of John Tyler." *Tyler's Quarterly Historical and Genealogical Magazine* 13 (October 1931): 73–80.
Lewis, James E. *The Burr Conspiracy: Uncovering the Story of an Early American Crisis*. Princeton, NJ: Princeton University Press, 2017.
Linklater, Andro. *An Artist in Treason: The Extraordinary Double Life of General James Wilkinson*. New York: Walker Publishing Co., Inc., 2009.
Lomask, Milton. *Aaron Burr: The Conspiracy and Years of Exile, 1805–1836*. New

York: Farrar, Straus, Giroux, 1982.
Lover, Samuel. *Songs and Ballads*. Philadelphia: Lea & Blanchard, 1847.
Lumpkin, Wilson. *The Removal of the Cherokee Indians from Georgia*. 2 vols. New York: Dodd, Mead, & Co., 1907.
Mahon, John K. and Romana Danysh. *Army Lineage Series—Infantry, Part I: Regular Army*. Washington, DC: Office of the Chief of Military History, U.S. Army, 1972.
Mahon, John K. *History of the Second Seminole War*. Revised edition. Gainesville: University of Florida Press, 1985.
Malone, Dumas. *Jefferson the President: The Second Term, 1805–1809*. New York: Little, Brown and Company, 1974.
Martin, Douglas D. *Yuma Crossing*. Albuquerque: University of New Mexico Press, 1954.
Matloff, Maurice, gen. ed. *American Military History*. Washington: Office of the Chief of Military History, U.S. Army, 1969.
May, Robert E. "Invisible Men: Blacks and the U.S. Army in the Mexican War." *The Historian* 49/4 (1987): 463–77.
McCall, Colonel George Archibald. *New Mexico in 1850: A Military View*. Edited by Robert W. Frazer. Norman: University of Oklahoma Press, 1968.
McCrary, Royce C. "Georgia Politics and the Mexican War." *Georgia Historical Quarterly* 60/3 (Fall 1976): 211–27.
McElroy, Robert McNutt. *The Winning of the Far West*. New York: G.P. Putnam's Sons, 1914.
McFaul, John M. *The Politics of Jacksonian Finance*. Ithaca: Cornell University Press, 1971.
McGrane, Reginald Charles. *The Panic of 1837*. Chicago: University Press of Chicago, 1924.
McRae, Lt. J. H. "The Third Regiment of Infantry." In Theodore F. Rodenbough and William L. Haskin, eds., *The Army of the United States: Historical Sketches of Staff and Line with Portraits of Generals-in-Chief.* New York: Maynard, Merrill, & Co., 1896.
McWhiney, Grady, and Parry D. Jamieson. *Attack and Die: Civil War Military Tactics and the Southern Heritage*. Tuscaloosa: University of Alabama Press, 1982.
McWilliams, Mary E. "Golden Ball Historical Report, Block 17 Building 6A Lot 53, Originally entitled: 'Craig's House and Shop Block 17-1, Lot #53.'" 1942. Colonial Williamsburg Foundation Library Research Report Series—1357. 1990. Colonial Williamsburg Foundation Library, Williamsburg, Virginia. Available online: https://research.history.org/DigitalLibrary/view/index.cfm?doc=ResearchReports%5CRR1357.xml&highlight=craig,%20james.
Meade, Bishop William. *Old Churches, Ministers, and Families of Virginia*. 2 vols. Philadelphia, J. P. Lippincott, 1861.

Meed, Douglas V. *The Mexican War, 1846–1848*. Oxford: Osprey Publishing, 2002.

Merk, Frederick S. *Manifest Destiny and Mission in American History: A Reinterpretation*. New York: Vintage Books, 1966.

Miller, John Chester. *The Wolf by the Ears: Thomas Jefferson and Slavery*. Charlottesville: University Press of Virginia, 1991.

Miller, Stephen F. *The Bench and Bar of Georgia: Memoirs and Sketches*. Philadelphia: J. B. Lippincott & Co., 1858.

Missall, John, and Mary Lou Missall. *The Seminole Wars: American's Longest Indian Conflict*. Gainesville: University Press of Florida, 2004.

Montagu, Ashley. *The Anatomy of Swearing*. New York: The Macmillan Co., 1967.

Moore, M. E. J. Staunton, ed. *History and By-Laws of Richmond Royal Arch Chapter, No. 3, A. F. & A. M., Richmond, Virginia*. Richmond: Williams Printing Company, 1911.

Morales-Vázquez, Rubil. "George Washington, the President's House, and the Projection of Executive Power." *Washington History* 16/1 (Spring/Summer 2004): 36–53.

Mordecai, Samuel. *Richmond in By-Gone Days*. Richmond: George W. West, 1856.

Morgan, Forrest. "General William Eaton, The First American Imperialist." *Americana* 6 (January–December 1911): 586–614, 697–713.

Moseley, Edward H., and Paul C. Clark, Jr. *Historical Dictionary of the United States-Mexican War*. Lanham, MD: The Scarecrow Press, 1997.

Motte, Jacob Rhett. *Journey into Wilderness: An Army Surgeons Account of Life in Camp and Field during the Creek and Seminole Wars, 1836–1838*. Edited by James F. Sunderman. Gainesville: University of Florida Press, 1963.

Mueller, Edward A. "East Coast Florida Steamboating, 1831–1861." *Florida Historical Quarterly* 40/3 (January 1962): 241–60.

Mueller, Edward A. "Steamboat Activity in Florida during the Second Seminole Indian War." *Florida Historical Quarterly* 64/4 (April 1986): 407–31.

Mueller, Jerry E., ed. *Autobiography of John Russell Bartlett (1805–1886)*. Providence: John Carter Brown Library, 2006.

Murphy, Douglas A. *Two Armies on the Rio Grande*. College Station: Texas A&M University Press, 2015.

Murray, Sterling E. "Weeping and Mourning: Funeral Dirges in Honor of George Washington." *Journal of the American Musicological Society* 31 (Summer 1978): 282–308.

Nardini, Louis Raphael. *No Man's Land: A History of El Camino Real*. New Orleans: Pelican Publishing Co., 1961.

Narrett, David E. "Geopolitics and Intrigue: James Wilkinson, the Spanish Borderlands, and Mexican Independence." *William and Mary Quarterly* 69/1 (January 2012): 101–46.

Nelson, John K. *A Blessed Company: Parishes, Parsons, and Parishioners in Anglican Virginia, 1690–1776*. Chapel Hill: University of North Carolina Press, 2001.

Northen, William J., ed. *Men of Mark in Georgia*. 7 vols. Atlanta: A. B. Caldwell, 1907–1912.

Nuckols, R. R. *A History of the Government of the City of Richmond, Virginia*. Richmond: Williams Printing Co., 1899.

Olmert, Michael. *Official Guide to Colonial Williamsburg*. Williamsburg: Colonial Williamsburg Foundation, 1985.

Olson, Alison G. "The Virginia Merchants of London: A Study in Eighteenth-century Interest-Group Politics." *William and Mary Quarterly* 40/3 (July 1983): 363–88.

[O'Sullivan, John L.] "Annexation." *The United States Magazine and Democratic Review* 17 (July–August 1845): 5–10.

Paisley, Clifton. *The Red Hills of Florida, 1528–1865*. Tuscaloosa: University of Alabama Press, 1989.

Patch, Joseph Dortch. *The Concentration of General Zachary Taylor's Army at Corpus Christi, Texas*. Corpus Christi: Mission Printing, 1962.

Paul, Joel Richard. *Without Precedent: Chief Justice John Marshall and His Times*. New York: Riverhead Books, 2018.

Paulus, Robert D. "Pack Mules and Surf Boats: Logistics in the Mexican War." *Army Logistician* (November–December 1997): 34–40.

Payne, Darwin. "Camp Life in the Army of Occupation: Corpus Christi, July 1845 to March 1846." *Southwestern Historical Quarterly* 73/3 (January 1970): 326–42.

Peskin, Allan. *Winfield Scott and the Profession of Arms*. Kent, Ohio: Kent State University Press, 2003.

Peterson, Merrill D. *Thomas Jefferson and the New Nation: A Biography*. New York: Oxford University Press, 1970.

Phillips, U. B., ed. *The Correspondence of Robert Toombs, Alexander H. Stephens, and Howell Cobb*. 1913. Reprint, New York: Da Capo Press, 1970.

Pletcher, David M. *The Diplomacy of Annexation: Texas, Oregon, and the Mexican War*. Columbia: University of Missouri, 1973.

Porter, Albert Ogden. *County Government in Virginia: A Legislative History, 1607–1904*. New York: Columbia University, 1947.

Porter, Kenneth W. *The Black Seminoles: History of a Freedom-Seeking People*. Gainesville: University Press of Florida, 1996.

Posey, Walter B. "The Protestant Episcopal Church: An American Adaptation." *The Journal of Southern History* 25/1 (February 1959): 3–30.

Potter, Woodburne. *The War in Florida*. Baltimore: Lewis & Coleman, 1836.

Price, Jacob M. "Who Was John Norton? A Note on the Historical Character of Some Eighteenth-Century London Virginia Firms." *William and Mary Quarterly* 19/3 (July 1962): 400–407.

Procyk, Richard J. *Guns across the Loxahatchee: An Archaeohistorical Investigation of Seminole War Sites in Florida*. Melbourne, FL: Florida Historical Society Press, 1999.

Prucha, Francis Paul. *The Sword of the Republic: The United States Army on the Frontier, 1783–1846*. New York: Macmillan Co., 1969.

Quinn, Arthur Hobson. *Edgar Allan Poe: A Critical Biography*. 1941. Reprint, Baltimore: Johns Hopkins University Press, 1998.

Rabun, James Zachary. "Alexander H. Stephens, 1812–61." Ph.D. diss., University of Chicago, 1948.

Ravenswaay, Charles van. *Saint Louis: An Informal History of the City and Its People, 1764–1865*. St. Louis: Missouri Historical Society Press, 1991.

Reavis, L. U. *The Life and Services of Gen. William Selby Harney*. St. Louis: Bryan, Brand & Co., 1878.

Reid, Mayne. *Osceola the Seminole*. New York: Robert M. De Witt, 1858.

Remini, Robert V. *Andrew Jackson and the Course of American Democracy, 1833–1845*. New York: Harper & Row, 1984.

Remini, Robert V. *Andrew Jackson and the Course of American Empire, 1767–1821*. New York: Harper & Row, 1977.

Remini, Robert V. *Henry Clay: Statesman for the Union*. New York: W. W. Norton & Co., 1991.

Remini, Robert. *Andrew Jackson and His Indian Wars*. New York: Viking, 2001.

Ripley, R. S. *The War with Mexico*. 2 vols. New York: Harper & Brothers, 1849.

Ripley, William Z. *The Financial History of Virginia, 1609–1776*. New York: Columbia College, 1893.

Rives, George Lockhart. *The United States and Mexico, 1821–1848*. 2 vols. New York: Charles Scribner's Sons, 1913.

Roberson, Jere W. "The South and the Pacific Railroad, 1845–1855." *Western Historical Quarterly* 5/2 (April 1974): 53–86.

Robinson, Fayette. *An Account of the Organization of the Army of the United States*. 2 vols. Philadelphia: E. H. Butler & Co., 1848.

Rodenbough Theophilus F., and William L. Haskin, eds. *The Army of the United States: Historical Sketches of Staff and Line with Portraits of Generals-in-Chief*. New York: Maynard, Merrill, & Co., 1896.

Rodenbough, Theophilus F. *From Everglade to Canyon with the Second United States Cavalry*. 1875. Reprint, Norman: University of Oklahoma Press, 2000.

Rogers, Benjamin F. "Florida Seen through the Eyes of Nineteenth Century Travelers." *Florida Historical Quarterly* 34/1 (October 1955): 177–81.

Rozbicki, Michael J. *The Complete Colonial Gentleman: Cultural Legitimacy in Plantation America*. Charlottesville: University Press of Virginia, 1998.

Ruhlen, George. "Fort Rosecrans, California." *San Diego Historical Society Quarterly* 5 (October 1959): 60–69.

Russell, J. Thomas. *Edgar Allan Poe: The Army Years*. West Point, NY: United

State Military Academy, 1972.
Schlesinger, Arthur M. *The Colonial Merchants and the American Revolution*. New York: Atheneum, 1968.
Schott, Thomas E. *Alexander H. Stephens of Georgia: A Biography*. Baton Rouge: Louisiana State University, 1988.
Scott, Col. H. L. *Military Dictionary*. 1861. Reprint, New York: Greenwood Press, 1968.
Scott, Mary Wingfield. *Houses of Old Richmond*. Richmond: Valentine Museum, 1941.
Scott, Sir Walter. *The Life of Napoleon Buonaparte, Emperor of the French*. 3 vols. New York: Collin S. Keese & Co., 1839.
Scott, Winfield. *Infantry-Tactics*. New York: George Dearborn, 1835.
Seale, William. *The President's House: A History*. 2 vols. Washington: White House Historical Association, 1986.
Sheldon, Marianne Buroff. "Black-White Relations in Richmond, Virginia, 1782–1820." *The Journal of Southern History* 45/1 (February 1979): 27–44.
Shockley, Martin Staples. *The Richmond Stage, 1784–1812*. Charlottesville: University Press of Virginia, 1977.
Sibley, Joel H. *Party over Section: The Rough and Ready Presidential Election of 1848*. Lawrence: University Press of Kansas, 2009.
Silverman, Kenneth. *Edgar A. Poe: Mournful and Never-Ending Remembrance*. New York: HarperCollins, 1991.
Skelton, William B. *An American Profession of Arms: The Army Officer Corps, 1784–1861*. Lawrence: University Press of Kansas, 1992.
Smith, Ethel M. "The Llangollen School for Boys, Spotsylvania County, Virginia, 1814–1832." *The Magazine of Virginia Genealogy* 22 (February 1984): 3–14.
Smith, Justin. *The War with Mexico*. 2 vols. New York: Macmillan Co., 1919.
Sprague, John T. *The Origin, Progress, and Conclusion of the Florida War*. 1848. Original text with introduction by John K. Mahon. Tampa: University of Tampa Press, 2000.
Statutes at Large and Treaties of the United States of America... / by Authority of Congress. Vol. 9 (December 1, 1845 to March 3, 1851)–v. 11 (December 3, 1855 to March 3, 1859). Boston: C. C. Little and J. Brown, 1851–1859.
Stephenson, Mary A. "Golden Ball Historical Report, Block 17 Building 6A Lot 53, Originally entitled: 'Craig's House and Shop Block 17-1, Lot #53.'" 1946. Colonial Williamsburg Foundation Library Research Report Series—1357. 1990. Colonial Williamsburg Foundation Library, Williamsburg, Virginia. Available online: https://research.history.org/DigitalLibrary/view/index.cfm?doc=ResearchReports%5CRR1359.xml&highlight=craig,%20james.
Sterne, Laurence. *The Life and Opinions of Tristram Shandy, Gentleman*. New York: Penguin Books, 2003.

Stubbs, Mary Lee, and Stanley Russell Connor. *Armor-Cavalry, Part I: Regular Army and Army Reserve.* Washington, D.C.: Government Printing Office, 1969.

Sturdivant, M. K. "Dover's Powder and Its Modifications." *The Medical Summary* 11 (December 1889): 215.

Sully, John M. "The Story of the Santa Rita Copper Mine." *Old Santa Fe* 3 (April 1916): 135–38.

Sweeney, Edwin R. *Mangas Coloradas: Chief of the Chiricahua Apaches.* Norman, University of Oklahoma Press, 1998.

Taylor, Alan. *The Internal Enemy: Slavery and War in Virginia, 1772–1832.* New York: W. W. Norton & Co., 2013.

Thomas, William S. *The Society of the Cincinnati, 1783–1935.* New York: G. P. Putnam's Sons, 1935.

Thompson, G. R., ed. *The Selected Writings of Edgar Allan Poe.* New York: W.W. Norton & Co., 2004.

[Thompson, John Reuben.] "The Late Edgar A. Poe." *Southern Literary Messenger* 15 (November 1849): 694–97.

Thonhoff, Robert H. "Taylor's Trail in Texas." *Southwestern Historical Quarterly* 70 (July 1966): 7–22.

Traas, Adrian George. *From the Golden Gate to Mexico City: The U.S. Army Topographical Engineers in the Mexican War, 1846–1848.* Washington, DC: Government Printing Office, 1993.

Tyler, Lyon Gardiner, ed. *Narratives of Early Virginia, 1606–1625.* New York: Charles Scribner's Sons, 1907.

United States Military Academy. *The Centennial of the United States Military Academy at West Point, New York, 1802–1902.* 2 vols. Washington: GPO, 1904.

Upton, Dell. *Holy Things and Profane: Anglican Parish Churches in Colonial Virginia.* Architectural History Foundation Books 10. New York: Architectural History Foundation and Cambridge, MA: MIT Press, 1986.

Upton, Emory. *The Military Policy of the United States.* Washington: Government Printing Office, 1917.

Virginia Historical Society. "The Virginia Society of the Cincinnati." *Virginia Magazine of History and Biography* 6/1 (July 1898): 22–29.

Wadsworth, Richard. *Forgotten Fortress: Fort Millard Fillmore and Antebellum New Mexico, 1851–1862.* Las Cruces, NM: Yucca Tree Press, 2002.

Wallace, Edward S. *The Great Reconnaissance: Soldiers, Artists, and Scientists on the Frontier, 1848–1861.* Boston: Little, Brown and Company, 1955.

Walthall, David K. *History of Richmond Lodge, No. 10, A.F. & a.m., 1790–1909.* Richmond: Ware & Duke, Printers, 1909.

[Waterhouse, Edward.] *A Declaration of the State of the Colony and Affaires in Virginia*.... London: G. Eld, 1622.

Watson, Samuel J. *Jackson's Sword: The Army Officer Corps on the American*

Frontier, 1810–1821. Lawrence: University Press of Kansas, 2012.

Wayland, Francis Fry. *Andrew Stevenson: Democrat and Diplomat, 1785–1857*. University of Pennsylvania Press, 1949.

Weigley, Russell. *History of the United States Army*. New York: Macmillan Publishing Co., 1967.

Wellman, Paul I. *Death in the Desert: The Fifty Years' War for the Great Southwest*. 1935. Reprint, Lincoln: University of Nebraska Press, 1987.

Wensyel, Col. James W. "The Old Guard." *Army* 46/8 (August 1996): 36–45.

Whiffen, Marcus. *The Public Buildings of Williamsburg*. Williamsburg: Colonial Williamsburg, 1958.

White, Frank L., ed. "The Journals of Lieutenant John Pickell, 1836–1837." *Florida Historical Quarterly* 38/2 (October 1959): 142–71.

White, William Carter. *A History of Military Music in America*. New York: The Exposition Press, 1944.

Williams, John Lee. *The Territory of Florida: Or Sketches of the Topography, Civil and Natural History, of the Country, the Climate, and the Indian Tribes, from the First Discovery to the Present Time*. 1837. Gainesville: University of Florida Press, 1962.

"Williamsburg Lodge of Masons." *William and Mary College Quarterly Historical Papers* 1/1 (July 1892): 1–33.

Wilson, John B. *Maneuver and Fire Power: The Evolution of Divisions and Separate Brigades*. Washington: Government Printing Office, 1998.

Winders, Richard Bruce. *Mr. Polk's Army: The American Military Experience in the Mexican War*. College Station: Texas A&M University Press, 1997.

Wolfe, Charles. "The Burial of Sir John Moore after Corunna." *The Oxford Book of English Verse* Oxford: Oxford University Press, 1940.

Wood, Peter H. "The Changing Population of the Colonial South: An Overview by Race and Region, 1685–1790." In *Powhatan's Mantle: Indians in the Colonial Southeast*, rev. ed., edited by Gregory A. Waselkov et al., 57–132. Lincoln: University of Nebraska Press, 2006.

Wright, Marcus J. *General Scott*. New York: D. Appleton and Co., 1894.

Index